50+

Also by Joe Graedon and Teresa Graedon

The People's Pharmacy: Totally New and Revised

**Joe Graedon's The New People's Pharmacy #3:
Drug Breakthroughs of the '80s**

The People's Pharmacy-2

(Available from Graedon Enterprises, Inc.
P.O. Box 52027
Durham, N.C. 27717-2027)

50⁺

The Graedons' People's Pharmacy for Older Adults

Joe Graedon
and
Teresa Graedon

BANTAM BOOKS
TORONTO · NEW YORK · LONDON · SYDNEY · AUCKLAND

50+: THE GRAEDONS' PEOPLE'S PHARMACY FOR OLDER ADULTS

A Bantam Book / June 1988

*This book was published simultaneously in
hardcover and trade paperback.*

Library of Congress Cataloging-in-Publication Data

Graedon, Joe.
 50+ : The Graedons' people's pharmacy
for older adults.

 Includes bibliographies and index.
 1. Geriatric pharmacology—Popular works.
I. Graedon, Teresa, 1947–   . II. Title.
III. Title: Fifty plus. IV. Title: Graedons'
People's pharmacy for older adults.
RC953.7.G72 1988   616.5´8   88-3304
ISBN 0-553-05245-4
ISBN 0-553-34485-4 (pbk.)

Published simultaneously in the United States and Canada

PRINTED IN THE UNITED STATES OF AMERICA

FG   0 9 8 7 6 5 4 3 2 1

THIS BOOK IS DEDICATED TO:

SID GRAEDON
Whose tragic experience gave us personal insight into the problems of aging and the courage it takes to endure a chronic and debilitating disease

HELEN GRAEDON
An amazing lady who could easily pass for someone twenty years younger. Her vigor, enthusiasm, compassion, and perseverance have spurred us on over the years

BRIAN WEISS
A loyal friend and colleague who inspired us to tackle this project and helped us over the humps

OLDER PEOPLE EVERYWHERE
Who deserve better treatment and more information about the medicines they are expected to swallow so conscientiously

Acknowledgments

Many people over the years have helped us in so many ways it would be impossible to list them all. Here are just a few of the friends and colleagues who have provided inspiration, imagination, encouragement, support, and assistance.

George Brett, our own personal wizard, who helped us take a big bite of the Apple. We never could have made it on time without George's sense of humor, skill, and computing genius.

Tom Ferguson, a wonderful friend and colleague who keeps our hands warm and our hearts happy.

Robert Temple, a dedicated and brilliant FDAer who provided us with an insider's view of drug testing and approval.

Lou Wolfe, who believed in us and gave us the support we needed to keep on trucking.

Toni Burbank, an extraordinary editor who understood the importance of this effort and encouraged us to do our best.

Bill Pinna, a loyal friend who generously includes us in his dreams of Montana.

David and Alena Graedon, the best kids two parents could ever want.

Hugh Tilson, who punctuates his clear thinking on pharmaceutical risk with charm and wit.

Carole Dombach, a dedicated and loyal assistant who always came through when we needed her most.

Ralph Scallion, a wise and wonderful doctor and a good friend who really cares about people's health.

Jere Goyan, one of the giants who's never afraid to shake the pillars of the professional establishment. Our hero!

Dean Edell, a real soul mate and friend who sets some pretty tough standards for us to follow.

Pedro Cuatrecasas, just about the best scientist and most able administrator in the pharmaceutical industry. His vision and integrity are a model for others to follow.

Al Kligman, our favorite dermatologist! A fearless, frank, and funny physician who has tackled some of the most fundamental skin problems known to man.

Robert Gilgor, a real gentleman and a heck of a nice guy who always comes to our rescue with a smile and insightful comments.

Stanley B. Levy, friend, perfect tennis partner, and physician who really provides us with an excellent dermatological perspective, especially into the world of cosmetics.

Cliff Butler, a model for what the ideal pharmacist should be.

Carol Hogue, a close friend and colleague who provided us with valuable insight into the confusing issues of osteoporosis.

John McHugh of the AARP, a dedicated pharmacist and administrator who really cares about providing older people with a service they so desperately need.

Ed Domino, a supportive, kind, and wise researcher who offered important information on the spur of the minute.

Tad Smith, who we hope is getting wiser and nicer in his old age.

Hank Swain, a really brilliant man who taught us to ask tough questions and notice when the emperor wears no clothes.

John Doorley, a noble representative of the pharmaceutical industry. We feel privileged to call him friend.

Carolyn Glynn, a super lady who has persevered and won her spurs. We always knew you would!

Fred Eckel, one of the finest pharmacist educators in the country and a person who really cares about older people.

Marcia and Ricardo Hofer, wonderful friends who really know firsthand that snails travel on their stomachs. Thanks for the valuable comments!

Chuck Fenimore and Vicki Gardner, who came to our rescue in the nick of time.

Betty and Bonnell Frost, who know what it's like to live with a nonagenarian.

Melva Okun, a great producer whom we sorely miss.

Miriam Berg Varian, the best, most thorough copy editor we've ever worked with.

Thanks also to:

Abel Arango, Leo Ars, Kathy Bartlett, Deborah Bender, Molly and Frederick Bernheim, Chuck and Alice Cambron, Bob Day, Mary Dorsey, Judi Fitzpatrick, Jeannette Frost, Jim and Eva Greenberg, Kathe Gregory, Joanne Hall, Alan Handelman, Linda Hart, Marilyn and Don Hartman, Helen Langa, Michael McClung, Will and Deni McIntyre, John and Christopher McLachlan, Robert Mendelsohn, Frank and Olga Michl, Mike Naimark, Barney Nietschmann, Tom Pritchard, Shirley Reynolds, Sanford Roth, Eva Salber and Harry Philips, Gail Schmidt, David Sedwick and Marty Veigl, Tom Smigel, Hector Tenorio and Amanda Weinsheim.

Attention

The health and drug information contained in this book represents a review of the medical literature and personal interviews
with knowledgeable health experts. Scientists do not always agree
about the benefits and risks of various treatments, especially with
respect to any particular individual. Every reader must consult
with his or her physician before starting or stopping any medicine and before implementing any other therapy discussed in this
book. Most important, any side effects should be reported promptly
to a physician.

Contents

Beware of Subtle Shifts in Side Effect Sensitivity • Dangers of Digitalis Overdose • **Tagamet** May Trigger Confusion • Don't Play Russian Roulette with Multiple Medicines • The Vicious Cycle Syndrome • Breaking the Hippocratic Oath: Doctors Do It All the Time • Dealing with Drug-Induced Dry Mouth • Squeeze Life Now—The Future Is Uncertain • Don't Let Lifesaving Drugs Make You Miserable • Capitalizing on Quality: **Capoten**, **Cardizem**, **Feldene**, **Procardia**, **Tenormin**, and **Zantac** • Plotting Your Course for Good Health • Things to Remember

Stereotypes Are Stumbling Blocks to Communication • Don't Suffer in Silence • Is a Good Doctor Really Hard to Find? • Precautions for Self-Protection • How to Talk to Your Doctor • Getting Him to Listen • Tips for Taking Notes • Holding Off Hospital Hazards • Things to Remember

12   STAYING SEXY AFTER SIXTY   335

How Important Is Sex Anyway? • Drug-Induced Impotence •
Going for the Gold: Drugs Less Likely to Cause Sexual Problems
• Maybe an Aphrodisiac? • The Stamp Test: Assessing Impotence
at Home • Papaverine Injections for Impotence • Oh That Pesky
Prostate • Women Have Problems Too • Things to Remember

TIPS, TOOLS, AND TABLES:

13   DEVELOPING YOUR RUBBER DUCKY DETECTOR   360
(QUACK QUACK)

Who's Watching Out for You? • Watchdogs Have More Bark
Than Bite • When Is a Claim Not a Claim? • The Fantasia Pharma-
copoeia: Biotin, **Gerovital, Blue-Green Manna** • The Magic
Potion Effect • Ten Claims That Are Hardly Ever True • Things to
Remember

14   FINDING THE FOUNTAIN OF YOUTH   379

The Fascination with Extending Life • Why Do We Age? A Survey
of Theories • Taking Steps to Stay Young • Zapping Free Radicals
• Eating Less for Longer Life • Afterword

Foreword

To be honest, I was more than a little skeptical when I learned in 1976 that someone named Joe Graedon had written a drug self-help book called *The People's Pharmacy*. Part of my skepticism had to do with the title, which was suspiciously similar to slogans uttered by those who operate in the fringe zones of health care. Then there was the matter of the author's reputation: he didn't have one. Nowhere on the hallowed pages of the Book of Names of Those in the Know About Drugs could his be found.

Besides, he was a pharmacologist and not even a clinician as might reasonably be expected of anyone who presumes to address seriously matters of drug therapy. (For those who are not aware of the distinction, pharmacologists are basic scientists who are skilled in investigating how drugs work, but who usually know very little about which ones are best or how to use them effectively. A clinician is just the opposite.) Finally, the shelves of book stores were already overloaded with such compendia, most of them by people who really should not have written them in the first place. So, I was prepared not to like his book.

Of course, I was entirely wrong; both Joe and *The People's Pharmacy* turned out to be delightful and knowledgeable in every regard and I quickly became a member of his fan club.

Recently, I learned that along with his wife, Teresa, Joe had written the book now in your hands. Once again I was skeptical, primarily because of the paucity of knowledge relating to the drug therapy of older persons. If you find that peculiar, you are not aware that only a few years have passed since we first realized that aging bodies tend to respond differently to drugs than younger bodies. The differences can be extreme and because much research remains to be done, there are many skilled and dedicated *clinicians* who do not know a lot about this phenomenon. Despite my respect for the authors, I found myself wondering if they hadn't gotten ahead of the knowledge base available.

I have now read it and to be frank, one must have a highly sophisticated understanding of drug therapy in order to fully appreciate *50+ The Graedons' People's Pharmacy for Older Adults.* On the other hand, one needn't know a thing about drug therapy to fully appreciate it. If these statements seem contradictory, the bridge between them is the Graedons' imaginative writing style and ability to translate the complicated information it covers into easily understood English. Only those of us who know how difficult this field is—how steeped in mind-boggling jargon, complex ideas, and controversy—have the ability to measure the magnitude of their accomplishment in this regard. And they do it in an entertaining manner that does not, as often happens, sacrifice accuracy.

There are so many good features about this book that it is difficult to sort out any one as more meritorious than others. The chapters on obtaining adequate information from prescribers, on aging of the skin, on forgetfulness, and on sexuality are unique state-of-the-art communications that everyone, regardless of age, should heed. The chapter on saving money on medicines illustrates the Graedons' agreement with me that the state of the patient's pocketbook is part of their health status. The overall theme, however, is worth mentioning again and again: we serve ourselves poorly if we do not take advantage of every opportunity to participate more actively in the decision processes that put drugs into or onto our bodies. This book is an excellent step in that direction.

But what I especially like about *50+* is its special sensitivity and responsiveness to the audience it addresses. We over-50s people are too often lectured to, patted on the head, and patronized by those who appear to view us as the next generation of children. Never once do the Graedons—neither of them 50 plus—convey this attitude. The reason is obvious to anyone who knows them: they respect us not because of clichés having to do with age and wisdom but because they are caring individuals who recognize that within our ranks are people who, through no choice of our own, have discovered that our bodies just don't work the way they used to. Because of this we have become the brunt of jokes, stereotyped in an unfair fashion, and bombarded with misinformation from many different sources. This book provides a breath of fresh air in an important area of the lives of everyone over fifty. We owe the authors a vote of thanks.

Jere E. Goyan, Ph.D., Dean
School of Pharmacy
University of California, San Francisco
Former Commissioner,
Food and Drug Administration

Why We Had to Write This Book

**It's not how long we live,
but *how* we live that counts!**

Growing older ought to be wonderful. With age should come wisdom and well-being. After all those years of work, work, work, at long last there's time for the luxury of doing things at our own pace without anyone setting deadlines or breathing down our neck. Instead of worrying about everyone else, we should be able to take care of ourselves and enjoy life. But even with good planning, time, and a measure of economic security, growing old can turn into a nightmare.

The problem is health. They say if you've got your health, you've got it all. What good is money in the bank and time to enjoy it if arthritis or heart disease makes it painful to walk across the room? How can you enjoy grandchildren if you can't remember their names?

It has broken our hearts to see a vibrant, joyful grandfather who loved to play with our children slowly robbed of his zest for life and his interest in his grandchildren. As his brain disease progressed, we watched helplessly as Sid's athletic coordination, natural talent for communication, and buoyant self-confidence disappeared. Confusion and clumsiness have insidiously gained the upper hand. Now he is confined to a wheelchair and dependent on Helen, his wife, or us for the simplest decisions.

We have watched Helen and Amanda, two energetic and fiercely independent octogenarians whom we love, restrict their activities and begin to isolate themselves because the pain of arthritis has interfered with their ability to get around. Although they rarely complain, the daily torment they must endure takes its toll. Just the struggle to get up in the morning requires more grit than most younger people can ever imagine.

We had to write this book for Helen and Sid, Leo, Amanda, Jeannette, Adele, Molly, Frederick, Grace, and our other friends and relatives. We got fed up with insensitivity and inflexibility of the health care system in dealing with the older members of our family. It infuriated us when Sid had to wait over six hours in the hospital lobby to be admitted.

When Leo suffered a dangerous blood clot in his lungs, his doctors twice disregarded his discomfort, not taking into consideration the fact that he isn't a complainer. When this 84-year-old retired dairy farmer showed up in the emergency room at midnight with a stabbing pain in his chest, you'd better believe there was something wrong. But the doctors didn't take him seriously. He was sent home with a pain reliever even after he suggested it could be a blood clot in his lungs caused by the medicine he was taking. It took precious weeks before they finally figured out Leo was right.

Please understand that these were able, caring, thoughtful physicians at a major medical center. But they just didn't listen. We're sick and tired of this condescending attitude toward older people. It's high time physicians, nurses, pharmacists, and everyone else start really listening and paying attention. People who have reached their seventies or eighties have a powerful lot of living behind them and may have a darn good understanding of how their bodies respond.

We're living longer today than ever before, but are we enjoying it less? Drugs lower our risks of heart attacks and strokes, fight off pneumonia and flu, and ease the pain of arthritis. When medicines work well to cure or relieve our ills without causing complications, they're a wonderful blessing.

But sometimes the gain is offset by pain. Are we trading a few extra years for a life barely worth living? Drug-induced depression, disorientation, dizziness, forgetfulness, and fatigue are not uncommon, but are often mistaken for inevitable signs of aging. Because such side effects usually come on gradually, it's often difficult to distinguish them from age-related changes.

Just because you're a "senior citizen" doesn't mean you have to throw in the towel. Fight back! Anyone who makes it well into retirement these days is pretty darn tough. So use your strength. "Good patient points," even if your doctor gives them out, won't make your life better. If you suspect you are having a problem with your prescription, don't suffer in silence. The quality of life is just as important as the quantity. The doctor may insist you take your medicine even if it causes "minor" side effects. (Those are the ones that don't kill you.) But a dry mouth, dizziness, constipation, or confusion can become a constant torment. If you are suffering, let your doctor know. There's often more than one way to skin a cat and more than one medicine for a given condition. It may take a while to find the right alternative for you, but it can make an extraordinary difference in the way you feel.

We wrote this book for you, whether you are over 50 yourself or looking out for an older person you love. Our goal is to help people learn how to use drugs carefully to improve their lives while simultaneously looking out for serious side effects. No one wants the "cure" to become worse than the disease. It's wonderful to have drugs that can lower the risk of strokes, heart attacks, seizures, kidney disease, and blindness, but that doesn't mean you have to be held hostage to their side effects.

Finding the right medicine and getting the correct dose is a difficult balancing act. Think about Goldilocks tasting the three bears' porridge, trying to avoid the bowl that was too hot and the one that was too cold. Just like Goldilocks, you and your doctor will have to make an effort to get it "just right."

That includes getting the right price. Many of the older people we know have spent their lives scrimping and saving for retirement. Plenty of folks are trying to live on Social Security or a modest pension. Leo gets by on $268 a month, so when he gets two prescriptions that cost $61.88, there goes his budget. He's already hunting for bargains on stale bread and specials on chicken backs and there's no room for extra economizing. And Medicare's little help when it comes to drugs, even for people who can manage somehow to make their way through the confusing maze of paperwork needed for reimbursement.

In this book we'll provide money-saving tips on how to get the best deal at the drugstore. We will try to help you balance the benefits of drugs against the dangers. We evaluate many popular medications, from high blood pressure drugs and estrogen treatment to antidepressants and sleeping pills.

Do you know exactly how to take your medicine—with meals or on an empty stomach? We were shocked to discover that most people, including plenty of doctors, don't have a clue as to what's best. Of course, that's not their fault. Until recently, the Food and Drug Administration (FDA) paid little attention to this issue, so the *Physicians' Desk Reference (PDR)* doesn't contain adequate information on interactions between foods and various drugs. We have combed through books, journals, newsletters, and reports to find the most complete information on which drugs mix well with food and which do not. We'll also give you the guidelines you need to be able to tell if some new, highly touted treatment is a real advance or a shameful scam.

As people grow older they become more vulnerable to a large number of medications. We have done our best to list many of the drugs that are especially likely to cause problems and what side effects to be alert for. You will find this extensive table at the end of this book. We'll give you some survival strategies for dealing with your doctor—ways to speak up for your rights with dignity. And we'll try to untangle the maze of confusing and conflicting information surrounding so many health issues these days.

Are you worried about your cholesterol levels? With contradictory reports appearing in medical journals almost monthly, it's hardly any wonder most folks don't know what's good and what's bad, which foods to eat and which to avoid. We'll give you the latest scoop on diet and drug treatments to keep your cholesterol under control. You'll find an easy-to-use chart that will allow you to monitor your own blood lipids. And we'll analyze some of the newest approaches to blood pressure control.

Osteoporosis, or weakened bones, has gotten nearly as much attention as cholesterol lately, and the rapidly changing recommendations have been hard to follow. Are calcium supplements the answer or is estrogen replacement therapy the solution? And what about arthritis? We've had first-hand experience in our family with these cruel and debilitating diseases. We'll discuss most of the medicines that are prescribed and help you evaluate their benefits and risks.

If you're worried about forgetfulness, you will want to check out our chapter about drugs that can make this problem worse. You will also find a discussion of experimental new treatments for Alzheimer's disease and other organic brain disorders. No one is more interested in these tragic ailments than us because they've affected our family so profoundly. There is as yet no cure, but some promising drugs may soon offer important advances against these mind slayers. Researchers are even starting to talk about "smart pills" that might improve memory and learning in healthy people.

That's not the only bright spot on the horizon. This book is filled with good news about exciting developments in dermatology, maybe even an effective wrinkle reverser. This drug, **Retin-A**, also may be helpful against some skin cancers and boost the effectiveness of the anti-baldness cream **Rogaine**. There are a number of new medications for blood pressure that have advantages over the old standbys, and new antidepressants with a positive effect on sexuality, and weight control may become a reality before long.

Finally, we will review some of the latest theories on aging. Is there a Fountain of Youth in a bottle? In recent years we have been overwhelmed with books, diets, and products that promise to erase wrinkles, improve sex drive, and add years to our lives. We'll do our best to separate fact from fiction.

We firmly believe that as you get older it is possible to have your cake and eat it too. We've received lots of letters from retired folks who are leading active lives and taking good care of themselves. We salute H. B., who is in better shape now that he's in his sixties than he's been since he was 16. He's eating healthier foods and exercising more than many younger men (15 miles a day on his bike). And we toast the couple who called our radio show to tell us that sex is better for them in their seventies than ever before.

Many of today's medicines are crucial to helping people live longer and enjoy life more fully. But too often drugs have boomeranged and brought complications and tragedy. That's why we had to write this book—for ourselves, for our loved ones, for our friends who are taking care of older relatives, and for you. We got angry at a health care system that in many ways has turned its back on older citizens. Too many physicians push high tech tests, sophisticated surgery, and potent prescriptions. All too often they focus on organs—gallbladders, kidneys, hearts, and lungs—without considering the whole person and the simple respect and dignity older people deserve.

We hope this book will challenge you and help you and your family get the most out of the medications you need. Ultimately, we hope it will help improve the quality of your life.

Avoiding Drug
Dangers

Older people are different. Now we're not talking bifocals, bunions, wrinkles, or white hair. Those are just the things that you can see. It's what you can't see that matters most, especially when it comes to medicine. As we age, the body's internal machinery changes.

Think about your car for a moment. No matter how well you pamper it—feeding it high-test gasoline, tuning the engine to perfection, and rotating tires—there will come a time when parts start to wear out. The tires become bald, the water pump begins to leak, or the engine starts to burn more oil and get fewer miles to the gallon.

Much the same thing can happen to critical organs inside your body. Kidneys and livers may not work as efficiently as we age. Sometimes the plumbing springs a leak. And that great engine in your chest may not push blood around as smoothly. We rarely notice these declines, because they usually come on slowly and insidiously. Unlike the aches and pains we feel or the white hair we can see, the inner changes give off few signals and often go undetected.

All else being equal, we could probably put up with a little less efficiency. After all, when your car gets over 100,000 on the odometer, you make a few allowances. As long as old Betsy gets you where you want to go, who cares if she burns a little extra oil or gets a few less miles to the gallon?

The trouble is that all else isn't equal when it comes to your body. Every time we swallow a pill, we throw a monkey wrench into our internal works. Even when the medicine is supposed to help us regulate our heart rate, blood pressure, or fluid balance, improve our ability to breathe or relieve the pain of arthritis, the possibility exists that the medicine may do harm.

As we grow older, we become much more vulnerable to medication. Our liver and kidneys may have a devil of a time getting rid of drugs and that may mean that the medicine that is supposed to help can build up to toxic levels instead. Imagine what would happen if everytime you flushed your toilet, instead of returning to the regular level, the water built up an extra quarter inch. Gradually, almost imperceptibly, the water would accumulate and eventually flow over the top and cause a flood. If your body can't keep up with the amount of medicine you take in, you can slowly flood your system.

This could happen with digitalis heart drugs like digoxin and digitoxin. It's not uncommon for these medications to build up almost imperceptibly over months or even years as kidney function gradually begins to diminish. Other drugs that also may accumulate include lithium for manic depression, **Tagamet** (cimetidine) for ulcers, **Procan** and **Pronestyl** (procainamide) for irregular heart rhythms, and **Diabinese** (chlorpropamide) for diabetes. This might even happen with a relatively new heart and high blood pressure medicine called verapamil (**Calan** and **Isoptin**). Researchers have found that this drug lingers longer in older people. As a result it may lower blood pressure and slow heart rate a little more than in younger folks.[1]

Doctors are not always informed about special dosing requirements for their elderly patients. With some drugs, a buildup in the bloodstream could eventually lead to adverse reactions. Unfortunately, side effects are not always easy to detect. Sometimes doctors chalk up a patient's complaints to "old age," when in reality they may be brought on by a medication.

Take Catherine's case, for example. At 76 she was in great shape. She always took great pride in her appearance and was delighted that most people mistakenly assumed she was in her late fifties or early sixties. Catherine was full of energy, participated actively in her church and women's club, and was involved in community affairs and local politics. She was an avid gardener and loved to walk and stay physically fit.

Like a lot of older people, though, Catherine began to have trouble falling asleep. It annoyed her that she would lie awake for hours watching the clock as the hours slowly ticked by. She was reluctant to get up for fear it would wake her husband, so she suffered in silence. One day she mentioned the problem to her doctor. Without a second thought he wrote her a prescription for a sleeping pill.

The insomnia disappeared, but soon Catherine's sparkle started to fade. She became lethargic, and her driving got so bad her friends were scared to ride with her. Usually sharp and insightful, Catherine became confused, uncertain, and forgetful. Her children feared she was becoming senile and were bracing for a diagnosis of Alzheimer's disease.

But Catherine was not losing her mind. She had suffered a drug overdose from her sleeping pills. Although her physician had prescribed a "normal" dose that probably would have been safe ten years earlier, her body was not capable of handling it. She may have looked 60, but her liver and kidneys weren't fooled. The medicine she took to get a good night's sleep gradually accumulated in her system. Because her brain was more susceptible to sedation, she became sluggish and driving was dangerous.

Figuring out what had happened to Catherine was actually pretty easy. She had felt a little guilty about her inability to fall asleep and hadn't mentioned the insomnia to her husband or her children for fear it would make them worry. As a result no one knew she was on sleeping pills. But when one of her daughters happened to discover the pill bottle by accident, the mystery was solved. Once the drug was eliminated, Catherine regained her old vigor and vitality.

Sleeping pills, sedatives, tranquilizers, or "nerve" pills are all relatively easy to track. People are aware that they can affect the brain and cause confusion if the dose gets too high. But who would ever expect a heart medicine could cause personality changes? After we wrote a newspaper column on the dangers of digitalis overdose, a reader responded:

I wanted to let you know that reading a letter in your weekly column led to a dramatic improvement in the condition of my mother-in-law, with whom we live.

She had been increasingly feeble, having delusions and hallucinations, unsteady on her feet, incontinent, sleeping far too much. When I read about the possible effects of too much Lanoxin, I suspected that all that confusion might not be just "old age" or Alzheimer's, so I contacted her doctor.

He had a blood level test done, and sure enough, the Lanoxin dose was much too high for her. He cut it in half, and in three weeks the change in her behavior, physical condition, and mental state improved unbelievably. The only bad part is that instead of acting docile and "out-of-it," she is now as critical and demanding as she used to be!

Lanoxin (digoxin) can be a life-saving heart medicine. But getting the dose right is not always easy. In excess, this drug can cause delusions, depression, hallucinations, and changes in personality. If not carefully controlled, digoxin can even cause life-threatening reactions. Don wrote to us to relate a very close call:

Three weeks ago I had to take my wife, who is 88 years old, to the doctor because of vomiting, stomach gas, loose stools, and a rapidly deteriorating general physical condition. The doctor took one look at her and had her put in the hospital.

Diagnosis, toxic poisoning caused by over-prescription of digoxin! Her doctor had prescribed a dosage of 0.25 mg of digoxin daily. According to the lab tests and her specialist's assessment, she shouldn't have been prescribed more than 0.10 to 0.125 mg of digoxin per day because her kidneys couldn't pass off the surplus.

While in the hospital, they found her dangerously deficient in potassium brought on by a diuretic. Without a special diet there was no way to replace the potassium being leached from her system by the diuretic. Naturally, I am disturbed that a doctor would prescribe such a heavy dosage for an elderly person without monitoring the results when all advice warns against such practice.

Don is certainly right in believing that his wife should have been monitored much more closely. If he hadn't recognized the danger and acted promptly, he might have lost her. Such a close call should have been prevented in the first place. *Goodman and Gilman's The Pharmacological Basis of Therapeutics*, the gold standard in pharmacology textbooks, warns: "The single most frequent cause of intoxication with digitalis is the concurrent administration of diuretics that cause potassium depletion ... If unrecognized or improperly treated, such reactions frequently are fatal ... physicians must exercise every precaution in prescribing digitalis; patients should be monitored carefully."[2]

Digitalis-type drugs like **Lanoxin** are prescribed so often that by now, most doctors should be aware of the dangers, especially for older people. That may not be the case with another doctor favorite. **Tagamet** (cimetidine) has become one of the most popular drugs in the physician's black bag. It makes doctors look good because it takes away ulcer pain almost like magic. Maybe that's the trouble. **Tagamet**, and its kissing cousin **Zantac** (ranitidine), are so good they are sometimes used inappropriately, almost like super antacids for heartburn and indigestion.

Although **Tagamet** is generally quite safe, it can cause unexpected complications in some older people. Who would ever suspect that a stomach medicine might cause psychological side effects? But mental confusion, restlessness, disorientation, agitation, slurred speech, and hallucinations have been reported with **Tagamet**.[3–6]

Until recently, it was assumed that such reactions were extremely rare. But a fascinating study carried out at Buffalo General Hospital suggests that mental problems may be more common than most people think. The researchers studied 124 surgical intensive care unit (ICU) patients who received **Tagamet** and compared them to 93 who did not get the drug. Twice as many of the **Tagamet**-taking patients (33 percent) had changes in mental status, usually within two days of starting the drug. If their kidneys and livers weren't up to snuff, 80 percent suffered signs of mental confusion.[7] Symptoms included disorientation, apprehension, restlessness, and depression.

Now these were some pretty sick bunnies to start with. You don't generally end up in an intensive care unit for a routine hemorrhoidectomy. But even so, it suggests that **Tagamet** may sometimes affect the mind, especially if you are sick, debilitated, or elderly. And there is now evidence that **Zantac**, that other popular ulcer drug, may also cause confusion for some vulnerable elderly people.[8]

The last thing anyone, especially an older person, needs is disorientation or slurred speech. Life is difficult enough without adding extra anxiety or confusion. When people feel nervous about their ability to communicate or get about, they may pull into a shell. As they isolate themselves from friends and relatives, a vicious cycle sets in, leading to more apprehension and disorientation and more seclusion.

What's so tragic is that drug-induced mental confusion or personality changes often go unrecognized because they may come on gradually and are so hard to prove. Even worse, they are often chalked up to "normal" aging. Doctors who prescribe drugs like **Tagamet** or **Zantac** to young or middle-aged patients see so few side effects or complications and get such good results that they may not realize older folks may be more sensitive to such ulcer medicine.

By now you've got the point. As we age, we change. We have relatively less muscle and more fat. The kidneys, liver, and digestive tract lose some oomph and the circulation may not be what it once was. The synapses slow down and we become more vulnerable to drugs that zap the nervous system.

So what's the big deal? Why are we flogging this sawhorse so hard? You'd think common sense should dictate that doctors would tread lightly when it comes to prescribing for older people. Surely, drug companies have carefully computed specialized dosage regimens for seniors. Oh, if only it were so.

The sad truth is that for many, if not most, of the medicines commonly prescribed to older people, there is a surprising lack of information on how the drugs are handled in their bodies.[9] Such "pharmacokinetic" studies are, to quote the FDA (Food and Drug Administration), "carried out principally in small numbers of normal males."[10] Read "normal" as young and healthy. If you're a woman and you're past 40, no one knows if your system would respond differently to most of the pharmaceuticals on drugstore shelves.

Only within the last year or so has the FDA actively encouraged drug companies to start checking new medications for an effect on the elderly. That means that for almost 30,000 prescription drugs marketed before 1986, there is precious little data on special sensitivity in seniors.[11] People past 70 or those with several chronic ailments like diabetes, hypertension, and arthritis may be skating on rather thin ice.

It is entirely possible, maybe even likely, that no one quite like you received the medicine you are taking while it was being tested. The human "guinea pigs" for drug testing programs are usually selected carefully to keep the data nice and simple. People with more than one health problem, taking more than one medicine or with questionable kidney or liver function are usually screened out. Subjects are supervised carefully and usually take the medicine on an empty stomach. As a result, there may be very little information about how the drug will act in the real world in patients who have more than one ailment. What's the right dosage for someone with your particular health problems? When and how you should swallow your pills? Your doctor may not have good answers to these fundamental questions. If you are taking more than one medicine for more than one condition, you have just added complexity on top of chaos.

Don't Play Russian Roulette

The older we get, the more likely it is for things to start to go wrong. Once we get past retirement, 86 percent of us will suffer from one or more chronic ailment.[12] It's not uncommon to have high blood pressure, chest pain, arthritis, and constipation all at the same time. Or maybe it's glaucoma, gout, diabetes, and indigestion. No matter what combination of conditions hits, the chances are good that you will end up taking more than one medicine at a time.

When you start mixing and matching, there's no telling what will happen. Think of it as a game of Russian roulette or Pop Goes the Weasel—except it's your health that may go pop. Here is a letter we received that demonstrates what can happen:

> **My father-in-law is 79 years old and his age is catching up with him quickly. He is showing signs of senility. His behavior has become highly erratic at times. We realize much of this can be attributed to the aging process, but we are concerned that the**

combinations of medications he takes (for numerous health problems) are contributing to his behavior.

The biggest problem is arthritis of the back and hip. They put him through physical pain at all times. He has had several heart attacks, suffers some breathing trouble and has a light case of diabetes. He occasionally has a problem with ulcers.

In recent months he has begun to have headaches, trouble sleeping, and trouble with his memory. If he is not working or sleeping, he sits in his recliner all day and watches TV. He is suspicious of everyone and has even accused his wife of 50 years of being unfaithful. (She is a saint.) He has become antisocial and has almost no close friends, although he is still well liked and respected in the community.

We are afraid the possible combinations of medicines could be a cause for his behavior. Here are the drugs he has lined up in front of his plate at the dinner table:

Orinase (tolbutamide) [for diabetes]
Motrin (ibuprofen) [for arthritis]
Procardia (nifedipine) [for heart]
Deltasone (prednisone) [for lungs and arthritis]
Quinaglute (quinidine) [for heart]
Gris-PEG (griseofulvin) [for fungal infection]
Tagamet (cimetidine) [for ulcer]
Mylanta (aluminum & magnesium hydroxide, simethicone) [for stomach upset]
Ornade (chlorpheniramine and phenylpropanolamine) [for cold or allergy]

This is an example of the walking drugstore phenomenon—a situation that is a lot more common than you would think. People over 65 get an average of 12 prescriptions filled each year—more than twice as many as folks between the ages of 25 and 44.[13] You don't need to be a Las Vegas oddsmaker or have a Ph.D. in pharmacology to realize that you increase your risk of suffering side effects the more pills you pop. Take up to five drugs, and your risk of experiencing an adverse reaction is about 4 percent.

Take 11 to 15 medications simultaneously, and your likelihood of running into toxicity rises to 24 percent.[14]

So what about the elderly father-in-law who is on nine different drugs? He was having trouble sleeping, showing signs of senility, complaining of headaches, and was suspicious and antisocial? Could his medicine be contributing to his problems?

There is no simple answer to such a question. He may be showing early signs of Alzheimer's disease. But as we mentioned earlier, **Tagamet** can occasionally cause mental confusion in older people. When it is added to antihistamines like the one found in **Ornade**, someone could easily end up feeling sluggish and foggy.

Then too, **Tagamet** interacts with many other medications to make them more dangerous. The effects of both heart drugs—**Procardia** (nifedipine) and **Quinaglute** (quinidine)—may be increased if they are taken with **Tagamet**.[15] Regular use of antacids may also make quinidine more potent. Signs of quinidine toxicity include digestive tract upset, headache, apprehension, confusion, vertigo, and delirium. Stomach pain and nausea could lead to more **Mylanta** and more **Tagamet**, which in turn could make quinidine more dangerous. Things could quickly get out of control. Frequent blood tests and careful monitoring can go a long way toward preventing such side effects.

The only way to truly prevent dangerous drug interactions in the first place is to make sure your physician and pharmacist have checked their reference books or computer programs to make sure your medications are compatible. (My favorite guide, by the way, is *Drug Interaction Facts* published by J. B. Lippincott. It's edited by Dr. Richard J. Mangini and can be ordered by calling 1-800-223-0554. You might ask your librarian to keep this reference on hand.)

Another way to reduce your risk is to make sure you don't get caught up in the "vicious cycle syndrome." One woman wrote to relate her experience with **Tenormin** (atenolol), a beta blocker prescribed for high blood pressure. A year or so after she was put on the medicine, she developed a cough and severe asthma.

Since **Tenormin** can bring on wheezing and asthma in susceptible individuals, you would think the doctor would have switched medications to something less likely to cause a breathing problem. But, oh no! Out came a prescription for prednisone, a potent cortisone-like medicine to counteract the asthma brought on by **Tenormin**.

Prednisone can have complications of its own. Like all steroids, it can bring on stomach upset and fluid buildup and deplete the body of potassium. So add an antacid, a diuretic, and potassium pills. But the antacid could well reduce the effectiveness of the **Tenormin**, so now add another blood pressure medicine, which has different side effects, which require additional treatment, which ... Get the picture? All of a sudden, you're on half a dozen different drugs all because the first medicine wasn't changed at the outset.

And don't forget that over-the-counter medications are just as likely to zap you as the ones the doctor hands out. Antihistamines found in cold and allergy remedies don't mix well with many prescription medicines, especially "nerve" pills like **Ativan** (lorazepam), **Centrax** (prazepam), **Librium** (chlordiazepoxide), **Paxipam** (halazepam), **Serax** (oxazepam), **Tranxene** (clorazepate), **Valium** (diazepam), or **Xanax** (alprazolam). Taken together with an antihistamine, such drugs can make you feel spaced out and confused.

Regular use of certain laxatives (especially those with phenolphthalein, like **Alophen**, **Correctol**, **Ex-Lax**, **Feen-A-Mint**, and **Phenolax**) may mess up absorption of vitamin D and calcium, which could lead to weakening of the bones. If relied on too frequently, aluminum-based antacids (such as **Amphojel**, **Alterna-GEL**, **Basaljel**, **Camalox**, **Gelusil**, **Maalox**, **Mylanta**, **Riopan**, and **Tempo**) may also affect bone strength.

Such antacids may also interact with tetracycline antibiotics and beta blocker medicines like **Tenormin** (atenolol) and **Inderal** (propranolol) to reduce their effectiveness.[16] The doctor might not understand why these antihypertensives aren't able to control blood pressure adequately and add more potent medication instead of recommending a different kind of antacid.

What you need to remember about all this is that when it comes to drugs—the more the messier. In one study of patients admitted to geriatric units, "27 percent of those on six or more drugs were suffering from adverse reactions."[17,18] It is absolutely essential that you have your various medicines reviewed periodically to make sure you aren't taking anything unnecessary or incompatible. Why not pack up everything (including nonprescription remedies and vitamins) in a big bag and take it in to the doctor *and* the pharmacist? This is the only way to make sure you aren't getting dangerously close to the twilight zone.

Breaking the Hippocratic Oath

The Hippocratic oath states quite unequivocally *"Primum non nocere"*—first do no harm. Yet every time a doctor prescribes a drug, he risks breaking that promise. There is no medication that doesn't have the potential to cause some side effects in some people, and older people are especially vulnerable.

People over the age of 65 make up only 12 percent of the population. But they take 25 to 30 percent of the prescriptions filled each year in this country.[19] They also face the greatest danger of suffering serious side effects. It has been reported that one out of four hospitalizations of older people may be linked to an adverse drug reaction.[20]

Now, most of the complications of drug therapy are not particularly dangerous. They may range from frequent urination and dry mouth to indigestion and dizziness. Such side effects may seem so trivial that many doctors don't even think to warn their patients about them. Take dry mouth for example. Hardly a life-threatening problem. But imagine what it would be like to have such a parched mouth that it felt like you had chewed a fuzzy cotton ball after walking 10 miles through the Sahara Desert.

Over 200 drugs can cause dryness of the mouth, cracked lips, and a change in tongue texture. The culprits include antihistamines and decongestants found in cold remedies and allergy medicine. Antidepressants (like **Adapin**, **Amitril**, **Aventyl**, **Doxepin**, **Elavil**, **Endep**, **Janimine**, **Pamelor**, **Sinequan**, **Surmontil**, **Tofranil** and **Vivactil**), some blood pressure medicines, and certain GI (gastrointestinal) drugs (**Bentyl**, **Pro-Banthīne**, **Combid**, **Librax**, **Donnatal**) can also be trouble.

No amount of water slurping will make the feeling go away. And if allowed to continue, this condition can make speaking and eating more difficult. People with dentures suffer the most. The gums can become very painful and may shrink so that dentures no longer fit properly. Artificial saliva sold as **Xero-lube** may help temporarily, but it's far from a cure.

Squeeze Life Now—
The Future Is Uncertain

A dry mouth won't kill you but it sure can hurt the quality of your life. **Quality of life**—that's a phrase that many physicians don't like to talk much about. Remember the Hippocratic oath—first do no harm. It has to cause doctors a little twinge every time a patient complains about stomach pain from an arthritis drug or dizziness from a blood pressure medicine. But instead of discussing the problem and trying to diminish the discomfort, many doctors call such patients whiners, complainers, or the worst epithet of all—noncompliers—which means they won't take their medicine. To us, that's always sounded a lot like blaming the victim.

Now we sincerely believe that most physicians are committed to healing people and keeping side effects to a minimum. They want to preserve and prolong life. But trying to balance these goals may be tricky. Some things can't be "fixed," and the drugs that may add years can cause real problems. Faced with this dilemma, a physician might find it hard to exercise the candor and joint decision making that many patients have come to expect. A reader of our newspaper column related the following experience with **Inderal** (propranolol), one of the most frequently prescribed drugs in the country. It is taken for everything from high blood pressure and irregular heartbeats to angina and migraine headaches.

> **I am a 66-year-old man who is taking Inderal for a heart condition. I have been on this medication for approximately five years and since taking this drug, my sexual urge has steadily decreased and I now find myself to be impotent. I've discussed this problem with my doctor and he claims my problem is psychological. However, I know that it is not, and that Inderal can have that effect on a person's sex drive.**

Most patients are smart enough to figure out such side effects for themselves. Insisting that impotence is "psychological" is ludicrous, especially when the doctors' bible, the *Physicians' Desk Reference (PDR)* states quite clearly that "male impotence" is a potential adverse reaction from **Inderal**. Some doctors may assume that sexuality shouldn't matter to anyone over 60. We beg to disagree. That's as much a part of your quality of life as anything else.

Another reader also reported problems with **Inderal**:

> **My family doctor put me on Inderal about three years ago, as a hedge against an irregular heart beat. As for doing what it was supposed to do, the drug did its job, most of the time, but not all of the time.**
>
> **However, it also clobbered me with the worst and deepest and blackest depression I ever had in my life. This went on for a year and a half, with the doctor being in the dark as to what was causing the problem. The depression became so black and deep I tried to end my life several times, and failed only because my wife discovered what I was trying to do.**
>
> **Finally, my family doctor eased me off Inderal, and started a program with Lanoxin, which turned out to be a better control for my heart condition, and lo and behold, the terrible depression lifted almost overnight.**

It's incredible that it took one and a half years in this case to discover that **Inderal** could cause depression. Quoting from the *PDR* under the heading **"Adverse Reactions"**:

> *Central Nervous System*: **Light-headedness; mental depression manifested by insomnia, lassitude, weakness, fatigue, reversible mental depression progressing to catatonia; visual disturbances; hallucinations; an acute reversible syndrome characterized by disorientation for time and place, short-term memory loss, emotional lability, slightly clouded sensorium, and decreased performance on neuropsychometrics.**[21]

Fortunately, **Inderal** does NOT cause such problems for most people. Millions have benefited from this medication without complications. It reduces blood pressure, controls irregular heart rhythms, takes away anginal pain, prevents migraine headaches, and averts repeat heart attacks. Undoubtedly, **Inderal** has also warded off countless strokes and saved thousands of lives. But physicians must balance the benefits against the side effects. An article in the *New England Journal of Medicine* says it best:

> **In treating patients with hypertension, physicians who are successful in controlling blood pressure may be unaware of the negative effect that antihypertensive drugs can have on the quality of life—on the physical state, emotional well-being, sexual and social functioning, and cognitive acuity—of their patients. Some patients perceive the use of antihypertensive medications to be more troubling than their seemingly symptomless disease, resulting in noncompliance and ineffectual long-term treatment.[22]**

And there's the double bind, dear reader—the ultimate in pharmacological paradoxes. You feel fine but the doctor says you have hypertension. Left untreated, it could increase your risks of heart and kidney disease, not to mention stroke. The last thing you want is to suffer paralysis or speech impairment from a blood clot or a bleeder in the brain. But you don't want to drag around for the rest of your life feeling miserable because of drug side effects.

Is it possible to control blood pressure without mucking up your life? Of course it is. Not all drugs are created equal. And people respond individually to various medicines. The researchers who wrote about quality of life in the *New England Journal of Medicine* studied the differences between **Capoten** (captopril), **Aldomet** (methyldopa), and **Inderal** (propranolol). They discovered some impressive variations: people taking methyldopa were more likely to experience fatigue, dry mouth, and blurred vision than those on captopril. The **Capoten** patients "scored significantly higher on measures of general well-being, had fewer side effects, and had better scores for work performance, visual-motor functioning, and measures of life satisfaction."[23]

People on propranolol also did better than those on methyldopa when it came to work performance. But patients "taking captopril reported fewer side effects and less sexual dysfunction than those taking propranolol."[24]

Now this doesn't mean that you should immediately call your doctor and demand a prescription for **Capoten**. It's not appropriate for everyone, and some people will experience unpleasant, if not dangerous, side effects on this drug too. What's more, a great many people do just fine on **Inderal** and **Aldomet**. Finding the right drug for you in the right dose may take some tinkering. No matter what your condition—diabetes or diarrhea, hypertension or heart disease—it may take plenty of persistence and patience from both you and your doctor to come up with the right therapeutic combination to keep you going strong. Just like Betsy, our old car, when you get a few miles on you, you deserve a little special treatment.

Capitalizing on Quality

Only in the last few years have drug companies come to realize that pampering pays. Squibb, the manufacturer of **Capoten**, has converted the "quality of life" issue into a major marketing bonanza. Dr. Charles Sanders, Executive Vice President for Science and Technology of Squibb Corporation, summarized:

> **The emerging picture of captopril came at a time when world opinion was paying more and more attention to the idea that advances in medicine should be judged not only on the medical outcome of a particular treatment regimen, but also on the impact of that treatment on a patient's life.**
>
> **Scientists attribute this attitudinal shift to four decades of social and technological changes, including the revolution in medical technology and the aging of the population in developed countries, which has contributed to the significant growth of chronic disease. The result is that people today not only live longer but expect more out of life.**[25]

Drugs that can deliver on this promise become shooting stars. Not suprisingly, **Capoten** was one of the brightest, with a 55 percent jump in sales in recent years.[26] Other high fliers include the heart medicines **Procardia** (nifedipine) and **Cardizem** (diltiazem), the ulcer drug **Zantac** (ranitidine) that sounds like it came from outer space, the high blood pressure medication **Tenormin** (atenolol), and the arthritis remedy **Feldene** (piroxicam). Sales of just these six drugs brought in well over $1 billion to their manufacturers.

What all these compounds have in common is that they treat chronic conditions that often affect older people. They also appear to be either more convenient or better tolerated than many of their predecessors. It should come as no surprise that drug companies love senior citizens. They are focusing on ailments of aging because that's where the big bucks are. According to financial expert Monte Gordon:

> **The elderly constitute the fastest-growing sector of the population, increasing at more than twice the rate of the total population. In the past 100 years the total U.S. population has multiplied five times, while the over-65 sector has multiplied an astonishing 15 times. Not only are *more* people living past age 65; our average life expectancy has grown from 45 years in 1880 to about 75 years today, and still advancing. Today, nearly 80% can expect to live through much of their seventh decade! On July 1, 1983, for the first time in our history, people over 65 surpassed in number those under 25: a watershed—we are no longer a nation of teenagers.[27]**

Experts predict that "drugs used by the elderly are likely to show a huge sales increase as these historic demographic changes make themselves felt in the market."[28] Already the pharmaceutical industry is devoting a large part of its research to the special needs of the elderly.[29] This "drug boom" will lead to the development of safer and more effective medicines for the ailments of aging—high blood pressure, heart disease, arthritis, and diabetes. More important, we will see treatments for conditions that until now have resisted therapy. Drug companies are scrambling to come up with what have variously been called "mind rectifiers, performance enhancers," or more to the point, "memory pills." Such medicine may not cure Alzheimer's disease, but there is hope that they might be able to hold the line against further deterioration. They may even help so-called benign forgetfulness that so often comes with aging.

Drug company executives have noted that prostate enlargement is one of the most common complaints of older men. More than half the men over 70 suffer with some symptoms of urinary difficulty. Each year approximately 300,000 prostate operations are performed.[30] Occasionally they lead to incontinence or impotence. An effective drug would go a long way toward ending the physical, not to mention the psychological, discomfort. And speaking of psychological, there are expectations for better and safer antidepressants. There should also be improvements in the prevention of atherosclerosis, osteoporosis, and cancer. The future looks pretty darn good. For all their problems, when drugs are used prudently, they not only prolong life but improve the quality as well.

In the pages that follow, we'll try to give you the information you need to make more intelligent decisions about the drugs you may take. Think of yourself as a co-pilot about to take off on a long flight. The captain (your doctor) is in charge, and your task is to go over the checklist to make sure every contingency is covered. What's the destination and when will you know you have arrived? Knowing the goal of drug therapy is crucial but often overlooked. Do you know when and how to take the medicine? What are the most common side effects—and which ones are serious enough to trigger an emergency phone call? Are there any foods or other medicines you must avoid? Armed with this kind of information, you should be able to avoid a bumpy flight, not to mention a crash landing.

Although older people must be especially vigilant with any medicine, some have developed a reputation for being particularly tricky. Many are found in the table at the end of this book from pages 393 to 419. We encourage you to check this list, and if you are taking one or more of these medications, make sure your physician and pharmacist are monitoring you closely.

Things to Remember

1. As we age our bodies change. It's hard to detect subtle declines in kidney and liver function, but they can have a profound impact upon the effectiveness and toxicity of many drugs.

2. Disorientation, confusion, or personality changes may result from reactions to drugs—including **Lanoxin** (digoxin), a heart medication, and **Tagamet** (cimetidine), an ulcer drug. What's more, they can come on so gradually that the connection to the drug may not be obvious.

3. There is a shocking lack of information about how older people respond to most medications. Until recently the FDA has not required special testing, so drug companies and physicians may be unaware of differences. If you suspect you are more sensitive to "normal" doses, let your doctor know.

4. Combining several drugs at once can lead to unexpected and disastrous consequences. Even over-the-counter medications like laxatives, antacids, and cold remedies could interact dangerously with prescription medicine. ALWAYS have your physician and pharmacist double-check to make sure the drugs you are taking are compatible.

5. Watch out for the "vicious cycle syndrome." That's when you start taking one medication to overcome the side effects of another. If your medicine is making you miserable, it's better to try to find an alternative rather than popping more pills, which may have side effects of their own.

6. Some blood pressure drugs can interfere with the quality of a person's life. Newer (and unfortunately more expensive) compounds may be less likely to cause fatigue, depression, sexual problems, sleep disturbances, and forgetfulness.

References

1. Abernethy, D., et al. "Verapamil Pharmacodynamics and Disposition in Young and Elderly Hypertensive Patients." *Ann. Int. Med.* 105:329–336, 1986.
2. Gilman, Alfred Goodman; Goodman, Louis S.; Rall, Theodore W.; and Murad, Ferid, eds. *Goodman and Gilman's The Pharmacological Basis of Therapeutics*, 7th ed. New York: Macmillan, 1985, pp. 738–739.
3. Schentag, Jerome J., et al. "Pharmacokinetic and Clinical Studies in Patients with Cimetidine-Associated Mental Confusion." *Lancet* 1:177–181, 1979.
4. Basavaraju, Nerlige G. "Cimetidine-Induced Mental Confusion in Elderly." *New York State J. Med.*, July, 1980, pp. 1287–1288.
5. "Cimetidine (Tagamet): Update on Adverse Effects." *Med. Let.* 20:77–78, 1978.
6. "Van Sweden, B., and Kamphusen, H.A.C. "Cimetidine Neurotoxicity." *Eur. Neurol.* 23:300–305, 1984.
7. Cerra, Frank B., et al. "Mental Status, the Intensive Care Unit, and Cimetidine." *Ann. Surg.* 196:565–570, 1982.
8. Mani, Ranjit B. "H2-Receptor Blockers and Mental Confusion." *Lancet* 2:98, 1984.
9. Greenblatt, David J., et al. "Drug Disposition in Old Age." *N. Engl. J. Med.* 306:1081–1088, 1982.
10. Temple, Robert. "Guidelines for Studying Drugs in the Elderly." Presented at The Drug Information Association Workshop on Geriatric Drug Use, Washington, D.C., Feb. 28, 1984.
11. Faich, Gerald A. "Adverse-Drug-Reaction Monitoring." *N. Engl. J. Med.* 314:1589–1592, 1986.
12. Federal Council on Aging. U.S. Dept. of HHS: The Need for Long Term Care: Information and Issues. DHHS Publication (OHDS) 81–20704. Washington, D.C., U.S. Government Printing Office, 1981.
13. Williams, Paul, and Rush, David R. "Geriatric Polypharmacy." *Hospital Practice* Feb. 15, 1986, pp. 109–120.
14. Ibid.
15. Mangini, Richard J., ed. *Drug Interaction Facts*. St. Louis: Lippincott, 1986.
16. Ibid.
17. Pearson, M. W. "Prescribing for the Elderly—An Audit." *The Practitioner* 229:85–86, 1985.
18. Williamson, J., and Chopin, J. M. "Adverse Reactions to Prescribed Drugs in the Elderly: A Multi-Centre Investigation." *Age and Ageing* 9:73–80, 1980.
19. Farley, Dixie. "Protecting the Elderly from Medication Misuse." *FDA Consumer* 20(8):28–31, 1986.
20. "Drug Use Problems Hospitalize Elderly." *Medical World News* 27(22):16, 1986.

21. Huff, Barbara B., ed. *Physicians' Desk Reference,* 40th ed. Oradell, N.J., Medical Economics Co., 1986, p. 624.
22. Croog, Sydney H., et al. "The Effects of Antihypertensive Therapy on the Quality of Life." *N. Engl. J. Med* 314:1656–1664, 1986.
23. Ibid.
24. Ibid.
25. O'Donnell, William, and Sokolowski, Gail. "Captopril: Quality of Life." *Squibline,* Fall, 1986 pp. 6–14.
26. Glaser, Martha. "Which Rx Brands Shone the Brightest." *Drug Topics* 130(5):43–54, 1986.
27. "The Greying of America." *Letter from the Lion,* Winter, 1986, No. 22.
28. Dickinson, James G. "Elderly Explosion Should Set Off Drug Boom." *Drug Topics,* Jan. 17, 1983, pp. 50–52.
29. "Drug Search: Meshing Costs, Regs." *Medical World News,* Mar. 10, 1986, pp. 114–115.
30. Goldstein, George S. "New Leads in Product Development." Presented at "Pharmaceuticals for the Elderly: New Research and New Concerns." Feb. 13, 1986.

2

Surviving the System by Speaking Up

We're tired of being told to "act your age." When we were kids we knew that kind of reprimand meant we'd better stop having fun and start behaving. As adults we're supposed to live up to an image of responsibility and maturity. And when we retire and are expected to be "older and wiser," people become downright uncomfortable if we don't fulfill their ideals.

Let's face it, Norman Rockwell didn't do us any favors. It's wonderful for people to imagine gray-haired grandparents smiling benevolently as they preside over the holiday table with all the family gathered round. Everyday life isn't nearly so idyllic, but a lot of people still feel they have to struggle to satisfy everyone else's expectations. Commercials on television reinforce the idea that we should tough out our aches and pains without letting on that we're hurting.

Doctors, like other people, love the Norman Rockwell vision of the elderly. Most of the people who go into medical school are pretty idealistic in the first place, and they can get enormous satisfaction out of making people better, whether they're repairing a hernia, removing a gallbladder, or pulling someone through a nasty bout of pneumonia. But a doctor who loves to "fix things" and see his patients get better may feel frustrated treating older people with chronic conditions that don't clear up and go away.

Once in a while a doctor who's not having much success easing a patient's pain may react to his own unhappiness about that by "blaming the victim." If Helen, Jeannette, or Adele don't smile, nod, and act charming, if they ask tough questions, demand answers, and air their difficulties and strong opinions, they may be considered "tough old birds."

There's got to be some middle ground between silver-haired graciousness and the cranky old lady, but these stereotypes don't leave much room. Categories like this can really get in the way when people are trying to communicate with each other. If older patients worry about asking the doctor questions or mentioning the side effects that have been bothering them for fear of being seen as grumpy old geezers instead of the angelic elders the media like to show off, then this kind of pigeonholing has done far too much damage.

We may feel, with some justification, that the doctor will be pleased and treat us better when we smile, don't complain, and act like "good patients." But you don't visit the doctor just to make *him* feel better. No, the point is to help you feel better—and no doctor can do that unless he knows exactly what's bothering you, and unless you understand exactly what he's asking you to do. While we'd never suggest that you be rude or nasty to your doctor, remember that "good patient points" don't add up to good health.

Don't Suffer in Silence

There's a common myth that old folks gripe a lot about drug side effects. Doctors also complain that their elderly patients are "noncompliant"—that they don't take their medicine. Wrong on both counts! A study by Johns Hopkins researchers Drs. Lawrence Klein and Pearl German proves that older patients are actually *less* likely to blame their medications for any problems they may be having.[1] Although they may be even more vulnerable than "youngsters" of 40 or 50 to drug side effects, older people are less likely to blame their medications.

Why not? How is it that patients don't recognize that their drowsiness, dizziness, diarrhea, insomnia, or urinary problems might be caused by the drugs they are taking? Part of the reason may be that too many doctors hear no evil, see no evil, and, above all, *speak* no evil about the medicine they prescribe. Study after study suggests that the majority of patients are not informed about potential problems.[2,3]

Maybe doctors are afraid that if they mention side effects, patients won't swallow their pills. But the Johns Hopkins investigators discovered that surprisingly few older people actually stopped taking their drug, even when they realized it was causing them difficulty.[4] What's more, some don't even complain when they are having this kind of trouble, partly because they have a hard time getting in touch with their doctor, partly because they don't think the doctor would understand, and partly because they don't think it's important enough to "pester" the doctor about.

If a reaction to a drug doesn't bother you, then perhaps it really isn't important enough to make a fuss about. But if it's interfering with your life, by all means speak up. Your doctor may assume that if you don't mention any problems, you don't have any. If you suspect that the dizziness, forgetfulness, or constipation that has been troubling you lately could be related to that drug you started last week or last month or even last year, why not ask? The doctor just might have some other treatment options, or some ideas on minimizing the discomfort, but he won't think to suggest them if he believes everything is going just fine. Of course, if you can't get through to your doctor or he doesn't seem to pay attention, you might need to consider some tactics beyond just speaking out. More about those later.

The truth is, prescribing for elderly people can be pretty tricky. Because our bodies do handle drugs differently as we get older, both underdosing and overdosing are common pitfalls for the physician writing out a prescription.[5] In fact, according to Dr. Peter Lamy, one of the world's leading experts on geriatric prescribing, "The normal adult dose is quite often an 'overdose' in the elderly."[6] But it may not look like an overdose. For example, doctors know that a patient on barbiturates may get very sleepy. If the dose is a bit too high, such a person may be heavily sedated and hard to rouse. A physician who is not aware that in elders barbiturates can occasionally lead to exactly the *opposite* response—agitation and hyperexcitement—might be tempted to conclude the patient needs more of the drug. That's why, for so many drugs, frequent monitoring is needed to make sure the dose is right. One of the standard mottos for prescribing for seniors is "start slow, go low," or even, "say no."

Dr. Henry Wieman, an expert in geriatrics at Upstate Medical Center in Binghamton, New York, believes that the risks of adverse reactions to medicines in older patients are high enough that doctors should try to minimize them by prescribing nondrug therapies whenever possible.[7] He recommends support groups, clergy counseling, or an exercise program for a patient with anxiety, for example, rather than tranquilizing medications such as **Valium**, **Tranxene**, **Xanax**, or **Ativan**.

That's especially true if the doctor is no more familiar with these drugs than a group of medical students, residents, and psychiatrists were with **Valium** about ten years ago. These docs were given a written quiz to check their knowledge of the action and usage of this popular anti-anxiety drug. No tricks: "all questions had a direct and immediate bearing on such clinically relevant decisions as when to prescribe or withhold a drug, choice of administration route, establishment of a proper dose, administration schedule, and indications for discontinuation of a drug."[8] The results were shocking, to say the least. More than two thirds of the doctors tested did not know that **Valium**, like similar drugs that have become more popular recently, can hold special dangers for older people. And only about 20 percent were able to set up a dosage schedule that would maintain appropriate levels of the drug in the body.

Now, that was back in 1978. How much do doctors know today about prescribing for senior citizens? A sobering study completed not long ago in Pennsylvania suggests that far too many don't know nearly enough.[9] The researchers contacted doctors who had been reimbursed by Medicare during the previous year and asked them to take a multiple choice test on drugs in older people. If you can believe it, less than a third of the doctors who returned the test got enough answers right to show they really know how to prescribe for older patients. Even worse, the experts who determined what score would demonstrate "adequate" knowledge weren't demanding perfection: 63 percent was "passing." Ask any schoolteachers you know how they'd feel if two thirds of their class got less than 63 percent on a test. Do you think those students would be allowed to go on? Yet these were doctors who treat older people, and when they make a mistake, there's a good chance that we, their patients, suffer the consequences. That's outrageous!

If we had our choice of those doctors, we'd rather pick one who passed. But there isn't any diplomatic way to test our docs before they write us a prescription or two. The investigators running this study took a look at which doctors did much better than the rest, and here's what they found: Doctors in group practice and those with practices in which a quarter to a half of all their patients were elderly tended to do well. So did those who believed professional meetings were the most important source of information about prescribing for older people, and those who thought doctors need to keep learning more about drugs and the elderly. Board-eligible or -certified physicians did better, too. Doctors who relied on drug advertising and company "detailers" fared worse.[10] But a lot of this information isn't any more likely to be listed in the phone book next to the doctor's name than his score on such a test.

Is a Good Doctor Really Hard to Find?

The first step in protecting yourself against drug dangers and making your medicine work best for you is to pick your doctor wisely. You may have to investigate several and interview a few before finding the physician who is right for you. That's right—you will be doing the investigating and interviewing, just as though you were an executive in some important company looking over the candidates for the job. It's amazing, but some folks check out a prospective housekeeper, hairdresser, or moving company far more carefully than they do their doctor. Yet who will have a greater impact on your life?

When we are hunting down a doctor, we ask the following questions.

Is the doctor in a group practice with other physicians? You'll be able to tell this just by looking at the listing in the Yellow Pages or the sign on the office door. The reason a group practice is an advantage is that you are covered all the time. There seems to be some kind of law that medical emergencies happen on weekends and holidays, not to mention the middle of the night. In a group practice, one of the doctors is likely to be on call during those times, and that means if you run into trouble while your doctor is away on vacation, you won't be taken care of by a total stranger. Instead, it will be one of your doctor's partners, who has access to your medical history.

Does the doctor see quite a few older patients? If you are seeing a doctor for the first time, look around when you walk into the waiting room. Do you see mostly pregnant women and babies, or young executives waiting for their yearly physicals? If so, you might be in the wrong place. But if you know that a number of friends your age go to this doctor and are pleased with her, and you see a few other older people in the waiting room, you may have found a doctor with enough experience in treating patients in the upper age brackets to be aware of the pitfalls in prescribing for them.

Does the office have a policy allowing patients to "drop in" without appointments for blood pressure checks, flu shots, and such things? This kind of help, which doesn't require a doctor's personal attention, should be available when you need it.

How do the receptionist and nursing staff treat patients? You'll probably end up seeing more of these people than you see of the doctor, so it's nice if they are friendly, helpful, and willing to answer questions. It also gives you a hint or two about the doctor who picked them out. If the physician has a receptionist who "protects" him from his patients or makes you feel like you're imposing when you have a question, you may find it difficult to get through to ask about that problem you think your medicine may be causing.

Does the doctor seem to listen when you are talking to him? This is probably the most important criterion. You will be able to communicate most effectively with someone who listens to you and answers you in terms you can understand. If you don't feel comfortable enough with your doctor to ask her questions, you could run into trouble later on.

Does the doctor return your phone calls? No patient should expect that the doctor would interrupt an office visit with another patient to take a telephone call; you wouldn't like it if your doctor did that to you. But a doctor who cares about communication will return your call and answer your questions. You have a right to expect that.

Precautions for Self-Protection

It is estimated that 125,000 Americans die every year because they don't take their prescription medications properly.[11] As many as half of the medicines prescribed during a year are taken incorrectly. As a result, people suffer unnecessarily from avoidable side effects or drug interactions, or lengthier illnesses; their work or family life may be affected, and they may need extra doctor visits, more prescriptions, or even hospitalizations. It defies logic, for sure, why anyone would go and spend hard-earned money on medicine and then take it improperly. But a big part of the reason may start right in the doctor's office when he tears the prescription off his pad.

The trouble is communication, or rather a lack of it. Sometimes, what doctors think they are saying is not what patients hear. When one research team asked doctors whether they told their patients about potential side effects of the drugs they prescribed, two thirds said yes. But when patients were asked if they had been told about possible side effects, only about 8 percent said they had.[12] That's a giant gap! What other information may be falling between the cracks as well?

How to Talk to Your Doctor

If you want to make the most of your trip to the doctor, you'll need some strategies for bridging that big gap. The first step is to make sure the doctor understands why you're there to see him. This may sound simple, but it's not so easy. You'd be surprised how often people get tongue-tied in the presence of a white coat and fail to tell the doctor what brought them in. Whether you know it or not, you have a *lot* to tell the doctor. What you say, and how you say it, will make a big difference in how well your problem gets diagnosed and treated. You need to tell the doctor as completely and precisely as possible why you're there.

Believe it or not, the hardest thing may be getting him or her to listen to your complaint. Research on doctor–patient interactions at Wayne State University suggests you may not have much time to speak before your doctor cuts you off.

> **... Many patient complaints may never be discussed because doctors simply don't give patients the chance to say all that is on their minds. In 52 of the 74 videotaped interviews, doctors interrupted their patients a mean time of 18 seconds after they had begun describing their problems. Half the patients were interrupted right after mentioning the first symptom. Later, when some of the doctors who participated in the study listened to themselves, they explained that their interruptions were in the interest of time. But the interviews fail to support this notion. Patients generally reported two to four symptoms and, when uninterrupted, finished within a minute. Even the most long-winded of the group finished in 150 seconds flat.[13]**

If you want to use the precious time you have with your doctor effectively, you're going to have to be well organized. The best way to avoid being struck dumb in the presence of your physician is to sit in the quiet and comfort of your home and make a list of what's bothering you. Put down what hurts and when, and whether the problem is constant or variable in intensity. If you see any pattern to it (always before meals, or always after exercise, or worse on hot days), write that down, too.

Describe the complaint in as much vivid detail as you can muster. If it's pain, what's the nature of the pain? Sharp or dull? Throbbing or constant? If you have weakness, is it mild or moderate? Disabling or just annoying? Write down everything you can think of that describes the problem. Think of these as all being good clues for the physician–detective to use in solving what's often a complicated and confusing puzzle.

And now that you've got everything on paper, get out another page. It's time to arrange your list of questions, problems, or complaints in order, and that means the most important should be Number 1, right at the top. If you could get your doctor to address only *one* issue, which one would it be? That's where you need to start, because the doctor expects you to begin with the problem that's troubling you most. Patients often "build up" to their major complaint, but if you leave it pretty far down the list, you may never get to tell the doctor about it—or, if you do, he may not understand just how important it is.

Once doctors were taught that patients who appeared with lists had psychological problems. No more. A recent article in the country's most prestigious medical journal[14] told doctors to encourage rather than discourage the list-bearing patient. He or she isn't crazy, just competent. And that's precisely what you want to be.

While you've got the pad and pen at hand, make a list of *every* medication you're taking. Or if that looks like an impossible task, get out your shopping bag and truck it all with you. Don't stop with just the prescription drugs. Take in the over-the-counter remedies (including vitamins) you are using, too. Doctors often forget to ask patients about these; we patients may forget to mention them. Yet they too can interact with other medicines, and may have an important bearing on some of your medical problems.

When you get in to see the doctor, take your list with you. Tell the doctor you'd like to get her opinion on all of the issues you've written down. Some doctors will want to read the list. Fine. Others will let you use it as "notes." Whichever, politely insist on getting answers to all your questions, especially how to take your medicine correctly, what side effects to watch out for, and what other medicines won't mix well with your prescription.

One thing your list shouldn't include is a conclusion about what the doctor ought to do. Your job, as a patient, is to present the symptoms. The doctor gets paid for diagnosis and treatment. Doctors tell us that a lot of the people they see have already decided what's wrong with them and what they want done about it. Most physicians believe that what patients want, 80 percent of the time or more, is a prescription.[15] But in fact, research shows that patients are actually *less* satisfied with their doctor visits— especially when it comes to getting their questions answered— when they get a prescription than when they do not.[16]

Please, dear reader, look on the doctor who says you don't need a prescription as a boon, not a bane, to your health. She has saved you money, spared you the risk of adverse reactions, and undoubtedly improved your life considerably. When patients plead, "What can you give me for this, doctor?" it creates a pressure to act that harried physicians sometimes can't or won't resist. It's easier just to write a prescription for a seemingly innocuous antibiotic than it is to convince an insistent Joan Q. Patient that her problem will go away by itself, thank you very much, or that it won't go away by itself but that nothing medical science has yet devised will really make any difference.

Now here comes the really important part. Full attention, please! Make sure you have brought along something to write with, so you can get the answers to those questions down on paper. Admit it, now: How many times have you walked out of a doctor's office thinking that it all made sense, only to discover later that some crucial details had become fuzzy? Were you supposed to take two pills three times a day, or three pills two times a day? Which pill goes with meals and which one on an empty stomach? There was one medicine that was supposed to be taken at bedtime, and another one before breakfast, but which was which? Incredibly confusing, isn't it? That is why you've got to **WRITE IT DOWN**.

All right, we can hear you saying, get serious. Shorthand isn't my speed, not speedy shorthand anyhow, so how can I ask all these questions *and* write the answers down too? Here's where you'll have to be clever. Get help, if you need it. Bring along a trusted relative or close friend who can sit in on the visit, except for the physical exam. Besides giving you the moral support you may need, he or she can be taking the notes. Perhaps the nurse will write things down for you. Or you may want to sit down in the waiting room after you've seen the doctor and get everything down right then, while it's still all fresh in your mind. Another advantage is that you can check on any details you're not quite clear on then and there.

If you've really got *chutzpah*, you could bring along a little tape recorder and ask the doctor if it would be all right to record his explanations and recommendations. Just tell him that your memory isn't what it used to be and you want to keep everything straight. Now this tactic might completely freak him out, if he's afraid of a malpractice suit. But it sure would make things easier all the way around.

If your doctor gives you a prescription, make sure you can read it. If his handwriting isn't clear, ask the nurse to print it out in plain English on a separate piece of paper.

Once you're out of the office (isn't it great to have all your questions answered and in writing?), you've got one more job ahead of you. For safety's sake, double-check all the information about your medicine—instructions, side effects, interactions, and so on—with your pharmacist. He or she went to school for years just to be able to answer questions like this, and most will be delighted to help. There is a distinct possibility that the pharmacist may know even more about your medicine than your doctor. After all, that's all the pharmacist has to concentrate on.

You're going to have to be cagey, though. Don't tell the pharmacist what the doctor said. That will only preprogram her to parrot back what you've already been told. Pharmacists often feel uncomfortable adding to or contradicting what physicians tell their patients. So play dumb. That way you get to compare notes. If there are any important discrepancies, you'll need to follow up with the doctor.

In fact, if you get home and find that anything is not clear, you need to check back with your physician's office. The nurse may be able to answer your question. But if you're not satisfied, ask to have the doctor call you. If you're still unhappy with the information you've received about your medicine, take matters into your own hands. Go to your local library and ask the reference librarian for help finding information on your medicine.

Books that we've found helpful include:

The Pill Book. (Bantam Books)

The Essential Guide to Prescription Drugs, by James Long, M.D. (Harper & Row)

Physicians' Desk Reference (PDR). (Medical Economics)

Advice for the Patient (USPDI: vol 2). (United States Pharmacopeial Convention, Inc.)

You may also find our *People's Pharmacy* collection of three books useful. You should be able to find them in your library or bookstore.

Holding Off Hospital Hazards

"At least in the hospital," you may be thinking, "I will be in good hands." If only that were always true! Unfortunately, older people may be as vulnerable in the hospital as anywhere else. One physician protested the treatment of a 79-year-old friend:

> **"What bothered me most," my friend said, "was that no one in that hospital would talk to me. No one gave me information about what to expect, and**

> I couldn't ask questions because I knew nothing
> about my disease. They just assumed I knew all I
> wanted to know."
>
> Did my friend experience ageism? I think so.
> Though no one overtly discriminated against him,
> he received substandard care in these major ways.
> First, his physician delayed the diagnosis by slough-
> ing off his symptoms as the quirks of an old man.
> Second, the staff didn't treat him well. No one
> laughed at him or deprived him of customary ser-
> vices, but they didn't talk to him and didn't be-
> friend him . . .
>
> The third source of substandard medical care for
> my friend was . . . "a liability in power dynamics."
> Older patients don't know how to work the system
> or stand up to authoritative physicians.[17]

No doubt about it, hospitalization is sometimes necessary for a serious health crisis, but being in the hospital is hard on the elderly. Problems that don't have anything to do with the original medical emergency may crop up and be treated, increasing the risk of side effects and further difficulties.

Researchers at Boston City Hospital found that fewer than 10 percent of patients younger than 70 developed "hospitalization" problems such as falling, confusion, incontinence, or not eating. But more than 40 percent of those over 70 had one or more of these symptoms.[18] What's more, older people are more likely to be treated for these troubles with restraints, antipsychotic medi-cines, or tubes. As you might guess, some of these treatments, unpleasant enough in their own right, can make people more susceptible to other problems!

One reader of our column had a hair-raising tale to tell:

> Last August my wife, who is 62, weighs 100 lbs and
> has an artificial heart valve, suddenly developed a
> terrible headache, very high blood pressure, dizzi-
> ness and weakness. I took her in to the hospital,
> where she was given innumerable tests. They turned
> up nothing, and after a few days her blood pressure
> dropped and the headaches were less severe. Sud-
> denly, she lost the power of speech. She knew, for

example, that "cat" meant a cat, but she couldn't say the word.

She completely recovered her speech in a few days (which astounded her doctors), but then she suffered hallucinations for several days. Strangely, she knew she was hallucinating and to this day can recall the details of each one. When they stopped, she was sent home, but we still don't know what was wrong in the first place. According to the doctors, their tests showed she did *not* have a stroke.

The hospital statement lists the following drugs she was given:

> Valium
> Kaon-Cl
> Mephyton
> Aldomet
> Phenergan
> Omnipen-N
> Furosemide
> Tylenol-3
> Inderal
> Coumadin
> Vistaril
> Heparin
> Garamycin
> Dulcolax
> Mylanta
> NaCl
> Cathlon
> Metanephrine
> Isoptin

Naturally, we wonder whether all this medicine could have contributed to the problems she had in the hospital. When we are buying our own medication, we always look it up first, but the hospitalized patient never sees a prescription. I had no idea what she was taking until I got the itemized hospital bill.

Now that is one impressive list—18 different drugs. Did her medicine cause the bizarre mental reactions? That's a hard thing to prove, but it certainly wouldn't be out of the question. Combine that many medicines in a 62-year-old woman who weighs only 100 pounds, and you increase the likelihood of strange or unpleasant side effects.

Not all patients get so many drugs, but it is usually true that folks in the hospital get more medications than they do at home. And it *is* hard to keep track of what's being given, especially if the patient is feeling nervous (and who doesn't) or stressed and a little disoriented. With so many drugs prescribed, it's hardly any wonder that hospital patients sometimes get drugs that may interact with one another.[19]

Even in the hospital, nobody should have to take anything without knowing what it is. If you are feeling strong enough, as the patient, make sure you tell whoever brings the pill in to you, politely but firmly, that you have a policy of not taking anything until you know exactly (1) what it is, (2) what it's for, (3) *precisely* how and how often the doctor meant you to take it, (4) what side effects it might produce, and (5) how it will interact with the other medications you are undoubtedly being asked to take during your stay. And then, make sure you understand the answers and are satisfied with them before you take it. If what it is and what it's for don't seem to make sense to you, have someone double-check that it's really meant for you. Hospitals are complicated places, and if you are lying in the bed Mr. Smith was in yesterday, the pharmacy might not know it's you there. Somebody could have sent up Mr. Smith's medications—and goodness knows, you'll have enough of your own to take without his, too!

One other thing you may want to check: Did the doctor prescribe the pill to be taken routinely, or only when you need it? Hospitals sometimes run smoother when patients are given all the medicines they might possibly need on a set schedule, rather than only if and when they need them. That's convenient for hospital staff but not necessarily the best thing for the patients. It may take some negotiation, but if a drug is prescribed "as needed," you shouldn't have to take it if you don't feel you need it. For example, if someone comes around at 10 P.M. and wakes you up to give you a sleeping pill, you might want to tell him what to do with it. (When it comes to pain medication, though, don't be too stoic. Analgesics work much better if you take them before the pain is *so* bad you're at the end of your rope.)

If you're not feeling tough enough to do all this by yourself, enlist some help. A spouse, a brother or sister, a child, or a friend who visits regularly can ask these kinds of questions, make sure the answers are written down, and leave the paper with you for reference. All of us need moral support when we're sick, and a "patient advocate" can give that support in a concrete way.

The patient's advocate may have to exercise a fair bit of persistence to get the information, and that may not make him or her altogether popular with the staff. But if the patient is able to avoid a serious drug problem as a result, it's well worthwhile. In one case, a daughter's persistence uncovered a prescription drug overdose before it had serious, lasting consequences.

The patient, an 87-year-old victim of Alzheimer's disease, was becoming difficult to manage in the nursing home. The doctor prescribed **Valium** to try to keep her from hitting at the staff, but it didn't seem to make much difference in her behavior. About a week after she started on the medication, her family visited and found her hard to waken. They were alarmed, and her daughter in particular did not accept the explanation that this was simply a sign that her disease was getting worse. She persisted until the doctor ordered a blood test and discovered that, to everyone's surprise, the patient had dangerously high levels of **Valium** in her body.

Both the doctor and the nurses had assumed that her lack of response to the drug meant the dose wasn't high for her. But because of her age, her liver couldn't handle the "normal" dose of the drug.[20] Thank goodness her daughter was alert enough to notice the change in her mother, and was willing to "make a pest of herself" so that the overdose was discovered.

Let's assume you've made it over all the hospital hurdles without any problems. Once it's time to go home, you would think everything would be downhill. Not so fast. Most people are so anxious to get going, they may forget to ask crucial questions. And who do you ask? Everything can get so confused just before you check out that sometimes it's hard to know if the person you are talking to is a medical student, a nurse, an intern, or a pharmacist. Who's in charge? Sometimes it may seem as if the right hand doesn't know what the left hand is doing. Just make sure you get everything you need to know down in writing. If your doctor wants you to start some new medicine at discharge, get detailed instructions before you get caught up in packing up and paying the bill.

Things to Remember

1. Don't take anything for granted. Drugs can accumulate gradually and cause serious side effects even after you have been taking them a long time. If you have a troublesome symptom, let your doctor know. If you have been taking a drug for many years, it's wise to ask your doctor to reevaluate your therapy from time to time, to make sure it's still appropriate.

2. If possible, pick a doctor you feel comfortable with. You should be able to ask questions and get back answers you understand. Your doctor and his staff should be willing to take the time for you to get everything straight in your mind.

3. Make a list of what's troubling you before you get to the doctor's office. Be sure to put the most important symptom first, and be as specific and detailed as you can.

4. Stick to your list in the office. If you get distracted by other topics, you may not remember what you wanted to ask about.

5. Don't let the doctor brush you off. If you have three problems you want to discuss and she's only addressed one, don't let her off the hook. But don't necessarily expect her to have an answer for everything either. If a doctor says, "I don't know exactly what's causing that, but I don't think we need to do anything about it now. Let me know if it gets worse," that may be a perfectly reasonable response. Not everything can be "fixed."

6. Get a trusted friend or relative to help you ask questions or get the answers down. This can be helpful for doctor visits or in the hospital.

7. Don't demand a prescription. If your physician suggests a nondrug treatment or coping strategy, be grateful and give it a fair trial.

8. If you are given a new prescription, be sure to ask about how it should be stored and precisely when and how it should be taken, as well as what it is and what side effects and interactions you should watch for. Also ask how long you should take the medicine. Sometimes a drug that's intended for a time-limited problem ends up being taken for the rest of someone's life, just because they don't ask when they should stop it. Get the answers on tape or in writing.

9. Double-check with the pharmacist about how to take your medicine, about precautions, interactions, and side effects. The pharmacist can also tell you how the drug should be stored. If you are having trouble taking your medicine for some reason—you can't pry that child-proof cap off, or that liquid potassium tastes so foul you gag on it—your pharmacist may be able to help you come up with a solution. And if you can't read that teeny print on the label, ask if there isn't a large-print label.

10. If you discover you don't understand one of your doctor's instructions, or you notice a new symptom shortly after starting the medication, get back in touch with his office promptly. If it's an emergency, say so when someone answers the phone, but don't cry wolf. Most of the time a call back at the doctor's convenience should be just fine.

11. Be patient as well as persistent. It is not easy to prescribe safely for older people, and your doctor probably needs all the help you can give him.

References

1. Klein, Lawrence E.; German, Pearl S.; Levine, David M.; Feroli, E. Robert; and Ardery, Joan. "Medication Problems Among Outpatients: A Study with Emphasis on the Elderly." *Arch. Intern. Med.* 144:1185–1188, 1984.
2. Consumer Product Safety Network (Consumer Federation of America). Letter to members, Aug., 1986.
3. Miller, Roger W. "Doctors, Patients Don't Communicate." *FDA Consumer* 17(6):6–7, 1983.
4. Klein, et al., op. cit., p. 1186.
5. Wieman, Henry M. "Avoiding Common Pitfalls of Geriatric Prescribing." *Geriatrics* 41(6):81–89, 1986.
6. Lamy, Peter P. "Comparative Pharmacokinetic Changes and Drug Therapy in an Older Population." Paper presented at the Washington conference, "Pharmaceuticals and the Elderly: New Research and New Concerns," Pharmaceutical Manufacturers Association, Feb. 12, 1986.
7. Wieman, op. cit.
8. Gottlieb, R. M.; Nappi, T.; and Strain, J. J. "The Physician's Knowledge of Psychotropic Drugs: Preliminary Results." *Am. J. Psychiatry* 135:29–32, 1978.
9. Ferry, Margaret E.; Lamy, Peter P.; and Becker, Lorne A. "Physicians' Knowledge of Prescribing for the Elderly: A Study of Primary Care Physicians in Pennsylvania." *J. Am. Geriatr. Soc.* 33:616–625, 1985.
10. Ibid., p. 619.
11. Consumer Product Safety Network (Consumer Federation of America). Letter to members, Aug. 1986.
12. German, Pearl S.; and Klein, Lawrence E. "Adverse Drug Experiences Among the Elderly." *New Research and New Concerns: Pharmaceuticals for the Elderly.* Washington, D. C.: Pharmaceutical Manufacturers Association and Hill and Knowlton, Nov. 1986, p. 45.
13. Pfeiffer, John. "Listening for Emotions." *Science 86,* June, 1986, pp. 14–16.
14. Burnum, J.F. "La Maladie du Petit Papier: Is Writing a List of Symptoms a Sign of an Emotional Disorder?" *N. Engl. J. Med.* 313:690–691, 1985.
15. German and Klein, op. cit., p. 42.
16. Ibid.
17. Preston, Thomas A. "Ageism Undermines Relations with Elderly." *Medical World News* 27(23):26, 1986.
18. Gillick, Muriel R.; Serrell, Nancy A.; and Gillick, Laurence S. "Adverse Consequences of Hospitalization in the Elderly." *Soc. Sci. Med.* 16:1033–1038, 1982.
19. Gosney, Margot, and Tallis, Raymond. "Prescription of Contraindicated and Interacting Drugs in Elderly Patients Admitted to Hospital." *Lancet* 2(8402): 564–566, 1984.
20. Wieman, op. cit., p. 86.

3

Taking Your
Medicine

Your doctor has a dark little secret he's been hiding—he really doesn't know *exactly* how most of the medicine he's prescribing ought to be taken. And don't look to your pharmacist for help. She may not know much more than your doctor. It's not that they're dumb, or don't work hard, or don't care. To be fair, it's not all their fault. The FDA and most of the drug companies have let them down.

Until fairly recently, almost everyone assumed it really didn't make much difference how, or when, or with what you swallowed your little pill. The drug companies are happy to tell you how many hoops they have to hop through to get their medicine approved by the FDA, how many millions they spend developing each new medication, and to the fourth decimal place what amount of the drug is in each pill. But they usually can't tell you if it's better to take their medicine with meals or on an empty stomach.

Sure, some pills have long been known to cause heartburn or irritate the digestive tract, so those got prescribed "with meals," even if they didn't always work quite as well that way. But in general, you popped your pill and were assumed to be getting your medicine. It's a classic case of the manufacturers not seeing the forest for the trees.

Start asking around, as we did, about the ins and outs of taking popular prescription products with various foods and be prepared to draw a lot of blanks. It's a question that neither the drug industry nor the FDA really gave much consideration to until recently. One FDA honcho admitted to us that the failure to require the drug companies to gather data on food–drug interactions as part of their licensing tap dance was a major oversight.[1]

Does that sound incredible, or what? How is it possible that the most fundamental information about how to take your medicine has been left pretty much up to chance. Oh, you don't believe us? Check it out. Go to your local library and ask for a copy of the PDR (*Physicians' Desk Reference*). This book is supposed to provide doctors with comprehensive information on prescribing—side effects, precautions, drug interactions, and most important of all, dosing instructions. What you'll find in the PDR is a lot of fine print, all of it approved by the FDA. In fact, there is so much data, it's almost overwhelming, for doctors as well as patients. But you won't find much, if anything, about whether or not such commonly prescribed drugs as **Aldoclor** (methyldopa, chlorothiazide), **Bactrim** (trimethoprim, sulfamethoxazole), **Calan** (verapamil), **Darvon** (propoxyphene), **Dilantin** (phenytoin), **HydroDIURIL** (hydrochlorothiazide), **Inderal** (propranolol), **Isoptin** (verapamil), **Procardia** (nifedipine), **Septra** (trimethoprim, sulfamethoxazole), or **Tenormin** (atenolol) should be taken with meals or on an empty stomach. There are thousands of medications without this most basic information.

Sometimes they have instructions that sound reasonable until you try to figure out what they mean. Take **Cardizem** (diltiazem), for example. The manufacturer suggests you take this heart medicine "before meals and at bedtime." That seems clear enough, but do they mean 10 minutes, 30 minutes, or an hour before you eat? And what do they mean by bedtime? Some folks pack it in by 9:00 P.M., while others stay up past midnight. And have you ever wondered whether "take four times a day" means you should get up in the middle of the night?

If it sounds like we're making a big deal out of taking a simple little pill, you're right. We are. And there's a reason for that. After many years of writing and speaking about medications, we've become convinced that great gobs of money are being wasted every year because patients aren't given the details on how to take their medicine. What's worse is that in many cases the way they take it actually decreases the drug's effectiveness, thus prolonging the problem rather than giving the promised relief. Sometimes certain foods may even make drugs more dangerous.

According to the FDA and the National Council on Patient Information and Education, "Up to half of the 1.6 billion prescriptions dispensed annually are taken incorrectly."[2] And in a lot of cases, patients make mistakes in taking their drugs because no one bothered to do the proper homework. Doctors may assume that if there are no details in the PDR, it doesn't much matter exactly how a medicine is given.

Yet in the last couple of years a whole host of factors have emerged as major influences on the amount of drug that actually gets to work in a person's body after he swallows a pill. The food you eat, the time of day you take the medication, age, weight, sex, other drugs, individual variability—all these are factors that can contribute to inconsistencies in the way a drug works in different people.

The more we learn, the more we come to respect the complexity of the human system, and the more leery we become of "one-size-fits-all" prescribing. To read the books from which doctors get most of the information they pass on to you, a person could reasonably conclude that the majority of medications usually get dispensed at some standard dosage. It rarely says anything about considering your age or sex, and even more rare is any comment on foods with which the drug can (or can't) be mixed.

Even the amount of fat in a meal can make a big difference in how the medicine is absorbed. If your doctor says you should take **Dyazide** (hydrochlorothiazide, triamterene—original formulation), one of the most frequently prescribed drugs in the country, does he know that a recent study has shown that bacon and eggs and butter on your toast can boost the levels of this diuretic to almost double what they would be with a low-fat breakfast?[3] A bacon and egg breakfast with hash browns could speed absorption of the asthma medicine **Theo-24** (slow-release theophylline) so much that toxicity could become a real problem.

Very few researchers have been interested in these questions. What little work has been done is often contradictory. For example, the most commonly prescribed drug in this country, if not the world, is hydrochlorothiazide (HCTZ). This diuretic is sold as **HydroDIURIL, Esidrix**, and **Oretic**, and can be found in dozens of combination blood pressure medications. We have located three studies on the interaction of this drug with food, and they all disagree. One says HCTZ is best absorbed with meals,[4] while another insists the drug works best when taken on an empty stomach.[5] To muddy matters even more, the third study suggests that it makes no difference.[6]

There are thousands of drugs for which there is no data about food and drug interactions. According to Dr. Peter Welling, a leading expert in the field, "the problem with a lot of these studies is that the companies don't want to rock the boat because the drugs are selling well. The universities can't do them because the companies won't finance them, and the NIH (National Institutes of Health) doesn't think they have sufficient scientific merit. So there's a catch-22 here—who the hell wants to do the studies? This is the problem we face with all of these older drugs."[7]

All of this sounds pretty depressing. But we've gathered up all the information we could on these critical issues to help make sure you take your medicine the best way.

Read the Label

Perhaps you know people who rarely take the time to read the instructions that come with an electronic gadget or a toaster. They tear open the box, assume they know how it works, plug it in, and sometimes watch it go up in smoke. Since we don't want *you* to get burned, let's start by reading the label.

Actually, we hope you'll be *able* to read the label, but we won't be surprised if you can't. Pills come in small bottles, which quite reasonably have small labels with small print. Reading one of those things is like decoding the fine print in a contract from a loan shark. One study found that 60 percent of the patients being discharged from a hospital had trouble reading their medication labels, a similar percentage had trouble understanding the directions, and the purpose of 54 percent of the medications was a mystery to those asked to take them.[8]

Assuming you can read it, the label on your prescription contains some valuable information, though not nearly as much as we'd like. The pharmacist has translated the doctor's instructions for taking the medication into English, so the label says something like "Take one tablet three times a day." That sort of information is woefully inadequate, but what is there should be followed carefully. It's the only guidance you have, and not adhering to it can in some instances have catastrophic consequences.

The goal of most drug therapy is to achieve and maintain a certain level of medication in your bloodstream. That is a lot easier said than done, and in fact, even under the best of circumstances the levels of most drugs will fluctuate considerably. Spacing the drug dose out over the course of the day is an attempt to make this roller coaster ride a bit more even.

If you skip your morning pill and instead double up at noon, there are several possible outcomes. One is that your body, unable to absorb any more, will simply shed the excess drug. Another is that you will have suffered a prolonged period in which there was no medication in your bloodstream and will now trade it for a wretched excess. These are relatively benign outcomes. Things can get a lot more dangerous if we're talking about medications that have a powerful effect on the heart, kidneys, or hormones. In some cases, the distance between "just enough" and "too much" isn't all that great. Doubling up can mean double trouble.

Generally speaking, if the directions say "Take two tablets twice a day," the intent is that you take them at evenly spaced intervals. Keep in mind the goal—a more or less constant supply of the drug in the bloodstream—and you'll see how to time your pills.

There are other things of interest on the label. One, of course, is the drug's name. A lot of people—most, we'd guess—leave the doctor's office knowing they have a prescription for something, but not really knowing what it is. Oh, they might know it's "an antibiotic" or "a painkiller," but it isn't until they get the little brown bottle home and look at the label that they know they'll be taking "Tetracycline, 250 mg."

Knowing what you're taking is vitally important for a number of reasons. First, you will almost certainly want to use some supplemental sources of information (including this book and others such as our *The People's Pharmacy*, *The People's Pharmacy-2*, and *The New People's Pharmacy-3*) to find out more about the drug you're taking—its possible adverse effects, dangerous interactions with other medications, and typical dosages. In fact, you might want to first check and see if what has been prescribed seems to be appropriate. Ridiculous? Consider this. We've received far too many letters from people taking drugs that don't make sense for their conditions. One study of pharmacists reported that an astounding 80 percent of them saw apparently inappropriate prescriptions by physicians at least some of the time.[9] And the journals are crammed with instances of unreadable physician handwriting leading the pharmacist to fill a request for one drug with another whose name was similar.

In 1985 we received a letter from a reader of *The New People's Pharmacy—3* who had exactly such an experience:

> **Just yesterday I purchased your book. I barely skimmed through the first few pages but luckily I glanced at your chapter on Prescription Super-Bloopers.**
>
> **My husband, aged 73, went to the pharmacy to have three prescriptions filled. When he returned home, I checked each of the medications as labeled on their bottles and noted that one drug was totally unfamiliar to me and did not correspond to the prescription. The drug the doctor had prescribed was "Clonidine" (which we know as "Catapres") and the pill bottle was labeled QUINIDINE SULFATE 200 mg. My husband had specifically asked the pharmacist if he were getting a generic brand rather than the Catapres. He was told that he was not prescribed Catapres—generic or otherwise.**
>
> **You can see from the copy of the handwritten prescription I've enclosed that it might be possible to mistake the "Cl" for a "Q," but I can't see how it would be possible to interpret 0.2 mg to read 200 mg. Why take such liberty if it didn't make sense for the drug you thought was being prescribed? Obviously, Quinidine doesn't come in 0.2 mg, so why not question the prescription to begin with?**
>
> **I telephoned the pharmacist when I discovered the error and he wanted to know how I knew the drug was Clonidine. Did I have a duplicate of the prescription? I had photocopied the prescriptions, so I did have a duplicate. When he heard that, he apologized and had my husband return to the drugstore for the correct medication.**
>
> **It scares me to think that here I am reading your**

book about some cases of mistakenly filled prescriptions and that we too might have become a
"statistic."

It frightens us too to think of what might have happened if this
woman had not been so alert. Not only might her husband have
ended up taking a drug he didn't need, one with a number of
potential side effects (quinidine, prescribed for the heart, can
modify heart rhythms as well as cause headache, dizziness, nausea, rash, blurred vision, and other symptoms); even more serious,
he would have *stopped* getting the **Catapres** (clonidine) he had
been taking. Here's the warning in the PDR about **Catapres**:

> **Patients should be instructed not to discontinue
> therapy without consulting their physician. Sudden
> cessation of clonidine treatment has resulted in
> subjective symptoms such as nervousness, agita-
> tion and headache, accompanied or followed by a
> rapid rise in blood pressure ... Rare instances of
> hypertensive encephalopathy and death have been
> reported.**

How fortunate that our conscientious reader was so careful—at
the very least she probably saved her husband a headache, and
possibly even his life. Though few of us photocopy all our prescriptions, we can't say it too strongly: Know *exactly* what you
are supposed to be taking.

Exhibit A is the actual prescription our reader photocopied
before sending her husband off to the pharmacy. It says Clonidine
0.2 mg #100 ♀ tid. Exhibit B is what he got: Quinidine Sulfate,
200 mg, #100. Take 1 Tablet 3 Times A Day. As you can see, there
is a big difference.

The number of look-alike and/or sound-alike drugs is truly
frightening. Digoxin is a heart drug. So is digitoxin. But they
behave differently in the body and mistaking one for the other
could be quite dangerous. Who'd be surprised at the pharmacist
who read a scrawled prescription for **Cyclapen** as **Cyclopar**, or
Reglan as **Regulax**, or **Temaril** as **Tepanil**? It's a bad case of
what you might call "too close for comfort."

Or suppose the doctor phoned in a prescription for **Elavil**, an
antidepressant, and the druggist heard **Mellaril**, a major tranquil-

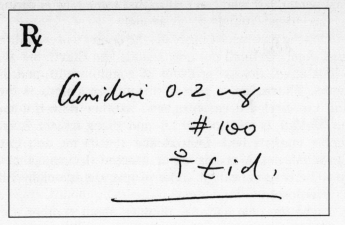

TAKE 1 TABLET 3 TIMES A
DAY

QUINIDINE SULFATE (RUGB
200MG   #100

izer. The hazard is particularly high on phone-in prescriptions. There are hundreds of drug names that are distressingly similar, and some that are spelled very differently actually sound quite alike. Whether the weak link is the doctor's handwriting or the telephone connection, the bottom line is that what's in the bottle stands a chance of being something you are NOT supposed to be taking. Check it out and make certain that what's in the bottle bears some relationship to what's wrong with you.

Next, check the dose. Why should you want to know about the typical dose if the pharmacist has neatly spelled out the instructions for taking the medicine? For one very important reason. You, the patient, are the *final* quality control inspector. After the doctor writes the prescription, and the pharmacist fills it, you are the last person left who can realize that something is wrong. And believe us, friends, things do go wrong.

Perhaps the pharmacist misreads the doctor's prescription by a decimal point. **Mellaril** not only sounds like **Elavil**, but also has the "look-alike" dosage problem of coming in 10- and 100-mg strengths. **Thorazine**, a potent tranquilizer, comes in 30- and 300-mg timed-release capsules, and another powerful antipsychotic, **Haldol**, is available in 1.0- and 10-mg tablets. Burroughs Wellcome markets both **Lanoxicaps** at 0.05 mg and **Lanoxin** tablets at 0.5 mg. A misplaced or misread decimal point could prove to be *very* unhealthy. Older people are especially vulnerable to overdoses.

Or maybe the pharmacist is thinking about another prescription while filling yours, and puts on its instructions instead. The point is, there are a multitude of possible sources of error. That's why *you* need to take your inspection seriously. Nobody else cares as much about you. You can and should always ask yourself, before taking a medication, "Does this make sense?"

Use every source of information available. Find out what a reasonable range of doses is for the drug you're being asked to swallow. If the amount prescribed for you doesn't add up, run, don't walk, to the phone and call the pharmacist. Ask her to double-check the prescription. If she insists it was filled correctly, call the doctor. It's your body that will suffer if somebody has made a mistake. Be polite, but firm. Tell the doctor you note that the amount you're being asked to take is three times the amount usually prescribed and you just want to make certain that's what he intended. If he's made a mistake, he may feel embarrassed and get defensive, but that's better than your putting your life on the line.

Another bit of information on the label that could prove invaluable is the expiration date. But it's rarely there. People often ask us if they can safely use a drug (especially an expensive one) they've had for a while—maybe an antihistamine left over from last year's hay fever season or a potent pain reliever they were given for a toothache. Of course there's no way to tell if a medicine has gone bad unless there's an expiration date on the bottle.

Although nothing magical happens on the last day the drug is supposed to be "good," the expiration date is in a sense the end of the manufacturer's promise that that pill will deliver a certain amount of medication to the bloodstream. Beyond that, you become an unpaid chemical test pilot by taking the medication. It might work. It might not. It might deliver full dose, or half. Or it might deliver some useless (or even harmful) by-product of the chemical breakdown of the drug. On balance, we'd have to say it's a risk not worth taking. If the label says it's dead, bury it. But the only way to know when to discard a drug is to make sure the pharmacist puts that expiration date right on the bottle.

Finally, you might find one or more stick-on labels added by the pharmacist containing warnings or limitations such as "Do not take with dairy products," or "May cause drowsiness." These should be considered part of the instructions, so pay attention to them.

If taking care of yourself rather than just trusting it all to the doctor and pharmacist seems either unnecessary or somehow disrespectful, consider the study that found that people over 60 pretty consistently got the short end of the information stick from health professionals. They received less information about drugs from their physicians than younger people. They also got less verbal information and less important information than younger patients when receiving a prescription drug. Younger people, for instance, received four times as much information about possible side effects as their over-60 counterparts. "It appears," said the researchers, "that the elderly, as more frequent users of drugs, are limited in the quantity of information they receive, including critical information that relates to side effects."[10]

Sit Down, Stand Up, Fight, Fight, Fight!

Having assured yourself you've got the right drug in the right amount, it's now time to swallow your medicine. And there's definitely a right—and a wrong—way to go about that seemingly mundane task.

Have you ever had trouble swallowing a pill? Almost everyone has, and older people often have a particularly hard time of it. There are a few tricks of the trade we'd like to pass along, in the hope that they'll help.

Ever watched most people take a pill? They slip it in their mouth, take a gulp of water, throw their head back, and pray it goes down. There's only one problem. Most capsules float when turned loose in a mouthful of water. So throw your head back and guess where the pill goes? Yup. It pops to the top, which in this case is the part of your mouth farthest from the throat, which is where you want the darn thing to go. You'll find it a bit hard to master at first, but try tipping your head slightly forward after taking that sip of water. If the capsule floats, it will rise to the top, which is now near the back of your mouth, and down she goes.[11]

But our favorite tip came from a doctor in Kentucky.[12] He calls it the "pop-bottle method." It's based on the fact that swallowing involves both voluntary and involuntary muscular actions. Eliminate the voluntary part and voila! The swallowing reflex takes over. To try it, proceed as follows. Get your pill ready. Open a bottle (no cans, please) of your favorite beverage (cola, juice, bottled water—carbonation seems to help). Put the pill in your mouth. Take a drink from the bottle, keeping contact between the bottle and your lips, using a sucking motion. This action activates the reflex swallowing motion. Good-bye pill. You won't even know it's gone.

Another way around the getting-it-down dilemma might be to crush a tablet (or, in the case of a capsule, spill out the little granules of medication) and take it in some gooey food. However, you should never do this without consulting either the doctor or pharmacist. The reason is that certain drugs undergo chemical changes when placed in very acid or alkaline environments (erythromycin and some of the penicillins, for example, are worth zilch if dredged in something like applesauce first— they don't like the acidity).[13]

Other drugs, such as those designed to release their properties slowly over a long period, must be taken in the original tablet or (more often) capsule. Any drug that has LA (long-acting), SA (sustained action), SR (slow release) or "Slo" or "Dur" as part of its trade name should be left as is. Still others, such as special formulations of aspirin, have what is called an enteric coating— one designed to minimize the impact of the drug on the stomach. Here again, the pill must be taken as is, or you could suffer the severe stomach irritation the pill was supposed to spare you.

The next trick in getting your medicine down is not to take it lying down ... and we mean that literally. One person wrote to tell us of feeling a sensation in his chest "like a red hot ember" within moments of taking a capsule. Thinking the medication was "stuck," he tried to "wash it down," but no amount of liquid would wash away the pain. What happened to him happens to thousands of people every year. The gelatin capsule *had* stuck in his esophagus. (To see how easily that can happen, try pressing your tongue lightly against a capsule and see what happens—just like it was put there with glue.)

What caused the pain, however, wasn't that the pill was stuck, but rather that it had released its irritating contents onto some extremely sensitive tissues. When some researchers looked into the question of how to take medication, they found 221 reported cases of throat injury caused by pills. The injuries ranged from hemorrhage and perforation of the tissue to five cases in which death resulted.[14]

Some 26 different pills were involved in the injuries, with almost half accounted for by doxycycline. There have been additional reports of injury by that medication[15,16,17] as well as tetracycline, theophylline, and a variety of other drugs. Tablets as well as capsules have caused problems. And such familiar friends as aspirin and vitamin C can be troublemakers.

The first step to happy pill taking, then, is to take your medication standing up and with plenty of liquid. The standing position gives the pill its best opportunity to keep right on rolling, and plenty of liquid will help the journey. If after all these tips you are still having trouble, maybe you need a different pill. Researchers have found that large round tablets are more likely to stick in your gullet than long thin ones (like capsules or caplets).[18] If you just can't choke down the pills your doctor says you should take, why not talk it over with her? You'd be amazed at the wide array of alternate formulations on the market these days.

When it comes to the antibiotic doxycycline, your doctor can choose between large capsules and little tablets—go for little every time. If the pain reliever **Wygesic** (propoxyphene, acetaminophen) looks intimidating, you could ask the doctor for **Darvon** (propoxyphene) and just pop several **Tylenol** Caplets (acetaminophen) on the side. You'd be getting the same ingredients in **Wygesic**, but in slightly smaller pills. Or say your doctor has prescribed **Inderal LA** (propranolol, long-acting). This formulation allows for convenient once-a-day dosing. But if you find the capsule keeps getting stuck, you might be better off going for regular **Inderal** in smaller tablet form. It's less convenient but could be easier to swallow.

No matter what size pill you're gulping, you should take it standing up and you should remain standing or sitting as long as possible, to get the pill past the esophagus and into your stomach. Taking medication with a gulp of water seconds before climbing into bed is really asking for it. Gravity is no longer in your favor, salivation decreases as sleep approaches, and trouble is just around the corner. The medication bomb gets about halfway down, you lie down, and bingo, end of journey. There it lies, in and on your tender esophageal tissue, the gelatin melting. You'll sure know it when the bomb goes off! Stand up and be counted. Your medicine will go down more easily.

The Numbers Game

If you have only one medication to take, count yourself lucky. And also unusual. The vast majority of older persons take more than one type of medicine.[19] This leads to a host of problems, ranging from simply being unable to remember and keep track of all the pills, to the even more difficult situation of conflicting instructions.

Lets see how that can happen. You're asked to take the ulcer medicine **Tagamet** (cimetidine) four times a day (at evenly spaced intervals . . . remember our discussion above), and the heartburn drug **Reglan** (metoclopramide) four times a day, but not within two hours of taking **Tagamet**, whose effect it will cancel. Oh, by the way, you *should* take **Tagamet** with food, but you *can't* take **Reglan** except on an empty stomach—30 minutes before meals. Getting confused?

That's just two drugs. Many seniors have multiple chronic (long-term) conditions that require three or more prescriptions. The bookkeeping would be enough to drive a corporate accountant up the wall.

You might find some assistance in the **People's Pharmacy Medication/Meal Wheel.**™ Here's how it can help you figure out when to take your pills. The wheel shows 16 hours in an average waking day. Let's say your day usually starts at 8:00 A.M. Then the wheel runs from 8:00 until midnight. Color in a pie-shaped segment for each meal. If you eat breakfast at 8:00, color the wedge from 8:00 to 9:00. Write any medications that must be taken "with meals" on a line touching the meal segment. A half hour one way or the other is still considered with food.

For any medications due "on an empty stomach," there must be at least one blank segment before the line on which you write. And for any drugs you've been instructed not to take with others, there must be at least two segments between the lines on which the drugs appear.

Visualizing your medication plan this way (and using a pencil with a good eraser) makes it a lot easier to resolve what may seem like a confusing hodgepodge of instructions. And it can also help make it clear to both you and your doctor when he or she has truly created a situation in which it's simply impossible to follow all the directions.

You can photocopy the blank Medication Meal/Wheel shown here and use it for your own schedule. Or you can write for a larger format wheel: Send $1 per copy with $1 postage and handling along with your name and address, clearly printed, to Graedons' People's Pharmacy, Medication Meal/Wheel, P. O. Box 52027, Durham, NC 27717–2027.

Use the bottom portion to note any symptoms you experience. Some of these might be adverse reactions from the drugs. Save the Medication Meal/Wheel and you will have an excellent record for discussing your medication and condition with the doctor, who will be astounded at your incredible organization and interest in your drug regimen. We have filled out an example to show you how it's done.

We have also prepared a **People's Pharmacy Medication Chart**. This monthly calendar will help you keep track of which medications you have taken so that you will know whether you miss a dose or not. We received a phone call recently from a woman who had panicked because she couldn't remember whether she had already taken her blood pressure drug **Lopressor** (metoprolol) that morning. She didn't know whether to risk having her blood pressure rise uncontrollably or suffer potential side effects from an overdose by taking an extra pill.

To keep yourself out of this kind of pickle, check off each dose on the calendar as you take it. The blank monthly Medication Chart here can also be copied or, if you prefer to receive a year's supply on a pad, send $1 plus $1 for postage and handling along with your name and address, clearly printed, to People's Pharmacy, Medication Chart, P. O. Box 52027, Durham, NC 27717–2027.

The Medication Meal Wheel

Date: MARCH 17   **Day:** TUESDAY

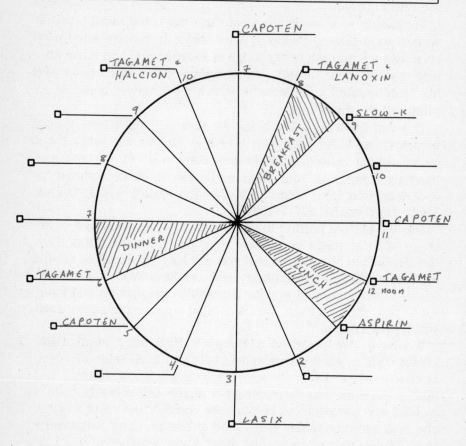

Time	Symptom
2:30	HEADACHE, DIZZY
9:40	ITCHY RASH

The Medication Meal Wheel

Date:	Day:

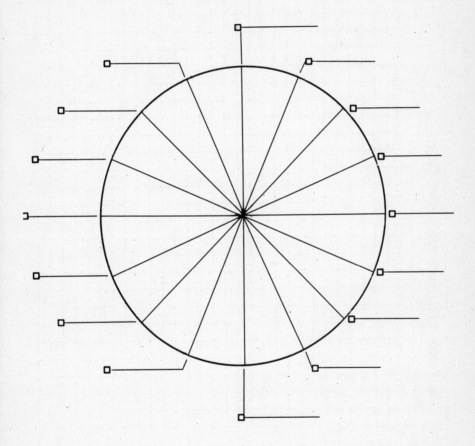

Time	Symptom

The People's Pharmacy Medication Chart

Month: _____

Drug Name	With Meals	1	2	3	4	5	6	7	8	9	10	11	12	13	14	15	16	17	18	19	20	21	22	23	24	25	26	27	28	29	30	31
Take ☐ times a day	☐																																
Take ☐ times a day	☐																																
Take ☐ times a day	☐																																
Take ☐ times a day	☐																																
Take ☐ times a day	☐																																
Take ☐ times a day	☐																																
Take ☐ times a day	☐																																

The People's Pharmacy Medication Chart

Month: _MARCH_

Drug Name	With Meals	1	2	3	4	5	6	7	8	9	10	11	12	13	14	15	16	17	18	19	20	21	22	23	24	25	26	27	28	29	30	31
CAPOTEN — Take [3] times a day	☐	✓✓✓	✓✓✓	✓✓✓	✓✓✓	✓✓✓	✓✓✓	✓✓✓	✓✓✓	✓✓✓	✓✓✓	✓✓✓	✓✓✓	✓✓	✓✓	✓✓																
TAGAMET — Take [4] times a day	✓	✓✓✓✓	✓✓✓✓	✓✓✓✓	✓✓✓✓	✓✓✓✓	✓✓✓✓	✓✓✓✓	✓✓✓✓	✓✓✓✓	✓✓✓✓	✓✓✓✓	✓✓✓✓	✓✓✓	✓✓	✓✓																
LANOXIN — Take [1] times a day	✓	✓	✓	✓	✓	✓	✓	✓	✓	✓			✓	✓	✓	✓																
SLOW-K — Take [1] times a day	✓			✓	✓	✓	✓	✓	✓	✓	✓		✓	✓		✓																
ASPIRIN — Take [1] times a day	✓	✓	✓	✓	✓	✓	✓	✓	✓	✓	✓		✓	✓		✓																
LASIX — Take [1] times a day	☐	✓	✓	✓	✓	✓	✓	✓	✓	✓	✓		✓	✓		✓																
HALCION — Take [1] times a day	☐	✓	✓	✓	✓	✓							✓		✓																	

The Meal Deal

Oil and water don't mix. That you know. But do you know which prescription medications don't mix well with food? Over the years there have been occasional sightings (like UFOs) in the literature of food–drug interactions, but nobody seemed to pay much attention. A few drugs were known to be highly irritating to the stomach, so doctors generally prescribed these to be taken "at meals." Other than that, there wasn't a whole lot of talk about food doing much to or for drugs.

Things are slowly changing.

The growing study of pharmacokinetics (the real measure of what happens to drugs after they enter your body) has led to an appreciation that a lot of things have an influence on how a drug gets absorbed and used (or not used) by the body. Among those factors, food turned out to play a significant role for many medications. Some foods delay the entry of drugs into the bloodstream, or prevent it entirely. Others actually enhance the drug's ability to get out and get to work.

For example, many antibiotics are less effective if taken with food. Take your ampicillin or penicillin (**Amcill, Omnipen, Pentids, Pfizerpen, Polycillin, Principen, Totacillin,** and many other brand names) with food, and you may not get rid of your infection. Acidic drinks like wine, soda pop, coffee, and fruit juice may also be a problem.

The exact formulation of the drug can make a big difference too. Erythromycin comes in various guises, including erythromycin stearate (**Bristamycin, Eramycin, Erypar, Erythrocin, Ethril, Pfizer-E,** and **Wyamycin S**), erythromycin estolate (**Ilosone**), and erythromycin ethylsuccinate (**E.E.S., EryPed,** and **Pediamycin**), all broad spectrum antibiotics often prescribed for a variety of infections, including those in the ear, throat, and urinary and reproductive tracts. Erythromycin stearate is less effective if taken with food. But studies have shown that the other two forms are absorbed at least as well (if not better) with meals as on an empty stomach. Acidic beverages are also a problem with erythromycin, so don't wash your pills down with O.J. or cola.

Griseofulvin (**Fulvicin, Grifulvin V, Grisactin, Gris-PEG**), on the other hand, gets a boost in doing its job against difficult fungal infections if swallowed with a meal containing a fair amount of fat. So live a little. Swallow your pill with a milk shake or take it at lunch when you're having tuna salad, pizza, or a burger and fries. If dessert's your thing, go ahead and indulge in a slice of pie or cheesecake. Take your tetracycline (**Achromycin, Cyclopar, Sumycin, Terramycin, Tetrex,** and others) with meals, though, and as little as half of it may get to work. Make that a meal containing milk products—or take a calcium supplement at the same time—and you can reduce that effectiveness to about 10 percent. You'd be paying a buck to get 10 cents' worth of help. Worse than that, 10 cents' worth is perhaps worse than no help at all, because it can mean the elimination of the weakling bacteria and the enhanced growth of the more resistant strains. You can wind up with an infection that's incredibly resistant to cure.

Laxatives containing bisacodyl (**Carter's Little Pills, Dulcolax, Fleet, Theralax**) shouldn't be taken with dairy products, either. They are designed to dissolve and go to work in the intestine; but when you wash them down with milk, they tend to dissolve in the stomach and cause irritation.

Calcium carbonate supplements (**BioCal, Calcitrel, Cal-Sup, Caltrate 600, Os-Cal, Suplical, Tums,** and others) are tricky. People with normal amounts of stomach acid probably don't have to worry about how they swallow this nutrient. But older folks often have lower than normal levels and this can make a profound difference in calcium carbonate absorption. Dr. Robert Recker of Creighton University found that patients with little, if any, stomach acid absorbed only one-fifth as much calcium when they took their supplements without food (*New England Journal of Medicine,* vol. 313, 1985, pages 70–73).

So to be on the safe side, take your calcium carbonate with meals, but watch out for foods that interfere with their absorption. Fruits and vegetables that contain oxalates, such as spinach, rhubarb, beets, green beans, gooseberries, and blackberries, should not be eaten within two hours of taking a calcium pill. That goes double for whole wheat bread. Not only does it contain oxalates, but it is also rich in phytic acid, as are other whole grain foods like oatmeal, barley, and rye. Black beans, almonds, limas, brown rice, soybeans, and peanuts are also full of phytate. Imagine the woman who sits down to a healthy breakfast of oatmeal, shredded wheat, or bran cereal and then pops down her calcium supplement. These foods will interfere with the effectiveness of her calcium and less will get into her body.

People with underactive thyroid glands are often put on thyroid supplements like **Cytomel, Euthroid, Levothroid, Synthroid,** and **Thyrolar.** Certain foods, however, can interfere with the action of the thyroid gland and compromise an already sluggish system. Do not overdo on cabbage, kale, kohlrabi, cauliflower, rutabagas, turnips, brussels sprouts, spinach, and soybean products like tofu.

People who have had blood clots (thrombophlebitis, pulmonary embolism, heart attack, or stroke) are often prescribed an anticoagulant such as **Coumadin** (warfarin). It works to thin the blood by blocking the action of vitamin K. If you eat large quantities of foods high in this nutrient, you could undo the benefits of your medicine and end up in the hospital with another clot. It's ironic that many of these foods are especially healthy and are often recommended for low-fat diets. Don't pig out on cauliflower, brussels sprouts, spinach, cabbage, broccoli, green beans, peas, leafy greens (turnip, mustard, collard), beef liver, soybean oil, and green tea. But don't eliminate all these foods, either, because you need some vitamin K to prevent hemorrhaging. To be on the safe side, have periodic blood tests run to make sure your blood is clotting properly.

Gout can cause episodes of excruciating pain when uric acid crystals build up in joints, especially in the big toe. Drugs that are commonly prescribed to control uric acid levels include **Zyloprim** and **Lopurin** (allopurinol), **Benemid** (probenecid), and **ColBENE-MID** (probenecid and colchicine). For these drugs to work most efficiently with the least risk of kidney stones, people taking them should avoid foods high in purines like anchovies, sweetbreads, brains, kidney, liver, gravies, scallops, herring, mackerel, sardines, spinach, broth (beef and chicken), lentils, and other legumes.

We could go on and on, but by now you have begun to get the idea that food and drug interactions can be extremely important. The following table lists drugs known to be adversely affected by food. We'd like to tell you that this list is complete, but we know that it isn't. When we began our quest for the information, it soon became apparent just how great the information gap is when it comes to food–drug interactions. We checked out standard references including *USPDI Drug Information for the Health Care Provider, PDR (Physicians' Desk Reference)* and *Drug Facts and Comparisons.* We scoured journal articles and we talked to ex-

perts in the field.[20-27] If your drug is not included, it may mean
that food does not interfere with it. But more likely, it means
there's not much research available. What's worse, physicians,
pharmacists, researchers, and drug companies don't always agree
or know how to interpret the data.

When we found scientific reports showing that peak blood
levels of **Procardia** (nifedipine), a popular heart medicine, were
delayed and reduced by almost 50 percent when the drug was
taken with meals, we thought the manufacturer would recommend taking this medicine on an empty stomach to get maximum
results. But some sales reps took it upon themselves to tell
doctors **Procardia** *should* be given with food—to minimize side
effects. Headquarters reined them in, but as of this writing, the
people at Pfizer still have not decided what instructions should
be provided, and have not convinced us that the drug will work
as expected if it is taken with meals.

Procardia is just one example, but confusion and controversy
about this issue are widespread. For now, all we can do is
suggest that you consult this list, and also press your doctor and
pharmacist to give you some definite information about the subject whenever they hand you a prescription or fill it. If they can't,
ask them to find out about any interactions of this drug with food
by asking the drug company directly. Perhaps if pharmaceutical
manufacturers get enough inquiries from enough doctors and
pharmacists on behalf of enough patients, they will gather the
information we all need.

Drugs Better Taken Without Food*

Meals may interfere with the absorption of many medicines,
either slowing down the rate at which the drug gets into the
body or reducing the amount that gets in. Your physician or
pharmacist should give you specific instructions for the medicine you are taking. If you are told the medicine must be taken
on an empty stomach, generally you should swallow it at least
an hour before meals or two hours after. Following it with a
full glass of water is usually a good idea.

*Brand names appear in **boldface**; generic names are in plain type.

Some medications can upset the digestive tract. Medicines such as the heart drugs procainamide and quinidine, aspirin and other arthritis remedies, iron supplements, the Parkinson's disease drug levodopa and others may need to be taken with meals to reduce irritation, even though food may limit their absorption somewhat. If any drug causes nausea, heartburn, or stomach upset and pain, or other side effects, this should be discussed with the physician and pharmacist. Because individuals differ, a drug that causes irritation for one may not bother someone else. Likewise, although the following drugs are better absorbed on an empty stomach, some people still obtain therapeutic benefits even when their medicines are taken at meals.

A.S.A. Enseals (aspirin [coated])
acetaminophen**
Achromycin V (tetracycline HCl)
Agoral (mineral oil)
Amcill (ampicillin)
ampicillin
APAP
Anacin-3** (acetaminophen)
aspirin (enteric-coated)
Azo Gantanol (sulfamethoxazole, phenazopyridine)
Azo Gantrisin (sulfisoxazole, phenazopyridine)
Bactocill (oxacillin sodium)
Bactrim (trimethoprim, sulfamethoxazole)
Beepen-VK (penicillin VK)
Betapen-VK (penicillin VK)
bethanechol
Bicillin (penicillin G)
Bristamycin (erythromycin stearate)
Capoten (captopril)
Carafate (sucralfate)
Cardizem (diltiazem)
Ceclor (cefaclor)
Citracal (calcium citrate)
Cosprin (aspirin [coated])
Cuprimine (penicillamine)
Cycline (tetracycline HCl)
Cyclopar (tetracycline HCl)
Datril** (acetaminophen)

Declomycin (demeclocycline)
Deltamycin (tetracycline HCl)
Deltapen-VK (penicillin V)
Depen (penicillamine)
dipyridamole
Dopar† (levodopa)
Dulcolax (bisacodyl)
Duvoid (bethanechol C)
Easprin (aspirin [coated])
Ecotrin (aspirin [coated])
Epsom salts (magnesium sulfate)
Eramycin (erythromycin stearate)
ERYC (erythromycin [coated])
Erypar (erythromycin stearate)
Erythrocin (erythromycin stearate)
erythromycin
erythromycin stearate
Ethril (erythromycin stearate)
Evac-Q-Kwik (bisacodyl)
Gantanol (sulfamethoxazole)
Gantrisin (sulfisoxazole)
INH (isoniazid)
isoniazid
Isordil (isosorbide dinitrate)
Keflex (cephalexin)
Laniazid (isoniazid)
Larodopa† (levodopa)
Lasix (furosemide)
Ledercillin VK (penicillin V)
levodopa†
Levothroid (T_4 thyroxine)
Lincocin (lincomycin)
Milk of Magnesia (magnesium hydroxide)
mineral oil
Mysteclin-F (tetracycline, amphotericin B)
Nadopen-V (penicillin V)
NegGram† (nalidixic acid)
Nizoral (ketoconazole)
Nor-Tet (tetracycline HCl)
Norpanth (propantheline bromide)

Nydrazid (isoniazid)
Omnipen (ampicillin)
oxacillin
oxytetracycline
P-I-N Forte (isoniazid)
Panmycin (tetracycline HCl)
Penapar VK (penicillin V)
penicillamine
penicillin G
penicillin V
pentaerythritol tetranitrate
Pentids (penicillin G potassium)
Pentol (pentaerythritol tetranitrate)
Pentritol (pentaerythritol tetranitrate)
Pen-Vee K (penicillin VK)
Peritrate (pentaerythritol tetranitrate)
Persantine (dipyridamole)
P.E.T.N. (pentaerythritol tetranitrate)
Pfizer-E (erythromycin stearate)
Pfizerpen-A (ampicillin)
Pfizerpen-G (penicillin G)
Pfizerpen-VK (penicillin V)
phenacetin
Pondimin (fenfluramine)
Posture (calcium phosphate)
Preludin (phenmetrazine)
Principen (ampicillin)
Pro-Banthīne (propantheline bromide)
procainamide†
Procan SR† (procainamide HCl SR)
Pronestyl† (procainamide HCl)
propantheline
Prostaphlin (oxacillin sodium)
Reglan (metoclopramide)
Retet (tetracycline HCl)
Rifadin (rifampin)
Rifamate (rifampin, isoniazid)
rifampin
Robitet (tetracycline HCl)
Rondomycin (methacycline)

Septra (trimethoprim, sulfamethoxazole)
SK-Ampicillin (ampicillin)
SK-Erythromycin (erythromycin stearate)
SK-Penicillin G (penicillin G potassium)
SK-Soxazole (sulfisoxazole)
SK-Tetracycline HCl (tetracycline HCl)
Sorbitrate (isosorbide dinitrate)
sulfamethoxazole
sulfisoxazole
Sumycin (tetracycline HCl)
Supen (ampicillin)
Synthroid (levothyroxine)
TAO (troleandomycin)
Teebaconin (isoniazid)
Tenormin (atenolol)
Tenuate (diethylpropion)
Terramycin (oxytetracycline HCl)
Tetra-C (tetracycline HCl)
Tetracap (tetracycline HCl)
tetracycline
Tetracyn (tetracycline HCl)
Tetrex (tetracycline HCl)
Theo-24 (theophylline)
Theo-Dur Sprinkle (theophylline)
Tolectin† (tolmetin)
Totacillin (ampicillin)
Tylenol** (acetaminophen)
Unipen (nafcillin)
Urecholine (bethanechol)
Uri-Tet (oxytetracycline)
Urobiotic-250 (oxytetracycline, sulfamethizole;
    phenazopyridine)
Uticillin VK (penicillin V)
V-Cillin K (penicillin VK)
Veetids (penicillin VK)
Wyamycin S (erythromycin)

**Absorption of acetaminophen is delayed by food. For more immediate
relief, take without food.
†If stomach upset occurs, take with food.

Certain drugs interact with particular foods in a much more alarming way. Tuberculosis is on the rise among older people, and isoniazid is the drug of choice for treating TB in this age group. But besides working better on an empty stomach, isoniazid could provoke a disastrous reaction if you happened to take it with certain foods high in an amino acid called tyramine, especially the following:

High Tyramine Foods
pickled herring
Stilton cheese
Camembert cheese
cheddar cheese
Emmentaler cheese
brick cheese
Roquefort cheese
Gruyère cheese
salted dried fish, like salt herring
mozzarella cheese
meat extract, gravy base, Marmite, etc.
Parmesan cheese
beef liver (stored)
Romano cheese
Brie cheese
chicken liver (stored)
provolone cheese
processed cheese
avocado
Chianti[28]

This list is arranged with the foods highest in tyramine at the top. If someone were to indulge or overindulge in one of these foods while taking isoniazid or the antidepressants **Marplan** (isocarboxazid), **Nardil** (phenelzine), or **Parnate** (tranylcypromine), the result could be a very dangerous reaction, pushing blood pressure through the ceiling. Isoniazid has another little-known quirk. It would be wise to stay away from fish, especially tuna and skipjack, while on this medication.[29] This interaction may not be as life threatening as if one were eating pickled herrring, but a person going through the histamine response that would result could easily feel like he were dying!

Now let's take a walk on the other side of the street. There are also drugs that aren't affected by food and even a small group whose activity is enhanced if you take them with meals. In some cases that's because the food cushions the stomach from the effect of the harsh drugs, which might otherwise cause anything from mild upset to a roaring case of nausea or diarrhea. In other cases the fats or other substances in a meal aid in absorption of the drug by giving the chemicals in it a piggyback ride into areas of the body that would otherwise be inaccessible.

Drugs that are better absorbed or less irritating when taken with food are listed in the table that follows.

Drugs That Are Better Absorbed or Less Irritating When Taken with Food*

Some medicines are actually absorbed best when taken with food. Although this is relatively uncommon, we have done our best to locate these drugs and they are highlighted below with capital letters and this symbol ☞.

In many other cases medications that upset the digestive tract are easier to handle if you swallow them at mealtime. This may occasionally reduce absorption, but your doctor or pharmacist will tell you if this trade-off is worthwhile.

If you are advised your medicine should be taken "with meals," that generally means right before, during, or immediately after you eat. Make sure you double-check instructions about pill taking with both your doctor and pharmacist; they know your case best and may need to tailor a medication schedule just for you.

acetazolamide
Actifed (triprolidine, pseudoephedrine)
Adapin (doxepin HCl)
Advil (ibuprofen)
☞**ALAZINE** (hydralazine)
☞**ALDACTAZIDE** (spironolactone, HCTZ$^\Delta$)

*Brand names appear in **bold face**; generic names are plain. CAPITAL LETTERS and this symbol ☞ mean a drug is better absorbed with food.
ΔHCTZ = hydrochlorothiazide

☞**ALDACTONE** (spironolactone)
☞**ALDOCLOR** (methyldopa, chlorothiazide)
Aldoril (methyldopa, HCTZ$^\Delta$)
Allerest (chlorpheniramine maleate, PPA$^\emptyset$)
allopurinol
Alupent (metaproterenol)
aminophylline
amitriptyline
Anaprox (naproxen sodium)
Antivert (meclizine)
Anturane (sulfinpyrazone)
A.P.C. w/Codeine**
☞**APRESAZIDE** (hydralazine HCl, HCTZ$^\Delta$)
☞**APRESODEX** (hydralazine, HCTZ$^\Delta$)
☞**APRESOLINE** (hydralazine HCl)
☞**APRESOLINE-ESIDRIX** (hydralazine HCl, HCTZ$^\Delta$)
Aristocort (triamcinolone)
Artane (trihexyphenidyl HCl)
Ascriptin w/Codeine** (aspirin, aluminum hydroxide,
    magnesium hydroxide, codeine)
Asendin (amoxapine)
aspirin*
Atabrine (quinacrine)
Ativan (lorazepam)
Atromid-S (clofibrate)
Aventyl (nortriptyline)
Azolid (phenylbutazone)
Azulfidine (sulfasalazine)
Benadryl (diphenhydramine HCl)
$^\Delta$**HTCZ-hydrochlorothiazide**
$^\emptyset$**PPA-phenylpropanolamine**
Benemid (probenecid)
Bentyl (dicyclomine HCl)
Benylin (diphenhydramine)
benztropine
betamethasone
BioCal (calcium carbonate)
Bonine (meclizine)
Brethine (terbutaline)

Bricanyl (terbutaline)
brompheniramine
Bronkodyl (theophylline)
Butazolidin (phenylbutazone)
Calcitrel (calcium carbonate)
calcium carbonate supplements
Cal-Sup (calcium carbonate)
Caltrate 600 (calcium carbonate)
Cardioquin (quinidine)
Celestone (betamethasone)
Centrax (prazepam)
☞CHLOROTHIAZIDE
chlorpheniramine
chlorpromazine
Chlor-Trimeton (chlorpheniramine maleate)
chlorzoxazone
Clinoril (sulindac)
clofibrate
codeine
Cogentin (benztropine mesylate)
Colace** (docusate sodium)
ColBENEMID (colchicine, probenecid)
Compazine (prochlorperazine)
Compoz (diphenhydramine HCl)
CORGARD (nadolol)
Cortef (hydrocortisone)
cortisone
CORZIDE (nadolol, bendroflumethiazide)
☞**DARVOCET N-100** (propoxyphene napsylate,
   acetaminophen)
☞**DARVON** (propoxyphene HCl)
☞**DARVON COMPOUND** (propoxyphene HCl, aspirin,
   caffeine)
Decadron (dexamethasone)
Delta Cortef (prednisolone)
Deltasone (prednisone)
Depakene (valproic acid)
desipramine
Desyrel (trazodone)
dexamethasone

Diabinese (chlorpropamide)
Dialose† (docusate)
Diamox (acetazolamide)
☞**DICUMAROL** (bishydroxycoumarin)
dicyclomine
digoxin
☞**DILANTIN** (phenytoin)
dimenhydrinate
Dimetane (brompheniramine maleate)
Dimetapp (brompheniramine, PPA⌀)
diphenhydramine
☞**DIUPRES** (chlorothiazide, reserpine)
☞**DIURIL** (chlorothiazide)
docusate†
☞**DOLENE** (propoxyphene HCl)
Dolobid (diflunisal)
doxepin
doxycycline
Dramamine (dimenhydrinate)
Drixoral (dexbrompheniramine, pseudoephedrine)
Duraquin (quinidine)
☞**DYAZIDE** (HCTZ$^\Delta$, triamterene)
Dymelor (acetohexamide)
☞**DYRENIUM** (triamterene)
Edecrin (ethacrynic acid)
E.E.S. (erythromycin ethylsuccinate)
Elavil (amitriptyline HCl)
Elixophyllin (theophylline)
Empirin w/Codeine** (aspirin, codeine)
Endep (amitriptyline HCl)
Equanil (meprobamate)
☞**ERYPED** (erythromycin ethylsuccinate)
☞**ERYTHROMYCIN ESTOLATE**
☞**ERYTHROMYCIN ETHYLSUCCINATE**
Esimil (guanethidine, HCTZ$^\Delta$)
☞**ESKALITH** (lithium carbonate)
Feldene (piroxicam)
Femiron (ferrous fumarate)
Feosol (ferrous sulfate)
Fergon (ferrous gluconate)

Fer-In-Sol (ferrous sulfate)
Fiorinal w/Codeine** (codeine, butalbital, caffeine, aspirin)
Flagyl (metronidazole)
Flexeril (cyclobenzaprine)
☞**FULVICIN** (griseofulvin)
☞**FURADANTIN** (nitrofurantoin)
☞**FURALAN** (nitrofurantoin)
☞**GRIFULVIN V** (griseofulvin)
☞**GRISACTIN** (griseofulvin)
☞GRISEOFULVIN
☞**GRIS-PEG** (griseofulvin)
Haldol (haloperidol)
haloperidol
Haltran (ibuprofen)
Hematinic (ferrous sulfate)
Hexadrol (dexamethasone)
☞HYDRALAZINE
hydrocortisone
Hygroton (chlorthalidone)
Ibuprin (ibuprofen)
☞**ILOSONE** (erythromycin estolate)
imipramine
Imuran (azathioprine)
☞**INDERAL** (propranolol)
☞**INDERIDE** (propranolol, HCTZ$^{\Delta}$)
Indocin (indomethacin)
Indomethacin
iron
Ismelin (guanethidine)
Kaochlor (potassium chloride)
Kaon (potassium gluconate)
Kato (potassium chloride)
Kay Ciel (potassium chloride)
Kenacort (triamcinolone)
K-Lor (potassium chloride)
Klorvess (potassium chloride, potassium bicarbonate)
Klotrix (potassium chloride)
K-Lyte (potassium chloride)
☞LABETALOL

Lanoxin (digoxin)
Legatrin (quinine)
Libritabs (chlordiazepoxide)
Librium (chlordiazepoxide)
☞LITHIUM
☞**LITHANE** (lithium carbonate)
☞**LITHONATE** (lithium carbonate)
☞**LITHOBID** (lithium carbonate)
☞**LITHOTABS** (lithium carbonate)
Lo/Ovral (norgestrel, ethinyl estradiol)
☞**LOPRESSOR** (metoprolol)
☞**LORELCO** (probucol)
Ludiomil (maprotiline)
☞**MACRODANTIN** (nitrofurantoin)
Mandelamine (methenamine mandelate)
maprotiline
Marax (theophylline, ephedrine, hydroxyzine HCl)
Marplan (isocarboxazid)
Maxzide (triamterene, HCTZ$^\Delta$)
meclizine
Meclomen (meclofenamate sodium)
Medipren (ibuprofen)
Medrol (methylprednisolone)
Mellaril (thioridazine HCl)
meprobamate
methenamine
methylprednisolone
Meticorten (prednisone)
metoprolol
metronidazole
Metryl (metronidazole)
☞**MEVACOR** (lovastatin)
Micro-K (potassium chloride)
☞**MIDAMOR** (amiloride HCl)
Miltown (meprobamate)
☞**MODURETIC** (amiloride HCl, HCTZ$^\Delta$)
Motrin (ibuprofen)
Mysoline (primidone)
Nalfon (fenoprofen)
Naprosyn (naproxen)

Nardil (phenelzine)
Navane (thiothixene)
niacin
Nicobid (niacin [nicotinic acid], timed release)
☞NITROFURANTOIN
Noctec (chloral hydrate)
☞**NORMODYNE** (labetalol)
Norpramin (desipramine)
nortriptyline
Nuprin (ibuprofen)
Orinase (tolbutamide)
Ornade (PPA⁰, chlorpheniramine)
Os-Cal (calcium carbonate)
Oxalid (oxyphenbutazone)
☞**OXSORALEN** (methoxsalen)
Oxycodan (oxycodone, aspirin)
oxyphenbutazone
PAS (paraminosalicylic acid)
PBZ (tripelennamine)
Pamelor (nortriptyline)
papaverine
Paraflex (chlorzoxazone)
paraminosalicylic acid
Parnate (tranylcypromine)
Pavabid (papaverine)
Paxipam (halazepam)
☞**PEDIAMYCIN** (erythromycin ethylsuccinate)
☞**PEDIAZOLE** (erythromycin, sulfisoxazole)
Percocet (oxycodone, acetaminophen)
Percodan (oxycodone, aspirin)
Periactin (cyproheptadine)
Permitil (fluphenazine)
Pertofrane (desipramine)
phenylbutazone
☞PHENYTOIN
Placidyl (ethchlorvynol)
Ponstel (mefenamic acid)
potassium
prednisolone
prednisone

Premarin (conjugated estrogens)
primidone
Priscoline (tolazoline)
probenecid
Prolixin (fluphenazine)
☞PROPRANOLOL
Protostat (metronidazole)
Quadrinal (ephedrine, phenobarbital, theophylline, potassium iodide)
Quibron (theophylline, guaifenesin)
Quinaglute (quinidine)
Quinamm (quinine)
Quinidex (quinidine)
quinidine
quinine
Quinora (quinidine sulfate)
Q-Vel (quinine)
Raudixin (rauwolfia serpentina)
Rauzide (rauwolfia serpentina, bendroflumethiazide)
Regroton (chlorthalidone, reserpine)
Renese-R (polythiazide, reserpine)
reserpine
Rufen (ibuprofen)
Salutensin (hydroflumethiazide, reserpine)
☞SER-AP-ES (reserpine, hydralazine HCl, HCTZ$^\Delta$)
Serax (oxazepam)
Serpasil (reserpine)
Sinequan (doxepin)
Slow-K (potassium chloride)
Somophyllin (aminophylline)
☞SPIRONOLACTONE
Stelazine (trifluoperazine HCl)
sulfasalazine
Suplical (calcium carbonate)
sulfinpyrazone
Surmontil (trimipramine)
Synalgos** (aspirin, caffeine)
Tagamet (cimetidine)
Talwin Compound** (pentazocine, aspirin)

Tedral (theophylline, ephedrine, phenobarbital)
Teebacin (paraminosalicylic acid)
☞**TEGRETOL** (carbamazepine)
Theobid (theophylline)
Theo-Dur (theophylline)
Theolair (theophylline)
theophylline
thioridazine
Thorazine (chlorpromazine)
Tofranil (imipramine HCl)
Tolinase (tolazamide)
☞**TRANDATE** (labetalol)
Tranxene (clorazepate)
triamcinolone
triamterene
Triavil (perphenazine, amitriptyline)
trifluoperazine
trihexyphenidyl
Trilafon (perphenazine)
Tuss-Ornade (PPA$^\emptyset$, caramiphen)
Tylox (oxycodone, acetaminophen)
☞**UNIPRES** (reserpine, hydralazine, HCTZ$^\Delta$)
☞**UNIPHYL** (theophylline)
Valium (diazepam)
valproic acid
Vibramycin (doxycycline hyclate)
Vicodin (hydrocodone, acetaminophen)
Vivactil (protriptyline)
Wyamycin E (erythromycin ethylsuccinate)
Wygesic (propoxyphene HCl, acetaminophen)
Xanax (alprazolam)
Zyloprim (allopurinol)

**Aspirin may be slightly less effective when taken at mealtime, but it is also less likely to irritate the stomach when taken with a full 8-oz glass of water or milk and some food.
†Be sure to drink at least 6 or 8 glasses of fluid daily if you are taking this laxative.
☞ This symbol indicates that a drug will be better absorbed with food.
$^\Delta$HCTZ = hydrochlorothiazide
$^\emptyset$PPA = phenylpropanolamine

A Peek at the Future

No doubt about it, taking your medicine can be a real hassle. But some things will be changing in the next few years that should make it easier to follow doctors' orders and get the maximum benefit from your drugs.

Physicians may soon prescribe not only a specific drug, but also the particular moment of the day when it will do you the most good! No more of this "Take two tablets three times a day" stuff. In the future it may well be "Take at 8:30 A.M., noon and 8:45 P.M.," and different hours may be specified for the same drug for a different person.

We're just beginning to learn about the body's complex rhythms, but we already know there are definite highs and lows in how the body uses different drugs. For example, **Indocin** (indomethacin) is a widely used anti-inflammatory drug for arthritis, bursitis, and tendinitis. In one study, people who took the drug between 7 and 11 P.M. had a very gradual rise in the blood level of **Indocin**. It never reached anywhere near the peak it did when they took it at other times of the day.[30] Those taking **Indocin** in the morning, between 7 and 11, showed peak blood values almost twice as high.

This is not just a peculiarity of **Indocin**. The absorption of other drugs, including digoxin, asthma medicine containing theophylline, antibiotics like erythromycin, aspirin, and alcohol, may also vary according to when the drug is taken. At the moment, our dosing technique is rather crude. It's a real sledgehammer approach, jamming in enough drug so that something is in the bloodstream at all times. Look for that to change as we come to a fuller understanding of the complex, interconnected rhythms that govern the rise and fall of the body's tides.

And look, too, for new and better ways to get that medicine down the hatch. In fact, in the future it may not go down the hatch at all. There are already a number of compounds (estrogen, nitroglycerin, scopolamine, and clonidine) available as patches that just stick onto a convenient place on the skin. While this route isn't suitable for all medications, advances in technology and pharmacology will probably enable it to be applied to many more drugs.

The advantages of a transdermal ("through the skin") patch are several. First, of course, there's obviously no problem swallowing it. Second, the patch tends to produce a more even distribution of drug in the bloodstream with its slow, timed, continuous release.

And since the patch is usually good for several days at a time, it greatly reduces the problem of having to remember to take your medication. Some folks develop a rash, however, and a few other glitches have to be worked out before dozens of drugs start showing up on your skin.

Other novel forms of medicine include chewing gums and nasal sprays. Eventually we may see implanted micropumps that will carefully release medicine as a sophisticated monitoring system determines actual blood levels. Patients can also look forward to the day when the wonders of genetic engineering produce drugs that are targeted to specific sites in the body. Instead of circulating in the blood stream from your nose to your toes, these drugs will go where they're intended and nowhere else.

Some of this is already reality. Until it becomes commonplace, though, it still remains a matter of popping pills. With the information in this chapter under your belt, we hope you'll feel a lot more ready to go about doing that with a sense that you're taking the right medicine at the right time in the right way.

Things to Remember

1. How medicine is taken *does* make a difference. If the doctor or pharmacist gives instructions on taking your drug, make sure you understand and follow them. If the directions are ambiguous, ask specific questions until you get a clear answer.

2. Ask your doctor whether the drug should be taken with meals or on an empty stomach (at least one hour before or two hours after eating). If the information isn't readily available, request that she contact the pharmaceutical manufacturer for specific data.

3. When you get your prescription filled, make sure the pharmacist puts the expiration date on the label. And check that the drug in the bottle corresponds to your doctor's prescription. Throw out any medicine that becomes dated. Why don't you check your medicine cabinet right now?

4. If you have trouble swallowing pills, you might want to try the "pop-bottle method." A carbonated beverage (preferably water) in a narrow-necked bottle is ideal. Put the pill in your mouth and take a swig straight from the bottle ... down the hatch she goes. Do not lie down after swallowing your medicine, as it could get stuck in your gullet.

5. For help in remembering whether you have taken all your medicine, get in the habit of checking it off on The People's Pharmacy Medication Chart.™ See page 64.

6. For tables on drugs that are best taken on an empty stomach, see pages 69 to 73. Drugs that are better absorbed or safer with food can be found on pages 75 to 83).

References

1. Temple, Robert. Personal communication, Dec. 22, 1986.
2. Farley, Dixie. "Protecting the Ederly from Medication Misuse." *FDA Consumer* 20(8):28–31, 1986.
3. Williams, Roger L., et al. "Effects of Formulation and Food on the Absorption of Hydrochlorothiazide and Triamterene or Amiloride from Combination Potassium-Sparing Diuretic Products." *Clinical Pharmacology and Therapeutics*. In press.
4. Beerman, B., et al. "Gastrointestinal Absorption of Hydrochlorothiazide Enhanced by Concomitant Intake of Food." *Eur. J. Clin. Pharmacol.* 13:125–128, 1978.
5. Barbhaiya, R.H., et al. "Pharmacokinetics of Hydrochlorothiazide in Fasted and Nonfasted Subjects: A Comparison of Plasma Level and Urinary Excretion Methods." *J. Pharm. Sci.* 71: 245–248, 1982.
6. Williams, et al., op. cit.
7. Welling, Peter. Personal communication, Nov. 22, 1986.
8. Zuccollo, Gerry; and Liddell, Helen. "The Elderly and the Medication Label: Doing It Better." *Age and Ageing* 14:371, 1985.
9. Bayne, J. Ronald, et al. "Pharmacists and Their Relationship with Elderly Patients." *Can. Med. Assoc. J.* 129:35, 1983.
10. Moore, Steve, et al. "Receipt of Prescription Drug Information by the Elderly." *Geriatrics & Gerontology* 17:920, 1983.
11. Kahn, G. "Capsule Swallowing: The Lean-Forward Technique." *Cutis* 36:144, 1985.

12. Fowler, Joseph F. "A Helpful Aid for Pill Swallowing: The Pop-Bottle Method." *Cutis* 37:461, 1986.
13. Rehmer, Karen. "A Spoonful of ... Applesauce?" *Hospital Pharmacy* 16:445, 1981.
14. Al-Dujaili, H.; Salole, E. G.; and Florence, A. T. "Drug Formulation and Oesophageal Injury." *Adverse Drug Reactions and Acute Poisons Review* 2:235–256, 1983.
15. Geschwind, A. "Oesophagitis and Oesophageal Ulceration Following Ingestion of Doxycycline Tablets." *Med. J. Aust.* 140(4):223, 1984.
16. Bokey, L.; and Hugh, T. B. "Oesophageal Ulceration Associated with Doxycycline Therapy." *Med. J. Aust* 1:236, 1975.
17. Schneider, R. "Doxycycline and Esophageal Ulcers." *Am. J. Dig. Dis.* 22:805, 1977.
18. Channer, Kevin S., et al. "The Effect of Size and Shape of Tablets on Their Esophageal Transit." *J. Clin. Pharmacol.* 26:141–146, 1986.
19. Gryfe, C. I., and Gryfe; B. M. "Drug Therapy of the Aged: The Problem of Compliance and the Roles of Physicians and Pharmacists." *J. Am. Geriatric Soc.* 32:301, 1984.
20. Welling, Peter. "Interactions Affecting Drug Absorption." *Clin. Pharmacokin.* 9:404–434, 1984.
21. Welling, Peter. "Nutrient Effects on Drug Metabolism and Action in the Elderly." *Drug–Nutrient Interactions* 4:173–207, 1985.
22. Lamy, Peter P. "How Diet Can Affect Drug Response." *Drug Therapy,* Aug., 1980.
23. Bergman, H. David. "Effect of Food on the Bioavailability of Orally Administered Drugs." *Hosp. Form.* 15:295–305, 1980.
24. Durgin, Jane M. "Drug/Food Interactions." *Pharmacy Times,* May, 1980, pp. 32–40.
25. Lehmann, Phyllis. "Food and Drug Interactions." *FDA Consumer,* March, 1978.
26. Welling, Peter. Personal communication, Nov. 22, 1986.
27. Morgan, Brian L.G. *The Food and Drug Interaction Guide,* New York: Simon and Schuster, 1986.
28. Roe, Daphne A. "Interactions Between Drugs and Nutrients." *Medical Clinics of North America* 63(5):958–1007, 1979.
29. Roe, Daphne A. "Drug–Nutrient Interactions in the Elderly." *Geriatrics* 41(3):57–74, 1986.
30. Reinberg; Alain; Smolensky, Michael; and Levi, Francis. "Aspects of Clinical Chronopharmacology." *Cephalgia* 3(suppl. 1):69, 1982.

4

Saving Money on Medicine

Drug companies are crying all the way to the bank. They are consistently one of the most profitable industries in the world. But they aren't content with the huge profits they are reaping. They constantly complain about the high cost of research and development, not to mention the inroads being made by generic competitors. In recent years they have waged a "smear and fear" campaign against generic substitution while increasing their prices dramatically. They have sent out an army of "detailmen" to try to convince doctors to stick with the familiar brand names. Many doctors buy the line, but we patients have to pay for the pills they prescribe.

Here's an expensive prescription for disaster. Take an older person on a fixed, limited income. Give that person one or two medical problems requiring daily medication. Let his medications be available only in patented, brand name forms.

The result will often be very hard to swallow. Complications can include a chronic shortage of money, inability to purchase necessary medicine, and a lingering sense that something is very wrong with a system in which people's problems are successfully diagnosed and properly prescribed for, and yet they can't get what they need to ensure their best chance at regaining and maintaining their health.

If you think this prescription isn't written very often, you should read our mail. We get heartbreaking letters from seniors who face the choice between buying proper medication and providing food and other necessities for themselves. These people are perplexed, confused, and angry.

Listen to Mary: "I don't know what we're going to do," she wrote. "My husband has to have his blood pressure pills every day, and we simply can't afford to spend $50 a month unless we eat less."

Another couple wrote to say that their combined medication bill came to more than $150 monthly ... no small sum even for those still earning a wage. Some write that they can't afford their medication some of the time; others say they can't afford it at all.

Even those of more ample means find that a constant outlay of one, two, or three dollars a day for medication, month after month and year after year, is depriving them of funds that would have meant those little extras that make life meaningful and happy rather than dreary and depressing. When drawing up a retirement budget, few people have a column for "medications."

Most folks, when they were younger, thought of prescription costs—if they thought of them at all—as something that might run a few bucks once or twice a year. But as we get older, the illnesses we're medicated for are much more likely to be ones that require daily (or even several-times-daily) dosing for the remainder of our lives. The bucks we're forced to spend are no longer so few and far between.

When it comes to help, there isn't much. Medicare, allegedly the great safety net, isn't about to break your fall from high prescription prices. While Medicare will pay to get your condition diagnosed, it doesn't cover all of the cost of the drugs needed to get you well. It's not sensible, it's not logical, and it's literally not healthy. But it *is* the way the system works.

What's more, many seniors just miss qualifying for state or local assistance programs. These people find themselves too rich for welfare, yet too poor to pay for the medicine they need. Given that reality, people say to us, what can we do?

A lot more than you might think. While we don't know of any pharmacies that are about to give their pills away, we do know a lot of ways you could be getting more for those precious dollars while at the same time making certain the medicine you receive is what you need, when you need it. As we see it, there are at least *ten major opportunities* to save money on your medication bill—without sacrificing quality. It's all a matter of knowing where to look and what to look for.

Saving money will take a bit of work, a lot of planning, some information (which we'll provide) and a measure of moxie. But you *can* do it! And the savings could be stupendous. The key to the strategy we're proposing is constant vigilance. The best way to save the most money on your medication bill is to take advantage of the savings available at every step.

The chances are excellent that you've already heard some of the easy and obvious ways to save money on medications, such as using generic drugs instead of their brand name brothers. We'll review these, just to make certain you haven't missed something. But to make this game plan work, to look at every phase of the health care process as a savings opportunity, may require a somewhat different attitude toward physicians and pharmacists than you might be used to.

Dealing with Doctors

Most accidents, it's said, take place near home. And most medication money, we say, is wasted not at the pharmacy but in the doctor's office. The reason is quite simple. The doctor is the one who specifies what drug you will receive. Most doctors do their best to get you well quickly, but that interest doesn't always extend to getting you well cheaply.

Many doctors are incredibly oblivious to the cost of almost everything from lab tests to medications. And even when they are aware, they could have trouble fully comprehending the fiscal and emotional impact of a $50-a-month medication bill on someone of meager financial means. Few doctors have ever been faced with making a choice between paying the rent and getting their medication. And because most seniors we hear from are proud people, the doctor may not appreciate just how much of a sacrifice that high-priced medication may call for.

Getting your doctor to understand your health concerns and your financial situation is crucial. But remember, you may only have 18 seconds to speak before your doctor cuts you off.[1] That's not much time to make yourself heard.

What should you be saying? To use his time and yours efficiently, don't forget to list all your symptoms and questions (see pages 37–39). This is **Step #1** to save big bucks, as well as to save yourself the embarrassment of forgetting some of the things you wanted to see the doctor about. And don't overlook seemingly trivial details. A skin rash, for example, can be a tip-off to a serious drug reaction.

Don't forget to make a list of every medication you're taking. This is **Step #2** to save money, and it's important. Many medications don't mix. If the doctor doesn't know what else you're taking, he may prescribe something that later has to be changed. You will have wasted money and time, but even worse, you will perhaps have risked a serious drug interaction. Remember that one study estimated that a quarter of the people taking more than ten drugs simultaneously end up with serious adverse reactions.[2]

Above all, don't ever demand a prescription. In fact, why not ask about nondrug approaches? If the physician takes the time to help you work out an alternative, count your blessings. It may be a bit more trouble, but if you can get your blood pressure down without medicine you will feel better and really save money. So there's **Step #3**—don't demand drugs. If you insist on getting a prescription, the doctor is likely to oblige, even if a pill is not the only solution.

Once your doctor has diagnosed the problem, perhaps even as she speaks, she may start writing. STOP HER. This is **Step #4** to protect your pocketbook. Don't miss it: Make sure you understand very clearly what the diagnosis is, and what treatment the doctor proposes. We say *proposes*, because most patients don't know that there is often more than one way to do battle against whatever ails you. From the way most doctors go about their business, patients have been led to the mistaken conclusion that there is always a single right answer—the one scribbled out on the prescription pad. BALONEY!

Docs, Doodads, and Dum-Dums

There's a distinct possibility that whatever ends up on the doctor's prescription pad wasn't necessarily chosen because it's the most economical way of solving your problem. Hundreds of millions of dollars are spent every year by pharmaceutical companies on glossy ads, traveling salespeople (the detailmen), imprinted pads and pens, and other devices designed to convince your physician to prescribe **Cheer-up** for your depression or **Flush-it** for your constipation.

Do you doubt that drug companies would stoop so low as to try and persuade docs with doodads? Well here is the famous "Dum-Dum" sucker case as reported in the *New England Journal of Medicine*:

ONE DRUG COMPANY'S SALES TECHNIQUES

To the Editor: A sales representative for a drug company inadvertently left a copy of a page from his manual of selling techniques in our office. I found it most enlightening and think that it may be of general interest. Among the devices recommended as "attention getters" were cookies with the shape and color of drug capsules, pizzas with drug initials picked out in pepperoni, Easter baskets containing eggs painted to resemble drug capsules, and Halloween baskets containing free samples and decorated with little ghosts made from Dum-Dum suckers in tissue. These last are to be accompanied with a little joke about haunting the doctor to write the correct prescriptions.

The instructions go on to say that any of the above can be made into "an annual event, and *they really enjoy them.*" Furthermore, they advise the representatives that it is vital to make the maximal impact in the limited time available. This is done by handing the doctor candy bars labeled "Powerhouse." Any initial mystification is quickly dispelled by then handing him one or two nostrums that are recommended as "powerhouses" for the treatment of common, chronic, and incurable conditions, such as chronic bronchitis and arthritis (type unspecified).

The original of this document, which I shall be glad to show to anyone interested, contains grammar and spelling that suggests that the standard of education among this company's sales force cannot be high. *BUT SALES TECHNIQUES ARE NOT USED UNLESS THEY WORK.* This drug company,

and perhaps others, obviously regard us as idiots
who respond to Easter baskets and italicized pizzas
by prescribing more of their products. Could it be
that they are right?

Patrick A. Murphy, M.D.
The John Hopkins University
School of Medicine[3]

[emphasis added]

It's hard to believe that drug companies could influence doctors with candy or pizza. But as Dr. Murphy says, sales techniques that are used repeatedly are usually the ones that work.
Another favorite trick of the industry is to sponsor luncheons,
dinners and conferences. At such affairs the food and drinks are
usually free and sometimes the entertainment can be extravagant.
One evening SmithKline Beckman rented Disneyland for the benefit of the assembled doctors and their families. But the niftiest
technique is the "seminar in paradise":

> Large firms regularly send the nation's most influ-
> ential specialists and their spouses on all-expense-
> paid trips to tropical climes. Last year, for example,
> Ciba-Geigy flew 100 gynecologists to Cancún, Mex-
> ico, to bone up on Estraderm, the company's new
> estrogen skin patch.
>   In 1985, the top 50 pharmaceutical companies
> officially spent $1.26-billion on "promotion," ac-
> cording to industry sources. But the total amount
> spent to influence doctors is actually far greater.
> According to FDA sources, drug companies often
> charge costly promotional activities, such as con-
> vention entertaining and the far-flung seminars, to
> their education or research budgets. The FDA
> sources estimate that total promotional spending
> by major drug companies exceeds $4-billion a year,
> or almost $9000 per doctor.[4]

Think about the problem the doctor faces. There are more than
30,000 prescription drugs, and sometimes 10 or 20 or more for
treating a given condition. Even the most conscientious doctor

doesn't have the time or energy to read all the latest scientific reports detailing studies on each and every one of those drugs.

So how do they decide what to use? Partly by talking to the drug company sales reps or reading the ads in medical journals. They may also make some decisions based on what they hear about a drug from their colleagues, or perhaps just by continuing to prescribe what they've always used, which might be what someone in medical school told them was good. A little less precise science than you thought, huh? That's why it's perfectly OK for you to jump in and ask the doctor to think about your prescription from a different perspective.

Tell the doctor, quite straightforwardly, that you're concerned about the cost of your medication. Then try pitching some of these questions toward the white coat:

- **Does he have any idea what the cost of the drug will be on a daily basis?**

- **If he's writing a brand name prescription, can it be filled with a generic** (more on this later)?

- **Is there any other drug, perhaps less expensive, that would accomplish the same end even if it's a bit slower?**

- **Could any OTC drug reasonably be substituted, or would a trial of an OTC medication be reasonable to see if that would solve the problem?** For example, you could give several OTC painkillers a try before popping for that expensive nonsteroidal anti-inflammatory drug. Aspirin is still the gold standard all these prescription powerhouses are compared to, and you couldn't find anything much cheaper. (With acetaminophen and ibuprofen available without prescription as well, there are any number of choices, and your doctor should be able to give you some guidance on what you might try.)

- **Does he have any samples of the drug you could take before having the prescription filled?** Sometimes people find, just after having their first expensive prescription for 100 capsules filled, that they can't tolerate the drug—it makes them nauseous or dizzy, gives them a hideous, itchy rash, or provokes an awful asthma attack. Too late. The pharmacist cannot take back the other 99 pills they haven't touched. The high cost of your medicine helps pay for a lot of things, including the "free" samples the drug company gives doctors. There's no reason not to get them, since you'll end up paying for them, indirectly, later. Trying a sample could save you from making an expensive investment in a drug you can't take.

By now you definitely have the doctor's attention, and he's probably convinced you're serious about saving money. That should have netted you the most economical prescription it's possible to write under the circumstances. But that's just the beginning.

Filling It

Prescription in hand, you leave the doctor's office. Into the hall, down the elevator, out at the ground floor and ... why, what a coincidence, there's a pharmacy. Gosh, it sure would be convenient to just pop in here and have them fill the prescription and not have to mess around with it later.

WAIT. Do you see what we see? Yes, it's **Step #5** in saving money on your prescription. What you have in your hand is an order from your doctor to anyone with a license to dispense drugs to give you what's ordered at whatever price they can get. Unlike supermarkets, pharmacies don't trumpet their prices in full page ads or generally do much at all to let consumers know that there are differences—sometimes very *big* ones—in the prices being asked by pharmacies for the identical drug.

When you shop for most things, you get (more or less) what you pay for. More money usually means better quality goods, a fancier store, or better service. In the case of drugs, however, prices often seem to bear little relationship to anything rational at all. Some of those economics textbook writers who dream of free markets and competition as the ultimate regulator of prices ought to go shopping at their corner drugstores.

Generalizations about drugstores don't necessarily hold for all of them, but here's a quick and simple guide to the major types of places you can purchase prescription drugs. They are (1) independent full-service pharmacies, (2) chain full-service pharmacies, (3) discount pharmacies, and (4) mail order pharmacies. Each offers services that you may or may not want or need. One of the keys to saving money is deciding which type of pharmacy is suited to your needs for each prescription.

The independent, full-service pharmacy is a local retail store. This is traditionally a "mom and pop" operation, where the pharmacist is the proprietor. Without a doubt, this is our favorite kind of establishment. You may find the highest level of personal attention and advice at such a pharmacy, plus the intangible benefit of dealing with a local merchant who may well know you and your health history personally. On the other hand, this type of store sometimes commands top dollar, since it can't always buy in the volume of a chain. However, on certain drugs, the independent pharmacy may have the best price.

The full-service chain store is often part of a nationwide network. Prices can be lower here than at the one-man-band operation, at the cost of some personal attention. Discount chains have a reputation for lower prices, but they're often volume operations with an "in-and-out" attitude. While it could happen, don't expect the pharmacist to linger for an hour discussing your health. In fact, in this type of operation the pharmacist is frequently stashed away behind a tall counter and you'll be waited on by a clerk who's not qualified to give advice on the ins and outs of taking your prescription. All the same, even at a discount store you could be lucky enough to find an excellent pharmacist who's willing to take time and help you with any questions you may have.

Finally, there are the mail order pharmaceutical services. The largest and best known of these is the one operated for members of the American Association of Retired Persons (AARP). Prices via mail order are generally rock bottom. However, there are two major costs to be paid for this discount. First, of course, you must accept the time delay involved in sending your prescription off and waiting for the drugs to return. For those taking the same drug month after month, who can anticipate their needs, this poses no difficulty and the cost saving is well worth the little bit of extra effort involved. On the other hand, if you need medication immediately, say for a strep throat or cystitis, mail order clearly won't work.

The second proviso is that mail order offers no chance to talk with a pharmacist, although AARP does offer informational brochures about many of the drugs it carries. While shopping locally is no guarantee that you'll get good advice (or any at all), it at least offers the opportunity to ask to see the person who has spent years being trained to understand the nuances of drug actions and interactions. One of the greatest disappointments to pharmacists is that they are too often seen by patients as "pill counters" rather than highly trained professionals who have much to contribute to the maintenance of their patients' health. Many a doctor has been quietly saved from misprescribing by a pharmacist who reminded him on the phone of an incorrect dosage or a combination that would cause an adverse reaction.

Those are your choices, roughly in order of cost. However, within any group there are still considerable variations. Enter **Step #6** for saving money.

Shop around. You have, we will assume, been told exactly what your prescription is (both the name of the drug, the size of the dose, and the number of tablets or capsules prescribed). Make certain to understand exactly what is prescribed. Many drugs are made in a variety of dosages, and the price for a 250-mg (milligram) capsule obviously won't be the same as it is for a 500-mg capsule. With this information in hand, start calling around.

Some pharmacies will probably tell you they don't quote prices on the phone. Fine. Don't do business with them. There is absolutely nothing unethical, unprofessional, or unfair about quoting prices on the phone. It's only bad for a pharmacy if their prices are out of line. Any pharmacy that won't tell a senior how much the bill will be before making him or her run across town to get a prescription doesn't get our vote. It is your absolute right as a consumer to know what something will cost.

Call several places before deciding where to shop. You're in for a real shock when you see the price variation. A 1985 survey of Boston-area pharmacies revealed the following price differences:

Pharmacy Price Variations:
High vs. Low Prices for Brand Name Products*

Drug Brand	Strength, Dosage Form	Low Price	High Price	% Difference
HydroDIURIL	50 mg tab	$ 6.29	$15.00	139
Lanoxin	0.25 mg tab	2.09	7.60	264
Persantine	25 mg tab	12.95	22.50	74
Lasix	50 mg tab	9.88	23.00	110
Isordil	10 mg tab	6.95	14.95	115
Diabinese	250 mg tab	13.98	50.92	264
Aldomet	250 mg tab	12.23	28.72	135

Prescription Drug Prices: Generic Vs. Brand-Name Products. Executive Office of Consumer Affairs and Business Regulation, Commonwealth of Massachusetts, Boston, MA, February, 1985. *Cited in:* Danielson, David A. "Influencing the Physician—Drug Industry Strategies." *Generics* 1(3):32–43, 1985.

If the price of an identical gallon of gasoline varied over 200 percent among service stations, you'd probably never patronize the high-priced garage. But because people often don't know exactly what the "market" price of their medication is, they may not realize when they are being charged too much. Just remember that the difference between highest and lowest is money in your pocket. For an expensive drug like **Diabinese** with a wide price spread, that can come to more than a little spare change.

You might, of course, choose to opt for a pharmacy that's not the "low bid" because it's closer to home, because they've offered you good service before, or because they'll deliver. All those are perfectly valid reasons for paying a bit more. The point of the game is not necessarily to get the rock bottom lowest price, but to let it be *your* decision as to how your money is spent. Pay a bit more and have it delivered, or pay less and drive. Pay a bit of a premium so you can talk it over with the pharmacist you trust, or go for low and wait it out via mail. The choice is yours.

Two additional thoughts about comparative shopping. First, don't assume that the pharmacy with the lowest price on one drug will be the most economical on another. Pharmacy A might have had a great price on the prescription you needed six months ago, but they may be sky-high on the drug you need now.

There are several reasons for this. Sometimes drugstores sell some of the more popular prescription drugs at a minimal markup, hoping that these "loss leaders" will bring in your other prescription business at a much higher markup. Other times a pharmacy might have been able to make a very good deal on a drug with one company, yet not have done as well because they didn't have sufficient volume or clout with another.

What all this adds up to is a strong argument for comparison shopping each and every time you have a prescription to be filled. There's one caution, however. If you play "musical chairs" with the pharmacies in your neighborhood, no one pharmacist will have a complete record of every drug you are taking. So, along with the savings you realize by shopping this way comes a certain responsibility. You yourself will have to check on potential drug interactions each time. Make sure the pharmacist is fully informed of *all* other drugs you are using.

Our second thought on comparison shopping by phone is that if the doctor has written a brand name prescription for a drug that's also available generically, some pharmacies might quote you a price on the generic version when you ask for the brand name. Which leads us to perhaps the largest and most contentious issue in medication marketing—brand name versus generic.

A Rose by Any Other Name Is . . .

When a drug company develops a new medication, it gets patent protection and the drug is marketed exclusively under that company's brand name for a period of years. Until recently, the length of the patent was 17 years, and the clock started running when the patent was granted. Since it might take the company several more years to thread the drug through the FDA's complex approval process and put it on the market, the period of protected sales was in fact less, sometimes quite a lot less.

Once the patent expires, other companies can ask the FDA to approve marketing of their chemically identical pills under the generic, or chemical, name (or sometimes a new and different brand name). These generic drugs are usually less expensive than the brand name version. The generic manufacturers did not, of course, have the heavy research and development costs associated with discovering, testing, and bringing to market the new drug, nor do they customarily advertise extensively since the market for the drug is already there ... it's just a question of who is going to sell the pills.

In 1984, Congress changed the rules of the drug game, to your benefit. After one of the most bruising lobbying and legislative battles in years, pitting the brand name manufacturers not only against the generic manufacturers but also against each other, Congress decided to make two major changes. First, the period of patent protection can now be extended up to five years to compensate drug companies for the time it takes to get the drug approved for marketing by the FDA. That was something the brand name manufacturers wanted.

The result (which they didn't all want) was a new set of rules for the approval of generic competitors once the drug comes off patent. Before, a drug company had to go through the whole tedious, time-consuming, and enormously expensive process of submitting clinical studies to demonstrate that its generic version did exactly what the brand name version did ... even though the two were chemically identical. This discouraged a great many of the generic manufacturers, who are generally smaller companies, from even trying in many cases. Those which did may have spent years getting their products to market.

Now the company can submit a much-abbreviated application that uses a small number of patients to simply confirm that the generic version of the drug gets into the bloodstream at the same speed and in the same quantity as the brand name product. This is known as bioequivalence, and it's your assurance that generic drugs really are identical and work the same as their brand name counterparts.

As a result, it's a whole lot easier and cheaper for a generic competitor to get into the race once a brand name drug's patent expires. In recent years we have seen some of the big sellers become available generically: **Aldomet** (methyldopa), **Atarax** (hydroxyzine), **Ativan** (lorazepam), **Bactrim** (trimethoprim, sulfamethoxazole), **Benadryl** (diphenhydramine), **Catapres** (clonidine), **Dalmane** (flurazepam), **Darvocet N** (propoxyphene, acetaminophen), **Desyrel** (trazodone), **Dyazide** (triamterene, hydrochlorothiazide), **Elavil** (amitriptyline), **Haldol** (haloperidol),

Inderal (propranolol), **Inderide** (propranolol, hydrochlorothiazide), **Keflex** (cephalexin), **Mellaril** (thioridazine), **Motrin** (ibuprofen), **Septra** (sulfamethoxazole, trimethoprim), **Tranxene** (clorazepate), **Valium** (diazepam). Since generics usually sell for a fraction of the cost of the brand name, it sounds like nothing but opportunity for us consumers.

In general, that's true. Substituting generic drugs for their brand name competitors will, by and large, save you a fistful of money. There are, of course, exceptions to every rule, and so you should not assume automatically that all generics are cheaper. A few may even cost more than their brand name equivalents.

As far as the active ingredient goes, generics and brand name drugs are the same. They have an identical dose of the self-same chemical, no ifs, ands, or buts. A 5-mg tablet of **Valium** contains 5 mg of diazepam; so does the generic tablet sold as diazepam. Bioequivalence testing assures you that other components of the pill (excipients, the ingredients added to make the pill a pill and make it hang together) haven't adversely affected the amount of drug that gets into the bloodstream. Are we sure? Well, here's the way the FDA states it: "No one has been able to demonstrate that the quality of generic drugs differs from that of the brand name counterparts ... FDA is not aware of a single documented bioinequivalence involving any generic drug product that has been approved by FDA as bioequivalent."[5]

There are a few cases where savings are modest and blood levels are critical enough that it may be worth sticking with a brand name or at least using care during the switchover. If your physician and pharmacist decide to go ahead with a generic, it would be wise to have your blood levels monitored to be sure you're getting the right amount. The drugs are **Coumadin** (warfarin), **Lanoxin** (digoxin), **Synthroid** (levothyroxine) and **Levothroid** (T_4 thyroxine). We also suggest caution with epilepsy medication.

Despite an excellent track record, the FDA decided to let the pharmaceutical industry air its case in the fall of 1986. The agency had heard enough bellyaching about inferior generics to give the industry a chance to put up or shut up. Here is how a spokesperson for the generic industry summed up his view of the conference. It was, he thought, the

> **... golden opportunity for the brand name drug companies to present, in a public forum of scientific peers, what they have so often argued about ge-**

neric drug effectiveness in subsidized publications, at closed conferences, and through detailmen. Here was the chance . . . to offer their scientific evidence.

. . . The PMA [Pharmaceutical Manufacturers Association] presenters conceded that the scientific evidence was not available, but they had a "feeling" it was out there, uncollected or unevaluated. This prompted the usually taciturn Robert Temple, M.D., who is responsible for approving new chemical entities at the FDA, to note wryly that if PMA's "desperate" search for such evidence of therapeutic inequivalence had not borne fruit, one might safely conclude it does not exist.

. . . Summing up the three-day hearing, FDA Commissioner Frank Young, M.D., said that he was shocked, as a scientist, by the lack of science and clinical data presented to justify the oft-repeated industry allegations.[6]

Others at the FDA seem to feel much the same. In an editorial for the *New England Journal of Medicine* in June 1987, some of the agency's key players wrote, "Although the FDA continues to seek evidence of unequal therapeutic effects between approved generic and brand-name products in healthy or sick persons, none has yet been received. . . . Criticisms of the FDA's bioequivalence criteria are usually anecdotal; often, decade-old problems with a few generic products not subject to current approval standards are cited."[7]

So there you have it, friends. To date there just hasn't been any evidence that generic drugs are inferior. If the truth were told, food and drug interactions have a far greater influence on blood levels of most medicines than any slight differences in formulation between brand-name products and their generic equivalents. But this is a subject most major pharmaceutical manufacturers would rather not discuss. As for the conditions under which generic drugs are manufactured, you should know that all companies producing medicine must meet and adhere to stringent FDA standards for quality control in their manufacturing and packaging facilities. Dark hints that drugs made by generic manufacturers come from some sort of sleazy facilities are absolute bullcrackle. In fact, many of the generic manufacturers have entered the business fairly recently and have the very latest in manufacturing and packaging equipment. Their facilities and personnel, like the product they produce, are fully equal (and sometimes superior) to the brand name competition. What's more, the big brand name companies themselves have entered the market with a vengeance and produce 70 to 80 percent of the generics on pharmacy shelves.[8]

This hasn't left the big boys a whole lot of room for legitimate arguments that the generics aren't as good, but that sure hasn't stopped them from trying. In expensive advertising (ultimately paid for, of course, by the patients who wind up buying the brand name drug) the companies seek to plant the seed of doubt without ever spelling out any specifics. Want to see how the drug game is played when it gets down and dirty? Read on.

Mellaril is Sandoz Pharmaceuticals's brand name for the chemical thioridazine. Sandoz wasn't any too happy to see the generic appear, and it proceeded to attack on several fronts. The company sent a telegram to pharmacists telling them that "The Sandoz Pharmaceuticals pharmacist's product liability protection policy will not defend or indemnify a pharmacist ... when the case involves substitution of the product of another manufacturer." It hardly took a genius to get the hint—dispense the generic version and you might get sued, and we won't be there to help. The company also told doctors and pharmacists that using the generic could result in "unpredictable results" because of widely varying blood levels of the generic.[9]

Sandoz pursued this attack in their promotional materials, in "Dear Pharmacist" letters, in advertising, and in personal presentations by their foot soldiers, the detailmen. The problem with this argument was that it had holes in it. And the FDA sent a regulatory letter ordering Sandoz to knock it off:

> **Representatives of Sandoz have had numerous opportunities to present their arguments to the FDA regarding the standards upon which the generic products are approved. Those arguments have been repeatedly rejected. Regardless of that, your firm has consistently refused to properly qualify your promotional materials by including the following material facts: (1) Differences in blood levels of thioridazine established by bioequivalence requirements have not**

**been demonstrated to be clinically significant; or
(2) That your product, Mellaril, produces similar
blood level variations.**[10]

Lots of other firms deserve the same kind of scolding, though
not all of them have gotten it. Medical magazines are peppered
these days with ads that in some way or another demean generics. Boehringer Ingelheim's ad for its **Persantine** brand of dipyridamole reminds doctors that it's "The Original ... the only
clinically-tested dipyridamole ... the experienced dipyridamole."[11]
The company fails to say, of course, why any of this makes one
iota of difference. Perhaps that's because it doesn't?

Another astounding ad comes from Roche, which manufactures **Valium.** Until quite recently, **Valium** was under patent protection, but it's now possible to buy diazepam for a fraction of the
cost. So what does Roche tell your doctor? That he or she should
write a prescription for the higher priced version because the
company needs the money! "Will the doctors of tomorrow have
the drugs of tomorrow?" the ad's headline says. "Only if manufacturers of brand-name pharmaceuticals like Roche can continue to
develop new products at a time when making them available is
both unpredictable and expensive."

The ad goes on to say that it's expensive to develop a new drug,
and then asks the doctor to help fund that research with *your*
bucks by writing the prescription in such a way that the druggist
must fill it only with the brand-name product.[12]

And the argument works. When asked, doctors who don't prescribe generic drugs often defend themselves by saying the companies need funds for research and development. As one physician put it bluntly, "Do you know what it costs to bring a drug to
the market? I write for brands; you don't starve a goose that lays
golden eggs."[13] This might wash if the large drug companies were
starving. But this kind of pitch is a little disingenuous. A congres-
sional investigation discovered that prescription drug prices rose
12.2 percent from July 1985 to April 1987, while the Consumer
Price Index went up a modest 2.7 percent. Subcommittee chairman Henry Waxman concluded:

**Most of the money generated by the recent enor-
mous price increases is *not* going to fund R&D.
Between the years 1982 and 1986, drug-price in-**

creases produced revenue gains of $4.7 billion. During the same period, R&D expenditures rose only $1.6 billion—or about a third of the revenue gains from price increases.

In short, the money was arriving in bucketloads, but was going to R&D in spoonfuls.[14]

But remember that this is one of the most profitable industries in the country, and brand name products may cost from two to ten times more than the generic version.

Are you outraged? We are. It's sure something to keep in mind the next time your doctor is writing out that brand name prescription. Perhaps a bit of outrage will make it easier for you to take **Step #7** and ask the doctor if the drug he or she is about to prescribe is available generically, and if so to please write the prescription for the generic version.

This request is necessary for two reasons. First, because in some states the druggist can not substitute just upon your request. If the doctor writes **Inderal,** the pharmacist must dish out **Inderal,** even though you and he both know that propranolol is equal and cheaper. Second, unless challenged, the doctor may easily fall prey to the advertising and mark his prescription with certain magic words ("Medically Necessary," "Dispense as Written," or "Do Not Substitute," depending on the state) that make it impossible for the pharmacist to give you anything but the brand name version.

Before any doctor does that, he owes you a very definite explanation of why it's necessary for you to spend several times as much money. Do not accept vague generalities ("This is the only form that's reliable," or "I haven't had any experience with the generic.") If the doctor can't cite specific evidence to justify the more expensive form, then maybe he's a victim of misleading advertising. There may be some situations where your doctor has a good reason to specify a particular brand name drug, but he ought to be able to tell you what it is.

You'll be dollars ahead by knowing what drugs are available generically. Since the generic drug companies don't have armies of detail people and spend far less on promotion than the big brand name houses, doctors sometimes don't even know whether a particular medication is available in generic form. You'll find a table of brand name drugs available generically at the end of this chapter. A number of other medicines are expected to appear in generic form sometime during the next several years, so you may want to be on the alert for **Adalat** (nifedipine), **Alupent** (metaproterenol), **Asendin** (amoxapine), **Blocadren** (timolol), **Carafate** (sucralfate), **Cleocin** (clindamycin), **Clinoril** (sulindac), **Colestid** (colestipol), **Loxitane** (loxapine), **Matulane** (procarbazine), **Minipress** (prazosin), **Nalfon** (fenoprofen), **Norpramin** (desipramine), **Paxipam** (halazepam), **Pertofrane** (desipramine), **Procardia** (nifedipine), **Proventil** (albuterol), **Tenormin** (atenolol), **Timoptic** (timolol), and **Ventolin** (albuterol).

Now it's time to get out your calculator and start toting up the savings. This is the fun part. Let's take our hypothetical example of Harry. He's got high blood pressure, diabetes, and some rheumatism, and he suffers from depression. His doctor has prescribed **HydroDIURIL** (50 mg twice a day), **Apresoline** (50 mg three times a day), **Diabinese** (250 mg), **Meclomen** (100 mg three times a day), and **Elavil** (50 mg twice a day). If he filled them at our local chain drug store, here is what a month's supply would cost: **HydroDIURIL ($7.85)** versus hydrochlorothiazide ($3.29); **Apresoline ($29.69)** versus hydralazine ($6.59); **Diabinese ($12.82)** versus chlorpropamide ($5.19); **Meclomen ($43.29)** versus meclofenamate ($35.39); **Elavil ($23.79)** versus amitriptyline ($6.29). The monthly total for the brand name drugs comes to **$117.44**. The monthly total for the generic equivalents comes to $56.75. That's a monthly savings of $60.69, or roughly two dollars a day. Suppose Harry started taking these drugs when he was 55 and put the difference in the bank to be compounded daily at 5 percent interest. By the time he was 75 he'd have about $25,000 in that account. Now that kind of money could really make a difference.

The following is a table of generic and brand name prices from the American Association of Retired Persons (AARP) Pharmacy Service. Look it over and you will get some idea of just how gargantuan the savings can be when you buy generic rather than brand name drugs. (Remember, these prices are for chemically identical drugs.) If you needed the steroid **Kenacort**, for example, you might have to shell out $79.50 to get 100 tablets from AARP. If your doctor prescribed it generically as triamcinolone, you could get it from AARP for $7.00. This may be one of the most extraordinary price differentials, but you'll have no trouble finding others. Perhaps you need to take **Artane**? You could order a hundred of the 5-mg brand name pills from AARP for $15.95, or get the generic equivalent from them for $2.85. The difference is over 400 percent. Or take **Antivert**, if that's what your doctor prescribes, and pay your $24.75 for every one hundred 25-mg pills that come in the mail. But buy it as meclizine, and AARP charges just $3.95 per 100. Same stuff, different name. The choice is yours.

The following table should also give you some ballpark figures about prescription costs. Keep in mind that drug prices fluctuate constantly, and it's unlikely that even AARP's prices will be exactly as shown here by the time you read this. (The generic prices listed were effective through February 1988; brand name prices are subject to periodic adjustment by the manufacturer. But, in general, you'll know whether you need to stop at the bank to mortgage the house before going to the pharmacy. You'll also have some sense of whether the local dispensers are getting anywhere near the going rate. If not, you might want to consider the mail order option if the nature of the prescription permits the delay. For an up-to-date AARP Pharmacy Service Catalog and price guide write to: One Prince Street, Alexandria, VA 22314. They will also be glad to provide a price quote if your drug is not listed in the price guide.

Meanwhile, Back at the Pharmacy . . .

Well, it hasn't been easy, but it hasn't been so hard, either. There you are at the pharmacy, getting ready to save yourself a fair bundle by getting the generic version of the right drug for the right problem. Before handing the prescription over to the pharmacist, or before sending it to the mail order pharmacy, take a look at the instructions. Notice how many pills the doctor has called for (this appears as #15 for 15 tablets, #25 for 25, etc. Not too complicated). This is **Step #8** in saving money, because you can ask the pharmacist to fill the prescription with less than the requested number of tablets.

Why do that? A couple of reasons. First, if it's your first time on the drug, and you haven't been able to get any samples to try, then there's still no assurance that this drug in this dosage is something you will be able to use. You might need a weaker (or

AARP Price Guide*

Brand Name	Generic Name	Generic Price	Brand Price
Aldactazide 25/25	Spironolactone 25 mg w/HCTZ** 25 mg	6.95	**21.95**
Aldactone 25 mg	Spironolactone	6.90	**20.95**
Aldomet 250 mg	Methyldopa	9.95	**20.95**
Aldomet 500 mg	Methyldopa	18.95	**36.95**
Aldoril 25	Methyldopa 250 mg w/HCTZ** 25 mg	17.75	**28.95**
	Aminophylline (generic) 100 mg	1.95	
	Aminophylline (generic) 200 mg	2.40	
Antivert 12.5 mg	Meclizine	3.25	**18.40**
Antivert 25 mg	Meclizine	3.95	**26.80**
Anturane 200 mg	Sulfinpyrazone	15.10	**34.95**
Apresazide 25/25	Hydralazine 25 mg w/HCTZ** 25 mg	12.00	**23.95**
Apresazide 50/50	Hydralazine 50 mg w/HCTZ** 50 mg	18.35	**33.95**
Apresoline 10 mg	Hydralazine	2.30	**13.20**
Apresoline 25 mg	Hydralazine	3.15	**18.50**
Apresoline 50 mg	Hydralazine	4.00	**25.65**
Apresoline 100 mg	Hydralazine	8.95	**35.95**
Aristocort 4 mg	Triamcinolone	7.00	**82.95**
Artane 2 mg	Trihexyphenidyl	2.45	**7.95**
Artane 5 mg	Trihexyphenidyl	2.85	**15.95**
Atarax 10 mg	Hydroxyzine HCl	7.95	**26.90**
Atarax 25 mg	Hydroxyzine HCl	10.95	**38.75**
Atarax 50 mg	Hydroxyzine HCl	12.95	**45.95**
Atromid-S 500 mg	Clofibrate	17.95	**29.95**
Azulfidine 500 mg	Sulfasalazine	6.50	**13.95**
Benemid 500 mg	Probenecid	6.50	**19.40**
Catapres 0.1 mg	Clonidine	9.95	**22.60**
Catapres 0.2 mg	Clonidine	11.95	**32.80**
Choledyl 200 mg	Oxtriphylline	6.80	**13.95**
ColBENEMID	Probenecid/colchicine	6.95	**22.90**
Compazine 10 mg	Prochlorperazine	12.65	**42.95**
Compazine 25 mg	Prochlorperazine	14.20	**52.95**
Cytomel 25 mcg	Liothyronine	3.95	**10.15**
Decadron 0.75 mg	Dexamethasone	7.70	**36.95**
Diabinese 100 mg	Chlorpropamide	7.95	**18.90**
Diabinese 250 mg	Chlorpropamide	8.50	**32.95**
Diamox 250 mg	Acetazolamide	6.95	**19.45**
Diprosone-0.05%, 45 gm	Betamethasone Dipropionate	10.50	**20.85**
Diupres-250	Chlorothiazide 250 mg w/reserpine 0.125 mg	4.70	**16.85**
Diuril 250 mg	Chlorothiazide	3.65	**8.45**

Brand Name	Generic Name	Generic Price	Brand Price
Diuril 500 mg	Chlorothiazide	5.70	**12.95**
Dyazide	Triamterene 50 mg		
	HCTZ 25 mg	15.95	**24.95**
Elavil 10 mg	Amitriptyline	3.70	**11.95**
Elavil 25 mg	Amitriptyline	4.95	**21.95**
Elavil 50 mg	Amitriptyline	6.00	**37.60**
Elavil 75 mg	Amitriptyline	10.65	**51.95**
Enduron 2.5 mg	Methyclothiazide	8.80	**16.90**
Enduron 5 mg	Methyclothiazide	10.95	**21.25**
Esidrix (See **Hydrodiuril**)			
Gantanol 0.5 gm	Sulfamethoxazole	7.15	**25.95**
Gantrisin 0.5 gm	Sulfisoxazole	3.95	**12.70**
Hydergine (Oral) 1 mg	Ergoloid Mesylates (Oral)	14.75	**31.90**
Hydergine sublingual 0.5 mg	Ergoloid Mesylates S.L.	8.75	**21.70**
Hydergine sublingual 1.0 mg	Ergoloid Mesylates S.L.	12.95	**38.50**
HydroDIURIL 25 mg	Hydrochlorothiazide (HCTZ)	2.80	**8.50**
HydroDIURIL 50 mg	Hydrochlorothiazide (HCTZ)	2.95	**11.95**
HydroDIURIL 100 mg	Hydrochlorothiazide (HCTZ)	3.35	**22.95**
Hydropres 25	Reserpine 0.125 mg w/HCTZ** 25 mg	3.00	**16.85**
Hydropres 50	Reserpine 0.125 mg w/HCTZ** 50 mg	3.15	**23.95**
Hygroton 25 mg	Chlorthalidone	8.95	**23.95**
Hygroton 50 mg	Chlorthalidone	9.45	**28.85**
Inderal 10 mg	Propranolol	5.50	**11.35**
Inderal 20 mg	Propranolol	7.95	**15.40**
Inderal 40 mg	Propranolol	9.95	**19.75**
Inderal 80 mg	Propranolol	17.95	**32.20**
Inderide 40/25	Propranolol 40 mg/HCTZ** 25 mg	19.95	**33.65**
Inderide 80/25	Propranolol 80 mg/HCTZ** 25 mg	28.95	**45.95**
Indocin 25 mg	Indomethacin	13.95	**31.95**
Indocin 50 mg	Indomethacin	21.95	**53.45**
Isordil (Oral) 5 mg	Isosorbide (Oral)	2.75	**11.35**
Isordil (Oral) 10 mg	Isosorbide (Oral)	2.95	**13.70**
Isordil (Oral) 20 mg	Isosorbide (Oral)	4.45	**20.65**
Isordil Tembids 40 mg	Isosorbide (Oral)	6.00	**24.60**
Isordil (S.L.) 2.5 mg	Isosorbide (S.L.)	2.70	**10.70**
Isordil (S.L.) 5 mg	Isosorbide (S.L.)	2.95	**11.50**
K-Lyte 25 mEq Eff	Potassium 25mEq Eff	15.95	**38.95**
Kenacort 4 mg	Triamcinolone	7.00	**79.50**
Lanoxin 0.25 mg	Digoxin	1.50	**5.40**
Lasix 20 mg	Furosemide	5.45	**8.95**
Lasix 40 mg	Furosemide	5.95	**11.95**
Lasix 80 mg	Furosemide	10.95	**21.10**
Mandelamine 0.5 gm	Methenamine mandelate	3.00	**14.40**

Brand Name	Generic Name	Generic Price	Brand Price
Mandelamine 1.0 gm	Methenamine mandelate	4.15	**21.70**
Marax	Ephedrine, theophylline,		
	hydroxyzine	5.95	**22.55**
Motrin 400 mg	Ibuprofen	7.95	**12.95**
Motrin 600 mg	Ibuprofen	10.95	**17.95**
Motrin 800 mg	Ibuprofen	14.95	**23.95**
Mycostatin Oral			
500,000 units	Nystatin Oral	18.95	**37.95**
Mysoline 250 mg	Primidone	5.45	**18.90**
Naqua 4 mg	Trichlormethiazide	3.45	**28.50**
Nitro-Bid 2.5 mg	Nitroglycerin T.D.	4.25	**15.10**
Nitro-Bid 6.5 mg	Nitroglycerin T.D.	5.50	**19.50**
Nitro-Dur II 30's,	Nitro Patch 30's,		
5 mg/24 hrs.	5 mg/24 hrs.	18.95	**30.40**
Norpace 100 mg	Disopyramide	18.95	**27.95**
Norpace 150 mg	Disopryamide	20.95	**31.95**
Orinase 0.5 gm	Tolbutamide	5.50	**14.85**
Pavabid 150 mg	Papaverine T.D.	4.05	**17.55**
Periactin 4 mg	Cyproheptadine	7.95	**24.45**
Phenergan 12.5 mg	Promethazine	2.75	**9.85**
Phenergan 25 mg	Promethazine	3.75	**17.40**
Polycillin 250 mg	Ampicillin	7.95	**18.95**
Polycillin 500 mg	Ampicillin	14.95	**31.05**
	Generic prednisone 5 mg	2.45	
Premarin 0.3 mg	Conjugated estrogens	5.95	**12.95**
Premarin 0.625 mg	Conjugated estrogens	6.95	**17.45**
Premarin 1.25 mg	Conjugated estrogens	8.45	**22.65**
Premarin 2.5 mg	Conjugated estrogens	15.00	**37.95**
Procan-SR 250 mg	Procainamide-SR	11.95	**18.40**
Procan-SR 500 mg	Procainamide-SR	16.95	**27.95**
Procan-SR 750 mg	Procainamide-SR	23.95	**40.95**
Pronestyl 250 mg	Procainamide	4.60	**19.95**
Pronestyl 375 mg	Procainamide	5.75	**28.95**
Pronestyl 500 mg	Procainamide	6.50	**33.95**
Quinaglute Dura-Tabs			
324 mg	Quinidine gluconate SR	19.95	**37.95**
Quinora (5 gr) 300 mg	Quinidine sulfate (5 gr)	14.50	**19.50**
Raudixin 100 mg	Rauwolfia serpentina	3.15	**34.95**
Reglan 10 mg	Metoclopramide	13.95	**24.95**
Robaxin 500 mg	Methocarbamol	4.95	**19.65**
Robaxin 750 mg	Methocarbamol	5.95	**26.35**
Ser-Ap-Es	Reserpine, hydralazine, HCTZ**	3.70	**28.40**
Serpasil 0.25 mg	Reserpine	2.45	**6.85**
Soma 350 mg	Carisoprodol	7.95	**52.95**
Sorbitrate Tablets			
(See Isordil)			
Stelazine 1 mg	Trifluoperazine	10.95	**29.80**
Stelazine 2 mg	Trifluoperazine	14.95	**42.95**
Stelazine 5 mg	Trifluoperazine	16.95	**52.85**
Stelazine 10 mg	Trifluoperazine	18.95	**22.95**

Brand Name	Generic Name	Generic Price	Brand Price
Synthroid 0.1 mg	Levothyroxine	2.15	**8.95**
Synthroid 0.15 mg	Levothyroxine	2.35	**10.95**
Synthroid 0.2 mg	Levothyroxine	2.45	**12.95**
Tegretol 200 mg	Carbamazepine	15.95	**24.95**
Thorazine 25 mg	Chlorpromazine	3.40	**24.25**
Thorazine 50 mg	Chlorpromazine	3.75	**29.25**
Tofranil 10 mg	Imipramine	3.55	**16.95**
Tofranil 25 mg	Imipramine	4.50	**25.90**
Tofranil 50 mg	Imipramine	5.45	**41.95**
Tolinase 250 mg	Tolazamide	17.95	**31.55**
Transderm-Nitro 30's 5 mg/24 hrs.	Nitroglycerin patch, 30's, 5 mg/24 hrs.	18.95	**30.95**
Urecholine 10 mg	Bethanechol	5.50	**37.95**
Urecholine 25 mg	Bethanechol	6.00	**55.65**
Urecholine 50 mg	Bethanechol	9.50	**76.30**
Valisone Cream 0.1% 15 gm	Betamethasone valerate cream	4.55	**9.45**
Valisone Cream 0.1% 45 gm	Betamethasone valerate cream	8.40	**17.25**
Vistaril 25 mg	Hydroxyzine pamoate	12.50	**39.35**
Vistaril 50 mg	Hydroxyzine pamoate	15.95	**46.95**
Zyloprim 100 mg	Allopurinol	5.95	**9.95**
Zyloprim 300 mg	Allopurinol	13.50	**23.75**

*American Association of Retired Persons Pharmacy Service. Prices given for quantities of 100, except where noted. Generic prices good through February 1988; brand name prices subject to periodic adjustment by the manufacturer.

**HCTZ = hydrochlorothiazide

stronger) form, or you might have an adverse reaction to the drug. Fill that entire prescription for 120 tablets and you could wind up with 119 wasted ones. There are no refunds on unused prescriptions.

If you choose to sample in this way, make certain the druggist notes it so you can come back and have the balance of the prescription filled. It is very important to take drugs in the prescribed way for the prescribed time. (This is particularly important with antibiotics. Patients sometimes slack off when they feel better. This is understandable, but it can lead to resistant bacteria, which are the toughies who survived the first chemical onslaught. Fail to deliver the knockout dose and these superbugs get to multiplying. The result can be real trouble.)

The second reason for getting less than the full prescription filled is to avoid inflated prices. If the local prices seem out of line, you might want to get just a week or ten-day supply for your immediate needs and then send the prescription off to a mail order service. You can do this in one of two ways. Either ask the doctor for a second prescription, or instruct the mail order pharmacy to call the pharmacy where you got your interim supply. (It cannot refuse to pass the prescription along).

Once you know you can handle a new drug safely and will have to take it for a long time, ask your doctor for a reasonably large quantity on the prescription. Like most other products, pills are cheaper when you buy in bulk.

Safe at Home

And here we are with **Step #9** to save money on medication. It's really very simple. Just take as directed. Every time we see the studies showing that most people don't take their medicine as prescribed, we're surprised. Why would folks spend their hard-earned cash to see the doctor, more money to get medicine that's supposed to fix them up, and then not take it as directed?

Playing medication hookey is like asking for a bigger bill. According to the National Council on Patient Information and Education:

> **Failure to take prescribed medicines safely and effectively kills an estimated 125,000 Americans each year. That's two-and-a-half times more Americans than are killed in motor vehicle accidents and six times more than are killed by accidental or deliberate use of firearms. Additionally, Americans spend $17 billion annually for prescription medicines. But studies indicate that 50% of the medicines are taken incorrectly. The widespread misuse of prescribed medications creates more than 225 million unnecessarily hazardous situations annually including:**
>
> • **prolonged illness**
>
> • **avoidable side effects**

- drug interactions

- absences from work or poor concentration at work

- increased hospitalizations

- additional prescriptions

- overutilization of health care services

Unfortunately, a 1982 FDA survey showed that patients are not getting the information they need about their drugs.

- **Nearly 70% of patients surveyed who had received a prescription within the last two weeks said their physicians and pharmacists did not tell them about precautions and possible side effects.**

- **40% said they were not told by their physician how to take the medication or how much to take.**[15]

If you don't get proper instructions and take the drug as you should, it may not accomplish the purpose for which it was prescribed. Then you go back to the doctor (spend more money), who may prescribe another medication (spend more money), which presents a new set of risks for adverse drug reactions, which can send you back to the doctor (spend more money).

So do what it says on the bottle. If the label says "Take three times a day, with meals," do it that way. From the last chapter, you already know why this is so crucial. If it says "Take as directed," then make certain you understood what the doctor said. If you don't remember, or aren't sure, do NOT be reluctant about calling and asking the nurse to find out. Doing it wrong could be costing you money as well as causing you problems.

Finally, **Step #10**. Store your medications properly. Having just shelled out some bucks for a container of capsules, don't render them useless (or even dangerous) by storing them unwisely. In general, medications do well in a cool, dark, and dry place. Of course, this does not describe the typical bathroom, with its steamy showers, yet that's right where the ill-named "medicine cabinet" can always be found.

We suggest using the medicine cabinet for soap, razors, rubber ducks, cotton swabs, or almost anything *except* medicine. Many medications change chemically upon exposure to high humidity or heat. It's like watching your money melt away. Find a quiet cabinet (out of reach of grandchildren) and put your medicine safely out of harm's way. That will save you the expense of having to refill the prescription, as well as the potential discomfort that could result from taking a drug that's not chemically what it was when dispensed by the pharmacist.

There you have the Graedons' People's Pharmacy prescription for saving money on your medicine. Take as directed, and you'll be able to keep more of your own hard-earned dollars in your pocket.

Things to Remember

1. Make a list and check it twice. Include everything that might help the doctor figure out what's wrong.

2. List all your medications or take them in with you when you go to see your doctor.

3. Don't demand a prescription. Nondrug alternatives, when appropriate, will save you money and surely reduce your risks of side effects.

4. Tell your doctor that you are trying to save money. Ask for the least expensive therapy that will safely do the job. Whenever feasible, request a free sample of a new prescription to make sure you can tolerate the medicine.

5. Could an OTC be tried initially? Don't forget that house brand OTCs (including vitamins) can often save you a bundle.

6. Shop around. Call the pharmacies in your area to get comparative prices. If your pharmacist provides special services and valuable information, it might be worthwhile sacrificing some savings.

7. Consider mail order. If you are taking the same medicine year in and year out with no variation, you may want to consider shopping by mail. The AARP Pharmacy Service is one of the oldest and largest. Many of their prescriptions come with free leaflets that provide valuable information about precautions and side effects. Braille labeling is available for people who cannot see. AARP will send you a free catalog and Money Saving Guide on request. Write to:

   AARP Pharmacy Service, Dept. J.G.
   One Prince Street
   Alexandria, VA 22314

8. Ask your doctor for generic equivalents whenever appropriate. The price differential between brand names and their generic counterparts can be astounding. Make sure the pharmacist does his or her homework and consults the FDA's *Approved Prescription Drug Products* book to be sure your prescription is filled with the exact same drug your doctor had in mind. (This list is available from the Superintendent of Documents, Washington, D.C. 20402.) Let the pharmacist know you are trying to save money, also, so that your generic prescription doesn't get filled with a brand name drug. Make sure she passes the savings on to you and doesn't pocket the difference.

9. When starting a new prescription, get a "trial size" first. If you can't get a free sample from your doctor, ask your pharmacist to give you a partial prescription. This way you get a chance to find out if you can tolerate the medicine.

10. Take your medicine properly. Make sure your doctor has provided complete instructions about how your pills should be swallowed—when, with what beverage, with or without meals—and whether there are any special precautions you should take.

11. Store your medicine properly and throw it out when it gets too old. Make sure your pharmacist writes the expiration date on the label of every prescription so you know when it will start to deteriorate. Ask about proper storage conditions. Request "easy-off" caps instead of child-proof ones—the medicine will stay airtight but you won't have a battle trying to open it. Just be sure to keep all drugs out of reach of children!

References

1. Shell, Ellen. "How to Talk to Your Doctor ... in 18 Seconds." *American Health*, Jan.–Feb., 1987, pp. 82–83.
2. Williams, Paul; and Rush, David R. "Geriatric Polypharmacy." *Hosp. Prac.*, Feb. 15, 1986, pp. 109–120.
3. Murphy, Patrick A. "One Drug Company's Sales Techniques." *N. Engl. J. Med.* July 25, 1985, pp. 270.
4. "The Big Lie About Generic Drugs." *Consumer Reports* 52, Aug. 1987, pp. 480–485.
5. "FDA Speaks Out About Generic Drug Quality." *NABP Newsletter*, Apr. 1986, pp. 53–54.
6. Haddad, William F. "Letter from the Publisher." *Generics* 2(3):4, 1986.
7. Faich, Gerald A.; Morrison, James; Dutra, Edwin V., Jr.; Hare, Donald B.; and Rheinstein, Peter H. "Reassurance about Generic Drugs." (editorial) *N. Engl. J. Med.* 316:1473–1475, 1987.
8. "FDA Speaks Out ... " op. cit.
9. Danielson, David. "FDA Bioequivalency Standards: Setting the Record Straight." *Generics*, Dec. 1985, pp. 21–34.
10. ibid.
11. *Emergency Medicine*, 18(18):120, 1986.
12. *JAMA*, 256(23):3184–3185.
13. Danielson, David A. "Influencing the Physician—Drug Industry Strategies." *Generics* 1(3):32–43, 1985.
14. "The Big Lie about Generic Drugs," op. cit., p. 484.
15. "Prescription Drug Misuse a Major Public Health Problem." *Talk About Prescriptions Month.* National Council on Patient Information and Education, Oct., 1986.

Brand Name Drugs Available Generically

Brand Name	Generic Name
*A and D Ointment	ointment with vitamins A and D
*A-200 Pyrinate	pyrethrins, piperonyl butoxide, ether
A/T/S	erythromycin (topical)
Achromycin V	tetracycline HCl
*Actidil	triprolidine HCl
*Actifed	triprolidine, pseudoephedrine
Adapin	doxepin HCl
*Advil	ibuprofen
*Afrin	oxymetazoline
Akne-mycin	erythromycin (topical)
Aldactazide	spironolactone, HCTZ**
Aldactone	spironolactone
Aldomet	methyldopa
Aldoril	methyldopa, HCTZ**
*Allerest	chlorpheniramine maleate, PPA[†]
Alpen	ampicillin
Alpha-Keri	mineral oil; lanolin, benzophenone-3
Ambenyl	codeine, bromodiphenhydramine
Amcill	ampicillin
Aminophyllin	aminophylline
Amoxil	amoxicillin
Amphicol	chloramphenicol
*Amphojel	aluminum hydroxide gel
*Anacin	aspirin, caffeine
Antabuse	disulfiram
Antepar	piperazine citrate
Antivert	meclizine HCl
Anturane	sulfinpyrazone
*Anusol-HC	hydrocortisone acetate, bismuth subgallate, bismuth resorcin compound, benzyl benzoate, balsam Peru, zinc oxide
Apresazide	hydralazine HCl, HCTZ**
Apresoline	hydralazine HCl
Aquatensen	methyclothiazide
Aralen	chloroquine phosphate

Brand Name	Generic Name
Aristocort	triamcinolone
Arlidin	nylidrin
Artane	trihexyphenidyl HCl
*Arthritis Pain Formula	aspirin, aluminum hydroxide, magnesium hydroxide
*A.S.A. Enseals	aspirin (coated)
*Ascriptin	aspirin, aluminum hydroxide, magnesium hydroxide
*Aspercreme	trolamine salicylate
Atarax	hydroxyzine HCl
Ativan	lorazepam
Atromid-S	clofibrate
AVC	sulfanilamide, aminacrine, allantoin
Azo Gantanol	sulfamethoxazole, phenazopyridine
Azo Gantrisin	sulfisoxazole, phenazopyridine
Azolid	phenylbutazone
Azulfidine	sulfasalazine
*Baciguent	bacitracin
Bactocill	oxacillin sodium
Bactrim	trimethoprim, sulfamethoxazole
Bancap	acetaminophen, butalbital
*Bayer Aspirin	aspirin
Beepen-VK	penicillin VK
*Benadryl	diphenhydramine HCl
Benemid	probenecid
*Ben-Gay	methyl salicylate, menthol
Bentyl	dicyclomine HCl
Benylin	diphenhydramine
*Betadine	povidone-iodine
Betapen-VK	penicillin VK
*Bonine	meclizine HCl
Brondecon	oxtriphylline, guaifenesin
*Bronkolixir	guaifenesin, ephedrine, theophylline, phenobarbital
Bronkometer	isoetharine
Bronkosol	isoetharine
*Bufferin	aspirin, aluminum magnesium
Butazolidin	phenylbutazone
Butisol	butabarbital sodium

Brand Name	Generic Name
Cafergot	ergotamine tartrate, caffeine
***Caladryl**	calamine, camphor, diphenhydramine HCl
Calan	verapamil HCl
***Caltrate 600**	calcium carbonate
Candex	nystatin
Catapres	clonidine HCl
***Chloraseptic**	phenol, sodium phenolate, etc.
Chlor-Trimeton	chlorpheniramine maleate
Chloromycetin	chloramphenicol
Choledyl	oxtriphylline
Cloxapen	cloxacillin sodium
Cogentin	benztropine mesylate
***Colace**	docusate sodium
ColBENEMID	probenecid, colchicine
Combid	isopropamide, prochlorperazine maleate
Combipres	chlorthalidone, clonidine
Compazine	prochlorperazine
***Compoz**	diphenhydramine HCl
***Comtrex**	acetaminophen, PPA† HCl chlorpheniramine maleate, dextromethorphan HBr
Cordran	flurandrenolide
***Coricidin**	aspirin, chlorpheniramine maleate
***Correctol**	docusate, phenolphthalein
***Cortaid**	hydrocortisone
Cort-Dome	hydrocortisone
Cortef	hydrocortisone
Cortisporin	polymixin B, neomycin, hydrocortisone
Cortone	cortisone
***CoTylenol**	acetaminophen, chlorpheniramine maleate, pseudoephedrine, dextromethorphan
Coumadin	warfarin sodium
Cyclospasmol	cyclandelate
Cytomel	liothyronine
Dalmane	flurazepam HCl

Brand Name	Generic Name
Darvocet-N 100	propoxyphene napsylate, acetaminophen
Darvon	propoxyphene HCl
Darvon Compound	propoxyphene HCl, aspirin, caffeine
*Datril	acetaminophen
Decadron	dexamethasone
Decapryn	doxylamine succinate
Delestrogen	estradiol valerate
Delta-Cortef	prednisolone
Deltasone	prednisone
Demerol	meperidine
Depakene	valproic acid
*Desenex	undecylenic acid, zinc undecylenate
Desoxyn	methamphetamine HCl
Desyrel	trazodone HCl
Dexedrine	dextroamphetamine sulfate
Diabinese	chlorpropamide
*Dialose	docusate
Diamox	acetazolamide
*Dietac	phenylpropanolamine
Dimetane	brompheniramine maleate
Dimetapp	brompheniramine, PPA[†]
Diprosone	betamethasone dipropionate
Diucardin	hydroflumethiazide
Dinlo	metolazone
Diupres	chlorothiazide, reserpine
Diuril	chlorothiazide
*Doan's Pills	magnesium salicylate
Dolene	propoxyphene HCl
Donnagel	belladonna mix, kaolin, pectin
Donnatal	belladonna mix, phenobarbital
Doriden	glutethimide
Doxidan	docusate, danthron
*Dramamine	dimenhydrinate
*Dristan Advanced Formula	phenylephrine HCl, chlorpheniramine maleate, acetaminophen
*Dulcolax	bisacodyl
Duotrate	pentaerythritol tetranitrate
Dyazide	HCTZ**, triamterene

Brand Name	Generic Name
Dycill	dicloxacillin sodium
Dymelor	acetohexamide
Dynapen	dicloxacillin sodium
*Ecotrin	aspirin (coated)
E.E.S.	erythromycin ethylsuccinate
Elavil	amitriptyline HCl
Elixophyllin	theophylline
*Emetrol	fructose, dextrose, orthophosphoric acid
Empirin	aspirin
Empirin w/codeine	aspirin, codeine
Empracet w/codeine	acetaminophen, codeine
E-Mycin	erythromycin (coated)
Endep	amitriptyline HCl
Enduron	methyclothiazide
Equagesic	meprobamate, aspirin
Equanil	meprobamate
ERYC	erythromycin (coated)
Eryderm	erythromycin (topical)
Erypar	erythromycin stearate
EryPed	erythromycin ethylsuccinate
Ery-Tab	erythromycin (coated)
Erythrocin	erythromycin stearate
Esidrix	hydrochlorothiazide
Eskalith	lithium carbonate
Ethril	erythromycin stearate
*Excedrin	acetaminophen, aspirin, caffeine
*Ex-Lax	phenolphthalein
Exna	benzthiazide
Fastin	phentermine HCl
*Feosol	ferrous sulfate
Fiorinal	butalbital, aspirin, caffeine
*Fergon	ferrous gluconate
Flagyl	metronidazole
Folvite	folic acid
Furadantin	nitrofurantoin
Gantanol	sulfamethoxazole
Gantrisin	sulfisoxazole

Brand Name	Generic Name
Garamycin	gentamicin sulfate
*Gaviscon	aluminum hydroxide, magnesium carbonate
*Gelusil	aluminum hydroxide, magnesium hydroxide, simethicone
Haldol	haloperidol
Halotestin	fluoxymesterone
*Haltran	ibuprofen
Hycodan	hydrocodone, homatropine
Hycomine	hydrocodone, PPA[†]
Hydergine	ergoloid mesylates
Hydrocortone	hydrocortisone
HydroDIURIL	hydrochlorothiazide
Hydropres	reserpine, HCTZ**
Hygroton	chlorthalidone
Ilosone	erythromycin estolate
Ilotycin	erythromycin
Inderal	propranolol HCl
Inderide	propranolol HCl, HCTZ**
Indocin	indomethacin
INH	isoniazid
Ismelin	guanethidine monosulfate
Isoptin	verapamil HCl
Isopto Carpine	pilocarpine HCl
Isordil	isosorbide dinitrate
Isuprel	isoproterenol HCl
Janimine	imipramine
Kaochlor	potassium chloride
Kaon	potassium gluconate
*Kaopectate	kaolin, pectin
Kay Ciel	potassium chloride
Kenacort	triamcinolone
Keflex	cephalexin
Kenalog	triamcinolone acetonide
K-Lor	potassium chloride
K-Lyte	potassium (effervescent)
Kolyum	potassium gluconate and chloride
Kwell	lindane

Brand Name	Generic Name
Lanoxin	digoxin
Larotid	amoxicillin
Lasix	furosemide
Librax	chlordiazepoxide, clidinium
Librium	chlordiazepoxide HCl
Lidex	fluocinonide
Limbitrol	amitriptyline, chlordiazepoxide
Lithane	lithium carbonate
Lomotil	diphenoxylate, atropine
Loniten	minoxidil
Lopurin	allopurinol
Ludiomil	maprotiline (availability expected)
Lufyllin-GG	dyphylline, guaifenesin
*Maalox	aluminum and magnesium hydroxide
Mandelamine	methenamine
Marax	ephedrine sulfate, theophylline, hydroxyzine HCl
Meclomen	meclofenamate sodium
*Medipren	ibuprofen
Medrol	methylprednisolone
Megace	megestrol acetate
Mellaril	thioridazine HCl
*Merthiolate	thimerosal
Metahydrin	trichlormethiazide
*Metamucil	psyllium (vegetable laxative)
Metandren	methyltestosterone
Meticortelone	prednisolone
Meticorten	prednisone
Midamor	amiloride HCl
Miltown	meprobamate
Modane	danthron
Motrin	ibuprofen
Mycifradin	neomycin sulfate
Mycodan	homatropine, hydrocodone
Mycolog-II	nystatin, triamcinolone acetonide
Mycostatin	nystatin
*Mylanta	aluminum and magnesium hydroxide, simethicone

Brand Name	Generic Name
*Mylicon-80	simethicone
Mysoline	primidone
Naldecon	chlorpheniramine, phenylephrine, phenyltoloxamine, PPA[†]
Naqua	trichlormethiazide
Naquival	trichlormethiazide, reserpine
Navane	thiothixene
NegGram	nalidixic acid
Nembutal	pentobarbital sodium
Neo-Cortef	hydrocortisone, neomycin
NeoDecadron	neomycin, dexamethasone
*Neosporin	polymixin B, bacitracin, neomycin
*Neo-Synephrine	phenylephrine
Neotrizine	trisulfapyrimidines
Nicobid	niacin (nicotinic acid) SR
Nicolar	niacin (nicotinic acid)
Nilstat	nystatin
Nitro-Bid	nitroglycerin
Nitro-Dur	nitroglycerin transdermal
Noctec	chloral hydrate
Norflex	orphenadrine citrate
Norgesic	orphenadrine citrate, aspirin, caffeine
Norpace	disopyramide phosphate
Norpramin	desipramine HCl
Novahistine DH	codeine, pseudoephedrine, chlorpheniramine
*Nupercainal	dibucaine
*Nuprin	ibuprofen
Nydrazid	isoniazid
*NyQuil	acetaminophen, dextromethorphan, doxylamine, pseudoephedrine
*Nytol w/DPH	diphenhydramine HCl
Omnipen	ampicillin
Oretic	hydrochlorothiazide
Orinase	tolbutamide
Ornade	chlorpheniramine, PPA[†]
Ornex	acetaminophen, PPA[†]
*Os-Cal	calcium carbonate

Brand Name	Generic Name
*Oxy-5	benzoyl peroxide
Panmycin	tetracycline HCl
Paraflex	chlorzoxazone
Parafon Forte	acetaminophen, chlorzoxazone
Pathibamate	tridihexethyl chloride, meprobamate
Pathocil	dicloxacillin sodium
Pavabid	papaverine
PBZ	tripelennamine HCl
Pediamycin	erythromycin ethylsuccinate
Pentids	penicillin G
Pen-Vee K	penicillin VK potassium
*Pepto-Bismol	bismuth subsalicylate
Percocet	oxycodone, acetaminophen
Percodan	oxycodone, aspirin
*Percogesic	acetaminophen, phenyltoloxamine
Periactin	cyproheptadine HCl
*Peri-Colace	casanthranol, docusate
Peritrate	pentaerythritol tetranitrate
Persantine	dipyridamole
*Phenaphen	acetaminophen
Phenaphen w/codeine	codeine, acetaminophen
Phenergan	promethazine
Placidyl	ethchlorvynol
Plegine	phendimetrazine tartrate
*Polaramine	dexchlorpheniramine
Polycillin	ampicillin
*Polysporin	polymixin B, bacitracin
Premarin	conjugated estrogens
*Preparation-H	live yeast cell derivative, shark liver oil derivative
*Primatene Mist	epinephrine
Principen	ampicillin
Pro-Banthine	propantheline bromide
Procan SR	procainamide HCl SR
Prolixin	fluphenazine HCl
Proloprim	trimethoprim
Pronestyl	procainamide HCl

Brand Name	Generic Name
*Propadrine	phenylpropanolamine
Prostaphlin	oxacillin sodium
Provera	medroxyprogesterone
Pyridium	phenazopyridine
Quibron	theophylline, guaifenesin
Quinaglute	quinidine gluconate
Quinamm	quinine
Quinora	quinidine sulfate
Raudixin	rauwolfia serpentina
Redisol	cyanocobalamin
Reglan	metoclopramide HCl
Restoril	temazepam
*Riopan	magaldrate
Ritalin	methylphenidate HCl
Robaxin	methocarbamol
Robaxisal	methocarbamol, aspirin
Robimycin	erythromycin (coated)
Robinul	glycopyrrolate
*Robitussin	guaifenesin
Rondec	carbinoxamine, pseudoephedrine
Rufen	ibuprofen
Saluron	hydroflumethiazide
Salutensin	hydroflumethiazide, reserpine
*Sebulex	sulfur, salicylic acid
*Sebutone	coal tar, sulfur, salicylic acid
Seconal	secobarbital sodium
*Selsun Blue	selenium sulfide
*Senokot	senna concentrate
Septra	trimethoprim, sulfamethoxazole
Ser-Ap-Es	reserpine, hydralazine HCl, HCTZ**
Serax	oxazepam (availability expected)
Serpasil	reserpine
Sinequan	doxepin
Sinutab	acetaminophen, chlorpheniramine, pseudoephedrine
*Sleep-Eze	diphenhydramine HCl
Soma	carisoprodol
*Sominex 2	diphenhydramine HCl

Brand Name	Generic Name
Somophyllin	aminophylline
Sparine	promazine
Staticin	erythromycin (topical)
Stelazine	trifluoperazine HCl
*Sudafed	pseudoephedrine
Sumycin	tetracycline HCl
Surmontil	trimipramine maleate
Sustaire	theophylline
Symmetrel	amantadine HCl
Synalar	fluocinolone acetonide
Synalgos-DC	dihydrocodeine, aspirin, caffeine
Synthroid	levothyroxine
Tandearil	oxyphenbutazone
*Tedral	theophylline, ephedrine, phenobarbital
Tegopen	cloxacillin sodium
Tegretol	carbamazepine
*Teldrin	chlorpheniramine maleate
Temaril	trimeprazine tartrate
Tenuate	diethylpropion HCl
Terramycin	oxytetracycline HCl
Tetracyn	tetracycline HCl
Theo-Dur	theophylline
Thorazine	chlorpromazine
Tigan	trimethobenzamide
*Tinactin	tolnaftate
*Titralac	calcium carbonate, glycine
Tofranil	imipramine HCl
Tolinase	tolazamide
Totacillin	ampicillin
Tranxene	clorazepate dipotassium
*Trendar	ibuprofen
*Triaminic	PPA[†], chlorpheniramine
*Triaminicol Syrup	PPA[†], chlorpheniramine, dextromethorphan
Triavil	perphenazine, amitriptyline HCl
Trilafon	perphenazine

Brand Name	Generic Name
Trimox	amoxicillin
Trimpex	trimethoprim
T-Stat	erythromycin (topical)
Tussend Expectorant	guaifenesin, hydrocodone, pseudoephedrine
*Tuss-Ornade	caramiphen, PPA[†]
*Tylenol	acetaminophen
Tylenol w/codeine	codeine, acetaminophen
Urecholine	bethanechol chloride
Valisone	betamethasone valerate
Valium	diazepam
Vancocin	vancomycin HCl
*Vaseline	petrolatum
Vasodilan	isoxsuprine
V-Cillin K	penicillin VK
Veetids	penicillin VK
Velosef	cephradine
Vermizine	piperazine citrate
Vibramycin	doxycycline hyclate
Vibra-Tabs	doxycycline
*Vicks Formula 44	dextromethorphan, doxylamine
Vicodin	hydrocodone, acetaminophen
Vioform-Hydrocortisone	hydrocortisone, iodochlorhydroxyquin
*Visine	tetrahydrozoline
Vistaril	hydroxyzine pamoate
Wygesic	propoxyphene HCl, acetaminophen
Wymox	amoxicillin
Zaroxolyn	metolazone (availability expected)
*Zephiran	benzalkonium chloride
Zyloprim	allopurinol

*Available without prescription
**HCTZ = hydrochlorothiazide
†PPA-phenylpropanolamine

5

Saving Your Skin

Would you like to look Younger? A lot Younger?" asks the ad. "New Discovery Seems to Stop the Effects of Aging from Showing on Your Face!" Another headline announces that an "Amazing New Formula from Beverly Hills Lets You Take up to 10 Years off Your Looks Without the Scars and Expense of Plastic Surgery." Then there's the "Miracle Eye Formula" that lets you "Eliminate Eye Wrinkles in 2 Days" to have the "beautiful wrinkle-free eyes of a 20-year-old."

Other products promise to rejuvenate, rebuild, nourish, and replenish. That sounds a little like fertilizer, the kind that comes from a bull. But people are desperate for "anti-aging" skin creams. Everyone wants to look younger these days. Americans are stocking up on creams, lotions, ointments, emulsions, activators, masks, and toners, many of which are supposed to erase wrinkles and make old skin look as smooth and tender as a baby's bottom.

The latest gimmick in this ever-expanding market is high-tech hype. Not content to offer simple moisturizers, the companies extol the wonders of aloe, collagen, cell extracts, hyaluronic acid, hydrorelectan, revitenol, and glycosphingolipids. The harder it is to pronounce, the more impressive it sounds. With trade names like **Biotherm, Age Zone Night Energizer, Trans Hydrex,** and **Ultima II ProCollagen Anti-Aging Complex Especially for the Eyes**, some manufacturers rely on the glamorous image of space age research, while others still go in for seductive models and good old-fashioned sex appeal with names such as **Estée**

Lauder Private Collection Silken Body Lotion or **Oscar de la Renta Body Lotion Activée.** Cosmetics pioneer Charles Revson realized that "hope in a bottle" springs eternal.

And price is no object. The more expensive a product is, the faster it seems to move off the shelf. According to *The Wall Street Journal*, "Americans spend about $1.9 billion a year on skin creams, almost double what they spent five years ago. At as much as $20 to $50 dollars an ounce, the most expensive creams have markups that can be 'hundreds of times more costly than the ingredients.' "[1] In fact, when one firm introduced a "cellular anti-aging cream" at $75 an ounce—as much as fine French perfume—sales of the stuff at Bergdorf's hit $50,000 in the first three weeks alone.

Now you have to understand that there is not much, if any, scientific evidence that any of the upscale skin creams are more effective than plain old petroleum jelly when it comes to moisturizing or even erasing wrinkles. But that doesn't seem to stop the folks on Madison Avenue. One product that has had the whole cosmetic industry in an uproar because of its marketing program is Glycel. Dr. Christiaan Barnard, the famous heart transplant surgeon, put his name and reputation behind Glycel.

> **Dermatologists have rebuked Dr. Barnard for trading on his name, and industry researchers have complained that the main ingredient in the "anti-aging" cream is merely one of a class of natural body fats with a fancy name. Furthermore, several cosmetic makers fear that the bold marketing of Glycel could bring the Food and Drug Administration down on them all ...**
>
> **"Everyone's worried that Barnard's claims, which sound as if he's got something to reverse aging, have stepped over the line and will spur the FDA to examine the entire industry's marketing methods," says Madeline Fleishman, a marketing executive at Jacqueline Cochran, an American Cyanamid Co. unit ...**
>
> **To avoid FDA scrutiny, cosmetics marketers are careful to claim that the benefit of their products is only skin deep. "We don't say we remove wrinkles, we say we diminish. We don't cure, we soften," says**

Pamela Fields, vice president of marketing and advertising for Biotherm, a skin care line sold by Cosmair, Inc., New York. "Sometimes, when we say 'diminish,' people think they hear 'gone,' " she says . . .

Alfin [maker of Glycel] and Dr. Barnard "have broken the rules, making claims that cannot be proven," says Dr. James Leyden, a researcher at the University of Pennsylvania, who tests new ingredients for many of Alfin's competitors.[2]

Wrinkled Raisins Give Us a Clue

The anti-aging hoopla has conveniently ignored the major causes of wrinkling, freckling, mottling, roughness, lines, dryness, and sagging skin. Besides genes (which you can't do anything about), facial expressions (like frowning or laughing), gravity, and smoking (which exaggerates crow's feet, wrinkles around the mouth, and lines on the cheeks),[3] the most significant reason for wrinkling and other signs of aging—including skin cancers, though they may also occur in younger people—is a lifetime of sun exposure.

According to Dr. Barbara Gilchrest, Chairman of Dermatology at Boston University School of Medicine and one of the world's leading researchers on the process of skin aging, "Almost all of the changes we think of as aging changes in the skin are caused by the sun. They are not caused by aging and they are not present in old non-sun-exposed skin.... This photoaging process or sun damage is indeed responsible for virtually all the changes that we call aging in the skin."[4]

We're not merely talking about sunbathing, though that is truly terrible for your skin. Just because you didn't lounge around a swimming pool your entire life doesn't mean you'll be protected. Your skin neither forgets nor forgives. Every time you strolled down the street, dug in the garden, hiked across a field, swatted a tennis ball, or hung up laundry on a clothes line you were accumulating ultraviolet radiation from the sun. In fact, you received a lot more sun exposure from daily activities like shopping than you did from a beach vacation or a trip to Florida. Little by little those rays did their invisible damage.

Oh, you don't believe us? Well, how about a few examples? Take Mom. She's a most extraordinary woman. She has had more than her share of stress and adversity over the years, but it doesn't show on her face. Although Mother is well into her eighties, you'd never guess her age to look at her. She has the skin of a woman at least 20 years younger. Her face is smooth and barely wrinkled.

What's the secret behind her youthful appearance? Well, we can guarantee you it's not some expensive face goo. She never went in for that sort of stuff. She has blue eyes and fair skin, which make her especially vulnerable to the sun's rays. Because she burned so easily, she shunned the sun her whole life. As a child she wore a hat and protective clothing outdoors. Mother was fortunate because during the early part of the century when she was growing up, there was no peer pressure to have a golden tan. In fact, the fashion of the day held that the fairer you were, the more beautiful. A "peaches and cream "complexion was admired. Even when she got older and fashions changed, Mom never saw much point in soaking up the rays. So today she still looks great!

You can't say the same thing for Carolyn [not her real name]. She loved the sun. Every chance she could she would lie spread-eagled in the backyard or on the beach sunbathing. She never wore a hat and took great pride in her beautiful tan. She's only 64 but she looks 84. Her face has a dried leather appearance with lots of lines and wrinkles. She's got sags and bags and blotches. Carolyn may be an extreme case, but she is by no means an exception.

Over the last several decades fashion has dictated that a tan is a mark of beauty. Generations have grown up worshipping the sun. Stroll onto just about any college campus in the country in May and you will find young men and women basting themselves to a golden glow. Even if you told them that the price they will pay for this indulgence is premature aging and wrinkling and a much greater risk of skin cancer, they'd probably ignore you. But visit a Buddhist monastery and you will see something quite amazing. Our favorite dermatologist, Dr. Albert Kligman, one of the pioneers in the field of aging skin, has done just that. He reports that if you look at the 80- and 90-year-old priests who have spent a lifetime indoors, "their skin is absolutely gorgeous, no tumors, no mottling, none of that stuff."[5]

Still not convinced? All right, time to take a test. Head for the bathroom and start stripping. Compare the skin on your breasts or the inside of your thighs with the skin on the back of your hands. Or look at the skin just under your armpit and compare it to the skin on your face. The differences in texture and wrinkling are due to the sun. Remember that it's all the same skin—same genes—same age. The only difference is that where your skin wasn't exposed to the sun, it looks a lot smoother and healthier.

If you could look at sun-damaged skin under a microscope, you would glimpse a most extraordinary sight. Dr. Lorraine Kligman (Albert Kligman's wife and colleague) is a scientist at the cutting edge of this kind of research. She describes a biopsy of Carolyn's face: "It is difficult to recognize this as elastic tissue. It is a swamp of degraded elastic material which has globbed on all kinds of garbage fibronectin. This is elastin that cannot serve the function to keep the skin in its normal bouncy healthy form."[6]

Instead of a nice orderly arrangement of cells and fibers, you see a "moth-eaten mess" under the microscope when you look at skin that has been repeatedly exposed to the sun. In addition to the nasty things that happen to elastic tissue, collagen can also be damaged by the sun. Just as a trestle holds up a bridge, so collagen forms a network of protein fibers that provides a foundation of supple support for cells and blood vessels just under your epidermis (the uppermost layer of skin).

Collagen is a word that is being hyped a lot these days. You will find all sorts of skin cream companies bragging about added collagen. But collagen doesn't work from the outside in. No amount of expensive anti-aging cream, with or without collagen, will erase wrinkles, restore youthful elasticity, and undo the damage. Putting beautiful icing on a cardboard cake won't improve the flavor of the cake. According to Dr. Albert Kligman, "Despite the many lush promises about inhibiting wrinkling and reduction of dryness, most 'moisturizers,' including the thousands of creams, ointments and lotions, prove to have only a trivial, transient effect. They may look good but the effect doesn't last. They don't affect the biology of aging."[7]

Retin-A to the Rescue

So what to do? By now you may be feeling a tad depressed. Let us reassure you that there is some good news. While it's true that your skin may have stored up a lifetime of sun damage, it doesn't mean that you should throw in the towel and give up. You may not be able to make sagging, wrinkled skin look young again, but you can certainly prevent further damage and perhaps even reverse some wrinkling and other aspects of photoaging. Experiments carried out by the Kligmans suggest that skin can begin to repair itself if you just "get the hell out of the sun or use sun screen."[8]

These days sunscreens are far more effective than they used to be. When we were growing up, about all that was available, besides a hat, which blocks only about half of the ultraviolet rays, was oil that acted more as a moisturizer than a protector. Such products could even have been counterproductive in that they may have actually allowed the ultraviolet rays to pass through the skin more easily. Now you can purchase sunscreens with high SPF (sun protection factor) numbers (15 or greater) that can virtually prevent sunburn and tend to slow down the tanning process.

The Kligmans' elegant experiments with hairless mice have demonstrated that "with use of sunscreens, further damage could be prevented and repair could occur, even in the face of continuing irradiation. Overall, the earlier application and higher SPF provided the greatest amount of protection to connective tissue."[9]

That's good news. Get out of the sun and the skin will gradually begin to show signs of natural repair. But lest you get a false sense of security from your sunscreen, there is a word of caution. Even the best sunscreens available can't block out all the sun's rays. Some ultraviolet and infrared radiation will still penetrate and do damage.[10] That's why we advise against hours of sunbathing even with good sunscreens. Although you won't get burned or even pink, you are still doing damage that could eventually lead to liver spots, wrinkling, and cancer. So cover up, wear a hat, or bring back that wonderful old invention, the parasol. Even light clothing can't completely protect your skin, as some sun will penetrate through loosely woven fabric.

All right, you're taking good care of your skin, staying out of

the sun as much as possible, and using a sunscreen regularly. Is
there anything else you can do about those wrinkles and blotches
caused by the sun? You betcha! The Kligmans have created quite
a stir of late with their research on **Retin-A** (known variously as
retinoic acid, vitamin A acid, and tretinoin). Retinoic acid is a
natural by-product of vitamin A. It's been available for more than
40 years and has been prescribed as an ointment under the brand
name **Retin-A** for over 15 years for the treatment of acne. Here's
how the Kligmans discovered its potential for improving sun-
damaged skin:

> **We came upon this coincidentally because the drug
> was first designed to treat acne. It is an anti-pimple
> drug. The medical profession has, I think, solidly
> endorsed it in the treatment of adolescent acne.
> For whatever reason, an increasing number of post-
> adolescent women have breakouts, they have pim-
> ples, and often little comedones, a disorder we have
> called acne cosmetica. As I have seen more and
> more of those people in their 20s and 30s I would
> give them retinoic acid, Retin-A. I'm trying to get rid
> of their pimples and they would come in and say,
> "Look, my face feels smoother, more lively, it's got a
> glow."
> In general, I didn't see that. I just thought these
> were nice ladies who wanted to say that we're pleased
> that we came to you. They thought you're a nice
> doctor, and we want to get better. It took me some
> years to pay attention specifically to what they were
> saying; that the skin really did have an improved
> texture, that it really did have more glow. And it's a
> result of those serendipitous observations that we
> came to see another application of Retin-A.[11]**

A 21-year-old model from Fort Lauderdale, Florida, is a perfect
example. Her dermatologist prescribed **Retin-A** three years ago
for acne, but it wasn't long before the young woman noticed that
her skin was younger looking. "I wake up in the morning and my
skin is fresh. It's completely different skin than when I went to
bed. I love it. People tell me my skin looks younger than it did
three years ago. It has a nice texture and even tone."[12]

Dr. Lorraine Kligman has found that **Retin-A** does indeed enhance the repair process and stimulate new collagen formation in photodamaged hairless mice.[13] **Retin-A** seems to stimulate the skin to turn on its cell-making machinery. Blood flow increases and new cells start migrating up to the surface, clearing the skin of dead cells and other debris.

> **The biologic effects begin almost immediately even though we can't see them. Within two days we can demonstrate that epidermal cell turnover has increased. There is the beginning of structural change. This activity goes on for some weeks before we can actually see the changes. Eventually, in a month or more, the skin becomes pinker, more turgid, less wrinkly. It has more elasticity, less blotching, and has a better color.**
>
> **Question.** *How long must you use retinoic acid to keep the skin younger looking?*
>
> **Answer. Probably forever. Any benefits depend on its continual use. It isn't like putting on rouge and lipstick and blushers where you have an instant change in appearance. It's a different game—one of maintenance, like brushing your teeth.**[14]

Before you get your hopes up too high, let us warn you that **Retin-A** is definitely *not* a fountain of youth. It won't make old skin look young again. But it does seem to increase blood flow, thicken the epidermis, improve texture, and enhance cell growth in the deeper layers of the skin.[15] Fine wrinkles, especially those around the eyes, may slowly fade. Even more exciting is the news that **Retin-A** appears to reverse precancerous skin lesions called actinic keratoses (pinkish or reddish scaly skin patches).[16] And some skin cancers (primarily basal cell) may also respond favorably to this drug.[17] Experiments are ongoing to see if this treatment will be helpful for scars, psoriasis, warts, or cervical dysplasia—a precancerous cellular change of the cervix. There are even reports that wounds heal faster with **Retin-A**.[18]

Before we continue our discussion of **Retin-A**, let us put in just a word about a nonprescription product that seems to speed the healing of a variety of skin sores: **Preparation H**. Now, we are not convinced yet that this product is a cure-all for shrinking hemorrhoids, but when we received the following letter from one of our newspaper readers, it really set off an enthusiastic response:

> **Early this year I acquired eczema. My hands would crack open and bleed. All callous areas would peel off on my palms and feet. The doctor prescribed Kenalog [a steroid cream]. After four prescriptions [at about $11 a tube] the results were nil.**
>
> **People advised me of all sorts of other oils to use and I tried several of my own. One day I tried Preparation H ointment [the stuff for hemorrhoids]. The day before I tried the ointment I had nine open areas on my hands. In two applications all openings had closed and started healing. Now after the third application I only have a few dry areas on my hands. I apply the ointment and wear plastic gloves when I sleep. I can only laugh at the results.**

At first we chuckled over this letter, but we're not laughing any more. After publishing it in our column, we were inundated with mail from other pleased readers:

> **I read your column about the benefits of Preparation H in healing sore open cracks on someone's hands. I was so impressed that I immediately purchased a tube of same. As soon as possible I applied the ointment to ugly sores on my brother's derriere (he is a stroke victim). Pure magic! They began healing—this after the failure of more sophisticated treatments in the hospital including a special bed.**

And another reader reported:

> **I had open heart surgery and while home recuperating the burning and itching of this 12-inch scar nearly drove me mad. After calling all three of my doctors, and getting no help, even with a cortisone ointment, and trying everything in the world, I discovered to my added misery Preparation H was called for for hemorrhoids. I decided "Oh, what the Hell"**

> and applied same to the scar, and Lo and Behold!!
> no more itching and burning from that point on. My
> husband also had open heart surgery and the same
> problem, so I slathered him with Prep H also, and
> he had no discomfort whatever after that! Guess it
> all depends from which end you attack the problem!

There is actually some scientific research that supports these testimonials. An article published in the *Archives of Surgery* by a doctor at the Alta Bates Burn Center in Berkeley, California, demonstrated that one of the same ingredients found in **Preparation H** (live yeast cell derivative) was capable of "accelerating wound healing beyond its normal rate."[19] The other ingredient in **Preparation H** is shark liver oil. Doubtless shark liver oil, like other fish liver oils, contains oodles of vitamin A, the original retinoid. All chemicals that are similar to vitamin A fall into this category. Now remember that **Retin-A**, Dr. Kligman's acne medicine and new approach to photoaged skin, is vitamin A acid—a topical retinoid. Ah ha! Maybe it all begins to make sense.

Whether or not **Preparation H** will do anything beneficial for wrinkles, **Retin-A** looks pretty good. Who should use it and when should it be used? Dr. Al Kligman believes that "Sport- and sun-loving persons who burn easily and tan poorly should start tretinoin prophylaxis in their twenties. People of Mediterranean origin who tan deeply and quickly may not wish to begin therapy until their thirties or forties...."[20] Anyone with fine wrinkling around the eyes (crow's-feet) would presumably be a candidate.

If you think you qualify, you will still need to talk to a dermatologist who knows how the drug works since **Retin-A** is available by prescription only. The FDA has approved this drug only for treating acne, so it's important to understand that if you follow through on such a program you are taking part in an experiment. Your doctor will have to do some homework if he decides it is appropriate to prescribe it for photoaged skin. Here are some hints for him to consider:

1. Go slow and go low. In order to reduce the risk
   of redness and peeling that often accompanies
   Retin-A acne treatment, the doctor may initially
   recommend that you start with a low concentration or apply the ointment every other night.

Although the usual formulation is 0.05% (cream) at bedtime, people with especially fair skin may need special dilution to 0.01%.

2. To avoid irritations never put **Retin-A** on wet skin. Wait at least 15 minutes after washing (always with a mild soap) before lightly applying the cream, or don't wash at all that night. Be careful not to get any **Retin-A** into the corners of the eyes, mouth, or nose as it can be irritating.

3. Make sure you apply a moisturizing cream religiously every morning to reduce the risk of peeling. **Moisturel** is a brand that Dr. Kligman recommends. **Lac-Hydrin** lotion may also be very effective, but more about other moisturizers in a moment.

4. If moderate redness or peeling occur and make you uncomfortable, give your face a break for several days before resuming treatment. After a few months this problem should disappear completely as your face adjusts to the medicine.

5. Some people may notice red, rough, scaly patches appearing after a month or so. These could well be precancerous skin lesions (actinic keratoses) that would have shown up eventually no matter what. The **Retin-A** brings them to the surface and may actually destroy them.

Skin cancer is related to sun exposure, and covering up or using an effective sunscreen is the best protection. When caught early, most skin cancers are curable. Be on the lookout for red, patchy, scaly spots that never seem to go away, or sores that don't heal. Shiny bumps with a pearly border should also be seen by a dermatologist.

Melanoma is a different kettle of fish. This kind of skin cancer is potentially life threatening. Have a dermatologist look you over from stem to stern periodically. Be alert for any moles that look "as American as apple pie." By that we mean a raised

mole that is red, white, or bluish, has a notched
border (like pie with a wedge cut out), and is not
symmetrical.

6. Always use a sunscreen when you go outdoors.
   Retin-A will make your skin more vulnerable to
   a sunburn. And you certainly don't want to undo
   any of the benefits of **Retin-A** by adding additional sun damage to that which has accumulated over a lifetime.

7. Finally, be patient. It will take at least six months
   to a year before you really see much improvement. Once the doctor is satisfied that your skin
   has achieved a better texture, she will probably
   recommend a maintenance schedule with applications two or three times a week.

As interesting as **Retin-A** may be, remember that it's not an
antidote to continued sun exposure and it's not for everybody.
Make sure you apply a good sunscreen, cover up, and generally
stay out of the sun as much as is reasonably possible. Plan your
outdoor activities before 10 A.M. or after 4 P.M. whenever possible.
Even on cloudy days there's plenty of damaging ultraviolet light
coming through, so make a sunscreen part of your daily ritual.
Don't forget your ears and neck. Although we can't turn back the
hands of time, we can certainly prevent them from going any
faster than they have to go.

Doing Something About Dry Skin

Cracking, scaling, and itching skin feels terrible and looks awful.
For reasons that no one seems to understand completely, we
become more vulnerable to these problems as we get older. In
the winter cold winds outside and heated air indoors pull moisture from our skin. In the summer air conditioning is the culprit.
Whenever the humidity drops, dry skin won't be far behind.
Strong soap, dish detergent, and harsh shampoos will all make
matters worse by stripping away natural oils in the skin that
normally act as a barrier. If dry skin comes on suddenly, though,

it could be a signal of something seriously amiss internally. Hypothyroidism is one possibility, and if your skin gets so dry it begins to look like fish scales, you'd better be seen by a dermatologist or internist to rule out lymphoma, lupus, and sarcoidosis, all serious conditions requiring medical treatment.

But for ordinary dry skin, the problem is usually evaporation. When skin is healthy and the air is relatively humid, the amount of water lost from the uppermost level is low and the skin feels and looks good. But when air becomes dry, the outermost layer of your hide (the stratum corneum, or horny layer) can lose more moisture to the air than the underneath cells can replenish. When this happens, the dead cells of the stratum corneum become dry, brittle, and scaly.

Enter moisturizers. What they are supposed to do is restore and hold water in your horny layer. Skin creams do this by first forming a barrier that prevents evaporation. Just think of what would happen if you put some sliced ham on a plate and left it open to the air for a few hours. It would dry out something fierce. But if you put some plastic wrap around the meat, you could preserve the moisture rather nicely. That's the first job of a good skin cream—to seal in water. The second task is to actually attract and trap moisture in the horny layer, either as it passes up from the deeper layers of the skin or from the air when there is some humidity available.

Not all moisturizers are created equal. This may come as a shock, but many of the leading brands are not very effective and what little benefit they do provide may wear off quickly. And a fancy price tag is no guarantee that you are buying increased quality. A survey of a wide variety of moisturizers carried out by *Consumer Reports* with 600 women showed that "Most of the expensive products are in the bottom half of the Ratings. In fact, out of a total of 48 products, the two most expensive—*La Prairie*, at $6.10 per ounce, and *Oscar de la Renta*, at $4.29 per ounce—finished in 46th and 47th place, respectively."[21]

Paradoxically, some moisturizers may actually make skin worse. Dr. Albert Kligman has observed that several highly promoted popular brands may be "irritating, especially when applied to the face. Some people with sensitive skin may complain of tightness, stinging, redness, and increased dryness. After stopping for a few days the skin can become chapped and scaling."[22]

So what *should* you do for dry skin? First, bathe less frequently, say every two or three days instead of daily, and don't make the water super hot. Remember that soap and detergents can actually rob your skin of valuable natural oils. A gentle sponge bath around skin folds can often get you by between regular showers or baths. Next, use gentle soaps. But that turns out to be a lot harder than you might think. And before you rely on your doctor for a recommendation, here again is straight-shooting Dr. Albert Kligman: "The naked truth is that physicians, dermatologists included, have no more knowledge than their spouses or patients concerning which soaps to recommend for 'sensitive' skins."[23]

Dr. Kligman found that for people who are especially vulnerable, **Dove** stood head and shoulders above the other brands he tested. It tends to melt away pretty fast though, which is a characteristic of the more gentle soaps that have added oils. Other soaps that dermatologists recommend these days include **Caress** and **Monchel**. We especially like **Monchel** because it is available in an unscented bar. Added fragrance in soaps, skin creams, cosmetics, shampoos, and even toilet paper can cause allergic reactions for people who have especially sensitive skin.

After your bath or shower gently pat yourself dry, leaving your skin just a little on the damp side. Immediately apply the moisturizer so you can trap that leftover water in your skin. But which brand to choose? All the dermatologists we have consulted over the years unanimously recommend petroleum jelly (**Vaseline**), otherwise known as petrolatum. Dr. Kligman says it in his usual blunt style—"the greasier and uglier the product, the better it is. If you are a mature person and you're not planning an amorous encounter that night, you should use petrolatum or **Eucerin**. If you are planning something romantic, then use **Lubriderm** or **Nivea**."[24]

Nivea Moisturizing Lotion was also one of the highest rated products in the *Consumer Reports* (*CR*) survey, coming in second out of 48 brands. At 23 cents an ounce it was also one of the best buys and had the added bonus of providing a moisturizing effect that "lasted a long time," which made it an excellent hand cream. Number one in the *CR* ratings was a moderately priced (83 cents an ounce), relatively new product from Clairol called **Sea Breeze Moisture Lotion**.

There are so many other moisturizers on the market that it really gets confusing. We would be hard put to say one is significantly better than another. Often the biggest difference is the price tag. Remember that *Consumer Reports* concluded that many of the classy, highly advertised, expensive brands actually showed up lower in the ratings than less-advertised, cheaper brands. Recognize too that dermatologists may not have any greater insight on this subject than anyone else. A few of the products that are often recommended by dermatologists, however, include **Aquaphor, Moisturel, Complex 15**, and **Curel**. Urea-containing skin creams (**Carmol, Nutraplus**, and **Aquacare**) are theoretically supposed to help remove scales and retain water well. Which moisturizer you select will depend to a great degree on personal preference and how much you are willing to spend. No matter what, avoid products that come in glass containers. The last thing you want when your hands are slippery is something that can break.

There is one category of skin cream that has caught our attention recently for treating serious dry skin that is visibly peeling and flaking. It combines both cosmetic acceptability (meaning you won't win first place in the greased pig contest) and a high degree of effectiveness. Not only do our dermatological consultants rate it highly, our personal experience has also given us a very good opinion of it. **Lac-Hydrin** contains an alpha-hydroxy acid (buffered lactic acid), which seems to normalize the structure of the outer horny layer of the skin. It's so special the FDA considers **Lac-Hydrin** more a drug than a cosmetic. You will need a doctor's prescription to buy it.

The manufacturer recommends using **Lac-Hydrin** twice daily for the first month, then once daily, especially after bathing. Even occasional use (such as every other day) seems to produce noticeable and lasting results. When it is used regularly, it may even lighten or help fade one type of thin age spot (seborrheic keratosis) that forms on the face.[25] For garden variety "liver spots," bleaching creams such as **Esoterica, Porcelana**, and **Solaquin** will do the job if you are patient enough. It will take a long time before you see a response, though, and you will have to keep smearing the stuff on your skin almost indefinitely to maintain the effect. Sun exposure will darken the spots again.

But back to **Lac-Hydrin.** It's not the only skin cream that contains alpha-hydroxy acid. Several over-the-counter products also contain this ingredient in lower concentrations. They are **LactiCare** and **AquaGlycolic** lotion (from a small company

called Herald Pharmacal in Richmond, Virginia). Some people
with especially irritated skin may notice a burning or stinging
sensation when they first start applying **Lac-Hydrin** or one of
these other products. It tends to go away after repeated applications, but keep the cream away from your eyes, nose, and mouth.

No matter which skin product you select, remember that dry
skin is best fought at its source. Anything that can restore moisture to the air and reduce the amount of water that evaporates
from the skin will be helpful. Humidifiers that can get relative
humidity up to at least 35 percent may be worth the investment.
But make sure they are easy to clean. You don't want them
collecting mold and dust; otherwise you could trade in a skin
problem for a breathing problem.

Dealing with Dastardly Dandruff

If you believe the commercials on television, you'd think that
dandruff is a dreadful disease, leaving its victims pariahs from
polite company. But most people, even those with snowy white
hair, will suffer a few flakes now and again. Like dry skin,
dandruff tends to get worse in the winter time when humidity is
low. But even the worst cases, including those considered seborrheic dermatitis, usually respond pretty well once you learn a few
tricks of the trade.

There are three basic types of dandruff shampoo. One kind
contains metal compounds such as zinc pyrithione (**Anti-Dandruff
Brylcreem**, **Breck One**, **Head & Shoulders**, **Sebulon**, and
Zincon) or selenium sulfide (**Selsun Blue**). These tend to slow
the growth of those hyperactive skin cells responsible for the
flakes.

Then there are the shampoos that scruff cells off the scalp
chemically, and break big flakes into smaller, less visible ones.
These usually contain salicylic acid or sulfur. Examples include
Cuticura Anti-Dandruff Shampoo, **Ionil**, **Klaron**, **Meted**,
Sebucare, and **Sebulex**.

Finally, you've got the coal tar products. These have been
around almost forever, but until recently they had a disagreeable
color and odor, and they tended to stain. They reduce the size of
skin cells, get rid of scales, and are helpful against itching. In

recent years they've been improved to make them nicer to use. You may want to look for **Ionil T Plus**, **Neutrogena T/Gel**, **Polytar**, **Sebutone**, **Vanseb-T**, or **Zetar**.

Now here's the inside scoop on how to get these dandruff shampoos to work most effectively for you. First, don't get in a rut. Many people pick a brand of shampoo and stick with it long past the time that it has stopped doing them any good. What happens, you see, is that your scalp seems to adapt to each type of product after a few months. It then loses effectiveness. When that occurs, it's time for a vacation from that one—move on to another type, preferably one from a different category. Alternating every few months should keep you from building up a "tolerance" to any of them.

So you might want to start out with a scruffer-type of shampoo like **Sebulex**. After a month or so you might want to go to a metal such as **Head & Shoulders** or **Breck One**. Then you could give a tar/scruffer combo a try—say **Ionil T Plus**. After a couple of months, back you go to a metal. This time, instead of zinc you might want to try selenium and give **Selsun Blue** a whirl.

To get the most for your money, pay careful attention to what follows. In the beginning you will probably want to shampoo every day or every other day. First, use a cheap, nonmedicated product just to wash off the oil and flakes that have collected. That should only take a minute or less. Now apply the antidandruff shampoo and let it stay on your scalp for five to ten minutes. Most folks rinse their medicated shampoo off far too quickly, before it has had a chance to go to work. Finally, dry your hair with a towel. Yes, we know blow dryers are faster, but the hot air can actually make dandruff worse. And try not to scratch or pick at your scalp, as that will also make things worse. Once you discover your flakes have pretty much disappeared, you can probably cut back your shampooing to two or three times a week.

If this regimen doesn't seem to be working, you may not have ordinary dandruff after all. Seborrheic dermatitis can easily be confused with dandruff, as it too produces itching and flaking. But with seborrheic dermatitis, there may be yellowish or reddish bumps on the scalp, and irritation and scaling may also affect the hairline, the eyebrows, the bridge of the nose, the folds in the ear and just behind it, and along the crease between the nose and the mouth. Sometimes even the eyelids may end up inflamed and scaling. Although dandruff often becomes less of a problem as people get older, seborrheic dermatitis seems to become more common as we age, especially for men.

Dermatologists have been arguing for years about what causes seborrheic dermatitis. Some say it's just an extension of dandruff and treat it with exactly the same medicated shampoos mentioned above. Others attribute the greasy scales to emotional or physical stress. Food allergy, vitamin B deficiency, and changes in the weather have also been blamed.

But now comes a Swedish researcher who believes that seborrheic dermatitis is actually linked to a kind of yeast infection. According to Dr. Faergemann from the Department of Dermatology at the University of Gothenburg, the bad actor in this play is a tongue twister called *Pityrosporum orbiculare*.[26] Although this yeastie beastie is a normal component of the flora and fauna of our skin and scalp, it seems to flourish in seborrheic dermatitis.

Dr. Faergemann has found that he can achieve spectacular results in clearing up and preventing recurrences of seborrheic dermatitis by combining a common antifungal athlete's foot remedy called miconazole (available over-the-counter as **Micatin**) with a hydrocortisone solution.[27] His success rate is over 90 percent and when people continue to use the solution twice a month prophylactically they can maintain the "cure."

There's only one problem. The miconazole/hydrocortisone liquid solution Dr. Faergemann used is not available in this country. But that doesn't mean you are left completely high and dry. Over-the-counter **Micatin** cream and any one of a dozen hydrocortisone products (**CaldeCORT**, **Cortaid**, **Dermolate**, **Hytone**, **Lanacort**, etc.) might be helpful for scaling, redness, and itching caused by seborrheic dermatitis on the face and behind the ears.

An over-the-counter acne cleanser containing benzoyl peroxide (**Fostex Wash**, **Oxy-10 Wash**, **Propa P.H. Liquid Acne Soap**) may also be helpful against this yeast infection. But be careful. Benzoyl peroxide can be very irritating and cause redness and peeling by itself. Make sure you keep it away from your eyes, mouth, and nose. Don't use it on inflamed skin, and start with a very light application.

Until Dr. Faergemann's miconazole-hydrocortisone liquid combo becomes available, you will probably have to stick with regular dandruff shampoos like **Ionil T Plus**, **Exsel**, **Neutrogena T/Gel**, **Selsun**, **Sebulex**, **Sebutone**, **Vanseb** and **Zincon**. If nothing works, you should certainly be seen by a dermatologist. She may have to prescribe a steroid solution like **Synalar** or **Valisone**. Another possibility may be that psoriasis is the culprit.

Halting the Heartbreak of Psoriasis

Psoriasis rarely kills, but it can make life miserable and for some it may get so bad that suicide becomes a real possibility. A Massachusetts reader said it eloquently:

> **You have no idea what *heartbreak* is until you've spent a night in a hospital, scaly, itching, sticky from tar treatments, and lonelier than you could have ever imagined because even your friends and family look at you funny and back away as if you're catching.**
>
> ***Heartbreak* is spending your whole summer in pants and sweatshirts so that people won't stare.**
>
> ***Heartbreak* is turning down social engagements for over six months because you've got red spots that you tell people are a rash or allergic reaction.**
>
> ***Heartbreak* is finding out that there are actually new methods out there that might help—but doctors don't know about them.**
>
> **I don't think I'd wish psoriasis on my worst enemy—it's the hardest thing I've ever had to go through. The last thing a psoriasis sufferer wants to hear is that "You know someone who had it a lot worse," or "Things could be worse," because that helps about as much as a kick in the pants.**
>
> **Psoriasis may not kill but antidepressants are prescribed quite often to try to combat the overwhelming desire to end the whole battle of skin disease. From what I hear suicide rates are very high among psoriasis patients.**

Now you have a partial idea of what psoriasis can do to a person's mind. Here is what happens to the body. For reasons that doctors do not yet understand, the skin factory starts working overtime. Cells that would normally replace themselves every four or five weeks start replacing themselves every four or five days—sort of like the Sorcerer's apprentice's problem. The result is salmon-colored patches of psoriasis covered with silvery scales. They usually appear on the arms, elbows, legs, hands, feet, and scalp. Any part of the skin that gets traumatized (bumped, chafed, scratched, picked) will be especially vulnerable. When it gets really bad, psoriasis can cover almost the whole body.

The goal of therapy is to slow down the out-of-control skin machine. Simple things like mild soaps and moisturizers can be helpful, especially when dry skin causes cracking and adds to the problem. More exciting, we have seen some revolutionary advances in recent years that are changing the way doctors treat psoriasis. While not a cure, these therapies should reduce the heartbreak for thousands of victims of this cruel disease.

The two newest drugs for severe psoriasis are **Temovate** (clobetasol) and **Tegison** (etretinate). These are both big guns that require careful instruction and monitoring from a knowledgeable dermatologist. **Temovate** is a cortisone-type cream that is more potent than any other steroid on the market. It is, in fact, so strong that if you were to use more than 1 1/2 ounces a week you could develop serious side effects, almost as if you were taking cortisone orally. It should probably be used only for short periods of time or intermittently—say only once every three or four days after the psoriasis starts to clear. It has been suggested that by using a skin moisturizing cream like **Lac-Hydrin** on the alternate days one could maintain a good response.[28]

Tegison is an oral retinoid, making it a synthetic cousin of vitamin A. It's a very powerful drug that is reserved for severe, recalcitrant psoriasis that hasn't responded to any other treatment. One side effect that appears to be quite common is calcification of tendons and ligaments leading to bone spurs. This can produce stiffness or restriction of movement in joints such as the ankles, knees, and pelvis. **Tegison** can also cause dry skin, itching, dry nose and nosebleeds, chapped lips, irritated eyes, dry mouth, and loss of hair. Headache, visual changes, or nausea should be reported to a doctor immediately. Obviously, **Tegison** is a pretty toxic drug, but for people with disabling pustular psoriasis, total body psoriasis, psoriatic arthritis or extensive psoriasis not responding to standard treatments, it can provide dramatic relief that may be worth the risks.

For garden variety and extensive psoriasis, a new–old treatment has one of our dermatological consultants very excited. Dr. Robert Gilgor in Chapel Hill, North Carolina, reports that almost 80 percent of his patients have responded very nicely to anthralin. This is an old drug that has been kicking around since 1916, but a new approach called "short-contact therapy " or AMEST (Anthralin Minute Entire Skin Treatment) makes it more effective and easier to use than ever before.

A study published in the *Archives of Dermatology* (December 1985, pages 1512–1515) by Dr. Thomas Schwarz reports that when fresh anthralin was spread on the entire body, including normal skin, left on for 10 minutes and then washed off in the shower, the results were quite impressive.[29] What makes this approach so nice is that it is quick, can be done at home (three or four days a week), and is less likely to stain skin or clothes than many other treatments. The anthralin does have to be made up fresh, however, and will require the dermatologist to do his homework and provide special instructions to the patient. Side effects seem tolerable—pink skin and itching are the most likely reactions. Kidney and liver function should probably be tested before and after treatment just to be on the safe side.

There are quite a few other psoriasis treatments being tried these days, from methotrexate to dietary supplements with fish oil to UVB light and special forms of vitamin D. Methotrexate is a powerful anticancer agent that in recent years has gained acceptance for use in treating rheumatoid arthritis and severe psoriasis as well. It's not the kind of drug that can be used casually, since it can produce many serious side effects (especially liver damage and blood abnormalities), and interacts dangerously with many other medications. Nevertheless, it can produce impressive results if patients are selected carefully.

Researchers at the University of California, Davis, and the University of Michigan report modest improvement with large doses of omega 3 fatty acids (EPA and DHA) found in fish oil supplements.[30] Of greater significance is the work of the Japanese who have been experimenting with both oral and topical (ointment) treatment of active metabolites of vitamin D_3.[31,32] What they have found is exciting because it suggests a new way to control and regulate the runaway cell division of psoriasis without producing serious side effects. Let's keep our fingers crossed that this discovery rapidly leads to the development of a safer and more effective vitamin/drug therapy.

Staving off Shingles with Zovirax

If you ever had chickenpox as a child, the seed has been planted for one of the most painful skin conditions we know of. Shingles is insidious. From the time we are infected with the virus as youngsters, it lurks hidden away deep within our nervous system. As we get older, for reasons no one seems to understand, it may flare up into an attack of shingles. Perhaps as the immune system loses its zip the virus comes out of hibernation to cause a painful rash, most frequently on the chest or belly, or around the belt line. But it's not just a garden variety rash like poison ivy or hives.

Initially, an attack of shingles can be easily confused with a flu bug. During the first three or four days you may notice chills and fever, fatigue, and lethargy. Somewhere around the fourth or fifth day red areas may appear, soon accompanied by groups of blisters. If you look carefully, you may see a little dip or depression in the middle of each blister. The rash usually spreads on one side of the body and is often incredibly sensitive and painful to the touch. In some cases the pain may come on before the blisters even appear. Pressure from clothes or even the weight of bed sheets may be excruciating. Sometimes there is nerve pain that lasts long after the blisters have disappeared. This "post-herpetic neuralgia" can be devastating, especially if it affects the face.

Until recently, physicians could do very little for victims of shingles. Cool compresses and skin creams were largely useless. Heavy doses of cortisone-type drugs sometimes helped, but there were always risks from the medicine, and no real cure. Pain was treated with aspirin, or even narcotics when it became intolerable.

Enter **Zovirax** (acyclovir). This antiviral drug has revolutionized the treatment of a whole range of herpes-related diseases, from cold sores and genital herpes to shingles (also known as herpes zoster). The trick to success is speed. To be effective, **Zovirax** has to be used at the very first sign of blisters. If you delay beyond two or three days, the drug cannot shut down the virus and speed healing. That's why you must immediately contact a dermatologist at the very first sign of blisters, tender skin, and a rash. Tell the receptionist it's an emergency and don't brook any delay. If it's a false alarm, you have wasted a trip to the doctor. If it's the real thing, the benefits could be impressive.

British researchers report that large doses (800 mg) of **Zovirax** taken five times daily for seven days improved recovery time and significantly reduced pain.[33] Such big doses can have side effects, though, including nausea, digestive tract upset, headache, and mental confusion. Some of those who have suffered with shingles may tell you that is a small price to pay for relief.

Help for the Hairless

No drug development in recent years has stimulated more headlines and excitement than minoxidil for baldness. Originally it was developed as an oral medicine for serious high blood pressure, but before long, patients started complaining that coarse hair had begun growing all over their bodies—on the forehead, arms, back, and yes, even on the head. At first it seemed like a liability. Here was one antihypertensive medication that was going nowhere fast.

And then some dermatologists got to thinking that if they made a lotion out of the pills and smeared it on people's heads they might be able to create a safe and effective treatment for baldness. Sure enough, preliminary research looked encouraging. Topical application of minoxidil did seem to produce noticeable hair growth on some people. The manufacturer of minoxidil (Upjohn) got interested and sponsored a large study at 27 centers around the United States. Over 1,800 patients completed the one-year program.

Did minoxidil work? Well, the success of a baldness remedy is very much in the eyes of the beholder. Some people—about a third—had noticeable new hair growth. But many others were disappointed. To say that minoxidil—now named **Rogaine Topical Solution**—was a cure for baldness would be a gross exaggeration. But even a hint that there was a way to stimulate hair growth sent Upjohn stock soaring. In early 1985 a share sold for about $35. By April 1985, the stock had climbed to almost $84 per share. It eventually zoomed to $169, split two for one, and kept right on climbing.

It's unlikely that hair growth stimulation will be as smashing as the stock performance. The drug seems to work best for those who have the least hair loss ... in other words, for people who

have just noticed the beginnings of a receding hair line. The
bald-as-a-billiard-ball look will probably not benefit much at all.
You can bank on the fact that **Rogaine** will not be cheap. And
people will likely have to keep using it for the rest of their lives.
When they stop applying **Rogaine**, chances are good that whatever new hair has managed to crop up will fall out once again.

That sounds discouraging, doesn't it? Well, hold the phone a
minute. There may be some good news after all. The dermatological grapevine has been reporting that if one were to *combine*
Retin-A (yes, Dr. Kligman's acne medicine for photoaged skin)
and minoxidil (**Rogaine Topical Solution**), results appear to be
far more impressive than when minoxidil is used all by itself. One
preliminary study using a dilute concentration of minoxidil
(0.5%—one fourth the usual dose) and 0.025% topical tretinoin
solution (**Retin-A**) produced a "good" response for 44 percent of
the subjects and a moderate response for 22 percent.[34] That
amounted to a total positive effect in 66 percent of the subjects—
about twice that which has been obtained from minoxidil alone.

We have a long way to go before we can say there is a "cure" for
baldness. But researchers are starting to unlock some of the
secrets to hair growth. Until they come up with something better,
it may turn out that a mixture of **Rogaine** and **Retin-A** will
actually produce acceptable results for a few people.

Gazing into the Crystal Ball

Dermatology is finally coming of age. In recent years we have
seen dramatic improvements in the treatment of all sorts of skin
conditions—from acne to herpes to psoriasis. Effective sunscreens
can prevent some of the problems caused by the sun's ultraviolet
rays. And drugs like **Retin-A** may even be able to undo part of the
damage. There are great developments on the horizon. Most
exciting are the skin growth factors that appear to speed wound
healing. Researchers have noted for a long time that animals lick
their wounds and that this seems to improve recovery. The reason it works so well is attributed to the growth factors found in
saliva. Similar compounds have now been isolated and tested,
and sure enough, wound healing is enhanced.[35] It may be too
much to expect cuts, scratches, and burns to disappear overnight,

but any improvement will be most welcome. We also look forward to better treatment of fungal infections of the fingernails and toes, and a topical ointment for excessive hair growth (hirsutism).

The skin is your window to the world. How it looks and feels will profoundly affect your self-image, not to mention the way others treat you. There are a lot of sharks out there waiting to rip you off with their anti-aging creams, wrinkle erasers, and hair restorers. Don't let the charlatans take you to the cleaners, especially now when medical science is coming up with legitimate approaches to these conditions and many others.

Things to Remember

1. Don't be snookered by sexy ads promising to take 20 years off your face in a hurry. Remember that fancy icing on a cardboard cake, no matter how yummy it looks, still won't make the cake taste good.

2. To keep your skin looking young, stay out of the sun! If the damage is already done, staying out of the sun and using a high SPF sunscreen may allow the skin to partially repair itself. **Retin-A**, a prescription acne medicine, could also be of some benefit.

3. Skin cancer is a common problem for people who have spent time in the sun. Be alert for any sores that don't heal. Melanoma, one of the most dangerous forms of cancer, is best treated if you detect it early. Have a dermatologist look you over periodically from stem to stern, especially if you have moles. Any change in the shape or color of a mole deserves immediate dermatological attention.

4. Dry skin is nothing to sneeze at. If your skin dries out suddenly, it could be a sign of something more serious going on internally. See a doctor!

5. Be wary of soap makers' claims that their products are mild and gentle for sensitive skin. Our recommendation, stick with **Dove**. It's still Dr. Albert Kligman's favorite brand. Other products that our dermatological consultants recommend include **Monchel** (unscented) and **Caress**.

6. If you're suffering from garden variety dry skin that gets worse when the humidity is low, there are lots of excellent moisturizers on the market. Price is no guide to quality. The greasier the product, the better it seems to work. Plain old petroleum jelly still tops the list. High on *Consumer Reports'* Ratings is **Nivea Moisturing Lotion**, and it's priced right. Other good moisturizers include **Eucerin**, **Lubriderm**, **Aquaphor**, **Moisturel**, **Complex 15**, and **Sea Breeze Moisture Lotion**. **Lac-Hydrin** contains a special ingredient (alpha-hydroxy acid) that actually seems to normalize dry skin. For people who really suffer, this may be the best choice of all. It is available by prescription only. Over-the-counter versions that are less concentrated include **LactiCare** and **AquaGlycolic** lotion. Remember that all moisturizers work best if you put them on fresh after you get out of the tub.

7. Dandruff is NOT a disease. It IS a normal part of living. Do not let the shampoo commercials make you feel guilty. There are three basic categories of dandruff shampoo—chemical scruffers, tars, and metals. Vary your medicated shampoo every couple of months to maximize the benefits. Leave the shampoo on your scalp for five to ten minutes to get the full effect.

8. Psoriasis *can* be treated successfully. There are so many new therapies available these days that it will take some careful evaluation to decide which treatment is best for any given patient. Dr. Robert Gilgor, a Chapel Hill, North Carolina, dermatologist, is excited about the new–

old "short-contact" anthralin approach. Intermittent use of strong steroids like **Temovate** may be appropriate for some. Combination therapy may also prove effective and easy to tolerate. For severe, recalcitrant psoriasis, methotrexate, **Tegison**, or PUVA (special ultraviolet light treatment in combination with drug therapy) have a place. Patience and persistence are the keys to success. And new experimental drugs may ultimately eliminate the heartache once and for all.

9. There is no cure for male pattern baldness. The FDA tells us that there are no over-the-counter products that will work to stimulate hair growth, so don't even think about anything advertised in magazines. That's the bad news. The good news is that tretinoin (**Retin-A**) combined with minoxidil (**Rogaine Topical Solution**) may work better than minoxidil alone. That's still not perfect, but for some desperate souls there's at last hope that modern medicine may actually come up with something for that receding hairline.

References

1. Waldholz, Michael. "Cosmetics Firms Fear Product Promoted as Anti-Aging Cream Invites FDA Probe." *The Wall Street Journal*, May 29, 1986.
2. Ibid.
3. "Facial Wrinkles: Another Reason Not to Smoke Cigarettes." *Mayo Clinic Health Letter* 5(1):8, 1987.
4. Gilchrest, Barbara A. "Problems of Aging Skin." Presented at the conference Cosmeceuticals: The Science of Beauty and Aging, hosted by Boston University Medical Center, Apr. 21, 1986.
5. Kligman, Albert M. "Cosmeceuticals: Medicine Explores the Riddles of Beauty and Aging." Presented at the conference Cosmeceuticals: The Science of Beauty and Aging, hosted by Boston University Medical Center, Apr. 21, 1986.
6. Kligman, Lorraine H. "Prevention of Aging Skin." Talk presented at the Westwood Conference on Clinical Dermatology: "Our Aging Population and Dermatology," Hilton Head Island, S.C., Oct. 8–12, 1986.

7. Kligman, Albert, op. cit.
8. Kligman, Lorraine H., op. cit.
9. Kligman, Lorraine H.; and Kligman, Albert M. "The Nature of Photoaging: Its Prevention and Repair." *Photodermatology* 3:215–227, 1986.
10. Kligman, Lorraine H., et al. "The Contributions of UVA and UVB to Connective Tissue Damage in Hairless Mice." *J. Of Invest. Derm.* 84:272–276, 1985.
11. Kligman, Albert, op. cit.
12. Snead, Karen. "New Skin." *Fort Lauderdale News*, Jan. 27, 1987, pp. 1E.
13. Kligman, Lorraine H. "Effects of All-*Trans*-Retinoic Acid on the Dermis of Hairless Mice." *J. Amer. Acad. Derm.* 15:779–785, 1986.
14. "Q&A on Photoaging: An Interview with Albert M. Kligman." Presented at the conference Cosmeceuticals: The Science of Beauty and Aging, hosted by Boston University Medical Center, Apr. 21, 1986.
15. Kligman, Albert M., et al. "Topical Tretinoin for Photoaged Skin." *J. Am. Acad. Dermatol.* 15:836–859, 1986.
16. Peck, Gary L. "Topical Tretinoin in Actinic Keratosis and Basal Cell Carcinoma." *J. Am. Acad. Dermatol.* 15:829–835, 1986.
17. Epstein, John N. "All-*Trans*-Retinoic Acid and Cutaneous Cancers." *J. Am. Acad. Dermatol.* 15:772–778, 1986.
18. Hunt, Thomas K. "Vitamin A and Wound Healing." *J. Am. Acad. Dermatol.* 15:817–821, 1986.
19. Kaplan, Jerold Z. "Acceleration of Wound Healing by a Live Yeast Cell Derivative." *Arch. Surg.* 119:1005–1008, 1984.
20. Kligman, Albert, op. cit.
21. "All-purpose Moisturizers." *Consumer Reports* 51:733–738, 1986.
22. Kligman, Albert M. Letter to Mr. Harvey Zimmerman, Key Pharmaceuticals, Inc., Mar. 19, 1981.
23. Frosch, Peter J.; and Kligman, Albert M. "The Soap Chamber Test." *J. Am. Acad. Dermatol.* 1:35–41, 1979.
24. "Q&A on Photoaging," op. cit.
25. Van Scott, Eugene J. "New Approaches to Dry Skin." Presented at the Westwood Conference, "Our Aging Population and Dermatology." Hilton Head Island, S.C. Oct. 8–12, 1986.
26. Faergemann, Jan; and Maibach, Howard I. "The *Pityrosporum* Yeasts: Their Role as Pathogens." *Int. J. Dermatol.* 23:463–465, 1984.
27. Faergemann, J. "Seborrhoeic Dermatitis and *Pityrosporum orbiculare:* Treatment of Seborrhoeic Dermatitis of the Scalp with Miconazole–Hydrocortisone (Daktacort), Miconazole and Hydrocortisone." *Br. J. Dermatol.* 114:695–700, 1986.
28. Van Scott, op. cit.
29. Schwarz, Thomas; and Gschnait, Fritz. "Anthralin Minute Entire Skin Treatment: A New Outpatient Therapy for Psoriasis." *Arch. Dermatol.* 121:1512–1515, 1985.
30. Ziboh, Vincent A., et al. "Effects of Dietary Supplementation of Fish Oil on Neutrophils and Epidermal Fatty Acids." *Arch. Dermatol.* 122:1277–1282, 1986.

31. Morimoto, S., et al. "An Open Study of Vitamin D3 treatment in Psoriasis Vulgaris." *Br. J. Dermatol.* 115:421–429, 1986.

32. Kato, T., et al. "Successful Treatment of Psoriasis with Topical Application of Active Vitamin D3 Analogue, Iα, 24-dihydroxycholecalciferol." *Br. J. Dermatol.* 115:431–433, 1986.

33. McKendrick, M.W., et al. "Oral Acyclovir in Acute Herpes Zoster." *Br. Med. J.* 293:1529–1532, 1986.

34. Bazzano, Gail S., et al. "Topical Tretinoin for Hair Growth Promotion." *J. Am. Acad. Dermatol.* 15:880–883, 1986.

35. Schultz, Gregory S., et al. "Epithelial Wound Healing Enhanced by Transforming Growth Factor-α and Vaccinia Growth Factor." *Science* 235:350–352, 1987.

6

Fighting Forgetfulness

Senility is what they used to call it. Now they use terms like "senile dementia of the Alzheimer's type" or "multi-infarct dementia" or "Binswanger's disease." By whatever name, it's devastating.

We, like so many others, have watched helplessly as someone we love dearly has slowly slipped away from us. We've seen the pain and the courage and the frustration first hand. Day by day we watch the inexorable decline—the empty stare, the agitation, the inability to communicate. The man who was once vigorous and bubbling over with a zest for life now hobbles from room to room bent over his walker, bewildered and confused. His mind has slipped away by inches and all that's left is a hollow shell. It makes us want to cry and rage and grieve.

Statisticians tell us that over two million people in the United States are affected. We suspect they're wrong and that the numbers are a lot higher. It has been estimated that 12 percent of those people between 75 and 85 years of age have Alzheimer's disease. But now experts believe 20 percent is more realistic and that as many as 40 percent of those over 85 may suffer this form of memory disorder.[1] As this country rapidly ages, we are facing an epidemic of incapacitating brain diseases.

Now don't let these numbers frighten you. Most older people who worry about their memories have what is known as benign senescent forgetfulness—the so-called "natural" forgetfulness many older people complain about. This condition doesn't become debilitating or develop into anything more serious than an inconvenience or an occasional embarrassing moment. You know what we're talking about—the keys that disappear, the acquaintance whose name you can't recall when you run into him in the grocery store, or the phone number that slips your mind when you need it.

One psychiatrist described people with benign senescent forgetfulness this way. "They forget—they remember they forgot—they remember what they forgot. Alzheimer's patients forget. Forget they forgot and couldn't care less what they forgot."[2]

We're not so sure it's that simple, but we do know that while it's frustrating not to be able to remember certain things, benign senescent forgetfulness doesn't end up affecting behavior, personality or motor coordination as an organic brain condition like Alzheimer's disease might.

It's disheartening that researchers still know so little about the causes of memory loss and confusion in older people. Ten years ago hardly anyone was even interested in Alzheimer's disease. Scientists were at Ground Zero and funding for research was virtually nonexistent. Today, money is still woefully inadequate, but at least scientists are beginning to unlock some secrets.

One of the biggest problems with Alzheimer's disease is that there is currently no good way to diagnose it until the patient dies and an autopsy can be performed to see whether the distinctive changes in brain tissue have occurred. And therein lies a very big problem. There's a strong suspicion among the experts that right now probably about 20 percent of the patients we classify as having Alzheimer's disease have another disorder—Pick's disease, multi-infarct dementia, etc.[3] (In our family, just such an error in diagnosis was made and not corrected for over three years.)

Don't Assume It's Alzheimer's

Neurological diseases have received most of the publicity, but there are a surprising number of other medical conditions that can also produce confusion, speech impairment, personality changes, disorientation, and memory loss. Someone who is suffering from unusual forgetfulness or confusion deserves a careful and complete medical workup to determine whether some treatable physical ailment is to blame. A thyroid condition may provoke symptoms that mimic those of Alzheimer's disease. So can deficiencies of vitamin B_{12} and folic acid. A severe thiamine deficiency, unlikely except after years of alcohol abuse, can also cause brain damage that may be mistaken for "senility." Abnormal levels of potassium or sugar in the blood may affect brain function and make a person appear forgetful or confused, and older people are especially vulnerable to becoming disoriented when they are dehydrated or suffering from an infection. Depression can bring on changes in appetite, sleep patterns, and other behavior, and is frequently the culprit when an older person appears forgetful or confused.[4,5] Many drugs can also complicate the picture. Here is a letter we received from one of our newspaper column readers:

I am now 75 years old. My wife and I retired to Florida five years ago. After we had settled in I felt so good I took a job and for a year everything was going fine except for some muscle aches. I assumed the heavy humid Florida climate was causing my problem and this "arthritis" was brought on by the fact that my body was unable to adjust to the humidity.

The doctor I went to immediately put all my problems down to high blood pressure, and brushing aside my aches, prescribed a diuretic and Inderal twice daily. But after a few nights using the Inderal I found myself having the most ghastly nightmares. I couldn't shake myself free of these "brain storms" and had to instruct my wife to wake me out of them.

I lost my concentration, had no memory and was completely vague. As time went by my mind became confused. I repeated everything I said several times—had to carry notes to help me with my daily routine—then I couldn't find my notes. After six months of trying to explain to my doctor my problems he decided to put me in the hospital. He thought I might

have a blood clot on my brain. After several exami-
nations and an angiogram I was found to have no
blood clot.

By now I am, as my wife said, talking like a senile
foolish idiot. My mind has gone completely. I don't
drive my car anymore because I don't know where I
am going. I really appreciated your column when
you mentioned disorientation and memory loss of
us senior people. We really are becoming lost souls.

It is unlikely that this gentleman's serious, rapid mental deterioration was caused by the **Inderal** he was taking for his high
blood pressure. He might have developed all of the same symptoms without swallowing a single pill. And yet it's not inconceivable that this medication may have added to the problem. Beta
blocker drugs like propranolol (**Inderal, Inderide**) and another
antihypertensive drug called methyldopa (**Aldoclor, Aldomet,
Aldoril**) have occasionally been associated with forgetfulness,
mental cloudiness, fatigue, sleep disturbances, and depression.
One small pilot study set out to measure the effects of these two
drugs on memory. The results were startling. The investigators
reported that:

When compared with the diuretic control group,
both methyldopa and propranolol groups showed
severe impairment in verbal memory scores . . .

Many of the study subjects were unaware of their
memory impairment. One patient receiving both propranolol and methyldopa was unaware of any memory problem, but his wife pointed out that since the
initiation of therapy, he had begun to make extensive lists to help remind himself of all his daily
tasks. Frequently the family, more than the patient,
first became aware of the deficit. The manifesta-
tions of this drug effect and the accommodations to
it can be subtle and easily missed. Many patients do
not attribute their memory difficulties to their medication, and several patients aware of having trouble remembering experienced a great sense of
emotional relief when told that their problem was
linked to the medication.[6]

How common is this reaction? No one knows. But wouldn't it be tragic if some people chalked up their forgetfulness to "old age" when in fact a medicine might be partly, if not totally, responsible? Of course, no one should *ever* stop his blood pressure medication to see if memory improves without first discussing the ramifications of such action with a physician. Abrupt withdrawal of beta blockers can lead to angina or even a heart attack. Uncontrolled hypertension may lead to a stroke. Although there are a number of blood pressure medications that do not seem to affect the brain, only a physician can devise an appropriate alternate therapy.

Antihypertensives aren't the only drugs that can affect memory. Some sleeping pills, sedatives, and anti-anxiety agents may also produce a kind of amnesia in which the person may not even remember doing certain things. Dr. Martin Scharf is a sleep researcher. He discovered that some of his anxious insomniac patients who received **Ativan** (lorazepam) at night to get to sleep experienced "marked and prolonged amnesia" to events occurring throughout the next day.[7]

> **One person lost the whole day. Another experience with amnesia occurred when a patient in a sleep laboratory study of Halcion (0.5 mg) experienced a gall bladder attack 30 minutes after drug ingestion with no recall whatsoever the next morning.[8]**
>
> **Our own experience involves a colleague who traveled to a meeting to give a presentation. Finding it difficult to fall asleep, he self-administered Halcion 0.5 mg at night. The next morning he arose and apparently presented his lecture on which he has subsequently received frequent compliments. He claims, however, total amnesia to any event that morning, including the lecture itself.[9]**

Other physicians have also reported strange episodes of amnesia the day after patients took **Halcion**:

> **Vignette 1: To ensure sleep during an overnight flight to Europe, a traveler ingested 0.25 mg of triazolam. The next night, he had amnesia for how he had gotten from the airport to his destination**

(only train and taxi receipts in his pocket clarified the mystery) . . .

Vignette 2. Because of work-related pressure, our next triazolam-taker had slept poorly for 5 nights. She took triazolam (0.25 mg) for the first time on night 6. The next day she used her bankcard in an automatic teller only to have it "eaten" by the machine. She had unknowingly given it the wrong six-letter personal code. Upon questioning by the bank manager, she could not state either her actual code (even though she knew it the day before and 48 hours after the incident) or what she had punched in. Several weeks later, after a second single-dose exposure, she found herself in an infrequently visited specialty grocery store unable to remember what she had gone in to buy . . .

We have perhaps unfairly pointed the finger at triazolam by citing these vignettes. Most other benzodiazepines clearly have been implicated in the production of anterograde amnesia . . . We recommend that a discussion of possible temporary loss of recall be part of the standard precautions provided by physicians to patients whenever benzodiazepines are initially prescribed.[10]

In recent years shorter-acting sleeping pills or anti-anxiety agents like **Ativan** (lorazepam), **Halcion** (triazolam), and **Xanax** (alprazolam) have become very popular, on the theory that such medications are less likely to cause "morning hangover" or mental side effects. Physicians are especially likely to prescribe these drugs to older people on the assumption that they will be safer than longer-acting sleeping pills such as **Dalmane** (flurazepam) or **Restoril** (temazepam).

But Dr. Scharf has reported that the shorter-acting compounds may actually be *more* likely to cause delayed memory impairment. What is so insidious here is that the effects of these drugs are supposed to fade quickly. Yet there are a growing number of articles that suggest they can have longer-term negative effects on memory.[11–14]

Dr. Scharf believes that this problem is under-recognized and under-reported.

Since geriatric patients consume a disproportionately large percentage of tranquilizers and hypnotics [sleeping pills], and considering that memory deficits in the elderly are common, a drug induced memory impairment might go altogether unnoticed or possibly misinterpreted as a normal consequence of aging.[15]

Now lest you get too nervous about all this, please keep in mind that no single drug is likely to produce all of the symptoms of Alzheimer's disease. Some forgetfulness, maybe. But there is no suggestion that medications actually cause a condition that leads to chronic debilitation. Nevertheless, you can easily imagine that people who begin to feel fuzzy-minded or forgetful could fear they were losing their minds.

What we really worry about, though, is the combination of a number of drugs that might work together to affect the mind negatively. Say an older person was taking **Tagamet** for an ulcer, **Xanax** for anxiety, and **Inderal** for high blood pressure. We know that **Tagamet** can sometimes cause mental confusion in seniors (see page 14). And according to Dr. Scharf, **Xanax** has on occasion been associated with memory impairment. Add to that the fatigue, forgetfulness, and depression sometimes brought on by **Inderal**, and it's not inconceivable that an older person could end up disoriented, forgetful, confused, listless, and apathetic, and have difficulty communicating. **Tagamet** can also interact with **Xanax** and **Inderal**, raising blood levels of these drugs and magnifying their effects.

Depression (whether drug-induced or spontaneous) can itself produce apathy, forgetfulness, and other symptoms that may mimic some of the signs of Alzheimer's and related diseases.[16] But watch out, there's quicksand out there. Some of the drugs used to treat depression may themselves cause problems. Those compounds that have strong "anticholinergic" action (like **Amitril**, **Elavil**, **Endep**, **Janimine**, **Surmontil**, **Tofranil**, and **Vivactil**) can cause blurred vision, severe dry mouth, constipation, and difficulty urinating. Such drugs may also cause speech impairment and stuttering, difficulty concentrating, confusion, mental fogginess, and forgetfulness in older people.[17,18] **Norpramin** and **Pertofrane** (desipramine), **Prozac** (fluoxetine), and **Wellbutrin** (bupropion) may be a little less likely to lead to such difficulties.

(For a more complete discussion of antidepressants for seniors, please see Chapter 7.)

Add sleeping pills to antidepressants and there is a potential for trouble, as one of our readers relates:

> For a year I have lived in fear I am losing my mind and I cannot talk to anyone for fear of going to a mental hospital. May I please explain.
>
> Ten years ago I had five major operations (two for cancer) and my 24-year-old daughter was killed— all in the span of fourteen weeks. I had a breakdown and was diagnosed depressive. I was finally put on one Noludar capsule and four Elavils at bed time. I take nothing throughout the day. My doctor is *always* telling me to increase the Elavil to six or seven at night. This has gone on for seven years. I stay at four and just put the extra away.
>
> I see the doctor once a month for twenty minutes. We talk about the weather, my family, and especially my beloved grandchildren and that's it. Exactly 20 minutes, not a minute more or less, and I give him a check for $35. This also never changes.
>
> I not only take care of my home but help my daughter out with her young children. Three days a week I take care of my son's daughter while her mother works. I make hand made painted ceramics, for which I get a nice fee, and I have managed to invest my husband's salary so we will retire comfortably. My point is that I manage quite well.
>
> For a year now I have become very concerned something is very wrong with my head. I'll be in the car or doing something and I'll become very confused and feel like I'm somewhere else and not really there. I have been cooking for 37 years and will stand at the stove and wonder "what goes in next" because I cannot remember. I meet people I have known 20 years and cannot recall their names so I call everyone "Dear" to cover up. I have misplaced an expensive diamond ring and tore the house up and cannot find it. I can't remember how to spell words I've used all my life. I am so scared I have even considered suicide to spare my family.

What a tragic story. We only wish we had a simple answer or a magic wand to wave over this desperate soul and make it all better. It's hard to say whether her mental condition represents the beginnings of Alzheimer's disease, or whether these symptoms are in part the result of years of medication. There is a study that suggests the antidepressant amitriptyline could be linked to some memory disturbances.[19] On the other hand, such symptoms may be spontaneous. They could well represent nothing more worrisome than benign senescent forgetfulness. That can certainly be annoying, sometimes even frightening, but it rarely develops into a serious handicap.

Although many of these drugs have been around for decades, researchers are just now beginning to ask questions about their long-term psychological and intellectual effects.[20,21] Investigators in the Department of Psychiatry at the University of Pennsylvania recently found that patients who had taken benzodiazepine-type anti-anxiety drugs like **Valium**, **Ativan**, **Tranxene**, and **Xanax** for more than five years did indeed appear to have some short-term memory impairment for a brief time following intake of their medication.[22] Other scientists have found that older people may be especially vulnerable to memory impairment with such drugs.[23] Add this to the fact that **Valium** and **Dalmane**-type medications can be addicting after long-term use and may, along with antidepressants and antipsychotics, also increase an older person's risk of falling and suffering a hip fracture, and you can see why we worry.[24]

Alzheimer's Advances

Clearly, it's important to evaluate drug side effects as a possible cause of memory problems. Once these have been considered and ruled out, a person experiencing memory loss, disorientation, speech impairment, confusion, or personality changes needs to see a competent neurologist. He or she will determine whether the symptoms are due to depression, thyroid problems, diabetes, strokes, pernicious anemia, Parkinson's disease, blood clots, infection, advanced alcoholism or hydrocephalus (fluid buildup in the brain).

Now the going gets even rougher. Separating Alzheimer's disease from multi-infarct dementia, Pick's, Creutzfeldt-Jakob, and Binswanger's disease is not always easy. All of these other neurological conditions can produce many of the same symptoms as Alzheimer's disease and are just as hard to treat. Even AIDS (acquired immune deficiency syndrome) can produce a dementia that is characterized by forgetfulness, confusion, disorientation, and speaking difficulties.

But let's first address Alzheimer's disease, as it is responsible for the majority of the cases of mental deterioration. We still don't know what causes this cruel, incurable, degenerative brain disorder. There are lots of theories, most of them marginal at best.

Some people worry about aluminum. Even though the brains of victims contain relatively high concentrations of aluminum, we are reasonably sure that aluminum pots and pans aren't responsible. It probably makes sense, just the same, not to cook acidic foods (tomatoes, sauerkraut, apples) in such cookware on the grounds that the extra aluminum that is leached into these foods from the pan is not desirable. And regular use of aluminum antacids is probably not a good idea for older people, though more because of their potential to weaken bones than for any effect on the brain. We also discourage everyone from using aluminum-containing antiperspirants in aerosols so that they do not inhale this metal. It's not particularly good for the lungs, and may be absorbed into the body.

Most researchers seem unconvinced that aluminum or any other environmental toxin causes this disorder, but certain chemicals may interact with or trigger chromosomes. There is growing evidence that a gene on chromosome 21 of Alzheimer's patients makes a unique protein that is linked to the twisted and tangled nerve cell fibers that clog their brains.[25,26] No one yet knows what triggers this gene to start making the protein, nor is it clear whether the protein is actually responsible for the destruction of neurons. A special protein (A68) does show up in parts of the brain affected by Alzheimer's disease, and it can also be detected in nerve cells before they appear visibly damaged and before the characteristic "neurofibrillary tangles" and plaque are formed.[27] Since it does not seem to appear in healthy older people, protein A68 is a prime suspect in the disease.

Another area researchers have concentrated much of their attention on is the role of neurotransmitters. These are chemicals that are important in passing signals from one nerve cell to another, much as letters were handed from one Pony Express rider to the next. Imagine what would happen if a horse broke its leg—the messages would not get through. In the brains of Alzheimer's patients, the crucial link could be an enzyme called CAT (choline acetyltransferase), which is dramatically depleted. This enzyme is needed for the brain to manufacture acetylcholine, a neurotransmitter originally believed to be the key to this disease. However, most attempts to increase levels of acetylcholine in the brain and improve memory have met with failure. Just supplementing the building blocks of acetylcholine by eating extra lecithin, or phosphatidylcholine, is ineffective.

Now investigators know that Alzheimer's disease is more complicated than they originally thought, and many other brain chemicals are affected. Ideally, successful treatment would prevent nerve cell destruction in the first place, perhaps by blocking the protein that is suspected of starting the whole mess.

Until that happens, though, there is still a lot of interest in alleviating some of the symptoms of Alzheimer's disease by preserving or increasing neurotransmitter levels. The most dramatic results to date come from a drug called THA (tetrahydroaminoacridine). On November 13, 1986, Dr. William K. Summers rocked the scientific community with a preliminary study published in the *New England Journal of Medicine.*

> **Twelve subjects have entered Phase III, in which the effects of long-term administration of oral THA are being evaluated. As of this writing, the first subject has been taking oral THA for 26 months; the average duration of oral THA administration is 12.6 months per patient. The degree of improvement has often been dramatic. One subject was able to resume most of her homemaking tasks, one was able to resume employment on a part-time basis, and one retired subject was able to resume playing golf daily. In other cases, there were improvements in activities of daily living, such as self-feeding at the family table, where total care had previously been required ...**
>
> **Prudence in judging these results is advised. THA is no more a cure for Alzheimer's disease than**

> levodopa is a cure for Parkinson's disease. Just as
> levodopa ceases to have effects in patients in the
> final stages of Parkinson's disease, we anticipate
> that oral THA will cease to have effects as Alzheimer's
> disease progresses. Indeed, two of our subjects have
> had some deterioration despite maintenance ther-
> apy with oral THA, one after 17 months and the
> other after 7 months of therapy. However, THA is a
> potential palliative treatment.[28]

Dr. Summers's report set off a firestorm of controversy. Many researchers were quick to criticize his conclusions as overly optimistic. Some questioned his methods. Whether their response was justified or in part due to professional jealousy is hard to tell. There is tremendous scientific competition in the quest for better understanding and treatment of Alzheimer's disease, and political in-fighting among investigators is not unheard of. Until his re-search was published in the *New England Journal of Medicine*, Dr. Summers had a low profile. Some of the heavy guns in Alzheimer's-related research undoubtedly felt one-upped by a relative unknown.

A positive result of the controversy is that researchers around the country are moving quickly to repeat the experiment and either confirm or reject Dr. Summers's results. And fortunately, THA is readily available. It is a drug that was discovered in 1909 and was once sold under the name **Tacrine**. It was originally used to counteract overdoses of barbiturates, muscle relaxants, and anesthetics. THA works in part by blocking the enzyme that destroys acetylcholine in the brain, thus allowing this crucial neurotransmitter to accumulate. That is one theoretical explana-tion as to why it produced positive effects in Dr. Summers's patients.

Although THA is no longer under patent and no drug manufac-turer currently sells it in this country, the Aldrich Chemical Company in Milwaukee, Wisconsin, is making the compound avail-able to qualified researchers who have special approval from the Food and Drug Administration (an Investigational New Drug Application). One such study was recently funded by the National Institute on Aging, with additional funding from the Alzheimer's Disease and Related Disorders Association (ADRDA) and techni-cal assistance and THA from the drug firm Warner-Lambert.[29]

Elevated liver enzymes in several patients have prompted the investigators to suspend this major study at the time of this writing. However, we expect that within several years we should know whether results from THA will justify the early enthusiasm.

If THA shows any positive effect at all, there will be tremendous pressure placed on the FDA to have the drug approved quickly for general use. Until then, the only access to this interesting compound be will through research centers that are carrying out approved experiments. ADRDA has staffed a toll-free number to provide information about THA and the study. The number is (800) 621-0379. People in Illinois can call (800) 572-6037.

So what to do in the meantime? First, there are no bankable breakthroughs, at least not yet. There are exciting scientific advances occurring at a rapid pace, and our understanding of the nature of this horrendous disease is increasing monthly. But a truly successful treatment or cure seems somewhat distant. **Hydergine** (ergoloid mesylates), the only drug approved by the FDA for senile dementia, is benign, but has produced inconsistent results and leaves a lot to be desired. **Hydergine** has not been clearly shown to "improve practical behavior (such as self-care, dressing, and prevention of incontinence) or to reduce hostile behavior."[30]

That doesn't mean you have to give up hope. Robert H. Rogge is a retired chemical engineer living in Chapel Hill, North Carolina. Over five years ago his wife Mary was diagnosed as an Alzheimer's patient. He has taken an active role in her care and has become as knowledgeable as many experts in the field. He has communicated with most of the key investigators and, in fact, traveled to California to enroll Mary in Dr. Summers's THA program. In addition to this experimental drug, Mary has been on **Trental** (pentoxifylline) for circulation, estrogen, and thyroid hormone. She also consumes numerous vitamins and minerals, along with extra amounts of the food supplement phosphatidyl choline (which is very much like lecithin). We have been impressed with Mary's condition over the years and share with you some of Robert Rogge's observations:

No miracles have resulted from this program but her general health is excellent and we lead a busy, athletic, creative, productive and happy life. We maintain a positive attitude about life and look forward

with anticipation and hope to our next day. This is not to say we don't have troublesome days, or periods within a day, but this is by far the minor part of the time.

There is more to the alleviation of problems in Alzheimer's, in my judgment, than nutrition and medication. I can summarize this non-drug therapy simply by saying: Keep the Alzheimer's person MOVING, BUSY, ALERT AND THINKING. It's good for the Alzheimer's person and what's good for him or her is good for the caregiver. It takes time, attention, effort and patience to make this program work. But the results are rewarding.

Of course there are great differences among Alzheimer's persons and I am aware of some of the special problems some of you have. But we all do have problems in different ways and one needs to find creative solutions for each individual case.[31]

Finally, a word for the family. We know firsthand how incredibly stressful a neurologic disease can be for the caregivers. Watching someone you love become more and more confused and disoriented is itself painful. The person's inability to make decisions, the difficulty with personal hygiene, the aimless wandering, fidgeting, agitation, sleeping and eating problems, can be awfully hard to cope with. Support and respite care is crucial. For the nearest Alzheimer's Disease and Related Disorders Association support group, write to the national headquarters at: ADRDA, 70 East Lake Street, Chicago IL 60601. Or call (800) 621-0379 (Illinois residents, (800) 572-6037).

What If It's Not Alzheimer's Disease?

There's a distinct possibility that the impaired judgment, memory loss, speech difficulty, and other symptoms of dementia are not caused by Alzheimer's disease. In the old days doctors used to think that "senility" was due to poor circulation and hardening of the arteries in the brain. So-called vasodilators (drugs thought to increase blood flow) were tried with few, if any, positive results.

Then the pendulum swung the other direction, and Alzheimer's disease grabbed the limelight. It was considered to be a problem of nerve cell destruction and neurotransmitter depletion. Blood circulation in the brain seemed irrelevant. But a significant number of patients (perhaps 20 to 30 percent) may indeed suffer mini-strokes (multi-infarct dementia or Binswanger's disease). For them, impaired cerebral circulation may be the first step in the destruction of brain tissue leading to what is called "vascular dementia." Since patients may not appear to have a full-blown stroke in the usual sense, a proper diagnosis may be missed till much later.

Doctors in the United States have little to offer such patients except blood pressure medications, which theoretically lessen the likelihood of further mini-strokes. However, doctors in Germany and Japan have been using a drug called **Trental** (pentoxifylline) for some cases of senile dementia. This medication is supposed to work by making the walls of red blood cells more flexible, so these oxygen-bearing cells can squeeze through narrowed capillaries. **Trental** has been approved in this country for treatment of intermittent claudication (painful leg cramps associated with exercise). Whether it will really prove to be useful for improving brain circulation still remains to be established.

One Italian study combined **Trental** and another drug called piracetam (under development by Syntex in the United States), which theoretically improves neuronal metabolism. Elderly patients with recent (less than six months') mental deterioration were tested on this regimen for 28 weeks and were found to have a modest 27 percent improvement in "psycho-intellectual performance."[32] Such studies will have to be repeated before these drugs will be taken seriously for similar uses in the United States. Harvard researchers have found that piracetam combined with lecithin was not effective for patients with Alzheimer's disease.[33] On the other hand, piracetam has been shown to improve reading and writing speed as well as reading and writing ability in dyslexic children.[34]

"Smart Pills" or "Memory Enhancers"— Whatever You Call Them, We're Excited

Another drug for the treatment of multi-infarct dementia that has a number of researchers excited is vinpocetine (**Cavinton**). It has been called a "cognitive activator," "mind rectifier," and "performance enhancer," and at the time of this writing is available in Japan (where it is selling spectacularly well), Eastern Europe (Bulgaria, Czechoslovakia, Hungary, Poland), the U.S.S.R., Hong Kong, Jamaica, Korea, Malaysia, the Philippines, Singapore, Syria, and parts of Latin America (Argentina, Mexico, Guatemala, Chile, Ecuador, Honduras, and Uruguay). Vinpocetine was originally developed by a group of Hungarian researchers who were looking to improve blood flow to the brain. They may have stumbled onto one of the first truly effective "memory pills."

> **In unpublished blind studies from Germany and Italy, involving over 700 patients, those with stroke and dementia showed "significant" improvements over placebo groups. Treated patients were discharged earlier from hospitals, and rated better on scales of depression and mental function by relatives, medical personnel and their own self-assessment. In at least one European clinical study, memory was found to be improved. In recent trials, the drug also improved the memories of rats used to model human impairment.[35]**

Vinpocetine is being developed by Ayerst Laboratories (a division of American Home Products) in this country. The company has funded considerable animal and human research, and the preliminary findings are encouraging. Dr. John Mullane is heading up the Ayerst research on this drug and their first multi-center investigations suggest that people with mild to moderate brain dysfunction who had normal blood pressure responded very nicely to the drug.[36] According to Dr. Mullane, this work was consistent with German studies that showed dramatically positive results. Japanese and Italian investigators have also reported that 70 to 80 percent of the elderly patients with "chronic cerebral dysfunction" treated with vinpocetine had a reduction in the severity of their illness.[37–40] In many cases the improvement was "good to excellent," especially with regard to speech and communication.

Another Ayerst scientist, Dr. Victor DeNoble, has devised animal experiments that model memory loss due to lack of oxygen in the brain. Again vinpocetine has proved effective.[41] He has even come up with a test that may "approximate a natural type of forgetting in humans." He teaches rats to choose between a dark and a light compartment.

> **After three days, most of the animals forget the correct response. "However, when we dosed those animals with vinpocetine, the number of rats that remembered the correct compartment after three days increased, from 15 out of 100 without the drug to over 70 with vinpocetine."**
>
> **Older people tend to forget things, even [those who are] not demented, he says. "We think this animal model approximates this natural type of forgetting in humans."[42]**

So far the drug seems reasonably safe, with no major side effects reported either in the animal or human studies. Preliminary research in humans also suggests that this drug may improve memory in healthy subjects.[43]

If all goes well with this compound, the company hopes it will win FDA approval by 1992. In the meantime, before you pack your bags for Mexico, Japan, or Jamaica, don't forget that we've been disappointed before. Initial excitement with some experimental drugs has given way to frustration when positive results couldn't be duplicated. But there is already a fair amount of good news with vinpocetine, enough to offer tentative encouragement. If this work can be confirmed, imagine the consequences. With a rapidly aging population, millions of people—perhaps as many as 85 percent—suffering from benign senescent forgetfulness will be anxious for anything that could improve their memories. Even for overcoming "normal" forgetfulness, the drug will be of extraordinary interest.

Pharmaceutical manufacturers realize that they have a tiger by the tail. "Smart pills" could become the hottest drugs on the market. Warner-Lambert, Lederle, and Syntex all claim to have something that looks encouraging. For the moment, though, Ayerst may have the inside edge with vinpocetine.

The brain remains the last frontier for medical research. Over the last decade enormous strides have been made in our understanding of learning and memory, but we have an awfully long way to go before we have a cure for Alzheimer's disease or any of the other memory disorders so common with aging. And time is running out. As our population ages, millions will begin experiencing confusion, disorientation, speech impairment, personality changes, and forgetfulness. The economic cost will run into the tens of billions of dollars. The human cost will be immeasurable.

Neither THA nor **Cavinton** (vinpocetine) will cure Alzheimer's disease, multi-infarct dementia, or any of the other severely debilitating diseases that used to be lumped together under the umbrella of senility. But if any of these new medications can offer any improvement in mental function or slow memory loss, they will truly represent a revolutionary breakthrough for older people.

Things to Remember

1. Confusion and forgetfulness may result from many causes, including treatable diseases. Make sure the confused or forgetful person gets a thorough medical workup from a neurologist experienced in diagnosing memory disorders.

2. Blood pressure drugs such as **Inderal** and **Aldomet**, sleeping pills and tranquilizers such as **Ativan**, **Halcion**, and **Xanax**, and certain antidepressants, including **Elavil**, **Endep**, **Surmontil**, and **Tofranil**, may cause confusion or forgetfulness, especially in older people. If you suspect that you or a loved one may be suffering from such side effects, talk it over with your doctor. Never discontinue any drug independently. There are many alternative medications for controlling blood pressure, and antidepressants such as **Norpramin**, **Pertofrane**, and **Wellbutrin** may be less likely to cause this kind of difficulty.

3. At this time, there are no drugs that can cure Alzheimer's disease, although THA has produced the most encouraging results to date. Research into the nature of this illness is proceeding at an impressive rate, but until there is a truly effective treatment, supportive care for the patient is crucial. For helpful information, you may want to consult a source such as: *The Thirty-Six-Hour Day: A Family Guide to Caring for Persons with Alzheimer's Disease, Related Dementing Illnesses and Memory Loss in Later Life*, by Nancy L. Mace and Peter V. Rabins (Warner Books, New York, 1981).

4. Support for the family and the principal caregiver is every bit as critical as care for the patient. The Alzheimer's Disease and Related Disorders Association can tell you how to contact the nearest chapter for information on local resources and support. Write to: ADRDA, 70 East Lake St., Chicago IL 60601.

5. If confusion and memory loss (not to mention other symptoms) are not due to Alzheimer's, but to other, mostly vascular, types of brain disease, some drugs that improve circulation or brain metabolism may prove helpful. Preliminary results with **Cavinton** (vinpocetine) are very encouraging. At the time of this writing, the drug is available in Japan, Eastern Europe (Bulgaria, Czechoslovakia, Hungary, Poland), the U.S.S.R., Hong Kong, Jamaica, Korea, Malaysia, the Philippines, Singapore, Syria, and parts of Latin America (Argentina, Chile, Ecuador, Guatemala, Honduras, Mexico, and Uruguay). If all goes well, it should be be approved by the U.S. Food and Drug Administration by 1992.

References

1. Khatchaturian, Zaven, Director, National Institute on Aging's Alzheimer's Disease Research Center Program. "Piecing Together the Puzzle of Alzheimer's Disease: A National Collaborative Approach." Presented at the First Joseph and Kathleen Bryan Alzheimer's Disease Research Center Conference, Feb. 10, 1987.
2. Blazer, Dan. Personal communication. Oct. 14, 1983.
3. Nemeroff, Charles B. "Recent Developments in the Neuro-chemistry of Alzheimer's Disease: Focus on Cholinergic and Peptidergic Systems." Presented at the First Joseph and Kathleen Bryan Alzheimer's Disease Research Center Conference, Feb. 10, 1987.
4. Gose, Kathleen; and Levi, Gloria. *Dealing with Memory Changes As You Grow Older.* Vancouver, 1985, p. 74.
5. Mace, Nancy L.; and Rabins, Peter V. *The Thirty-Six-Hour Day: A Family Guide to Caring for Persons with Alzheimer's Disease, Related Dementing Illnesses and Memory Loss in Later Life.* (Warner Books, New York, 1981.)
6. Solomon, Sanford, et al. "Impairment of Memory Function by Antihypertensive Medication." *Arch. Gen. Psych.* 40:1109–1112, 1983.
7. Scharf, M. B., et al. "Lorazepam—Efficacy, Side Effects and Rebound Phenomena." *Clin. Pharmacol. Ther.* 31:175–179, 1982.
8. Kales, A., et al. "Hypnotic Efficacy of Triazolam: Sleep Laboratory Evaluation of Intermediate Term Effectiveness." *J. Clin. Pharmacol.* 16:399–406, 1976.
9. Scharf, Martin B.; and Saskin, Paul. "Benzodiazepine Induced Amnesia—Clinical and Laboratory Findings." In press.
10. Shader, Richard I.; and Greenblatt, David J. "Triazolam and Anterograde Amnesia: All Is Not Well in the Z-Zone." *J. Clin. Psychopharmacol.* 3:273, 1983.
11. Kales, A., et al. "Comparison of Short and Long Half-life Benzodiazepine Hypnotics: Triazolam and Quazepam." *Clin. Pharmacol. Ther.* 40:378–386, 1986.
12. Scharf, M. B., et al. "Differential Amnestic Properties of Short- and Long-Acting Benzodiazepines." *J. Clin. Psychiatry* 45(2):51–53, 1984.
13. Scharf, M. B., et al. "Morning Amnestic Effects of Triazolam." *J. Clin. Psychiatry* 8:38–45, 1986.
14. Block, R.I.; and Berchou, R. "Alprazolam and Lorazepam Effects on Memory Acquisition and Retrieval Processes." *Pharmacol. Biochem. Behav.* 20:233–241, 1984.
15. Scharf and Saskin. "Benzodiazepine Induced Amnesia—Clinical and Laboratory Findings." op. cit.
16. Jarvik, L. K. "Depression: A Review of Drug Therapy for Elderly Patients." *Consultant* 22:141–146, 1982.
17. Bernstein, Jerrold G. "Pharmacotherapy of Geriatric Depression." *J. Clin. Psych.* 45(10, Sec. 2):30–34, 1984.

18. Glassman, Alexander H., et al. "Adverse Effects of Tricyclic Antidepressants: Focus on the Elderly." E. Usdin, et al., eds. *Frontiers in Biochemical Pharmacological Research in Depression.* New York: Raven Press, 1984, pp. 391–398.
19. Lamping, Donna L., et al. "Effects of Two Antidepressants in a Double-blind Study." *Psychopharmacology* 84:254–261, 1984.
20. Hendler, N., et al. "A Comparison of Cognitive Impairment Due to Benzodiazepines and to Narcotics." *Am. J. Psychiatry* 137:828–830, 1980.
21. Petursson, H., et al. "Psychometric Performance During Withdrawal from Long-term Benzodiazepine Treatment." *Psychopharmacology* 81:345–349, 1983.
22. Lucki, Irwin, et al. "Chronic Use of Benzodiazepines and Psychomotor and Cognitive Test Performance." *Psychopharmacology* 88:426–433, 1986.
23. Block, Robert I., et al. "Memory Performance in Individuals with Primary Degenerative Dementia: Its Similarity to Diazepam-Induced Impairments." *Exp. Aging Res.* 11(3):151–155, 1985.
24. Ray, Wayne A., et al. "Psychotropic Drug Use and the Risk of Hip Fracture." *N. Engl. J. Med.* 316:363–369, 1987.
25. Robakis, Nikolaos, et al. "Chromosome 21q21 Sublocalisation of Gene Encoding Beta-Amyloid Peptide in Cerebral Vessels and Neuritic (Senile) Plaques of People with Alzheimer's Disease and Down Syndrome." *Lancet* 1(8529):384–385, 1987.
26. Amato, I. "Alzheimer's Disease: Scientists Report Research Advances." *Science News* 130:327, 1986.
27. Davies, Peter. "The Genetics of Alzheimer's Disease." Presented at the First Joseph and Kathleen Bryan Alzheimer's Disease Research Center Conference, Feb. 10, 1987.
28. Summers, William Koopmans, et al. "Oral Tetrahydroaminoacridine in Long-term Treatment of Senile Dementia, Alzheimer Type." *N. Engl. J. Med.* 315:1241–1245, 1986.
29. "Warner-Lambert Is Supplying THA for Alzheimer's Trial." *FDC Reports* 49(30), July 27, 1987, p. T&G 1.
30. Cook, Peter; and James, Ian. "Cerebral Vasodilators." *N. Engl. J. Med.* 305:1560–1564, 1981.
31. Rogge, Robert H. "Some Observations on Recent Alzheimer's Disease Research." June, 1986.
32. Parnetti, Lucilla, et al. "Haemorrheological Pattern in Initial Mental Deterioration: Results of a Long-term Study Using Piracetam and Pentoxifylline." *Arch. Gerontol. Geriatr.* 4:141–155, 1985.
33. Growdon, J. H., et al. "Piracetam Combined with Lecithin in the Treatment of Alzheimer's Disease." *Neurobiol. Aging* 7:269–276, 1986.
34. Tallal, P., et al. "Evaluation of the Efficacy of Piracetam in Treating Information Processing, Reading and Writing Disorders in Dyslexic Children." *Int. J. Psychophysiol.* 4:41–52, 1986.
35. Bauman, Norman. "Maybe a Drug to Remember." *Med. Trib.* 27(16) June 4, 1986.
36. Mullane, John. Personal communication, Feb. 18, 1987.

37. Otomo, E., et al. "Comparison of Vinpocetine with Ifenprodil Tartrate and Dihydroergotoxine Mesylate Treatment and Results of Long-term Treatment with Vinpocetine." *Curr. Ther. Res.* 37(5):811–821, 1985.

38. Manconi, E., et al. "A Double-blind Clinical Trial of Vinpocetine in the Treatment of Cerebral Insufficiency of Vascular and Degenerative Origin." *Curr. Ther. Res.* 40(4):702–709, 1986.

39. Peruzza, Marino, et al. "A Double-blind Placebo Controlled Evaluation of the Efficacy and Safety of Vinpocetine in the Treatment of Patients with Chronic Vascular or Degenerative Senile Cerebral Dysfunction." *Advances in Therapy* 3(4):201–209, 1986.

40. Balestreri, Roberto, et al. "A Double-blind Placebo Controlled Evaluation of the Safety and Efficacy of Vinpocetine in the Treatment of Patients with Chronic Vascular Senile Cerebral Dysfunction." *J. Amer. Ger. Soc.*, May, 1987.

41. DeNoble, Victor J., et al. "Vinpocetine: Nootropic Effects on Scopolamine-Induced and Hypoxia-Induced Retrieval Deficits of a Step-Through Passive Avoidance Response in Rats." *Pharmacol. Biochem. Behav.* 24:1123–1128, 1986.

42. Bauman, Norman, op. cit.

43. Subhan, A.; and Hindmarch, I. "Psychopharmacological Effects of Vinpocetine in Normal Healthy Volunteers." *Eur. J. Clin. Pharmacol.* 28:567–571, 1985.

7

Overcoming Anxiety, Insomnia, and Depression

Everyone suffers from anxiety from time to time. In fact, in our household it happens every Friday like clockwork. That's when our newspaper column deadline comes due. In the ten years that we've been writing "The People's Pharmacy" (syndicated nationally by King Features), we have never once gotten ahead. And so every Friday for ten years we have had a mini-anxiety-attack. Sometimes the column just about writes itself. That's rare. Most times it comes with a little effort. But sometimes, trying to get the right words down can be as frustrating as trying to thread a needle with a tow line or to squeeze blood out of a turnip. As the clock gets closer to deadline, the pulse increases, hands start to sweat, and blood pressure climbs.

Why do we let it happen? We blame it on our incredibly hectic schedules. The truth is that we're deadliners. Always have been and probably always will be. With a little planning, though, we could probably get ahead and reduce the anxiety.

We're not the only ones. Much of the stress in people's lives is self-induced. Too many of us allow ourselves to get caught up in deadlines and details. Just take a look at the shopping malls on

December 24th. Tell me last minute shopping isn't stressful? The trouble is that we aren't taught how to relax or reflect, and so daily events become overwhelming. The waves may seem so ominous that we never catch a glimpse of the ocean. For many people, worrying can become a way of life.

Now please don't get us wrong. There are lots of things to worry about. Making ends meet can become a constant source of anxiety if you live on Social Security. Chronic illness and pain can make the most dedicated optimist desperate and despondent. And watching a loved one suffer is about as stressful as anything in the world. Such problems cannot be ignored or covered over with platitudes or a prescription.

But rather than try to get at the source of their patients' stress and anxiety, many doctors have been quick to prescribe "nerve pills," otherwise known as tranquilizers, sedatives, anti-anxiety agents, or "hypnotics" when taken at bedtime. If patients ask about addiction, far too often the question is brushed aside. And when people complain that they are having difficulty stopping, some physicians have a knee jerk response—"just keep taking your medicine." One of our newspaper column readers related the following:

> I have always been a somewhat nervous person, but about two years ago the anxiety level became unbearable. My doctor put me on Xanax.
>
> I felt better very quickly and continued to take the Xanax. But when I thought I could gradually withdraw from the medicine, I found out that the experience was terrible.
>
> I tried for two weeks, going through hell, thinking I was going crazy and not being able to sleep. My doctor tells me I'm not addicted, but I know I'm dependent upon the drug and it worries me. My doctor tells me I may have to take Xanax the rest of my life. He compares it to a diabetic having to take insulin.

Incredible! How can a doctor compare **Xanax** (alprazolam) or any other anti-anxiety agent to insulin? A diabetic would die without insulin, but drugs like **Valium** and **Xanax** are intended only for temporary relief. Even the drug company admits that:

> XANAX Tablets (alprazolam) are indicated for the
> management of anxiety disorders or the short-term
> relief of the symptoms of anxiety. Anxiety or ten-
> sion associated with the stress of everyday life usu-
> ally does not require treatment with an anxiolytic
> [tranquilizer] . . .
>
> The effectiveness of XANAX for long-term use,
> that is, more than four months, has not been estab-
> lished by systematic clinical trials. The physician
> should periodically reassess the usefulness of the
> drug for the individual patient.[1]

Unfortunately, all too often that "periodic assessment" results
in another prescription with half a dozen refills. And since the
name on the bottle doesn't say **Valium**, most patients believe
their doctor when he reassures them it isn't addicting. **Valium**
has taken most of the flack, but it is no worse than any of the
other anxiety agents. In fact, some of the newer, shorter-acting
drugs may produce a more rapid and dramatic withdrawal
reaction.

> A 50-year-old woman who was undergoing outpa-
> tient treatment for agoraphobia and panic attacks
> took alprazolam [XANAX], 3 mg tid [three times a
> day], for 18 months. She stopped taking the drug
> suddenly, of her own accord, and began to experi-
> ence drug withdrawal symptoms 18 hours later. Feel-
> ings of anxiety, restlessness, and apprehension were
> followed by palpitations and shortness of breath.
> Over the next three days she experienced paranoid
> thought patterns and visual and auditory hallucina-
> tions. She was tremulous, diaphoretic [sweating],
> anorexic [not eating], and insomniac. On the third
> day she was hospitalized.
>
> She was advised to resume taking alprazolam,
> starting with a 1-mg dose. Within three days she
> was back to her usual self.[2,3]

If patients take these drugs continuously for more than six or
eight months and then stop abruptly, many will suffer unpleasant
withdrawal reactions that include anxiety, headache, difficulty

concentrating, insomnia, fear, nerve jerking, tremor, depersonalization, perceptual changes, sweating, and fatigue.[4]

Isn't it ironic that the very symptom for which these drugs are often prescribed—anxiety—is one of the most common side effects produced by withdrawal of the medicine? No wonder, then, that people go right back to their drug if they begin to experience such unpleasant side effects when they stop.

Often, the glib response to the question of withdrawal is "gradual tapering." Just phase the patient off the drug gently. Well, let us tell you that for some people even a gradual reduction in dosage can be a problem:

> **With the short-acting benzodiazepines, even a gradual tapering-off is no guarantee against a withdrawal reaction. One recent case study described the occurrence of severe headache followed by grand mal seizures in a 19-year-old college woman who had taken alprazolam for the treatment of panic disorder. This young woman had followed her physician's instructions, reducing her drug dosage by 1 mg every three days.[5,6]**

A column reader reports an even more harrowing tale:

> **When I was in my early 40's I started having a problem with sleeping through the night. My doctor put me on Dalmane for only 30 days and the relief from sleeplessness was marvelous. At the end of the 30 days however, he would not re-issue the prescription because he did not want me to get addicted to it. So I changed doctors—finding one who simply wrote prescriptions for Dalmane and saw no reason not to.**
>
> **I stayed on Dalmane for more than ten years and would probably be on it yet had I not suffered a rather violent dizzy spell. The doctor said she believed it was caused by Dalmane taken over too long a period of time and suggested I attempt to withdraw from the use of it.**
>
> **She prescribed an over-the-counter sleep aid feeling that this would gradually reduce my dependence**

on Dalmane. The results were a total disaster. I did not sleep at all—I merely dozed lightly for short periods during the night. I found myself with tears running out of my eyes when I wasn't crying . . .

I gradually reduced the amount of Dalmane I took until I was taking none. All of the symptoms again returned and medication prescribed by the doctor to help just worsened the situation so I did not use them. At the end of three months there was a lessening of some of the symptoms but it was at least six months before there was a noticeable improvement in the way I felt. After three months, my doctor told me all the Dalmane would have been removed from my system and that any remaining side effects were psychological. He was wrong!!!

Two reactions remained for more than a year: I had a feeling in my head as though someone with pincers was applying pressure to both temples causing a momentary flash of pain to travel across my brain from one side to the other—this occurred constantly throughout the day. The second oddball reaction was a constant pressure in the left side of my head which somehow seemed related to a numbness in the ankle of my left leg. It took about a year for the first symptom to fade away and it has only been in the last month that the odd sensation in my head and ankle seem to be present less frequently.

I did indeed suffer (over a period of one and a half years) halting speech, itching, jerking nerves, confusion, insomnia, blurred vision, irritability and a metallic taste in my mouth (and many more bizarre and frightening side effects that do not readily come to mind). My withdrawal from Dalmane was a living hell for more than a year and [the drug] can indeed cause addiction.

There is no way I would ever take any type of sleeping pill again. For the first time in years I feel mentally alert, find that even my memory is improving. I am happier in disposition and optimistic in viewpoint. In other words, the negatives have been changed to positives.

Whew, what a nightmare! And to think the manufacturer insisted for years that **Dalmane** could not cause addiction. It took dozens of letters from our readers and countless phone calls to Hoffmann-La Roche to finally get the company to change the sentence on addiction in their package insert from "Physical and psychological dependence have not been reported or observed in persons taking recommended doses of **Dalmane**," to "Withdrawal symptoms have rarely been reported with **Dalmane**." A victory of sorts, eh?

Now please don't get the idea that we are just picking on **Dalmane**. **Ativan** (lorazepam), **Centrax** (prazepam), **Halcion** (triazolam), **Librium** (chlordiazepoxide), **Librax** (chlordiazepoxide, clidinium), **Paxipam** (halazepam), **Restoril** (temazepam), **Serax** (oxazepam), **Tranxene** (clorazepate), **Valium** (diazepam), and **Xanax** (alprazolam) all have the potential to produce side effects for some people if discontinued abruptly. And for a few unfortunate souls the symptoms can last a very long time, perhaps because of a change in the biochemistry of the brain.

Some doctors believe that it's no big deal. Just leave a patient on **Xanax** (or whatever) for life—like a "diabetic on insulin." Maybe that's appropriate for a few folks, but keep in mind the new concern that some of the shorter-acting drugs (**Ativan**, **Halcion**, **Xanax**) may have a negative effect on memory. There's also the very real danger of impaired driving ability while taking any of these medications. Then add to that the recent observation that longer-acting anti-anxiety agents (**Dalmane**, **Librium**, **Valium**), antidepressants (**Adapin**, **Elavil**, **Sinequan**, **Tofranil**), and antipsychotics (**Haldol**, **Mellaril**, **Thorazine**) may make people feel dizzy or unsteady and increase the risk of falls and hip fractures, and you can understand our concern.[7]

We are especially worried about the use of antipsychotic medications like **Compazine** (prochlorperazine), **Haldol** (haloperidol), **Loxitane** (loxapine), **Mellaril** (thioridazine), **Moban** (molindone), **Navane** (thiothixene), **Prolixin** (fluphenazine), **Serentil** (mesoridazine), **Sparine** (promazine), **Stelazine** (trifluoperazine), **Thorazine** (chlorpromazine), **Trilafon** (perphenazine), and **Vesprin** (triflupromazine) in people who don't have symptoms of schizophrenia.

Although these drugs are occasionally appropriate for severe nausea and vomiting, that is rarely why they are administered to nonpsychotic older adults. These medications can act as chemical straitjackets. That is, they may produce a kind of zombie-like state. An agitated nursing home patient may be very difficult for the staff to control and can make life difficult for other residents. A major tranquilizer will calm down such a person and make him or her more docile. But it can also cause drowsiness, weakness, unsteadiness, nasal stuffiness, dry mouth, breast enlargement, rash, glaucoma, blurred vision, and slurred speech. Another serious complication is tardive dyskinesia, which can be irreversible, even after the drug is discontinued. It manifests itself as uncontrollable jerking movements and muscle spasms. Often the neck may begin to twitch and no matter how hard someone tries to stop the motion, it won't go away. Sometimes there is a parkinsonian tremor and a shuffling walk. We've heard a horror story of a person diagnosed as having Parkinson's disease and treated with levodopa, when in reality the entire problem was created by antipsychotic medication.

Does that mean none of these drugs should ever be prescribed? Of course not. Anti-anxiety agents *do* have a place. If you consider them as chemical crutches to be used for short periods of time to get over an immediate crisis or for an occasional sleepless night, the chances are good that you won't run into trouble, especially if the dose is low—older people are more vulnerable to all drugs that affect the brain. Problems arise when they are used day in and day out or every night to fall asleep "just in case." Remember, they are not a cure for anxiety or insomnia, just temporary palliative therapy.

One relatively new anti-anxiety drug called **BuSpar** (buspirone) seems less likely than most other agents to cause sedation, driving difficulties, and confusion or to interact with alcohol. It may take a little longer to start working and there isn't much information about long-term reactions. Side effects to be aware of include dizziness, nervousness, and headache.

Although **BuSpar** may appear to be an attractive alternative to traditional nerve pills, there is one important caveat. People cannot be switched from **Valium**-like drugs directly to **Buspar** without risking withdrawal symptoms. And because it works differently, people may find that the anti-anxiety effect they obtain is not the same as they are used to with drugs like **Ativan**, **Centrax**, **Librium**, **Tranxene**, and **Xanax**. There is still no magic bullet that will wipe out symptoms of stress and nervousness, improve our outlook on life, and do all this without side effects or a risk of addiction.

So what should you do if you're feeling anxious and the weight of the world seems to be resting on your shoulders? We have no simple answers, but our best suggestion is to look for support. Talk out the problems. It's amazing how helpful a sympathetic ear can be. Friends, relatives, neighbors—whoever can lend a little time to listen. If you can afford it, a therapist (psychologist, psychiatric social worker, nurse, physician's associate, etc.) can also help.

But what do you talk about? First, make a list. What's got you worried? Is it money? Perhaps health is your biggest concern. Or maybe relationships with family and friends have you on edge. No matter how trivial you think they may be, try to get down on paper all the hassles that have been making your life miserable. Now rank them starting from the most stressful (#10) to the least stressful (#1). Next, try to describe how each problem makes you feel. If Cousin Mildred drives you up the wall with her constant bickering and complaining, write down anger and annoyance after Mildred's name. If arthritis keeps you awake at night and has you worried about your ability to get around, write down pain and frustration. And when Brother Clyde ignores you in his will and instead leaves everything to that good-for-nothing hussy he married last year, write down bitterness and resentment.

Okay, now that you have begun to identify the sources of the anxiety, you may be better able to deal with them and talk out the issues with friends. There's also a chance you may be better able to work out an effective escape strategy, especially with a little advice and assistance from helpers. Sometimes an objective bystander can come up with excellent suggestions that we would never think of on our own.

It might be as simple as avoiding Cousin Mildred's harsh voice by purchasing an inexpensive telephone answering device to screen out her calls. Perhaps a new prescription or exercise program will ease some of that arthritis pain. And a good lawyer might figure out a way to sue the hussy for half of Clyde's estate. The point is that sometimes there *are* solutions to what appear on the surface as insurmountable problems. Once you've dealt with what's been bothering you, you may be amazed to find you feel better. All the **Valium** and **Xanax** in Missouri won't take those troubles away, either. And even when answers don't come easily, it still pays to write down the source of the anxiety so that it doesn't sneak up on you unawares.

What are some other nondrug approaches to relieving tension? Regular exercise—especially walking—may help you feel rejuvenated. Music can be wonderful. You don't have to be a teenager to appreciate the marvels of modern electronics. An inexpensive portable Walkman-type cassette player will allow you to listen to relaxing music in your favorite chair. Or perhaps a book on cassette will help take your mind off your worries. Publishers are now making available an extraordinary number of classics on tape. You might also find Dr. Emmett Miller's relaxation tapes helpful. We find that his voice is one of the most soothing and healing sounds next to ocean waves and bird songs. Our favorite tapes for draining tension are "Letting Go of Stress" and the "Ten Minute Stress Manager." You can get order information from The Source, P.O. Box W, Stanford, CA 94305, or by calling toll free (800) 52-TAPES (California residents call (415) 328-7171).

Get involved with other people—whether in a volunteer group, local politics, or a senior citizens' center. Talking, discussing, arguing, caring—those are the things that make life meaningful. Loneliness makes any problem seem much worse. If you're stuck at home, think about a pet. The love and companionship an animal can give you can be a real comfort.

If you have an Alzheimer's patient to look after, contact the local ADRDA support group (see page 171). If another chronic condition is the problem, seek out others who know what you are going through and band together. There's strength in sharing.

Easing into Sleep

When it comes to insomnia, realize that as we get older our bodies usually seem to need less sleep. It takes us longer to doze off and we may find that we wake earlier. If you can function normally throughout the day, there's no need to worry about reduced sleep. Yes, we know it can be disturbing to watch the minutes tick by or to be up at 4 A.M. when the rest of the world is happily snoring away. Just count yourself lucky to be able to get by with less and read or listen to music or write letters to all those people who would love to hear from you.

Here are some other tips that may help a little:

- Stay away from caffeine! You've heard it before, but it bears repeating! From about 3 P.M. on don't indulge in caffeinated coffee or tea. Soft drinks with caffeine and over-the-counter diet pills or decongestants are also a mistake.

- Caffeine isn't the only drug that can be a problem. Find out whether any prescription medicines you are taking could cause insomnia. For example, beta blockers like Inderal and Lopressor and asthma drugs such as Theo-Dur, Theobid, and Slo-Phyllin occasionally aggravate sleeping problems.

- Don't get trapped in the habit of taking a nightcap. Alcohol may zonk you out so you fall asleep, but it will often disrupt sleep and actually make insomnia worse over the long haul.

- Exercise during the day. A brisk walk can take your mind off your problems and help make you feel pleasantly tired. But don't do strenuous exercise in the evening, as it may stimulate your nervous system or increase your aches and pains.

- A soak in the tub can be relaxing before bedtime.

- Try to have regular hours for sleeping. Late afternoon naps could interfere with nighttime ZZs.

- Warm milk and crackers (or a cookie if you're feeling indulgent) provide the amino acid tryptophan, which may help you feel drowsy. A favorite in our house is Cheerios and honey or a malted.

- Try to avoid late night television. Once you get caught up in an exciting movie or a talk show, you may find it hard to relax and unwind.

- Don't concentrate too hard on falling asleep or rehash the day's events. One way to let your mind unwind is to listen to Dr. Emmett Miller's relaxation tapes. "Easing into Sleep" is one of our favorites, along with "The Healing Journey." Order information for Dr. Miller's tapes can be obtained from The Source, P.O. Box W, Stanford,

CA 94305. You can call toll free (800) 52-TAPES
(California residents call (415) 328-7171).

Are You Dealing with Depression?

If nothing works and insomnia is making your life miserable, you
need professional help. A sleep disorder clinic might be helpful in
analyzing the nature of the problem and offering a successful
nondrug treatment program. Or perhaps you are suffering from
psychological depression. Sleep disturbances are one of the classic tip-offs that someone may be depressed. If insomnia is accompanied by feelings of helplessness and hopelessness, don't ignore
what could be a serious situation.

When you're down in the dumps, it's hard to even imagine
what it used to be like to feel good. The sense of uselessness and
despair isolate you from the world around you and it may seem
as if you are in a rut so deep you can't see over the top, let alone
climb out. Little problems appear insurmountable. Food loses its
appeal. Sex seems superfluous. Life just loses its vibrancy.

Now all of those feelings would be appropriate if a terrible
event had just occurred in your life. When you lose a loved one,
grief and depression are natural responses. But if you or someone you love feels terribly sad for no apparent reason, it's time to
take action. Get to a physician or therapist pronto! When this
kind of severe depression is allowed to continue it can produce
symptoms that even mimic senility. People can become forgetful,
uncommunicative, and lethargic. Some poor souls may even end
up being placed in a nursing home when in fact they are simply
depressed.

This kind of mental illness does not respond to exhortations to
cheer up. You can't just "pull yourself up by the bootstraps." You
need professional help. And when you make that trip to the
doctor's office, take along every single medicine you are swallowing, because the very first thing you're going to want to ask her is
whether you could be suffering from drug-induced depression.

Remember the Hippocratic oath?—*Primum non nocere*—"First,
do no harm." We are convinced that most physicians really do
want to help their patients get well and stay healthy, but far too
often doctors fail to warn people that psychological depression

can be a subtle side effect of a surprisingly large number of medications. This is the kind of adverse reaction that can sneak up on you slowly and insidiously.

A radio talk show host described it this way:

> **One morning I was reading the morning newspaper and I started to cry. I knew something was wrong because the news never affected me that way before. I had been feeling down for weeks and thoughts of suicide had even entered my mind. But I didn't think I was depressed and I never associated those feelings with the medicine I had started taking for blood pressure several months before.**

Allan Benson, a physician who himself experienced subtle psychological effects from his heart medicine, wrote a poignant letter to the editor of the *New England Journal of Medicine*, in verse. Here are some excerpts:

ODE TO PROPRANOLOL

Two hundred dawns,
Two hundred dusks,
Have passed through
Time's portals
Since my physician
Prescribed propranolol.

. . .

The watered grass remains
Green, and the fields
Are golden and full,
As is right, when
summer's fading warmth
Forecasts autumn's threat'ning breeze.

I have noted this
Sixty-seven times before.
And each autumn, since
Relatively rational mentation
Came to me, autumn's beauty
Was true and deep.

Now it is perceived
But there is no burst
Of mental, and physical
And sensual fulfillment
That, in times past,
Brought me contentment.

. . .

Truly, I continue,
I eat, I walk, and talk,
And, in a fashion, think.
And I worry less
About whether or not
I shall live longer.

But if a Chagall poster
Can no longer
Make me marvel,
Or a Chopin nocturne
Cannot conjure
A dream,

Why then, is the cost-benefit ratio
A proper one?[8]

This doctor was taking **Inderal**, one of the most frequently prescribed drugs in the world. It is used to treat high blood pressure, irregular heart beats, and angina, and to prevent heart attacks, migraine headaches, and even stage fright. It is a very useful medication and an important part of the physician's pharmacopoeia. But there are times when the cost-benefit question posed in the poem needs to be addressed.

Most doctors are probably unaware just how common drug-induced depression is. Harvard researcher Dr. Jerry Avorn and his colleagues set out to unravel the mystery by determining how often antidepressants are prescribed to people taking beta blockers (**Inderal**, **Lopressor**, and **Corgard**). What they found was shocking. After examining the medical records of 143,253 Medicaid recipients in Michigan and Minnesota, the researchers discovered that 23 percent (almost one out of four) of those people on beta blockers had also received antidepressant medication.[9]

Dr. Avorn and his colleagues believe that their research may actually underestimate the incidence of drug-induced depression.

The point is that doctors often give patients additional prescriptions to overcome side effects, sometimes without even realizing that the problems could be solved just by starting over again with a different medication for the initial problem. The following table lists just some of the medications that have been associated with psychological depression:

Drugs That May Trigger Depression*

Adalat (nifedipine) [rare]

Aldoclor (methyldopa, chlorothiazide)

Aldomet (methyldopa)

Aldoril (methyldopa, HCTZ*)

Alurate (aprobarbital)

Amipaque (metrizamide) [frequent and may persist awhile]

Amytal (amobarbital)

Antabuse (disulfiram)

Blocadren (timolol) [uncommon]

Butisol (butabarbital)

Catapres (clonidine) [may go away after regular use]

Corgard (nadolol) [uncommon]

Cortone (cortisone) [with higher doses or upon discontinuation]

Decadron (dexamethasone) [with higher doses or upon discontinuation]

Deltasone (prednisone) [with higher doses or upon discontinuation]

Demi-Regroton (chlorthalidone, reserpine) [frequent when dose is over 0.5 mg; may persist awhile after discontinuation]

Dilantin (phenytoin) [with high doses]

Digoxin [new information, needs to be confirmed]

Diupres (chlorothiazide, reserpine) [frequent when dose is over 0.5 mg; may persist awhile after discontinuation]

Diutensen-R (methyclothiazide, reserpine) [frequent when dose is over 0.5 mg; may persist awhile after discontinuation]

Dopar (levodopa)
Elspar (asparaginase) [frequent]
Fastin (phentermine) [upon discontinuation]
Flagyl (metronidazole)
Gemonil (metharbital)
Halcion (triazolam) [uncommon]
Hydropres (reserpine, HCTZ**) [frequent when dose is over 0.5 mg; may persist awhile after discontinuation]
Inderal (propranolol) [not infrequent]
Inderide (propranolol, HCTZ**) [not infrequent]
Indocin (indomethacin)
INH (isoniazid) [uncommon]
Ismelin (guanethidine)
Laniazid (isoniazid) [uncommon]
Lanoxin (digoxin) [new research, needs to be confirmed]
Larodopa (levodopa)
Lioresal (baclofen) [more common upon discontinuation]
Lopressor (metoprolol) [uncommon]
Lotusate (talbutal)
Luminal (phenobarbital)
Mebaral (mephobarbital)
Metatensin (trichlormethiazide, reserpine) [frequent when dose is over 0.5 mg; may persist awhile after discontinuation]
Minipress (prazosin) [uncommon]
Motrin (ibuprofen) [uncommon]
Mysoline (primidone) [with high doses]
Naqua (trichlormethiazide) [uncommon]
Naquival (trichlormethiazide, reserpine) [frequent when dose is over 0.5 mg; may persist awhile after discontinuation]
NegGram (nalidixic acid) [uncommon]
Nembutal (pentobarbital)
Normodyne (labetalol) [uncommon]
Pariodel (bromocriptine) [may persist weeks after stopping]
Pondimin (fenfluramine) [upon discontinuation]
Prednisone [with higher doses or upon discontinuation]
Preludin (phenmetrazine) [upon discontinuation]
Procardia (nifedipine) [rare]

Raudixin (rauwolfia serpentina) [frequent when dose is over 0.5 mg; may persist awhile after discontinuation]

Rauzide (rauwolfia serpentina; bendroflumethiazide) [frequent when dose is over 0.5 mg; may persist awhile after discontinuation]

Reglan (metoclopramide)

Regroton (chlorthalidone reserpine) [frequent when dose is over 0.5 mg; may persist awhile after discontinuation]

Renese (polythiazide) [uncommon]

Renese-R (polythiazide, reserpine) [frequent when dose is over 0.5 mg; may persist awhile after discontinuation]

Rifamate (rifampin, isoniazid) [uncommon]

Rufen (ibuprofen) [uncommon]

Salutensin (hydroflumethiazide, reserpine) [frequent when dose is over 0.5 mg; may persist awhile after discontinuation]

Sandril (reserpine) [frequent when dose is over 0.5 mg; may persist awhile after discontinuation]

Seconal (secobarbital)

Ser-Ap-Es (reserpine, hydralazine, HCTZ**) [frequent when dose is over 0.5 mg; may persist awhile after discontinuation]

Serpasil (reserpine) [frequent when dose is over 0.5 mg; may persist awhile after discontinuation]

Sinemet (carbidopa, levodopa)

Tagamet (cimetidine)

Talwin (pentazocine)

Tenormin (atenolol) [quite uncommon]

Tenuate (diethylpropion) [upon discontinuation]

Timoptic (timolol) [uncommon]

Trandate (labetalol) [uncommon]

Trecator-SC (ethionamide) [common reaction]

Tuinal (secobarbital, amobarbital)

Velban (vinblastine) [uncommon]

Visken (pindolol) [uncommon]

Zantac (ranitidine) [uncommon]

Zarontin (ethosuximide) [with high doses]

**HCTZ = hydrochlorothiazide

*Gerner, Robert H. "Present Status of Drug Therapy of Depression in Late Life." *J. Affective Disorders* Suppl 1:S23– S31, 1985.

"Drugs That Cause Psychiatric Symptoms." *Medical Letter* 28:81–86, 1986.

No drug should ever be discontined without careful discussion with your physician. If depression is drug-induced, it's possible that an alternate medication could be substituted. On the other hand, depression can often arise spontaneously, with no apparent cause. There is good evidence that this form of mental illness often runs in families, so a tendency toward depression may be inherited. A physical ailment can also bring on the blues. It's common for people to develop a severe, debilitating depression after suffering a stroke. If family members aren't prepared for this possibility, treatment could be delayed.

No matter what the reason, there are many effective antidepressants that can lift your spirits and lead to improved sleep. There is absolutely no reason to resist pharmacological help. We know a lot of folks who try hard never to take drugs, preferring instead to tough out discomfort on their own. When it comes to depression, that would be a terrible mistake. When you're suffering unrelenting despair, it is unlikely to go away all by itself. For reasons we don't understand, brain biochemistry seems to change. Correcting the imbalance that brings on depression is not something you can do easily by yourself. You may need a chemical life preserver that will help pull you out of the sinkhole.

But which medicines will be right for you? Normally we like to leave that sort of decision up to physicians, but some may not be aware that older people are especially vulnerable to antidepressants. Such drugs can accumulate in the body. **Vivactil** is particularly likely to build up and should probably be avoided. Drugs like **Amitril**, **Elavil**, **Endep**, **Janimine**, **Surmontil**, **Tofranil**, and **Vivactil** may make you feel confused, mentally foggy, and forgetful. Other side effects include dry mouth, dizziness, sedation, weight gain, constipation, sexual dysfunction, blurred vision, urinary difficulties, and weakness.

Fortunately, many of these side effects tend to diminish over time. Drowsiness, sedation, and weakness often disappear after several weeks. And since it usually takes that long for these medications to begin to go to work in the first place, a little patience is important during the first month or so of therapy. If six weeks go by and you're still down in the dumps, or if side effects are unbearable, contact your physician and start discussing alternatives.

One adverse reaction that you may not notice for several months is weight gain. It is not uncommon with such drugs, but is rarely mentioned. Doctors still don't know if this happens because of increased appetite, a craving for sweets, or a change in metabolism. Whatever its origin, weight gain can have serious consequences, not just physically, but also psychologically. Feeling fat doesn't boost your self-esteem. Dry mouth is often considered a minor annoyance, but it can have a major effect on one's quality of life. Not only that, dentures may stop fitting and the jaw may ultimately be affected.

Drugs such as **Norpramin** and **Pertofrane** (desipramine) and **Desyrel** (trazodone) are less likely to cause many of these "anticholinergic" side effects, and forgetfulness may not be as much of a problem either. **Desyrel** can cause considerable drowsiness, but if taken at night that may be an aid in falling asleep.

A new antidepressant, **Prozac** (fluoxetine), may also be helpful for some older people. It too is much less likely to cause dry mouth, constipation, weight gain, sexual difficulties, urinary retention, sedation, dizziness, and forgetfulness. If anything, this drug tends to cause weight loss, especially when pounds were added while on other antidepressants. **Prozac** may be mildly stimulating, however, and cause some jitteriness or insomnia. For people who are feeling lethargic and droopy, this energizing effect could be welcome. On the other hand, if you suffer from insomnia or tend to be nervous and uptight, **Prozac** may be inappropriate. Other side effects include nausea and diarrhea. **Prozac** is exciting because it is less likely to cause confusion, forgetfulness, sleepiness, or weight gain, but also because it is less likely than most other antidepressants to interact with medications for other problems. **Prozac** was finally approved by the Food and Drug Administration at the end of 1987 and arrived on pharmacy shelves early in 1988.

Another new antidepressant, still in the testing phase, is **Wellbutrin** (bupropion). Like **Prozac**, this drug appears to promote weight loss rather than weight gain. **Wellbutrin** also has been reported to stimulate sexuality and restore functioning that has been diminished by other medications. As with **Prozac**, the person taking **Wellbutrin** is more likely to feel stimulated or even a little anxious, instead of drowsy and confused. Dry mouth, urinary retention, constipation and the like are uncommon with **Wellbutrin**, but insominia may be a problem for some people. **Wellbutrin** was approved by the FDA in December 1985. But before it was actually put on sale, the manufacturer, Burroughs

Wellcome, voluntarily recalled the drug. A small study designed to test the benefits of **Wellbutrin** against an eating disorder called bulimia produced some alarming statistics. Four out of 50 women taking the drug experienced seizures. That incidence (8 percent) was high enough to scare the FDA into demanding further tests. Burroughs Wellcome resisted, insisting that thousands of patients had taken the drug safely and that the actual incidence of seizures was comparable to that of other antidepressants.

Until August of 1987, **Wellbutrin** languished in limbo. But an agreement between the company and the FDA allowed for further testing to resolve the seizure controversy once and for all. The results were to become available in late 1988. If the risk of seizures is low enough, doctors should be able to prescribe **Wellbutrin** sometime in 1989.

Until newer and better drugs become available, we will have to make do with what's available. Besides **Norpramin**, **Pertofrane**, and **Desyrel**, another option is a whole different class of antidepressants—the MAO (monoamine oxidase) inhibitors. **Parnate** (tranylcypromine) and **Nardil** (phenelzine) may be especially helpful for older people who are anxious as well as depressed.[10] Side effects to be wary of include dizziness when standing up quickly, weight gain, headaches, jitteriness, forgetfulness, and sexual difficulties. Some foods are dangerous with MAO inhibitors like **Parnate** and **Nardil** because they contain tyramine, a substance that could make blood pressure rise dramatically when combined with these drugs. Stay away from the following high-tyramine-containing foods: aged cheese (Brie, Camembert, cheddar, Gruyère, Parmesan, etc.), sour cream, yogurt, bologna, pepperoni, salami, summer sausage, dried fish, pickled herring, chicken liver, avocado, banana, canned figs, chocolate, caffeine, beer, ale, Chianti wine, and sherry. Refer also to the list of high-tyramine foods on page 74 And, of course, check with your physician and pharmacist about any other food or drugs to avoid while taking this kind of medicine.

No matter which antidepressant your doctor prescribes, make sure she follows the old saying, "Start low, go slow." To avoid undue side effects, older people often need lower doses of anti-anxiety agents, sleeping pills, and antidepressants.[11,12] Nondrug approaches to dealing with nervousness or sleeping problems should always be the first line of attack.

Things to Remember

1. Anxiety, stress, tension—no matter what you call it, a case of "nerves" can be awful. But a quick fix with sedatives, tranquilizers, or anti-anxiety agents is no cure. When drugs like **Ativan**, **Centrax**, **Dalmane**, **Halcion**, **Librax**, **Librium**, **Paxipam**, **Restoril**, **Serax**, **Tranxene**, **Valium**, and **Xanax** are taken for more than six or eight months, some people experience unpleasant withdrawal symptoms if their medicine is discontinued abruptly. "Gradual tapering off" may translate into weeks and months of reducing the dosage. Support from patient and caring health professionals is crucial.

2. Nondrug coping strategies for anxiety include listing your worries, talking them out, and seeking solutions whenever feasible. Professional help can sometimes be worth the investment if the counselor is skilled and sensitive. Exercise, music, relaxation, involvement with others, and self-help groups can all contribute to your sense of well-being.

3. There may be times when it is appropriate to take an anti-anxiety drug for one's entire life. But risks of falls and fractures must be taken into account in older people. Antidepressants and antipsychotics also increase this danger.

4. Sleeping difficulties are not uncommon as we age. As long as you're not uncomfortable, don't worry about fewer hours of sleep. If insomnia is making you miserable, however, try nondrug approaches first: cut back on caffeine, watch out for certain prescription drugs, forgo nightcaps, exercise earlier in the day, soak in the tub, avoid afternoon naps, have some warm milk and cookies, avoid exciting TV viewing before bedtime, don't worry about falling asleep, listen to relaxation tapes.

5. Depression can be drug-induced. If you suspect your medicine is dragging you down, ask your doctor if an alternative exists that will be less likely to affect your nervous system.

6. Some antidepressants can make you feel foggy, forgetful, and drowsy. **Norpramin**, **Pertofrane**, **Prozac**, and **Wellbutrin** (at this writing, still on hold at the FDA) may be less likely to cause such problems. **Desyrel** may be helpful at night when drowsiness is less likely to be unwelcome.

References

1. Huff, Barbara B., ed. *Physicians' Desk Reference*, 41st ed. Oradell, N. J., Medical Economics, 1987, p. 2070.
2. Vita-Herne, J., et al. "Another Case of Alprazolam Withdrawal Syndrome." *Am. J. Psychiatry* 142:1515, 1985.
3. "Review of Alprazolam Withdrawal Reaction." *Physicians' Drug Alert* 7:35, 1986.
4. Busto, Usoa, et al. "Withdrawal Reaction After Long-term Therapeutic Use of Benzodiazepines." *N. Engl. J. Med.* 315:854–859, 1986.
5. Noyes, R., et al. "Seizures Following the Withdrawal of Alprazolam." *J. Nerv. Ment. Dis.* 174:50–52, 1986.
6. "Review of Alprazolam Withdrawal Reaction," op. cit.
7. Ray, Wayne A., et al. "Psychotropic Drug Use and the Risk of Hip Fracture." *N. Engl. J. Med.* 316:363–369, 1987.
8. Benson, Allan. "Ode to Propranolol." *N. Engl. J. Med.* 313:123, 1985.
9. Avorn, Jerry, et al. "Increased Antidepressant Use in Patients Prescribed β-Blockers." *JAMA* 255:357–360, 1986.
10. Salzman, Carl. "Clinical Guidelines for the Use of Antidepressant Drugs in Geriatric Patients." *J. Clin. Psychiatry* 46:38–44, 1985.
11. Feighner, John P., and Cohn, Jay B. "Double-Blind Comparative Trials of Fluoxetine and Doxepin in Geriatric Patients with Major Depressive Disorder." *J. Clin. Psychiatry* 46[3, Sec. 2]:20-25, 1985.
12. Salzman, op. cit.
13. Lakshmanan, Mark, et al. "Effective Low Dose Tricyclic Antidepressant Treatment for Depressed Geriatric Rehabilitation Patients: A Double-blind Study." *J. Am. Geriatr. Soc.* 34:421–426, 1986.

8

Helping Your Heart

It used to be that if a doctor diagnosed clogged coronary arteries he struck fear into a patient's heart. Today, AIDS, cancer, and Alzheimer's disease scare us a lot more. Coronary bypass procedures are almost assemblyline operations. Angioplasty—inflating a balloon inside a coronary artery to reduce atherosclerosis—is becoming routine.

No one gets too worried these days if a friend or relative has a heart attack. A common question might be, "Will I have enough time to send a card before he gets out of the hospital?" Since we all know people who have survived heart attacks and gone on to live long and productive lives, it's hard to take a "coronary" as seriously as we used to. A heart attack no longer seems like a death sentence.

Over the last two decades deaths from heart disease have declined an impressive 30 to 40 percent.[1,2] The drop in deaths from strokes has been even more dramatic. We are eating healthier foods, smoking less, exercising more, and controlling blood pressure better than ever. That's the good news.

The bad news is that almost one million people still die each year from cardiovascular disease. About 350,000 heart attack victims don't even make it to the hospital.[3] Strokes affect another 500,000 people annually, often leaving the survivors crippled, depressed, and unable to resume a normal, productive life. We can do better!

Lowering Lipids

Cholesterol, lipid, fat—whatever you call the stuff, it's nasty, right? Well, not so fast. You will discover in Chapter 10 that there are good fats (olive and fish oil) and bad fats (the saturated kind found in coconut and palm oil and in marbled red meat and bacon). There is also good cholesterol (HDL, or high-density lipoprotein cholesterol) and bad cholesterol (LDL, or low-density lipoprotein cholesterol). And don't forget VLDL (very-low-density lipoprotein cholesterol). Confused? Stay put, the story gets even more complicated than that. Now scientists are all excited about apolipoproteins (apo A-1 is a good guy and apo-B can be a villain).

All right, let's give you the straight and skinny on cholesterol so it makes some sense. Say you eat the all-American lunch—a burger and fries plus an extra-thick milk shake, and maybe chocolate chip cookies for dessert. The fat in the food gets carried by your bloodstream to your liver. There the body converts a lot of that saturated fat into cholesterol. You must have cholesterol to make hormones and cell walls and other good stuff. Even if you somehow managed to completely avoid cholesterol in your diet your body would still make it from fat in your food.

In order to get the cholesterol from your liver to the parts of the body where it's to be used, the body needs a special protein "postman." The problem, as every schoolchild knows, is that oil and water don't mix. Since blood is mostly water and cholesterol is oily (actually waxy), you would have a devil of a time making a delivery unless the cholesterol got special packaging. That's where LDL comes in (low-density lipoprotein, remember?). It's the cholesterol carrier from the liver to body tissues. When LDL cholesterol arrives at its destination, that apo-B protein we mentioned rings the bell and transports the cholesterol into the cells.

After the cholesterol has done its job it becomes "used," sort of like tired old motor oil that has to be thrown out. For this to happen you need another protein (apo A-1), which extracts the old cholesterol from the cells and hands it over to our hero HDL. This HDL postman wraps up the used cholesterol and carries it back to the liver for garbage disposal.

Researchers now believe that the relationship between the

different HDL and LDL postmen and apo proteins has a lot to do with who will come down with atherosclerosis.[4-6] The more HDL cleaner-upper in your blood, the better off you are. While diet and exercise can have an important influence on these cholesterol carriers, so can heredity.

Ever wonder why some people live to a ripe old age while regularly indulging in fried eggs and sausage for breakfast, slathering butter on bread, gorping down steaks for dinner, and pigging out on ice cream for dessert, and on top of that doing virtually no exercise—while others exercise and eat carefully and still end up with heart attacks? Scientists suspect the explanation may be in the genes.

Take Winston Churchill. He smoked, avoided physical exertion, and loved to eat rich foods. He had as stressful a job as ever could be imagined, and yet with all that he lived to the age of 92. James Fixx was the quintessential athlete. He ran ten miles a day, was in great shape, and followed a prudent diet. He died at age 52 of a heart attack while jogging in Vermont.

The autopsy showed that Jim Fixx had severe coronary artery disease. One important blood vessel "was plugged to pinprick size—on the order of 97 to 99 percent. In addition, the right coronary artery was 80 to 85 percent occluded, or blocked— another severe narrowing. The third coronary artery was 40 to 50 percent shut."[7] And what about tennis star Arthur Ashe? He was a professional athlete in absolutely superb shape. No extra fat on that body. He suffered not one, but two, heart attacks before he reached the age of 40. Then there was the case of the two sisters:

> **Experience told the doctors the two patients shouldn't have heart disease. They were young women, just 31 and 29 years of age, and their overall cholesterol levels were normal. Yet there in the black and white of the X-rays was clear evidence that the coronary arteries of both patients—two sisters—were almost totally clogged ...**
>
> **Using techniques that didn't exist as recently as five years ago, they finally tracked the problem to the genes. Specifically, they tracked it to a gene on the tip of the 11th pair of chromosomes in each cell of the two sisters' bodies.**
>
> **The gene normally makes a protein [apo A-1] that**

enables blood to remove used cholesterol from tissues and carry it off for disposal. But in both sisters the gene wasn't working. Their blood never
picked up the cholesterol—and thus didn't show an
elevated reading. Meanwhile, the used cholesterol
piled up day after day in the tissues and artery
linings.[8]

The scientist who discovered the genetic defect responsible for
the sisters' heart disease, Dr. Jan Breslow, speculates that "the
Churchills of the world, we presume, have a genetic protection
against heart attack, whereas the Arthur Ashes have a genetic
susceptibility."[9]

Does that mean that you just give up and leave your destiny to
your genes? Of course not. The vast majority of us lie somewhere
between the Churchills and the Fixxes of this world. What we eat
and drink is very important. (For a discussion of beneficial foods,
see Chapter 10). Exercise, cigarettes, and drugs also influence
our lipids. Some medications raise blood fats in a bad way while
others lower them. How you live your life *does* make a difference!

Cracking Down on Cholesterol

By now you are probably feeling totally confused, what with
HDLs and LDLs and apo A-1s and apo-Bs and goodness knows
what else. While the story of heart disease is terribly complex,
we'll try to simplify things so that you can take some numbers to
the bank and really use them. For the moment, most cardiologists
seem to be relying on total cholesterol and HDL levels to determine people's risk of heart attacks. Lots of studies suggest that
the lower your total cholesterol and the higher your HDL levels,
the better off you are.[10,11]

But how low should those cholesterol levels be? Just a few
years ago doctors were pretty lenient. A middle-aged man with a
cholesterol of 250 was considered more or less normal. Most
doctors looked the other way if he climbed to 270, and they
didn't really start to worry until his cholesterol went over 300.
Today, however, most cardiologists believe that anyone with
cholesterol levels that high is in very big trouble.

Until 1987, cholesterol guidelines from the NIH (National Institutes of Health) were broken down by age. People 20 to 29 years of age with total cholesterol levels above 200 were considered at "moderate risk." Those between 30 and 39 were at such risk if their total cholesterol was over 220, and for people over 40 the cutoff was 240.[12]

The most recent guidelines, however, apparently do not take age into account. Instead, they call for all adults to somehow get their total cholesterol levels below 200. Cholesterol readings from 201 to 239 are now classified as "border line," requiring further testing and dietary treatment, and anyone with a level over 240 is now considered at high risk regardless of age, and is a candidate for drug treatment to get those blood fats under control.[13]

Our goal in this chapter is to help you get your risk down as low as possible. Over 60 million Americans have one or more forms of heart or blood vessel disease,[14] and almost one million people die of cardiovascular disease in this country each year. But perhaps the new guidelines are too stringent for people over 60. A reasonable target level probably should be 210 or lower.[15]

So the lower your cholesterol levels, the better off you are. Well, most of the time that's true. But let's not forget our old friend HDL cholesterol. Remember him? He's the good guy—the garbage disposal for used cholesterol. The more of this high-density lipoprotein cholesterol in our blood, the less likely we will develop coronary artery disease and heart attacks. Doctors generally feel happy when our HDL cholesterol levels are greater than 45. In fact, the HDL number may be more meaningful than total cholesterol.

Someone with a total cholesterol of 180 might feel quite proud of himself. But if his HDL levels were only 25, that individual would be at far greater risk of heart disease than the person with a total cholesterol of 220 who had an HDL level of 65.

Let's try and make it a little easier. Doctors now favor the ratio of total cholesterol to HDL cholesterol as a more accurate indicator of risk than either number alone. Anything below a four to one ratio of cholesterol to HDL is thought to be pretty darn good and represents a low risk of coronary artery disease. So someone with a total cholesterol of 200 and an HDL level of 50 would have a four to one ratio and be in good shape. A five to one ratio represents some risk (for example, a total cholesterol of 225 and an HDL of 45). If your total cholesterol-to-HDL-cholesterol ratio is six to one, the red flags start going up, and over seven to one (say 250 to 35) "probably means coronary artery disease is already present."[16]

If you really want to get sexy, you can calculate an LDL cholesterol to HDL cholesterol ratio. Here a ratio of less than three to one is good. A ratio between three and five is moderate, and if the ratio of LDL to HDL is over five, you're in big trouble.[17] How can you use all these numbers that we've been throwing around so fast and furious? First, keep a diary of your blood fats. We'll call it your "lipid profile." Having your own records is useful because laboratories are notorious for screwing up cholesterol measurements, especially HDL cholesterol.[18]

> When a physicians' group in 1985 asked 5,000 of the nation's top laboratories to run cholesterol tests on identical samples, nearly half produced results that a leading expert calls "unacceptable." Some labs weren't even close.
>
> In the test, the College of American Pathologists sent each lab a sample with a known cholesterol value of 262.6 milligrams per deciliter. The laboratories came back with reports ranging from 101 to 524 . . .
>
> Patients who falsely test low may forgo diet or drug regimens that their doctors otherwise would prescribe. Patients who falsely test high may face the unpleasant side effects of cholesterol-lowering drugs, to say nothing of an unnecessary cost of up to $125 a month.[19]

What this means is that neither you nor your physician should go nuts just because you come up with one high cholesterol reading. After all, it could easily be laboratory error. That's why you'll need a number of tests over months and years to get an accurate overview.

You are going to have to get involved! We're going to ask you to track your cholesterol levels, just as you keep track of your bank balance. First, you will snow your doctor with your new interest and knowledge. Second, you will have a much better idea of your dietary progress. It makes no sense to watch what you eat if you never see the fruits of that labor. You will also be able to assess the effects of medications on your cholesterol levels (more about that in a while). Finally, you will get a better sense of what's going on inside your arteries.

If you really want to impress your physician, you can ask her to simultaneously send your blood to several different labs. Tell her that you've read there are often mistakes and you would like to do some cross-checking. Sure, it will cost a little more, but keep in mind that a false result could land you on drugs that would be a whole lot more expensive.

Then, make sure your doctor gives you all the lab numbers—total cholesterol, HDL cholesterol, and LDL cholesterol. Every time you have a blood test run, get those numbers and then write them down in your **Personal Lipid Profile**. Just divide total cholesterol by HDL cholesterol to find that ratio (lower than 4.5 is good) and LDL by HDL to come up with your LDL/HDL ratio (lower than 3 is good). Here is an example and also a blank form for filling in your own values.

Personal Lipid Profile

Date:	7/11/85	3/17/87	5/6/88		Goal
Total cholesterol	240	220	200		210 or lower for people over 60
HDL	30	36	40		40 to 45 or higher*
LDL	180	174	160		150 or below, the lower the better*
LDL/HDL/ratio	6	4.8	4		3 or less
Total cholesterol/ HDL ratio	8	6.1	5		4.5 or less

*These numbers are somewhat arbitrary, as actual goals vary with age, sex, and laboratory.

Personal Lipid Profile

Date:					Goal
Total cholesterol					210 or lower for people over 60
HDL					40 to 45 or higher*
LDL					150 or below, the lower the better*
LDL/HDL/ratio					3 or less
Total cholesterol/ HDL ratio					4.5 or less

*These numbers are somewhat arbitrary, as actual goals vary with age, sex, and laboratory.

Feel free to photocopy the blank form so you can have additional copies available. If you would like to order a larger-size **Personal Lipid Profile**, send $1 per copy plus $1 for postage and handling along with your name and address, clearly printed or typed, to Graedons' People's Pharmacy, Personal Lipid Profile, P.O. Box 52027, Durham NC 27717-2027.

You also might want to send some to friends and relatives. We emphasize the relatives because, quite honestly, we have a hidden agenda here. We're going to be absolutely straight with you. If you're over 70 and have had angina for years, or maybe a heart attack or two, school is pretty much out. We still want you to eat healthy food and keep an eye on the cholesterol levels, but don't count on undoing what's already been done. Your children and grandchildren, however, need to take immediate action to keep their coronary arteries as clean as possible. You probably already know a lot more than they do about blood fats just by having read this far. So loan them this book, send them a **Personal Lipid Profile**, and tell them to get cracking before it's too late.

Okay, now you know more or less where you stand with regard to your lipids. If your total cholesterol is under 200 and your HDL cholesterol is over 45, you are sitting pretty. Thank your parents for passing along their good genes and thank yourself for eating sensibly. If, on the other hand, your cholesterol is consistently up above 240 and your HDL cholesterol is under 40, you'd better take some executive action now!

Read Chapter 10 for a list of good healthy foods. Things like olive oil, fish, onions, garlic, oatmeal, lentils, carrots, Chinese tree fungus, and even a little wine now and again can all have a positive effect on your blood lipids. If you lose excess weight, exercise, and cut back on ciggies, you'll be pleased with the results. Needless to say you will also want to cut back on saturated fats of all kinds. That includes nondairy creamers in your coffee.

Cashing Out on Coffee

Speaking of coffee, it might be a very good idea to cut back considerably on your coffee intake. There is mounting evidence that moderate to heavy coffee drinking can do some unpleasant things to your cholesterol levels, not to mention your heart.[20-23] Several years ago Norwegian researchers "examined the relation between coffee consumption and levels of serum total cholesterol, high-density-lipoprotein (HDL) cholesterol, and triglycerides in a population of 7,213 women and 7,368 men between the ages of 20 and 54 years."[24]

They found that moderate coffee drinkers (four cups or less a day) had cholesterol levels five percent higher than non-coffee-drinkers. People who drank five to eight cups a day had cholesterol levels 9 percent higher, and the real java junkies (more than nine cups of coffee daily) saw their cholesterol levels zoom over 12 percent compared to non-coffee-drinkers. The Norwegian doctors concluded that:

> **Our attitude toward the present finding of a coffee–cholesterol association changed from suspicious surprise to guarded belief as the relation seemed to withstand all adjustments. The association is strong and consistent, and its magnitude makes coffee one of the strongest determinants of serum cholesterol levels in the present population.[25]**

Researchers at Stanford University also studied the effects of coffee on "bad" LDL cholesterol and that other villain, apolipoprotein B (apo-B). They looked at male university employees between the ages of 30 and 55 and sure enough, they found that "coffee intake exceeding 2 1/2 to 3 cups per day is associated with elevated plasma concentrations of three well-established cardio-vascular risk factors: total cholesterol, LDL-cholesterol, and apo B concentrations in a sample of sedentary, middle-aged men."[26]

A team of investigators at the University of Texas, San Antonio, also confirmed a coffee–cholesterol link. They studied 1,288 women and 923 men. Here's what they found:

> **In women, mean serum cholesterol rose from 205.3 mg/dl among those who drank less than a cup of coffee a day to 223.1 mg/dl among those who drank eight or more cups. Serum cholesterol rose from 206.7 mg/dl in men who drank less than a cup of coffee daily to 226.5 mg/dl among those who consumed eight or more cups. Similarly, serum LDL rose from 128 mg/dl to 135.8 mg/dl in women and from 132.4 mg/dl to 147 mg/dl in men.[27]**

Those kinds of elevations are enough to take people at mild risk of heart disease and push them into the moderate range. To be fair, we have to admit that some studies do not confirm the coffee–cholesterol connection, but the majority do. Researchers are still arguing, though, as to whether it's the coffee or some other factor that's responsible. It may be for example, that coffee drinkers put cream in their coffee and it's the cream that's responsible. Or perhaps coffee drinkers are generally more stressed than non-coffee-drinkers and it's the stress that does it, or maybe they smoke more cigarettes. Then again, coffee drinkers may eat fattier foods and their diet is the culprit.

Most of these theories have been shot down. For example, neither the cream in the coffee, nor stress, nor cigarettes appear to be behind this cholesterol effect.[28] In fact, it would be hard to explain away a follow-up Norwegian study in which a group of men with high cholesterol levels were randomly assigned to three groups. One group drank coffee as usual. The second group gave up coffee for five weeks and then resumed coffee as usual. The third group abstained for ten weeks.

And the envelope please: Right again. The fellows who gave up coffee for five weeks saw their cholesterol levels "fall significantly." But when they went back to drinking coffee, their levels rose. Those who kept off java for ten weeks continued to see total cholesterol come down. The authors concluded that this positive effect could not have been psychosomatic or due to some unconscious dietary change:

> **The observed reduction in total cholesterol during abstention from coffee was considerable, uniform, and independent of concomitant use of sugar and cream, cigarette smoking, or tea drinking. Otherwise the diet was not monitored. The participants were, however, chosen from a group of hypercholesterolaemic men [with very high cholesterol levels] who, for the previous three years, had been trying without much success to reduce their cholesterol concentration by dietary means. The possibility that any sudden, unconscious dietary change could lead to a fall in cholesterol concentration of the magnitude seen here was therefore unlikely.[29]**

Okay, we hear you starting to mutter. Enough with the coffee and cholesterol already. So we'll switch to decaffeinated and everything will be hunky-dory. Would it were so simple. A number of these researchers examined tea and cola intake on the assumption that if the caffeine in coffee were to blame, they would see a similar elevation in cholesterol in tea and cola drinkers. Not so. The tea drinkers and cola guzzlers did not appear to have increases in cholesterol like the coffee drinkers.[30–34] This has led some investigators to conclude that caffeine is not the villain in causing elevated cholesterol levels.[35,36] While the last word is not in on the caffeine question, it's entirely possible that drinking only decaffeinated coffee may not eliminate cholesterol problems. Tea, on the other hand, might be a good substitute if a hot beverage is an important part of your routine.

Okay, by now we should have convinced you that moderate to heavy coffee consumption has been associated with elevations of the bad cholesterol actors in our play. But that's not all coffee does. It can also cause irregular heart beats and affect blood pressure. Several well-controlled, double-blind studies have demonstrated a significant increase in blood pressure.[37,38]

You may have noticed that we still haven't mentioned a thing about heart disease itself. If you have a good denial system, you could even come up with all sorts of excuses as to why these results don't mean anything. And after all, you only drink a couple or three cups a day, right? Get ready, here comes the smoking gun!

Dr. Caroline Bedell Thomas is a brilliant physician. Back in 1946 she came up with an extraordinary idea. She would study male medical students who graduated from Johns Hopkins Medical School from 1948 to 1964. Dr. Thomas had them fill out questionnaires on family history, how much coffee they drank and how many cigarettes they smoked. They were also given physicals and checked for blood pressure and cholesterol. Then she and her colleagues tracked these men for the next 19 to 35 years. Every five years they got follow-up questionnaires to see if they had changed their coffee drinking or smoking habits over the intervening years. Each year the researchers checked their doctor–subjects to see if any men had become sick or had died.

Believe us when we tell you that this kind of study is as good as it ever gets. There's research, and then there's research. Some of what ends up in the pages of medical journals these days is hardly fit for the bottom of the bird cage. But this Johns Hopkins coffee study, which was published in the *New England Journal of Medicine* in 1986, produced the kind of results you take to the bank.

Here is what the investigators found:

> **At the 30-year follow-up, subjects who drank five or more cups of coffee per day had the highest cumulative incidence of coronary disease (10.7 percent), as compared with subjects who drank three to four cups per day (8.8 percent), one to two cups per day (5.1 percent), or no coffee (1.6 percent) . . .**
>
> **Our findings support a strong, positive, dose-responsive, independent association between the risk of clinically evident coronary disease and coffee consumption in this group of predominantly non-smoking men. The magnitude of the relation sug-**

gests a twofold to threefold elevation in the risk of clinical coronary disease associated with heavy coffee drinking . . .

The present findings are in agreement with two earlier case-control studies that showed a twofold to threefold increased risk of acute myocardial infarction [heart attack] associated with heavy coffee consumption just before hospital admission for myocardial infarction. Also consistent with the present study was a recent report of a positive association between coffee consumption and mortality due to coronary disease among a predominantly nonsmoking cohort of male Seventh-Day Adventists who were followed for 21 years. In three other prospective studies, coffee was positively and significantly associated with coronary events or mortality.[39]

And there you have it. To us the evidence is clear that regular heavy coffee consumption elevates cholesterol levels, raises the risk of coronary artery disease, and ultimately increases the likelihood of heart attacks. Not all researchers would agree. And even Dr. Thomas and her colleagues dub their results "preliminary." Nevertheless, we are being extra cautious. Although we love a good cup of coffee as much as anyone, we are restricting our intake to one or two cups a day (max). And most of the time we have tea instead. In our household coffee has become something of a luxury, like an especially sinful dessert reserved for special occasions.

Drugs That Affect Cholesterol Levels

Coffee isn't the only "drug" to raise cholesterol. Your doctor isn't likely to mention this, but a surprising number of prescription medications, especially those for hypertension, actually boost cholesterol levels.

Stop and think about that statement for a minute. It's a bombshell. No, that's actually an understatement. It's more like a nuclear warhead just waiting to explode. Blood pressure medicines are supposed to *lower* your risk of coronary artery disease and heart attack. And yet some of the most commonly prescribed antihypertensives raise total cholesterol, dastardly LDL cholesterol, and triglycerides. What's even more depressing is that they lower our benefactor, the good HDL cholesterol that is supposed to act as the garbage man to keep our arteries clean. All this means is that while blood pressure may drop, the risk of heart attack could be climbing.

In other words, it's like driving with your foot on the brake and the gas pedal at the same time. The benefits of lowering blood pressure may be partially, if not completely, undone by adversely affecting the total cholesterol/HDL lipid ratio that most cardiologists now believe is so crucial. You do realize that such words are heretical. The medical profession implores patients to take blood pressure medicine to ward off the "silent killer." While it seems true that these drugs do indeed lower the risk of stroke, the track record against coronary heart disease is not good.

Take the "Oslo Study," for example. Drs. Paul Leren and Anders Helgeland from Oslo, Norway, reported on ten years of research with 785 mildly hypertensive Norwegian men.[40] Half received medicine—hydrochlorothiazide (**HydroDIURIL**, **Oretic**, **Esidrix**, HCTZ) alone or in combination with propranolol (**Inderal**) or methyldopa (**Aldomet**). The other half did not receive medicine for their high blood pressure. This untreated "control" group suffered a higher incidence of strokes than the men on drugs, who definitely seemed protected. But those taking medications had significantly more heart disease and coronary deaths than their nondrug compatriots. Here are the doctors' stunning conclusions:

> **Hypertension is a well-established coronary risk factor. This has led to the expectation that lowering elevated blood pressure by means of drug therapy would be an effective preventive measure against coronary heart disease. In that respect, the results of the Oslo Hypertension Study are disappointing; however, they are consistent with other randomized, controlled hypertension drug trials with placebo or untreated control groups that have also failed to show a definite preventive effect of antihypertensive drug therapy on the incidence of coronary heart disease . . .**
>
> **The fact that antihypertensive drug therapy has**

no demonstrated effect on the incidence of coronary heart disease is a major health problem and a challenge to the medical profession. Although the reasons for this phenomenon are unknown, some speculations have been made. It has been suggested that the adverse metabolic effects of commonly used antihypertensive agents counteract the beneficial effect ascribed to a reduction in blood pressure ... Diuretics have been the most commonly used drugs in a majority of these trials, and several studies have shown these drugs have adverse effects on blood lipids [cholesterol] ...

The fact that a reduction in the incidence of coronary heart disease has not been correlated with the reduction in blood pressure achieved with antihypertensive drug therapy should provide immediate and widespread concern over the drugs currently used.[41]

Bingo! And it's not the only study that suggests such drugs do not protect against atherosclerosis. Australian and British researchers have also carried out large-scale research that shows the rate of heart attacks and coronary heart disease does not decrease when people are treated with diuretics, beta blockers (like **Inderal**) or methyldopa (**Aldomet**).[42,43]

So on the one hand, the risk of coronary heart disease is lowered by lowering high blood pressure, while on the other hand, that risk appears to be raised by raising bad cholesterol levels. Now if that isn't the most incredible double bind, we don't know what is. Not only do drugs like **Aldomet** or beta blockers like **Inderal** sometimes make people feel mentally foggy, fatigued, depressed, and forgetful, they may also muck up the ratio of bad cholesterol to good cholesterol.[44-48] Additional drugs that have been reported to have a negative effect sometimes on blood fats include other beta blockers (**Lopressor**, **Tenormin**), male hormones (anabolic steroids), thiazide diuretics (possibly less of a problem in older people), synthetic progestins (nonestrogenic female hormones), danazol (**Danocrine** for endometriosis and fibrocystic breast disease), etretinate (**Tegison** for psoriasis), and cigarettes.[49,50]

Don't Panic, Help Is on the Way

Okay, we know that by now you are probably feeling confused and perhaps even a tad angry. We have just hit you with a double whammy. You get to pick your problem—if you reduce the risk of stroke and congestive heart failure with blood-pressure-lowering drugs, you might possibly counterbalance those benefits by increasing the risk of coronary heart disease. What a dilemma. Well, let's see if we can't come up with a strategy to improve the odds.

First, **DO NOT** stop any medicine because of what you have just read. You definitely do not want to suffer a stroke or heart attack! Sudden discontinuation of any blood pressure treatment could lead to one or both. Not all blood pressure drugs affect cholesterol and not everyone reacts in a negative way to those that do.

Second, it is important that you have a blood test for total cholesterol, LDL cholesterol, triglycerides, and HDL cholesterol before you start on blood pressure treatment. That way you and your doctor can get some idea of your normal cholesterol levels B.D. (before drugs). Periodically after starting on medication you should have additional blood tests to see what effect the drugs are having on your lipid levels. Remember to record all this data in your **Personal Lipid Profile** (see page 207).

There is a very good possibility that your cholesterol levels won't become a problem. But if the ratio of total cholesterol to HDL cholesterol starts to climb over 5 or 6, you will want to sit down with your physician and have a very long heart-to-heart talk about your blood pressure treatment.

Third, there *is* good news. Not all blood pressure medications are created equal. Some do not seem to affect cholesterol adversely. And others may even produce positive changes. **Minipress** (prazosin), for example, lowers all the bad guys—total cholesterol, LDL cholesterol, triglycerides, and VLDL (very-low-density lipoprotein cholesterol).[51-53] There is even some preliminary data that suggest **Minipress** may increase the beneficial HDL cholesterol.[54,55] It may also neutralize the negative effects of diuretics. Side effects from **Minipress** are generally tolerable and often disappear with continued treatment. Be especially careful after the very first dose—it can cause severe dizziness and fainting. For this reason the very first time such a drug is taken should be at bedtime. Other things to watch out for include drowsiness, dizziness, headache, weakness, palpitations, nausea, and stomach pain.

So now you know you *can* almost have your cake and eat it too. That is, you can lower blood pressure and reduce your risk of stroke and heart failure without mucking up your cholesterol level. And **Minipress** isn't the only drug that's getting good reviews these days. There are quite a few other antihypertensive medications that don't louse up your lipid levels. Here is an up-to-date list that has us excited:

Blood Pressure Drugs That Don't Raise Cholesterol*

Brand Name	Generic Name
Adalat	nifedipine
Apresoline	hydralazine
Calan	verapamil
Capoten	captopril
Cardizem	diltiazem
Catapres	clonidine
Isoptin	verapamil
Lozol	indapamide
Minipress	prazosin
Normodyne	labetalol
Procardia	nifedipine
Sectral	acebutolol
Trandate	labetalol
Vasotec	enalapril
Visken	pindolol
Wytensin	guanabenz

*Ames, Richard P. "Metabolic Disturbances Increasing the Risk of Coronary Heart Disease During Diuretic-based Antihypertensive Therapy: Lipid Alterations and Glucose Intolerance." *Am. Heart J.* 106:1207–1214, 1983.

Ames, Richard P. "The Effects of Antihypertensive Drugs on Serum Lipids and Lipoproteins: I. Diuretics." *Drugs* 32:260–278, 1986.

Dzau, Victor J. "Evolution of the Clinical Management of Hypertension." *Am. J. Med.* 82(suppl 1A):36–43, 1987.

This table is not written in stone. As we learn more, some drugs will be dropped from the list while others will be added. Some of these medications are just "lipid neutral," meaning they neither raise nor lower cholesterol, while others actually seem to be somewhat beneficial. What you must understand is that it has only been within the last several years that researchers have started taking the cholesterol-raising or -lowering effects of drugs seriously. There is an awful lot of work yet to be done before anyone can give a stamp of approval to the "ideal" blood pressure medicine.

Lowering Cholesterol Chemically

Okay, let's assume you have done your best to get those cholesterol levels into the safe range. You've lost the spare tire, you've cut back on cigarettes and coffee, you exercise as much as the body comfortably permits, and you are eating sensibly. Let's also assume that your doctor has made sure none of the medicines you are taking adversely affects lipid levels.

And yet with all of that it's possible that cholesterol ratios could remain dangerously high. Don't forget those genes. Every once in a while the body conspires to undo all our good efforts. James Fixx and Arthur Ashe proved that point. But you don't have to follow in their footsteps. There are drugs that can lower cholesterol levels when all else fails.

There is, however, one big risk with lipid-lowering medications. Some people may assume they can return to their old dietary indiscretions as long as there's a pill that will undo the damage. Wrong! These drugs are not magic bullets that will allow you to pig out on pie, pizza, ice cream, and cheese cake. They can help people who can't get their cholesterol levels down through diet or who have a genetic defect that makes them susceptible to abnormally high cholesterol levels.

One of the oldest drugs for lowering elevated cholesterol is actually a vitamin—vitamin B_3 to be exact, otherwise known as niacin or nicotinic acid (**Nicobid**, **Nicolar**, and lots of generics). In a slightly modified form it is available as niacinamide. Niacin will knock down total cholesterol, LDL cholesterol, and triglycerides. Better yet, it raises our old buddy HDL cholesterol by up to

20 percent. One well-controlled study proved that niacin could lower the risk of repeat heart attacks; what's more, the benefits persisted almost a decade after people stopped taking it. All that from a simple vitamin.

The trouble is that to be effective you have to take a whole lot more than the recommended dietary allowance (12 to 20 mg). Doctors often prescribe 3,000 mg (3 grams) or more a day to lower cholesterol. At that dose many people experience itching, digestive tract upset, dry skin, headache, and perhaps most disturbing of all, flushing and tingling. (This side effect may be diminished by taking one aspirin tablet about 30 minutes before popping down the niacin.) More serious adverse reactions include liver abnormalities, elevated uric acid levels, and sugar imbalance. People with active peptic ulcer, liver disease, severe diabetes, or glaucoma should avoid this compound.

Lots of folks might give up on niacin for obvious reasons. That would be a shame. This vitamin is by far the cheapest treatment for elevated blood lipid levels—a month's supply of generic niacin from Bronson Pharmaceuticals (4526 Rinetti Lane, La Canada, CA 91011-0628) will run under $5. Most of the other drugs used to control cholesterol cost significantly more, sometimes over $100 per month. Some people have been very pleased with the results they got from niacin. One of our radio show listeners offered his testimony:

> I am a 64-year-old man in good health who quit smoking 18 years ago. I quit eating eggs four years ago, eat meat no more than three times a week, and swim at least three times a week. But my cholesterol was still around 250. My doctor said that wasn't too bad for my age, and he wasn't worried about it, so I shouldn't either, but I was. He insisted that the medication to bring cholesterol down was terrible and expensive.
>
> My wife heard Dr. Art Ulene on the "Today" show highly recommend a book, *The 8-Week Cholesterol Cure*, by Robert Kowalski. I went on the program, which includes niacin and oat bran, and after 6 weeks I had to see my doctor about something unrelated.
>
> While I was there, I asked him to check my cho-

> lesterol. It was 174. The last time it was taken it
> was 248. My HDL went from 50 to 80, so my ratio of
> total cholesterol over HDL is now 2.18 whereas
> before it was 5. I'm inclined to believe that the
> mere mention of the word "vitamin" to an M.D.
> causes an immediate rejection and a closed mind.
>
> I have found that half an aspirin tablet takes care
> of the flushing. The cost, using time release cap-
> sules, is 30 cents per day. Haven't figured out the
> cost of the bran muffins we eat, but it might be
> about 30 cents also. Sure beats those high-priced
> drugs!!

Now that's pretty impressive. There's no guarantee everyone will get these kinds of results, but more and more doctors are looking at niacin as a first-line approach against elevated cholesterol. In combination with other drugs, it may be even more effective.

To be on the safe side, you probably should check in with your doctor before you start self-medicating with megadoses of niacin. You won't need a doctor's prescription, however, because niacin is available from mail order vitamin or pharmacy services or at any drugstore. Tablets range in size from 25 mg up to 1,000 mg. It is unclear how much people can benefit from low or intermediate doses (under 3,000 mg a day), but for someone who is exercising and watching his diet conscientiously, it is possible that a modest niacin supplement could make the difference in getting to an optimal total cholesteral/HDL ratio. There are reports that as little as 1,000 mg (1 gram) daily could be beneficial. This much niacin in a time-release form or spread throughout the day at mealtimes rarely results in troublesome side effects. If this doesn't work, larger doses can be tried (under your doctor's supervision of course). Or he may want to add another lipid-lowering drug to your regimen.

In recent years **Questran** (cholestyramine) and **Colestid** (colestipol) have become quite popular. A large ten-year study (Coronary Primary Prevention Trial, or CPPT) compared **Questran** to placebo in lowering cholesterol levels.[56,57] The 1,906 men in the **Questran** group started with cholesterols of 265 or greater. The drug lowered total cholesterol 8.5 percent and LDL choles-terol 12.6 percent compared to the men in the placebo group. More importantly, the drug lowered the incidence of heart attack or death from coronary heart disease from 8.6 percent in the untreated group to 7.0 percent in the **Questran** group.

Based on that research, lots of doctors have started prescribing **Questran** to patients with very high cholesterol levels. We have no doubt that lives have been saved as a result. But some physicians have pointed out that routine use of **Questran** may not be such a good idea. Dr. George V. Mann, a professor at Vanderbilt University School of Medicine, offers the following insights:

> **I would not recommend that all patients with high cholesterol levels be put on cholestyramine just because of the results of the CPPT [Coronary Primary Prevention Trial]. In the trial, there were 71 deaths in the placebo group, versus 68 in the treated group; the difference simply wasn't that significant.**
>
> **Moreover, cholestyramine is a difficult drug to take. I would encourage every physician who is considering using it to try taking it himself for a few days—just to see how bad it is.[58]**

When Dr. Mann says that **Questran** is a difficult drug to take, he isn't kidding. It comes as a powder that has to be dissolved in water. People complain that the drug leaves a gritty, grainy kind of aftertaste. In addition, **Questran** often causes constipation, heartburn, nausea, bloating, gas, flatulence, diarrhea, and loss of appetite. It also may interact with a number of drugs and vitamins (see page 288).

A slight increase in the incidence of digestive tract cancer cases was also reported in the CPPT study. This caused Dr. Michael F. Oliver, President of the British Cardiac Society, to comment:

> **I must say that I'm a bit disturbed about the incidence of gastrointestinal cancer in the cholestyramine-treated group. There were 21 cases of GI cancer in the cholestyramine group (including 8 deaths) versus 11 in the control group. I'm also disturbed by the 6 cases of cancer of the mouth and pharynx in the treated group.[59]**

Do you begin to get the idea that **Questran** leaves something to be desired? Now add to all that the cost—anywhere from $25 to over $120 a month, depending on the dose recommended by the doctor—and you can see why lots of folks have a hard time tolerating this drug.

Colestid (colestipol) is another cholesterol-lowering drug, similar in some respects to **Questran**. It made medical news when a major study, the Cholesterol Lowering Atherosclerosis Study (CLAS), found that **Colestid**, together with niacin and a low-fat diet, not only lowered cholesterol levels, but even reversed atherosclerosis.[60] An editorial in the *Journal of the American Medical Association* summarized the results: "A regimen of diet, colestipol hydrochloride, and niacin resulted in a 43 percent reduction in LDL cholesterol levels and a 37 percent increase in HDL cholesterol levels."[61] This is the most dramatic finding about coronary disease anyone has heard in years; bypass surgery has become widely used, but the problem is that the grafts tend to clog up with cholesterol-laden plaque after a few years, just as the original arteries had. In this study, bypass patients managed to keep their new blood vessels relatively clear and clean. In some cases there was actually marked improvement in overall coronary status.

Such success does not come easily, however. **Colestid** is granular and sandy-tasting and not much easier on the digestive tract than **Questran**. Constipation, bloating, nausea, heartburn, belching, gas, flatulence, and diarrhea are not uncommon. Rare but bothersome side effects include itching and skin rash, headache, dizziness, and arthritislike symptoms. A month's supply is about as expensive as **Questran**—running anywhere from $25 to $120, depending on the dose.

Another cholesterol-lowering drug is **Lorelco** (probucol). It is easier to put up with since it comes as a pill rather than a powder. Total cholesterol and LDL cholesterol are reduced by 10 to 15 percent. The trouble is that **Lorelco** also reduces good-guy HDL cholesterol proportionally more than it lowers bad-guy LDL cholesterol. The end result is that the lipid ratio may not be significantly improved. Once again we may be driving with one foot on the brake and the other on the gas pedal. This drug may also cause diarrhea, flatulence, nausea, and vomiting.

Lopid (gemfibrozil) is yet another drug for cholesterol. Next to niacin, this is the cholesterol drug we are most excited about. A study published in the *New England Journal of Medicine* (vol. 317, 1987, pp. 1237–1245) established that this drug could reduce heart disease by 34 percent. Over 4,000 Finnish men were followed for five years, and those on **Lopid** had noticeably fewer heart attacks, especially in the later years of the study.

Like niacin, **Lopid** reduces all the bad guys: triglycerides, LDL, and total cholesterol. Better yet, it raises HDL cholesterol. While it has some side effects, including stomach pain, diarrhea, nausea, vomiting, flatulence, dizziness, and blurred vision, the Finnish scientists found that the drug was well-tolerated overall and that digestive tract upset diminished after the first year. The only problem with **Lopid** is that it could possibly lead to a slight increase in the risk of gallbladder problems, though not as much as a similar medication called **Atromid-S** (clofibrate).[62]

Atromid-S was once quite popular. But a large long-term study sponsored by the World Health Organization (WHO) has cast a pall over **Atromid-S**. What happened was truly incredible. The men who received **Atromid-S** (instead of placebo) to lower their cholesterol levels had a death rate 47 percent greater than the men who got no medicine to lower their cholesterol.[63] Here was a case in which the cure was more dangerous than the disease. The men who took the drug had more cancer, gallbladder trouble, liver disease, digestive tract difficulty, and pancreatic problems than the men who got no medicine. Today, **Atromid-S** is reserved for rare patients rather than for routine treatment.

The latest development in the cholesterol contest is a brand new drug called **Mevacor** (lovastatin). It works by blocking an enzyme in the cholesterol-making chain of command and also seems to stimulate the liver to remove cholesterol from the blood more rapidly. People who suffer from a hereditary form of high cholesterol (hypercholesterolemia) have seen their total cholesterol and LDL cholesterol drop about 40 percent while taking **Mevacor**.[64,65] Now that's dramatic! Better still, the drug increases the good HDL cholesterol in the neighborhood of 5 percent.

People who do not suffer the genetic form of high cholesterol levels but still have elevated lipids (perhaps as many as 60 percent of Americans) also seem to benefit from **Mevacor**. For them the drop in bad cholesterol is between 32 and 39 percent.[66] And when **Mevacor** is combined with **Colestid**, the results are even better. Together, the drugs lowered LDL cholesterol almost 50 percent.[67]

Overall, a very impressive picture. But while the drug does seem to be better tolerated than many other anticholesterol compounds, some people have complained of flatulence, diarrhea, muscle tenderness, headaches, rash, itching, and insomnia. Of greater concern are reports of cataracts and changes in liver enzymes. Because **Mevacor** is still so new, it will take several years before we know if it will live up to Yale cardiologist Dr. Robert M. Stark's prediction that "It's going to be earth-shaking." Its widespread use will prevent "tens of thousands of heart attacks a year,"[68] but **Mevacor** will put a dent in most people's wallets. Depending on the dose and the drugstore, a month's worth could run roughly from $50 to nearly $200.

No matter what new miraculous medicines the drug companies come up with to lower cholesterol, the first and best approach to a healthy heart will always be diet and exercise. Losing weight, stopping cigarettes, eating heart-healthy (fish, olive oil, onions, garlic, oats, split peas), plus moderating alcohol intake, can go a long way to keeping the arteries clean. When all else fails, the drugs can be effective.

New Help for Hypertension

Next to controlling cholesterol, nothing gets more attention than reducing high blood pressure. It is, after all, another very important risk factor for stroke and heart disease. Pharmaceutical manufacturers are rapidly waking up to the fact that when it comes to treating hypertension, the quality of life has become as important as the quantity of life. Many of the newer antihypertensives lower blood pressure without causing depression, sedation, fatigue, nightmares, insomnia, impotence, asthma, cold hands and feet, forgetfulness, dizziness, dry mouth, or a host of other common side effects. It's too bad a lot of doctors aren't yet up to speed on some of these newer drugs.

Primum non nocere—first do no harm—is, as we have stated before, a key idea in the doctors' Hippocratic oath. Nowhere is this vow more important than in the treatment of high blood pressure, especially when it comes to older people. If the medicine makes people so dizzy they fall and break a hip, the doctor has certainly done no favors. If the antihypertensive drug raises bad cholesterol levels, increases the risk of coronary disease, makes someone impotent and depressed, it would be pretty hard to justify such treatment. And if the doctor is too aggressive in lowering blood pressure suddenly, he could precipitate a stroke.

Yes, we just dropped another bombshell. You read right. We know that lowering blood pressure is supposed to prevent strokes, but if doctors move too quickly to push blood pressure down in older people, they may actually cause a stroke. Now that's bizarre. In an effort to solve this apparent paradox, Dutch researchers carefully reviewed the cases of 30 nursing home patients who had experienced strokes or reduced blood flow to the brain soon after they were put on drugs to lower blood pressure.

Here is one poignant case history:

> **A woman aged 67 years used indapamide [Lozol] once daily for 2 weeks because of recently detected hypertension (earlier blood pressure level 170/90). A blood pressure of 210/120 was recorded and labetalol [Normodyne or Trandate] was added to the treatment. After 2 days the patient developed stroke and was admitted to hospital. Blood pressure at admission was 160/80. An infarction [clot] in the area of the right middle cerebral artery was diagnosed. After a few weeks she was transferred to a nursing home. There was no recovery from the left-sided hemiparesis [paralysis].[69]**

In reviewing all 30 cases the Dutch researchers found that almost all the patients had extremely high blood pressure that fell dramatically with drug treatment. In some cases pressure dropped as much as 53 percent. If high blood pressure is bad and causes strokes, why was lowering the extremely high blood pressure of these older people a danger?

The answer seems to lie with the changes that accompany aging. The brain, central as it is to our functioning, is well set up to protect itself against all sorts of insults. Let blood pressure fall, and the brain responds by widening the blood vessels and keeping blood pressure relatively constant. In people who have chronic high blood pressure, the point at which this mechanism comes into play is higher. But after about a 25 percent fall in blood pressure, the system has reached its limit in terms of making adjustments. After that, the brain is just getting less blood.

All this points to the need for caution when an older person with high blood pressure is started on drugs to lower that pressure. The trick is NOT to avoid treating high blood pressure, but simply to be aware that "easy does it." Using drugs whose action is milder, and using them gradually, in smaller doses, would appear to be the key to the safest treatment of hypertension in the elderly. Since people rarely develop high blood pressure overnight, the doctor shouldn't try to "cure" it that fast either.

In fact, doctors have been arguing for years about how high is too high and when to start treating high blood pressure in an elderly person. Part of the problem is that slapping a blood pressure cuff on doesn't always give an accurate readout of a senior's true pressure. One study found that the standard technique for measuring blood pressure gave a number that was 10 or more points too high in nearly 40 percent of the patients.[70]

Even if your doctor has an accurate idea of your true blood pressure, the criteria for treating people over 65 are different from those for people under 40. The 120/80 magic numbers that may be appropriate for a 30-year-old are too strict for someone over 65. Unless there are signs of organ damage, the Canadian Hypertensive Society doesn't worry about patients aged 65 to 74 until their blood pressure reaches 160/90 or thereabouts.[71]

Keep track of your own blood pressure. There are now some wonderful little digital machines on the market that make do-it-yourself monitoring pretty easy. For an in-depth discussion of high blood pressure, including measurement and treatment, you might want to take a look at "Hacking Away at High Blood Pressure," in *Joe Graedon's The New People's Pharmacy #3* (Bantam Books, $8.95). In that chapter, not only do we offer a number of nondrug alternatives for blood pressure control, we evaluate some of the most commonly prescribed medicines.

These days we are most excited about the calcium channel blockers. Drugs like **Cardizem** (diltiazem), **Calan** and **Isoptin** (verapamil), and **Adalat** and **Procardia** (nifedipine) can effectively lower blood pressure in older people, perhaps even better than the beta blockers.[72,73]

What makes these drugs so popular is that they have fewer side effects than many of the other more traditional antihypertensives. Sedation, forgetfulness, fatigue, depression, cold hands and feet, nightmares, and insomnia don't seem to be a problem with these drugs, and sexual side effects may also be less likely. Better still, the calcium channel blockers don't muck up cholesterol levels like many of the beta blockers. So they bring blood pressure down without increasing the risk of coronary artery disease. There is even some hope they may help prevent atherosclerosis.

There's an added bonus with calcium channel blockers. They are effective against angina and certain irregular heart rhythms. In addition, there is preliminary data that suggest some of these drugs may be beneficial against asthma, migraine headaches, and Raynaud's phenomenon (a painful circulatory problem that affects the hands, especially during cold weather).

Constipation is a fairly common side effect of **Calan** and **Isoptin**. It's annoying, but controllable. **Procardia** and **Adalat** can produce a rapid drop in blood pressure at the very first dose, so initially extra caution is necessary in case of dizziness. After that, the most common complaints are swelling of the ankles and feet (edema) and flushing. A few people experience headaches.

In our opinion, **Cardizem** is one of the best tolerated of the calcium channel blockers. Side effects are generally uncommon, though people with heart disease require careful monitoring by a physician. For a detailed review of these drugs and many other medications like **Aldomet** (methyldopa), **Apresoline** (hydralazine), **Catapres** (clonidine), **Dyazide** and **Maxzide** (hydrochlorothiazide, triamterene), **Minipress** (prazosin), and the beta blockers (**Blocadren, Corgard, Inderal, Lopressor, Normodyne, Tenormin, Trandate,** and **Visken**), pick up *Joe Graedon's The New People's Pharmacy #3.*

An Ace in the Hole

One class of compounds, the ACE (angiotensin-converting enzyme) inhibitors are catching on like gangbusters. **Capoten** (captopril) and **Vasotec** (enalapril) do not appear to raise cholesterol levels, so they too offer some advantages over the beta blockers.[74] Although these enzyme inhibitors are probably a little less effective against hypertension in older people than the calcium channel blockers, they are beginning to carve out a strong niche, especially if a patient also has congestive heart failure.

Harvard cardiologist Dr. Victor Dzau has gone so far as to call them "the gold standard in the treatment of chronic heart failure."[75] Given that there are growing concerns about the benefits and risks of digitalis-type medications (digitoxin, digoxin, **Lanoxin**) for this condition,[76] these enzyme inhibitors will doubtless continue to pick up steam.

Both **Capoten** and **Vasotec** are less likely than many other blood-pressure-lowering drugs to cause unwanted side effects. In one study in which **Capoten** was compared to **Aldomet** (methyldopa) and **Inderal** (propranolol), it was found that the enzyme inhibitor scored much higher when it came to "quality of life."

> **... patients taking captopril, as compared with patients taking methyldopa, scored significantly higher on measures of general well-being, had fewer side effects, and had better scores for work performance, visual–motor functioning, and measures of life satisfaction ... Patients taking captopril reported fewer side effects and less sexual dysfunction than those taking propranolol and had greater improvement on measures of general well-being.[77]**

Although **Capoten** and **Vasotec** are well tolerated, there are some side effects to be aware of. Temporary loss of taste while on **Capoten** can be annoying. Skin rash and itching are occasionally quite a problem for some patients. A dry cough has also been reported and may be unpleasant enough that some people will have to stop the medicine. Although relatively rare, side effects such as dizziness and light-headedness can be serious for older people.

Most important of all, be alert for signs of kidney damage. During the first months of treatment blood and kidney function should be monitored frequently. Insist that your doctor order serum creatinine and BUN tests. Kidney failure has been reported when **Vasotec** was combined with certain diuretics.[78] Potassium-sparing diuretics (**Aldactone, Dyazide, Maxzide, Moduretic**), potassium supplements (**Kay Ciel, Kaochlor, Kaon, K-Lor, KATO, Klorvess, Klotrix, K-Lyte, K-Tab, Micro-K,** and **Slow-K**), and salt substitutes (**Adolph's Salt Substitute, Morton Salt Substitute, NoSalt,** etc.) can also be a problem when combined with **Capoten** or **Vasotec**. Potassium may build up in the body to dangerous levels, and could lead to abnormal heart rhythms, difficult breathing, confusion, weakness, fatigue, anxiety, and numb or tingling sensations in the hands, feet, and lips.

Putting It All into Perspective

We've covered a lot of territory in this chapter, and if there's one message we'd like to have you remember, it's this: Watch out when doctors start treating numbers instead of patients. Just getting blood pressure down isn't worth a damn if in the process you don't improve your chances of escaping coronary artery disease or a heart attack. Blood pressure and cholesterol *are* important risk factors for heart disease, but we need to keep risk in perspective.

Dr. Peter Lamy, a world renowned expert in geriatric pharmacology and nutrition offers the following anecdote:

> **A 73-year-old man told me this story. His father is a 93-year-old immigrant from Russia, who likes pickles, salted herring, borscht, and other good, salty foods. His new physician cautioned him strongly: "How can you eat those foods? Don't you know they contain salt, and salt is a risk factor?" The 93-year-old man, trained to respect authority, was in fact told not to eat the foods he likes because of the potentially life-shortening risk factor. What we have now is a not-so-healthy 93-year-old because he does what the physician tells him and a 73-year-old son trying to get his father to eat.[79]**

If we can all make it to the ripe old age of 93 in good health and with an appetite for pickles, salted herring, and borscht, we've earned the right to a few indulgences. In fact, we should be congratulated! There's a lot we don't know about heart disease and high blood pressure, especially when it comes to older people. We hope that the information in this chapter has been helpful, not just in reducing risk factors but also in improving the quality of life. And despite all the nasty things we said about coffee, if you've made it to 93 in good health, don't worry too

much about giving up one of life's little pleasures. Who knows,
you might have inherited those same wonderful genes that kept
Winston Churchill going for so long.

Things to Remember

1. Heart attacks still kill more people each year
   than any other disease. How you live your life
   can make a difference to the health of your
   heart.

2. Cholesterol comes in many different forms—good
   guys and bad guys. The more HDL (high-density
   lipoprotein) cholesterol and apo A-1 you have,
   the happier your heart will be. Total cholesterol,
   LDL (low-density lipoprotein) cholesterol, VLDL,
   triglycerides, and apo-B are villains, and the
   less you have the better. The best way to assess
   your cholesterol status is to divide total cholesterol by HDL cholesterol. A ratio below 4.5 is
   good news.

3. Things that are bad for overall cholesterol ratios
   include smoking, overweight, lack of exercise, a
   diet high in saturated fat, coffee, and a number
   of other drugs. Some beta blockers and many
   diuretics, as well as certain other blood pressure
   medicines, may mess up blood fats while they
   lower blood pressure.

4. Things that are good for overall cholesterol ratios include fish oil, cold water fish, olive oil,
   onions, garlic, oatmeal, fiber, chromium, moderate alcohol consumption, cutting back on cigarettes, losing weight, exercise, and **Minipress**.
   Other medications that are either lipid "neutral"
   or beneficial can be found on page 217.

5. When all else fails, cholesterol-lowering drugs
   may be appropriate. Niacin and **Lopid** may be
   better for older people. **Mevacor** is the newest

of all the compounds, but it's still too early to tell whether it will prevent coronary artery disease and help prevent heart attacks.

6. Untreated hypertension can lead to strokes, but in older people, sudden dramatic drops in blood pressure may have the same effect. The old motto, "start low, go slow," is crucial. For elders, starting doses should be low and should be increased gradually with careful monitoring every step of the way.

7. New medications are revolutionizing the treatment of high blood pressure by preserving quality of life while simultaneously lowering risk factors. Calcium channel blockers (**Adalat, Calan, Cardizem, Isoptin, Procardia**) offer distinct advantages over the older beta blockers. ACE inhibitors (**Capoten** and **Vasotec**) are coming on strong, especially for people who suffer from congestive heart failure.

8. Take an active role in helping your heart. Keep track of your own blood pressure and monitor your cholesterol levels. Don't forget to fill in your **Personal Lipid Profile** (page 207).

References

1. American Heart Association, Jan. 19, 1987.
2. Marwick, Charles. "A Nation of Jack Sprats? Cholesterol Program to Stress Dietary Changes." *JAMA* 256:2775–2779, 1986.
3. *1987 Heart Facts*, American Heart Association.
4. Silberner, Joanne. "Artery Clogging and APO-B." *Science News* 131:90–91, 1987.
5. Hegele, Robert A., et al. "ApolipoproteinB-Gene DNA Polymorphisms Associated with Myocardial Infarction." *N. Engl. J. Med.* 315:1509–1515, 1986.
6. Bishop, Jerry E. "Scientists Are Learning How Genes Predispose Some to Heart Disease." *Wall Street Journal* 207(26):1, Feb. 6, 1986.
7. Pietschmann, Richard J. "Probing Death on the Run." *Runner's World*, Nov., 1984, pp. 38–94.
8. Bishop, op. cit.

9. Ibid.
10. Gordon, D. J. (for the Lipid Research Clinics Follow-up Study). "Plasma High-density Lipoprotein Cholesterol and Coronary Heart Disease in Hypercholesterolemic Men." *Circulation* 72:111–185, 1985.
11. Watkins, L. O., et al. (for the M.R.F.I.T. Research Group). "High-density Lipoprotein Cholesterol and Coronary Heart Disease Incidence in Black and White M.R.F.I.T. Usual Care Men." *Circulation* 71:417A, 1985.
12. Kashyap, Moti L. "Hyperlipidemia: Current Recommendations and Methods for Making an Accurate Diagnosis." *Modern Medicine* 55(2):56–60, 1987.
13. National Institutes of Health, Expert Panel on Detection, Evaluation, and Treatment of Blood Cholesterol in Adults. "Guidelines." U.S. Government Printing Office, Oct. 5, 1987.
14. *1987 Heart Facts*, op. cit.
15. "Wrap-up: Cholesterol." *University of California, Berkeley Wellness Letter* 1(10):4–5, 1985.
16. Pietschmann, op. cit.
17. Kashyap, op. cit.
18. Superko, H. Robert, et al. "High-density Lipoprotein Cholesterol Measurements." *JAMA* 256:2714–2717, 1986.
19. Bogdanich, Walt. "Inaccuracy in Testing Cholesterol Hampers War on Heart Disease." *Wall Street Journal* 209(23):1–24, Feb. 3, 1987.
20. Haffner, S.M., et al. "Coffee Consumption, Diet and Lipids." *Am. J. Epidemiol.* 122:1–12, 1985.
21. Curb, J.D., et al. "Coffee, Caffeine and Serum Cholesterol in Japanese Men in Hawaii." *Am. J. Epidemiol.* 123:648–655, 1986.
22. Mathias, S., et al. "Coffee, Plasma Cholesterol, and Lipoproteins: A Population Study in an Adult Community." *Am. J. Epidemiol.* 121:896–905, 1985.
23. Klatsky, Arthur L., et al. "Coffee, Tea and Cholesterol." *Am. J. Cardiol.* 55:577–578, 1985.
24. Thelle, Dag S., et al. "The Tromso Heart Study: Does Coffee Raise Serum Cholesterol?" *N. Engl. J. Med.* 308:1454–1457, 1983.
25. Ibid.
26. Williams, Paul T., et al. "Coffee Intake and Elevated Cholesterol and Apolipoprotein B Levels in Men." *JAMA* 253:1407–1411, 1985.
27. "Coffee Consumption Linked with Rising Serum Cholesterol." *Medical World News* 26(15):23–24, Aug. 12, 1985.
28. Curb, J.D., et al. "Coffee, Caffeine, and Serum Cholesterol in Japanese Men in Hawaii." *Am. J. Epidemiol.* 123:648–655, 1986.
29. Forde, Olav Helge, et al. "The Tromso Heart Study: Coffee Consumption and Serum Lipid Concentrations in Men with Hypercholesterolaemia: A Randomised Intervention Study." *British Med. J.* 290:893–895, 1985.
30. Curb, op. cit.
31. Klatsky, op. cit.
32. Naismith, D.J., et al. "The Effect in Volunteers of Coffee and Decaffeinated Coffee on Blood Glucose, Insulin, Plasma Lipids, and Some Factors Involved in Blood Clotting." *Nutr. Metab.* 12:144–151, 1970.

33. Little, J.A., et al. "Coffee and Serum Lipids in Coronary Heart Disease." *Lancet* 1:732–734, 1966.
34. Kark, J.D., et al. "Coffee, Tea, and Plasma Cholesterol: The Jerusalem Lipid Research Clinic." *Br. Med. J.* 292:699–704, 1985.
35. Haffner, Steven M., et al. "Coffee Consumption, Diet, and Lipids." *Am. J. Epidemiol.* 122:1–12, 1985.
36. "Coffee Consumption Linked with Rising Serum Cholesterol." *Medical World News* 26(15):23–24, Aug. 12, 1985.
37. Robertson, David, et al. "Effects of Caffeine on Plasma Renin Activity, Catecholamines and Blood Pressure." *N. Engl. J. Med.* 298:181–186, 1978.
38. Pincomb, G.A., et al. "Effects of Caffeine on Vascular Resistance, Cardiac Output and Myocardial Contractility in Young Men." *Am. J. Cardiol.* 56:119–122, 1985.
39. LaCroix, Andrea Z., et al. "Coffee Consumption and the Incidence of Coronary Heart Disease." *N. Engl. J. Med.* 315:977–982, 1986.
40. Leren, Paul; and Helgeland, Anders. "Coronary Heart Disease and Treatment of Hypertension: Some Oslo Study Data." *Am. J. Med.* 80(suppl 2A):3–6, 1986.
41. Ibid.
42. "The Australian Therapeutic Trial in Mild Hypertension. Report by the Management Committee." *Lancet* 1:1261–1267, 1980.
43. Medical Research Council Working Party. "MPC Trial or Treatment of Mild Hypertension: Principal Results." *Br. Med. J.* 291:97–104, 1985.
44. MacMahon, Stephen W., et al. "Plasma Lipoprotein Levels in Treated and Untreated Hypertensive Men and Women: The National Heart Foundation of Australia Risk Factor Prevalence Study." *Arteriosclerosis* 5:391–396, 1985.
45. MacMahon, Steven W.; and Macdonald, Graham J. "Antihypertensive Treatment and Plasma Lipoprotein Levels." *Am. J. Med.* 80(suppl 2A):40–47, 1986.
46. Ames, R.P. "The Effects of Antihypertensive Drugs on Serum Lipids and Lipoproteins. II Non-diuretic Drugs." *Drugs* 32:335–357, 1986.
47. Ames, R.P. "Metabolic Disturbances Increasing the Risk of Coronary Heart Disease During Diuretic-based Antihypertensive Therapy: Lipid Alterations and Glucose Intolerance." *Am. Heart J.* 106:1207–1214, 1983.
48. Lean, A.S., et al. "Plasma Lipid Changes with Aldomet and Propranolol During Treatment of Hypertension." *Circulation* 66(suppl 2):37, 1982.
49. Glueck, Charles J. "Nonpharmacologic and Pharmacologic Alteration of High-density Lipoprotein Cholesterol: Therapeutic Approaches to Prevention of Atherosclerosis." *Am. Heart J.* 110:1107–1115, 1985.
50. Ames, Richard P., op. cit.
51. Leren, Helgeland, op. cit.
52. Ames, R. P., op cit.
53. Glueck, op. cit.
54. Kokubu, T., et al. "Effect of Prazosin on Serum Lipids." *J. Cardiovasc. Pharmacol.* 4(suppl 2):S228–S232, 1982.

55. Velasco, M., et al. "Effects of Prazosin and Alphamethyldopa on Blood Lipids and Lipoproteins in Hypertensive Patients." *Eur. J. Clin. Pharmacol.* 28:513–516, 1985.
56. Lipid Research Clinics Program. "The Lipid Research Clinics Coronary Primary Prevention Trial Results: I. Reduction in Incidence of Coronary Heart Disease." *JAMA* 251:351–364, 1984.
57. Lipid Research Clinics Program. "The Lipid Research Clinics Coronary Primary Prevention Trial Results: II. The Relationship of Reduction in Incidence of Coronary Heart Disease to Cholesterol Lowering." *JAMA* 251:365–374, 1984.
58. Conference Call. "The Lipid-lowering Trial: Where Do We Go from Here?" *Modern Medicine* 52(3):267–269, 1984.
59. Ibid.
60. Blankenhorn, David H., et al. "Beneficial Effects of Combined Colestipol-Niacin Therapy on Coronary Atherosclerosis and Coronary Venous Bypass Grafts." *JAMA* 257:3233–3240, 1987.
61. Passamani, Eugene R. "Cholesterol Reduction in Coronary Artery Bypass Patients." *JAMA* (editorial) 257:3271–3272, 1987.
62. Dr. Robert Buchanan, Personal communication, Mar. 10, 1987.
63. Oliver, M., et al. "WHO Cooperative Trial on Primary Prevention of Ischaemic Heart Disease with Clofibrate to Lower Serum Cholesterol: Final Mortality Follow-up." *Lancet* 2:600–604, 1984.
64. "More Optimism for Lipid Lowerer." *Medical World News* 28(1):86, 1987.
65. "Merk's Mevacor (Lovastatin) Will be Targeted at Hypercholesterolemics at High Risk: Advisory Panel Recommends Approval, Frequent Liver Monitoring." *F-D-C Reports* 49(8):3–5, Feb. 23, 1987.
66. The Lovastatin Study Group II. "Therapeutic Response to Lovastatin (Mevinolin) in Nonfamilial Hypercholesterolemia: A Multicenter Study." *JAMA* 256:2829–2834, 1986.
67. Vega, Gloria Lena; and Grundy, Scott M. "Treatment of Primary Moderate Hypercholesterolemia with Lovastatin (Mevinolin) and Colestipol." *JAMA* 257:33–38, 1987.
68. Waldholz, Michael. "New Cholesterol Drug Enhances Merck's Role As a Leader in Research." *Wall Street Journal* 208(123):1–16, Dec. 23, 1986.
69. Jansen, P.A.F., et al. "Antihypertensive Treatment as a Possible Cause of Stroke in the Elderly." *Age and Ageing* 15:129–138, 1986.
70. Hla, Khin Mae, et al. "Overestimation of Diastolic Blood Pressure in the Elderly: Magnitude of the Problem and a Potential Solution." *J. Am. Geriatr. Soc.* 33:659–663, 1985.
71. Alexander, James K. "Managing the Elderly Patient with Hypertension." *Modern Medicine* 55(1):58–67, 1987.
72. Kirkendall, Walter M. "Treatment of Hypertension in the Elderly." *Am. J. Cardiol.* 57:63C–68C, 1986.
73. Cressman, Michael D., et al. "Geriatric Hypertension Controversies: Uses of Newer Agents." *Geriatrics* 40(11):53–65, 1985.
74. Dr. John Irvin, Personal communication, Mar. 11, 1987.

75. Dzau, Victor. "Evolution of the Clinical Management of Hypertension: Emerging Role of 'Specific' Vasodilators as Initial Therapy." *Am. J. Med.* 82(suppl 1A):36–43, 1987.

76. Mulrow, Cynthia D., et al. "Reevaluation of Digitalis Efficacy: New Light on an Old Leaf." *Ann. Int. Med.* 101:113–117, 1984.

77. Croog, Sydney H., et al. "The Effects of Antihypertensive Therapy on the Quality of Life." *N. Engl. J. Med.* 314:1657–1664, 1986.

78. Tatro, David S., ed. "Enalapril/Diuretics Interaction: Acute Renal Failure." *Facts and Comparisons Drug Newsletter* 6(8):61, 1987.

79. Lamy, Peter P. "Nutrition, Drugs and the Elderly." *Currents: The Journal of Food, Nutrition & Health* 1(2):21–28, 1985.

9

Clarifying the Osteoporosis Controversy

Ten years ago, most people had never even heard of osteoporosis. But with all the media attention it has received recently, almost everyone knows of the danger of weakened bones leading to fractures in the elderly. Broken bones are unquestionably serious: in 1985, there were 247,000 broken hips in older Americans.[1] Some of these unfortunate people, perhaps as many as one sixth of them, die within several months.[2] Many others never are able to get around by themselves again as they once did, and require wheelchairs or assistance to go anywhere. That's what makes broken hips even more serious than broken wrists or "crush" fractures in the spine—nothing to be sneezed at either, and probably associated with the same process of bone loss as hip fractures.

Unfortunately, when it comes to keeping bones strong, we still don't know nearly enough. For example, few people realize that there are actually two different "profiles" of osteoporosis. One affects only women, with bone loss actually beginning before menopause in most cases, but speeding up noticeably after the body stops producing estrogen. "Dowager's hump" usually results from this process. But there also appears to be an inexorable loss of bone with age, so that men as well as women in their eighth and ninth decades simply do not have bones as strong as youngsters'. As a consequence, elderly people of either sex are more vulnerable to broken bones even without risking their necks on ski slopes or diving boards. Can this bone loss be slowed somehow, or weak bones strengthened? Those are the questions everyone would like to answer.

Calcium Comes on Strong

Public awareness of osteoporosis has gotten a big boost from the advertising industry. While scientists study the problem and journalists treat it as a "hot" health story for newspapers, magazines, and even television, advertisers have discovered it's a gold mine. Perhaps no aspect of osteoporosis has gotten more attention than calcium supplements to keep bones strong and healthy. Drug manufacturers have run ads on TV and in magazines showing the contrast between a vibrant, active young woman and a withered, bent-over old lady. The implication is clear: To avoid the same fate, be sure to gobble down the calcium supplement being advertised. No wonder everyone is jumping on the calcium bandwagon before it passes them by.

The only trouble is, this bandwagon has been behaving more like a steamroller. Back in 1982, calcium supplements were a $47 million market, which sounds impressive enough.[3] But lately lots of new products touting their calcium content have appeared on drugstore and supermarket shelves, whether they are calcium supplements such as **Suplical**, calcium-containing antacids like **Calcitrel**, or diet aids like **Fibre Trim**,[4] or even whole wheat bread and diet cola. Manufacturers are spending millions on advertising, and Americans are shelling out $166 million a year for such products.[5] By 1990 that figure will probably skyrocket to over $200 million.[6] From the ads alone, it would be easy to infer that all a woman has to do to avoid a problem with brittle bones is to take her calcium supplement religiously. If only life were that simple!

You see, although we often tend to think of bone as being as solid and unchanging as a stone, it is actually living tissue. It is constantly being "remodeled," and, if you've ever remodeled your home, you already know that includes a fair amount of tearing down while the building is going on. There are at least 20 different chemicals that can affect this whole process, and many of them, including hormones secreted by the thyroid and parathyroid glands, estrogen (a female hormone), and vitamin D (also a type of hormone), are found naturally in the body.[7] In fact, the more scientists learn about osteoporosis, the more complicated the bone story seems to get.

It's tempting just to say, "Pass the calcium," and try not to worry about anything else. But don't be lulled into a false sense of security. The most recent research suggests that osteoporosis is not a "simple calcium-deficiency disease."[8] Taking calcium after menopause may make only a relatively small difference in the strength of the bones,[9] and there's even a possibility calcium supplements may sometimes be counterproductive.

The calcium wagon got its first shove when Robert Heaney did some careful metabolic studies and found that around menopause women's bodies don't hold on to calcium very well. To offset what they are losing, it seems that women need to take in 1,200 to 1,500 mg of calcium daily. Otherwise, like a bank account that has been overdrawn, they may have a "negative calcium balance." Since we know bones have a lot of calcium in them, it seems unwise to let the body "throw it away," but relatively few women actually eat foods supplying that much calcium.

To get 1,200 mg of this mineral, one could simply drink four glasses (8 ounces each) of low-fat milk every day. But for a lot of folks, that's easier to say than to swallow. The older we get, the less likely it is that our intestines still produce enough lactase, an enzyme that digests milk sugar, to handle that much milk. The result? Undigested milk sugar, or lactose, can be the source of bloating, cramps, diarrhea, or gas, uncomfortable symptoms that prevent some people from enjoying milk or even ice cream. Not too long ago, the only alternative would have been to give up on milk and drink something else—but whether you substituted soda, beer, apple juice, or plain old tap water, you wouldn't find anything with the same nutritional value as milk. Nowadays there are several products that tackle this difficulty so that someone who wants to drink milk can do so with less risk of untoward "side effects."

It is now possible to find milk on grocery store shelves that has been pretreated so that most of the sugar it contains has already been broken down. In our area, there are at least two brands, **Lactaid** and **Enjoy**. In other regions of the country, there are probably other brand names, but whatever it's called in your store, it will be labeled "lactose-reduced milk." Most likely it will contain only about 30 percent as much lactose as it did when it left the cow. Many people who can't handle ordinary milk may find that with these treated brands they can enjoy the benefits of this beverage without the bellyache.

In addition, the folks at **Lactaid** put out some other lactose-reduced dairy products, such as ice cream, cream cheese, and cottage cheese, although it's difficult to argue that cream cheese or ice cream, tasty as they may be, should have an important role in anyone's nutritional plan, and cottage cheese is not an especially rich source of calcium. But another **Lactaid** product, called **CalciMilk**, has been introduced in response to the interest in calcium. This low-lactose milk is fortified with calcium, so that just two glasses daily, instead of four, provide about 1,000 mg of this important mineral.

Now, what if you don't find high-calcium, low-lactose milk, by any brand name, in your supermarket? If you want to be able to drink regular milk, or eat foods made with it, check in with your pharmacist. Lactose-digesting enzymes are available in pills designed to be taken with the meal or snack containing milk. These products, under the names **Lactrase** and **Lactaid**, are moderately helpful, but if your system is quite sensitive to the effects of lactose, they may not be good enough.[10] One option to test is doubling the dose; if that doesn't work, it's time to hunt down some other way to get your daily calcium. The active cultures in yogurt digest lactose themselves, once they get inside your body and warm up to a good working temperature, so yogurt may be an option for some lactose-intolerant people. There is 400 mg of calcium in an 8-ounce container of plain yogurt, but it's hard to imagine spooning down three of those a day, every day.

Does a calcium supplement make sense? It may, but we're considerably less enthusiastic about this than we were a few years ago. It doesn't really look as though high doses of this mineral will turn out to be a magic bullet against osteoporosis, but scientists are uncovering other potential benefits of this common mineral. Calcium intake may have a role in maintaining normal blood pressure,[11,12] and recent research has indicated that precancerous abnormalities in the cells lining the colon may revert to normal when high-risk people take calcium supplements for several months.[13]

If you are already getting your three or four daily servings of milk, yogurt, cheese, or other dairy products, and perhaps have an unusual enthusiasm for canned salmon or sardines, complete with their bones, or for tofu (at least it doesn't have any bones!), you won't need a supplement. Don't worry if you don't love all the dark green leafy veggies like collard, turnip or beet greens, spinach, kale, and chard: some very sophisticated research using spinach that had been grown with radioactive calcium in its leaves has shown that the calcium in spinach is hardly absorbed at all.[14]

If the closest you get to milk is a little cream in your coffee, though, you might consider a supplement as "insurance" to make sure you are getting at least the recommended dietary allowance of 800 mg per day. Often a supplement providing 1,000 mg daily is recommended, unless you have experienced calcium-containing kidney stones or are at risk for them. But once a person is on the "wiser" side of forty, so to speak, it's not a bit clear that extra calcium is very protective. There have been, for example, at least eight studies in which postmenopausal women took calcium supplements. According to osteoporosis expert Dr. B. Lawrence Riggs of the Mayo Clinic, "half of these trials have shown a partial slowing of bone loss, whereas the others have shown little or no effect."[15] There is even some new evidence suggesting that calcium supplements (not dietary calcium) may interfere with other nutrients important for bone strength.

In any event, don't expect a calcium supplement to keep your bones strong on its own. Although there has been a lot of emphasis on calcium for mature women, this mineral is probably most critical in the diet during childhood and adolescence when bones are growing and the initial density of the bone is being established.[16,17] Several studies have shown that calcium supplements after menopause may help slow bone loss, especially from the arms and legs, but estrogen seems to be considerably more effective.[18,19] One bone scientist, Dr. Richard Mazess of the University of Wisconsin, has even characterized calcium supplements as "the laetrile of osteoporosis."[20] Though other researchers are less outspoken, many seem to agree with Dr. Riggs that "the advertisers are way out ahead of the scientific evidence."[21] Perhaps the calcium bandwagon is rolling out of control.

A state-of-the-art study completed recently on menopausal women in Denmark shows that although calcium is better than nothing, it can't come close to estrogen in preventing bone loss.[22] The researchers used the latest fancy technology to measure the density of bone very accurately several times over the course of two years in three groups of women who had just gone through menopause—14 who were given a calcium supplement of 2,000 mg a day, 11 who were given estrogen, and 11 who were given a placebo. The women taking calcium did lose less of the mineral from the hard outer shells around the tubelike long bones. But the supplements didn't have any impact on the spongelike bone tissue inside the tubes (trabecular bone), which is also the most important type of bone in the spine. Estrogen stopped the loss of both kinds of bone.

New evidence suggests that calcium is only part of the story. Other minerals, including both magnesium and manganese, may also be crucial. Magnesium is sometimes supplied in combination with calcium in a supplement, but calcium supplements seem to interfere with the absorption of manganese. This little-known mineral, the "Cinderella" of osteoporosis, is an essential element in an important bone-remodeling enzyme.[23] High levels of iron and magnesium, as in supplements (or in spinach), can also mess up the body's ability to absorb manganese.[24] But Mother was right after all. Milk is one of the better sources of manganese in our diet, and for reasons no one appears to understand very clearly, the calcium in milk doesn't interfere with absorption of manganese. Other sources of manganese in the diet include nuts and beans, whole grains, and eggs. If you judge your diet's not strong on these foods and decide to go for a manganese supplement, for goodness sake don't take it along with your iron or calcium pills. It would be a shame to pay a pretty penny for something like that, and then just waste it completely.

The "Sunshine Vitamin" Gets Under Your Skin

Manganese and magnesium aren't the only nutrients to consider. Vitamin D is also essential for the body to absorb and utilize calcium properly. This vitamin can be found in some foods (especially fish, cheese, and fortified milk), but the most fascinating thing about it is that human skin, when it is exposed to sunlight, manufactures this vitamin from a common "precursor" chemical. Usually, this doesn't require prolonged sunbathing. A baby with fair skin can make a day's supply of D in about half an hour of playing outside. But as we get older, the skin's ability to change the raw materials into vitamin D decreases by as much as 75 percent.[25]

If you were getting most of your calcium from milk products (with the occasional can of sardines thrown in), you'd be getting a fair bit of vitamin D at the same time. But if you were taking a calcium supplement—say, **Tums**, and staying out of the sun to protect your skin from damage, you just might be wasting the calcium supplement because you can't absorb it or use it without enough vitamin D. So if you are taking a calcium supplement and sitting inside or in the shade, you may need to make an extra effort to get vitamin D in your diet, either through fortified breakfast cereals (the "bran" brands seem to be fortified most), dairy products, fish, or a vitamin supplement. It would be wise to aim for the recommended dietary allowance of 400 IU as a minimum. (*IU* stands for "international units": there are 100 of these standard measures of vitamin D in a cup of fortified milk.)

Just to add another wrinkle, vitamin D from the skin or from food must be changed into more active forms, first by the liver and then by the kidney.[26] An ailing kidney has a harder time making this conversion; it seems plausible that the gradual decline in kidney function that often comes with aging might also affect the conversion of vitamin D to its active form (1,25-vitamin D). If older kidneys do have trouble with this biochemical task, it could help to explain why older people seem to need more calcium to stay "in balance." It doesn't take very much 1,25-vitamin D in the intestine to pull calcium into the body, but having too little interferes with the absorption of calcium, whether from the diet or from supplements.[27]

The kidneys are also crucial in handling another nutrient that complicates the picture in osteoporosis. When people eat a lot of protein, their kidneys kick more calcium out of the body.[28] It's been suggested that the high-protein American diet may contribute to osteoporosis.[29] Very likely steak lovers, egg addicts, and others whose diets are rich in protein need to pay a little attention to getting more calcium.

Sorting Out the Supplements

If you decide to take a calcium supplement, you may want to know about the many different kinds of pills you have to choose from. You see, calcium doesn't come in a "pure" or elemental form in a pill. The calcium supplements you'll find, like the calcium in food, have the mineral "hooked up" to other chemicals with names like carbonate, lactate, or gluconate, and these compounds all have different calcium contents. They may also differ in how readily the body can break them down, pick up their calcium, and put it to work. According to Dr. Louis Avioli of Jewish Hospital in St. Louis, calcium supplements vary widely in their bioavailability; he has found that some health food versions are virtually indestructible. [30]

Calcium carbonate, which is found in **Tums**, **Os-Cal**, **Caltrate**, and many other supplements, is generally the least expensive (especially if you hunt for a "house brand"). It should usually be taken with meals to make sure that it is absorbed well,[31] and if several tablets are needed, it would be best to space them throughout the day.[32] But don't take your calcium with foods high in oxalates or phytates: whole wheat bread; brown rice; barley; whole grain cereals, including bran cereals, shredded wheat, and oatmeal; lima beans; nuts and peanuts; beets; rhubarb; spinach; and corn.

The drawback to calcium carbonate is that it is sometimes constipating. Also, daily intake of this supplement should be limited to 4 or 5 grams or less. (This would provide 1,600 or 2,000 mg pure calcium.) Some women, like one reader's mother, may run a risk if they get carried away by the ads for calcium supplements and "go for broke":

> Is there such a thing as too much calcium? With all
> the publicity about osteoporosis, my mother's got-
> ten very nervous about brittle bones. She's gulping
> down almost a package of Tums a day for the extra
> calcium, but I am worried that she may be overdoing.

Our reader was right to worry about her mother. A person
getting more than 4 or 5 grams of calcium carbonate daily may be
vulnerable to "milk-alkali syndrome," a metabolic imbalance that
could have a serious effect on the kidneys. A whole package of
Tums would supply 6 grams of calcium carbonate—definitely
more than anyone should be using on a regular basis. As the table
below shows, however, **Tums** is a relatively inexpensive source
of calcium as a supplement.

Calcium lactate pills have less total calcium, so you have to
take more of them. To get the best absorption of this calcium
supplement, you should take it with milk[33]—of course, if milk
gives you digestive trouble, calcium lactate will, too. Calcium
gluconate is least likely to cause tummy trouble—but it is only 9
percent calcium, so to get enough to count for anything, you
could end up gulping an awful lot of pills. Calcium citrate is
absorbed better than calcium carbonate, especially in older people who make less stomach acid.[34] Advertising claims for calcium
citrate suggest that it may also be less irritating to the digestive
tract.

As you can see from the table below, there are some very
significant differences in price among the various calcium supplements. You'd spend $690.24 a year if you relied on Lilly's calcium
gluconate, but if you shopped around for the cheapest generic
calcium carbonate, your calcium supplement might cost you as
little as $15.84 for a year's supply, or even less.

Calcium Supplements

Type	Calcium in Pill	Number of Tablets for 1 Gram Calcium	Cost/Month*
Calcium carbonate			
BioCal	500 mg	2	8.85
Calcitrel	234 mg	5	7.04
Cal-Sup	300 mg	4	8.98
Caltrate 600	600 mg	2	6.99
Os-Cal 500	500 mg	2	6.99
Suplical	600 mg	2	7.58
Tums	200 mg	5	3.29
Titralac	168 mg	6	8.98
Generic (Bronson)	500 mg	2	1.32
Generic (Nature Made)	500 mg	2	5.99
Calcium gluconate			
Generic (Lilly)	93 mg	11	57.52
Calcium lactate			
Generic (Lilly)	84.5 mg	12	26.03
Generic (Nature Made)	84.5 mg	12	6.67
Generic (Bronson)	100 mg	10	8.10
Tribasic calcium phosphate			
Posture	600 mg	2	6.39
Calcium phosphate			
Fibre Trim with Calcium	40 mg	25	53.25
Calcium citrate			
Citracal	200 mg	5	10.49
Generic	250 mg	4	5.00

*Prices current as of 1987

Just because a calcium supplement is high-priced, it isn't necessarily better. In fact, price doesn't guarantee much of anything. That doesn't mean all calcium carbonate pills are created equal. Although the FDA carefully regulates calcium-containing antacids because they are drugs, the agency has not been quite so rigorous when it comes to nutritional supplements. Ralph R. Shangraw and his associates at the University of Maryland School of Pharmacy found that some calcium carbonate pills did not dissolve well in simulated gastric juices.[35] Some of the supplements flunking the test included: **BioCal, Calcium 600** (Medicine Shoppe International), **Calcium 600-D** (Plus Products Pathmark), **Calcium Plus** (General Nutrition Centers), **Extra Strength O.S. Calcium** (K Mart), and **Sea-Cal** (Natural Sales Co.). Some of the calcium carbonate products that passed Dr. Shangraw's dissolution test are: **Calcimax, Calcium 600** mg (Giant Food Inc.), **Calcium HiCal** (Rite Aid Corp.), **Caltrate 600, Os-Cal 500, Suplical,** and **Tums.**

Exercise Against Bone Loss

We are always on the lookout for ways to stay well without drugs, and when it comes to osteoporosis we've had plenty of company. Countless articles in newspapers and magazines have run hopeful headlines: "Women can fight osteoporosis with smart diet and exercise."[36] We've known for years that extreme inactivity or immobilization can lead to loss of bone,[37] and that young athletes generally have thicker, denser bones than their less active contemporaries.[38] From there it seemed a short leap to the belief that exercise may protect against bone loss, and a few studies have shown that older athletes, both men and women, also have greater bone density than sedentary people their age.[39,40] Indeed, in one study, putting middle-aged women into a regular exercise and fitness program slowed or even reversed the loss of calcium from their bones.[41]

Here again, though, as in the rest of the osteoporosis story, the more doctors learn, the more complicated the situation appears. It is possible for young women to exercise too much. A woman who exercises vigorously for at least an hour every day runs a substantial risk of having her ovaries quit for a while: no ovulation, no periods, no estrogen output.[42] Without estrogen, the female athlete begins losing bone, just as if she had just had a total hysterectomy or gone through menopause.[43] Luckily, easing back on the exercise a bit can get the system humming again, and the bones regain their minerals.[44]

Now, clearly, none of this is relevant for the woman who is already past menopause. But does moderate exercise really protect against fractures? It is still too early to tell for sure, but it doesn't look as though the daily constitutional will be the single simple solution everyone's been hoping for:

> **Randomized trials of the effect of brisk walking and other forms of exercise on bone mass in postmenopausal women are now under way. Preliminary findings reported to date indicate that any protective effect will not be marked.[45]**

In short, aerobics may not offer strong enough magic to keep older bones intact. And even a lifetime of activity may not make very much difference, according to researchers who questioned a group of college alumnae who graduated between 1925 and 1981.[46] These scientists concluded that those who were athletes in college (and often in later life) weren't at any greater risk of postmenopausal fractures than those whose favorite exercise might have been "a good sit." But they don't appear to be significantly better off, either. Apparently exercise strengthened their bones, all right, but it also made them thinner. And fatter women have higher levels of estrogen circulating in their bloodstreams after menopause, which also has a protective effect on bone. So the exercise factor came out a wash. If you happen to be a pleasingly plump former athlete, it just may be that the stars are on your side.

The alumnae study did identify a few risk factors, however; women whose diet contained little milk or milk products were somewhat more likely to experience fractures after age 40, and so were those who had never been pregnant. Women eating low-fat diets seemed less likely to report broken bones—goodness knows why! Estrogen replacement therapy (ERT) offered a little protection from fractures.[47]

At this point, frustration may be setting in. If you are past menopause and want to minimize your chances of broken bones, it looks as though many of the things you can do won't have much of an impact. The strongest risk factors are mostly out of our control. The older you are, the more likely you are to have osteoporosis, but what's your alternative? An early menopause or a total hysterectomy before then carries a higher risk of weakened bones, but there's little you can do about that, either.

If you were lucky enough to be born black, or to parents who kept strong bones into their eighties, congratulate yourself. A pregnancy at any point in your life history might help—but it's probably too late to do anything about that now! Many of us feel that our body build is more or less beyond our control as well—but at least here is one situation where it's better to be heavy rather than svelte.

Being bedridden or immobilized for a period of time increases the likelihood of bone loss, and so does long-term use of corticosteroid medications, such as **Aristocort**, **Celestone**, cortisone, **Cortef**, **Cortone**, **Decadron**, **Delta-Cortef**, **Deltasone**, dexamethasone, **Haldrone**, hydrocortisone, **Kenacort**, **Medrol**, methylprednisolone, **Meticorten**, prednisone, and triamcinolone. Aluminum-containing antacids such as **Amphojel**, **ALternaGEL**, **Aludrox**, **Di-Gel**, **Gaviscon**, **Gelusil**, **Maalox**, **Mylanta**, **Riopan**, and a few others can increase the amount of calcium the body "throws off." So it's probably wise not to use any of these more than once in a while, especially if your calcium intake is on the low side.[48] Scientists also believe that cigarettes and booze are bad for bones, as is a very low calcium intake.[49,50] In your bones' best interest, it would be prudent to try to get more calcium and less nicotine or alcohol.

Neither exercise nor calcium alone seems to offer a perfect solution, but they *are* positive steps a person can take into her (or his) own hands; besides, together they may work better than either one alone. The full story's not yet in, and until it is, moderate exercise (perhaps three hours a week) tailored to your abilities, together with a reasonable calcium intake and adequate vitamin D (don't forget the low-fat diet), are not going to do any damage and may have plenty of beneficial side effects. Many people find that a regular exercise program helps them feel better in general, whether or not it's making their bones measurably more dense.

The Estrogen Question

When it comes to osteoporosis, the big drug issue is estrogen. The evidence is certainly piling up that postmenopausal estrogen replacement therapy (ERT) can improve bone density. And denser should mean stronger. The latest research indicates that this effect reduces the risk of fractures.[51,52] In Framingham, Massachusetts, physicians tracked 2,873 women for more than 20 years. They found that women who took estrogen any time after menopause were significantly less likely to suffer hip fractures. There were only 28 broken hips in this group, compared to 135 among the women who had never used ERT. Many doctors now assume that nearly any older woman at risk for osteoporosis should be put on estrogen at menopause for the rest of her life, more or less. After all:

> **Estrogen therapy prevents or retards bone loss in peri- and postmenopausal women for as long as they continue its use . . . When estrogen therapy is stopped, cortical bone loss resumes at a rate similar to that observed immediately after menopause in women who are not treated with estrogen.[53]**

Here's the translation of that medicalese: Estrogen is much more effective than calcium in preventing bone loss after menopause, but as soon as a woman stops using the drug, she starts losing bone just as fast as if she never had taken it. But the decision whether or not to use this drug can pose a real quandary as Mrs. S. made clear in a letter:

> **I have heard of problems with estrogen for years, and when I started menopause I decided that none of the discomforts I had were great enough to warrant the risks of taking it. I'd tough it out. And sure enough, I did get through the discomfort, to my relief, without estrogen.**
>
> **Lately, though, I have had vaginal pain. My gynecologist, whom I trust, says the lining has atrophied and the irritation will probably worsen. She says estrogen is the only answer. When I said I was**

concerned, she said the only problem was taking it
alone. She would prescribe 15 days of conjugated
estrogen alone, then 10 days in combination with
progesterone. This way, she claims, I would be protected from estrogen's carcinogenic effect and also
from heart problems. Otherwise, she offered an estrogen cream which she said would be better than
nothing.

I am still a little leery of estrogen, so I asked my
internist about his approach. He believes in prescribing it in the lowest amounts for the shortest
time possible—one to three tablets weekly for three
weeks, then one week off. He doesn't think the
progesterone is needed and he says there's no proof
it will do anything for my heart at all.

I'm feeling very confused. I wish I knew whether
it is safe to take this drug at all, and if so, which
method is best.

It's really no wonder Mrs. S is confused, since even her doctors
don't seem to be able to agree. And they are not the only physicians wrestling with this problem. Reluctance to have absolutely
every woman gulping down estrogen after menopause is based
partly on the concern that it may predispose women to some
kinds of cancer, particularly cancer of the lining of the womb.
Some experts maintain that earlier studies suggesting this risk
were so badly designed that their results are worthless,[54] but
most others agree that the risk is real.[55] Dr. William A. Peck,
chairing a recent meeting on osteoporosis at the National Institutes of Health, suggested, "Because estrogen use is not uncom-
plicated, it is recommended only in women who are at high risk,
have no contraindications, and will adhere to a program of careful follow-up."[56] That means yearly mammograms, even though a
large study from the Centers for Disease Control has recently
shown that ERT does not make any significant difference in a
woman's susceptibility to breast cancer.[57] It will almost certainly
mean pelvic exams from time to time, too, because of worries
about cancer attacking the endometrium lining the uterus.

Many doctors go along with our reader's gynecologist in advis-
ing a different female hormone, progesterone (in its synthetic
form, progestin), in addition to estrogen for 12 or 13 days each

cycle to protect the uterus. In fact, one enterprising bunch of British researchers has worked out a simple way of telling when a woman is getting enough progestin for effective protection.[58] They recommend that the dose of this medication be adjusted so that the regular monthly bleeding (the "period" which goes with ERT) begins no sooner than the eleventh day of taking progestin. Their data indicate that an earlier period is associated with negative changes in uterine tissue.

Even with this regimen, clinicians are still debating the value of progestin therapy.[59] Although estrogen seems to have a beneficial impact on the levels of various fats in the blood, raising "good-guy" HDL cholesterol and lowering "bad-actor" LDL levels, progesterone may very well put this into reverse.[60] What's more, progestin has been known to trigger blood clots leading to phlebitis or pulmonary embolism (clots in the lungs). It has also been associated with allergic reactions, rash, and changes in weight, sleep patterns, or hairiness.

Even more crucial, how does hormone therapy after menopause affect a woman's chances of getting a heart attack or stroke? Confusion on this issue was underscored in 1985 when two studies published in the same issue of the *New England Journal of Medicine* answered this question—with contradictory answers.[61] One study came from the town of Framingham, Massachusetts, whose inhabitants are the unsung heroes of much of our medical understanding of heart disease. Women in Framingham using estrogens after the age of 50 were more than twice as likely to suffer a stroke than those who did not, and almost twice as likely to have a heart attack, unless they also smoked. Then they ran four times the risk of heart disease as those who neither smoked nor took estrogens.

The other study focused on 32,000 nurses who were past menopause. It found that women using replacement estrogens had only one third the heart attack rate of those who were not taking them. Even the smokers seemed to enjoy a lower risk of heart attack. Not even the researchers know quite what to make of these results, so we won't bother to splash in the water. Clearly, the question is wide open and of critical importance.

What about estrogen patches? Gallstones, high blood pressure, and clots all appear to be more likely when a woman is using ERT, but there is some hope that the relatively new **Estraderm** patches may be able to get around some of these risks[62] because the estrogen goes straight into the bloodstream instead of making its usual detour through the liver. Breast tenderness, irritability, and mid-cycle bleeding have been reported as side effects of the patch, which is known to work pretty well for hot flashes. We still don't have any solid data demonstrating that the estrogen patch prevents bone loss, but there's every reason to believe that it should work. Experts do suggest, though, that progestin be given along with **Estraderm**.[63]

The prospect of taking estrogen for the rest of your life may not be grim; it's just too bad that there are so many unresolved questions. For now, Dr. Robert C. Young of the National Cancer Institute cautions, "It's not possible to conclude from the existing information that postmenopausal estrogen therapy should or should not be routinely administered." He recommends that doctors individualize their estrogen prescriptions for each patient and give "the lowest dose that will produce the desired effect."[64] Right now, it appears that 0.625 mg is that dose, and that higher doses, such as 1.25 mg, are riskier but not a lot more effective.[65]

One possible way of getting the dose of estrogen even lower may come out of some tantalizing new research suggesting that maybe, just maybe, combining calcium (1,500 mg/day) and estrogen (0.3 mg—about half the usual dose) works better to strengthen bone than either pill could alone.[66] We'll be interested in seeing more studies on combination approaches like this, because so far there is no one, simple, sure-fire solution to the problem of broken hips and crushed vertebrae. Perhaps the treatment program that will emerge in the future, when we know more about bones and breaks than we do now, will include everything— estrogen, exercise, and diet.

None of these approaches can do anything to undo the damage of osteoporosis once it has occurred. There are a few drugs that have been approved for regulating bone formation in Paget's disease, a condition in which bone metabolism is quite abnormal. Paget's disease is not common, and investigators have been considering whether some of the medications for treating it might be useful for reversing osteoporosis.

Calcitonin (**Calcimar**, **Cibacalcin**, or **Miacalcic**) is being tried in some cases, but it has a few drawbacks. It must be injected and may cause serious allergic reactions in some people. It is also quite expensive. Another treatment for Paget's disease, **Didronel** (etidronate), is stirring up quite a bit of excitement now in studies both in the United States and in Europe. The idea behind its use is to give it in a timed treatment—14 days on, then 74 days off—to try to control the bone-remodeling process and stimulate more bone formation. Pilot studies are very encouraging, showing as much as a 17 percent increase in bone mass in postmenopausal women.[67] The last word is not yet in on this experimental treatment for osteoporosis, but doctors are hoping that several years of experience will show that **Didronel** can prevent fractures. Because it is taken orally and is not terribly expensive, some day it may prove more appropriate than calcitonin for osteoporosis reversal.

Keeping Humpty Dumpty Whole

In the meantime, the other approach to preventing broken bones is to try to avoid falls. No one is quite sure exactly why a fall that would be inconsequential for a younger person can result in a serious injury in an octogenarian. A couple of doctors who have given the osteoporosis problem a lot of thought, Drs. L. Joseph Melton III and B. Lawrence Riggs of the Mayo Clinic, suggest that weaker muscles, slower reflexes, or less "padding" in elderly persons may account for the fact that they are more likely to break something when they slide off a bed or a chair.[68] They believe that preventing falls would be very helpful, but they acknowledge that it's pretty difficult to do. In fact, at this point we know a lot more about how to increase an older person's risk of falling and breaking a hip than about preventing falls.

In a recent study of elderly Medicaid patients, Dr. Melton and several other scientists found that older people were nearly twice as likely to suffer broken hips if they were taking certain types of drugs: long-acting sleeping pills such as **Dalmane** (flurazepam), anti-anxiety drugs such as **Valium** (diazepam) or **Librium** (chlordiazepoxide), antidepressant medicines like **Elavil** (amitriptyline), **Adapin** (doxepin), and **Tofranil** (imipramine), and drugs for psychosis including **Mellaril** (thioridazine), **Haldol** (haloperidol), and **Thorazine** (chlorpromazine).[69] What's more, as the dose goes up, so does the risk of a fracture.

The researchers suggest that these medications have two undesirable features that could lead people to fall more often. They often make people feel drowsy and uncoordinated, even in the daytime; and they can lead to a dizzying drop in blood pressure when a person stands up suddenly.[70] The manufacturer of **Haldol** often advertises in the medical journals showing pictures of an older person labeled FRAGILE—HANDLE WITH HALDOL. The results of this study suggest that it might be more appropriate to run the legend FRAGILE, SO WATCH OUT FOR HALDOL!

Things to Remember

1. Bone loss in women begins even before menopause and speeds up afterwards. But the majority of crippling hip fractures occur in women in their seventies or eighties or older. Men this age are also susceptible to brittle bones and breaks.

2. It's important to get enough calcium (1,000 to 1,500 mg every day is usually recommended for older people), but the calcium supplement tablet is no panacea. If you can drink milk or eat dairy products, try to get some of your daily calcium that way. Other nutrients needed for bone strength, including vitamin D and manganese, are supplied in milk along with available calcium.

3. If you are staying out of the sun, be aware of your vitamin D intake. Drink milk, eat fish, or take a supplement.

4. If you want to take a calcium supplement, look at the price tags. Although calcium gluconate is less likely to be constipating or irritating to the digestive tract, it is the most expensive way you could possibly supplement your dietary calcium. Calcium carbonate is relatively cheap and doesn't require that a person swallow a huge handful of pills.

5. Exercise does not wield the magic to ward off osteoporosis, but it's good for you anyway. Be sensible: walk, play tennis, practice martial arts,

or do any other activity you enjoy, but don't overdo and break normal bones through carelessness or overexertion.

6. The person most at risk of osteoporosis is a thin white woman whose ovaries were removed before natural menopause. Other factors that can increase the risk include cortisone-type drugs, immobility, smoking, and heavy alcohol consumption. Be wary if a close relative had problems with spine or hip fractures.

7. Most doctors would want such a high-risk person to take estrogen starting as soon as possible after menopause and going for as many years as possible. To prevent bone loss, a dose of 0.625 mg per day works for most people, and a lower dose of 0.3 mg may prove helpful in conjunction with calcium. Lower doses mean less risk of uterine cancer, and also less likelihood of a monthly period.

8. Estrogen treatment cannot put back bone that has already been lost. Calcitonin (prescribed under the names **Calcimar**, **Cibacalcin** and **Miacalcic**) is being used to treat as well as prevent bone loss. However, it is quite expensive (around $200 a month), requires frequent injections, and has not been proven to keep bones from breaking.

9. For elderly men as well as women, preventing falls is essential to preventing hip fractures. Living space should be free of hazards, and drugs that can cause dizziness or affect coordination should be avoided unless absolutely imperative. Long-acting sleeping pills (**Dalmane**), antidepressants (**Elavil**, **Adapin**, **Sinequan**, **Tofranil**), anti-anxiety drugs (**Valium**, **Librium**), and antipsychotic agents (**Mellaril**, **Haldol**, **Thorazine**) may double the risk of hip fracture in older people.

References

1. Kelsey, Jennifer L.; and Hoffman, Susie. "Risk Factors for Hip Fracture." (editorial) *N. Engl. J. Med.* 316:404–406, 1987.
2. Cummings, Steven R.; Kelsey, Jennifer L.; Nevitt, Michael C.; and O'Dowd, Kenneth J. "Epidemiology of Osteoporosis and Osteoporotic Fractures." *Epidemiologic Reviews* 7:178–208, 1985.
3. Culliton, Barbara J. "Osteoporosis Reexamined: Complexity of Bone Biology Is a Challenge." *Science* 235:833–834, 1987.
4. "Food, Drug Makers Beef Up Products by Adding Calcium." *The News and Observer*, Raleigh, N.C., Feb. 1, 1987, p. 2–1.
5. Kolata, Gina. "How Important Is Dietary Calcium in Preventing Osteoporosis?" *Science* 234:519–520, 1986.
6. Culliton, op. cit.
7. Marx, Jean L. "Osteoporosis: New Help for Thinning Bones." *Science* 207:628–630, 1980.
8. Culliton, op. cit.
9. Kolata, op. cit.
10. Prescott, Lawrence M. "Lactase-Deficient Patients Aided by Oral Enzyme." *Medical Tribune* 29(8):13, 1987.
11. Grobbee, Diederick E.; and Hofman, Albert. "Effect of Calcium Supplementation on Diastolic Blood Pressure in Young People with Mild Hypertension." *Lancet* ii(8509):703–706, 1986.
12. McCarron, David A., et al. "Blood Pressure and Nutrient Intake in the United States." *Science* 225:1392, 1984.
13. Lipkin, Martin; and Newmark, Harold. "Effect of Added Dietary Calcium on Colonic Epithelial-Cell Proliferation in Subjects at High Risk for Familial Colonic Cancer." *N. Engl. J. Med.* 313:1381–1384, 1985.
14. Culliton, op. cit.
15. Ibid.
16. Kolata, op. cit., p. 520.
17. Riggs, B. Lawrence; and Melton, L. Joseph, III. "Involutional Osteoporosis." *N. Engl. J. Med.* 314:1676–1686, 1986.
18. Ibid.
19. Horsman, A., et al. "Prospective Trial of Oestrogen and Calcium in Postmenopausal Women." *Brit. Med. J.* 2:789–792, 1977.
20. Kolata, op. cit., p. 519.
21. Ibid.
22. Riis, Bente; Thomsen, Karsten; and Christiansen, Claus. "Does Calcium Supplementation Prevent Postmenopausal Bone Loss?" *N. Engl. J. Med.* 316:173–177, 1987.
23. "Calcium Supplements: Don't Depend on Them." *University of California, Berkeley Wellness Letter* 3(6):1, 1987.
24. "Hoop Star Walton vs. The Big 'O'." *Medical SelfCare* (39):12, 1987.
25. Gilchrest, Barbara A. "Problems of Aging Skin." Presented at the conference *Cosmeceuticals: The Science of Beauty and Aging*, hosted by Boston University Medical Center, Apr. 21, 1986.

26. "New Therapies, New Forms of an Old Vitamin." *Science News* 115:181, 1979.
27. Cummings et al, op. cit., p. 190.
28. Riggs and Melton, op. cit., p. 1680.
29. Blume, Elaine. "Overdosing on Protein." *Nutrition Action Health Letter* 14(2):1–6, 1987.
30. Culliton, op. cit.
31. "Calcium Supplementation with Antacids." Questions and Answers, *JAMA* 257:541, 1987.
32. "Calcium Supplementation in the Elderly." *Drug Therapy for the Elderly* 1(9):42, 1986.
33. "Absorption and Side-Effects Calcium Supplements." *Nutrition and the M.D., 1981.*
34. Recker, Robert R. "Calcium Absorption and Achlorhydria." *N. Engl. J. Med.* 313:70-71, 1985.
35. Quint, Laurie; and Liebman, Bonnie. "Putting Calcium into Perspective." *Nutrition Action Health Letter* 14(5):8–10, June 1987.
36. "Women Can Fight Osteoporosis with Smart Diet and Exercise." *Durham Sun*, Mar. 21, 1986.
37. Marx, op. cit., p. 630.
38. Cummings et al, op. cit., p. 191.
39. Lane, Nancy E., et al. "Long-distance Running, Bone Density and Osteoarthritis." *JAMA* 255:1147–1151, 1986.
40. Jacobson, P. C.; Beaver, W.; Grubb, S. A., et al. "Bone Density in Women: College Athletes and Older Athletic Women." *J. Orthopedic Research* 2:328–332, 1984.
41. Aloia, John F., et al. "Prevention of Involutional Bone Loss by Exercise." *Ann. Internal Med.* 89:356–358, 1978.
42. Green, Beverly B., et al. "Exercise as a Risk Factor for Infertility with Ovulatory Dysfunction." *Am. J. Public Health* 76:1432–1436, 1986.
43. Riggs, B. Lawrence; and Eastell, Richard. "Exercise, Hypogonadism, and Osteopenia," (editorial). *JAMA* 256:392, 1986.
44. Drinkwater, Barbara L., et al. "Bone Mineral Density After Resumption of Menses in Amenorrheic Athletes." *JAMA* 256:380–382, 1986.
45. Kelsey and Hoffman, op. cit., p. 405.
46. Wyshak, Grace, et al. "Bone Fractures Among Former College Athletes Compared with Nonathletes in the Menopausal and Postmenopausal Years." *Obstetrics & Gynecology* 69:121–126, 1987.
47. Wyshak et al., op. cit., p. 123.
48. Spencer, Herta; and Lois Kramer. "Antacid-Induced Calcium Loss," (editorial). *Arch. Intern. Med.* 143:657–658, 1983.
49. Kelsey and Hoffman, op. cit., p.405.
50. Culliton, op. cit., p. 834.
51. Weiss, Noel S. "Decreased Risk of Fractures of the Hip and Lower Forearm with Postmenopausal Use of Estrogen." *N. Engl. J. Med.* 303:1195–1198, 1980.
52. Keil, Douglas P. et al. "Hip Fracture and the Use of Estrogens in Postmenopausal Women: The Framingham Study." *N. Engl. J. Med.* 317:1169–1174, 1987.

53. Cummings et al., op. cit., p. 185.
54. Gordan, Gilbert S. "Estrogen and Bone: Marshall R. Urist's Contributions." *Clin. Orthopaedics and Related Research* 200:174–180, 1985.
55. Speroff, Leon. "Estrogen Update: New Dimensions." A medical writers' seminar held during The American College of Obstetricians and Gynecologists Annual Meeting, May 4, 1986.
56. Culliton, op. cit.
57. Wingo, Phyllis A., et al. "The Risk of Breast Cancer in Postmenopausal Women Who Have Used Estrogen Replacement Therapy." *JAMA* 257:209–215, 1987.
58. Padwick, Malcolm L., et al. "A Simple Method for Determining the Optimal Dosage of Progestin in Postmenopausal Women Receiving Estrogens." *N. Engl. J. Med.* 315:930–934, 1986.
59. Culliton, op. cit.
60. Speroff, op. cit.
61. Bishop, Jerry E. "Studies Conflict on Estrogen Tie to Heart Attack." *Wall Street Journal,* Oct. 24, 1985, p. 33.
62. Riggs and Melton, op. cit. p. 1683.
63. "Transdermal Estrogen." *Medical Letter* 28:119–120, 1986.
64. "Estrogen's Benefits Downplayed," op. cit.
65. Culliton, op. cit.
66. Gallagher, J. Chris. "Estrogen Update: New Dimensions." A medical writers' seminar held during The American College of Obstetricians and Gynecologists Annual Meeting, May 4, 1986.
67. Horwitz, Nathan. "Coax Bone to Amass 10 Percent Gain." *Med. Trib.* 28 July 1, 1987, pp. 1, 14.
68. Melton, L. Joseph, III; and Riggs, B. Lawrence. "Risk Factors for Injury After a Fall." *Clinics in Geriatric Medicine* 1:525–539, 1985.
69. Ray, Wayne A., et al. "Psychotropic Drug Use and the Risk of Hip Fracture." *N. Engl. J. Med.* 316:363–369, 1987.
70. Ibid., p. 367

10

Balancing Nutritional Needs Against Nutty Notions

Americans are taking nutrition very seriously these days. Scan the newsstands and you'll spot headlines on wonder vitamins and miraculous minerals. Bookstore shelves are crowded with titles touting the healing properties of foods. Not only are there eating plans virtually guaranteed to help a person lose weight, there are diets that are supposed to boost the immune system; food systems to maintain fitness, vim, and vigor well into the later decades; diet plans to conquer cancer and arthritis; and an uncounted number of articles about minerals, vitamins, and special ingredients reputed to do almost everything except give us all the sex drive of teenagers. (There are even a few advertisements hinting that *that* goal might be achievable, but only with the proper combination of expensive nutritional supplements.)

Are we all being a bit too gullible, and playing into the hands of the modern-day medicine showmen? Proper nutrition *is* important, but miracles are just too much to expect. In this chapter we'll take a look at the evidence for some of these claims, checking out whether fish oil really can fight heart attacks, if broccoli and brussels sprouts might help protect you from cancer, and whether you need to take a vitamin supplement.

Healthy Eating to Help the Heart

For years, doctors and dieticians have been talking about foods that are *bad* for us. In the television ads of the sixties, mean little Mr. Cholesterol used to rub his hands with glee as some unsuspecting diner prepared to spread butter on an English muffin. No doubt he would have chortled as he watched someone tear into a big dessert of ice cream and rich chocolate cake, and howled with delight in the morning while a hungry man polished off two eggs, over easy, with three strips of bacon and buttered toast. Yes, Mr. Cholesterol undoubtedly succeeded in making plenty of folks miserable at the table: either they felt guilty because they were indulging in some cholesterol-rich morsel—or they felt deprived because they weren't!

In the past several years, though, we've learned that, along with the dietary don'ts that litter the landscape, there are plenty of foods that may help promote a healthy heart. The Ireland–Boston Diet–Heart study was begun back in 1959, when Mr. Cholesterol was king of the mountain. After following about a thousand men for 20 years, the researchers found that those who ate more saturated fat and cholesterol were indeed at greater risk of a heart attack. No surprises there. Butter, eggs, bacon, burgers, cheese, ice cream, and many of the other foods we've been cautioned against over the years really can pack a nasty wallop. But unexpectedly, those who ate more vegetable foods (and as a result got more fiber, vegetable protein, and starch) seemed somewhat protected against fatal heart disease.[1]

What's this about fiber? Well, it turns out that although cholesterol in the diet is still considered a no-goodnik, the real culprit is the cholesterol in the bloodstream. And since our bodies make that themselves, the big question has been, how can we get them to cut back on production? In fact, the situation is even more complicated. Scientists have learned much more about cholesterol in the past several years. There are many different types of cholesterol, from the beneficial high-density lipoprotein (HDL) to the villains, low-density lipoprotein (LDL) and very-low-density lipoprotein (yup, you guessed it, VLDL). (Chapter 9 has all the details.) The trick is to boost HDL as much as possible while discouraging the others. This is a difficult assignment, no bones about it, but there are a number of dietary "stars" emerging that might help quite a bit. Please welcome ... fiber, fish oil, olive oil, and onions.

Fiber seems pretty simple. It's just roughage, right? Bran cereal for breakfast and all that. Well, almost. It turns out that, like cholesterol, there are more types of fiber than you ever may have thought possible. The ones most effective against cholesterol in the blood appear to be soluble fiber and pectin, and one of the best sources is oats. Not only can oatmeal and oat bran help lower cholesterol that is dangerously high, but researchers at Northwestern University School of Medicine reported recently that one to two ounces of oats or oat bran daily (one to two cups of hot cereal) helped bring "normal" blood cholesterol levels down as well.[2] And since researchers have decided that the risk of heart attack is directly related to the level of cholesterol coursing through the veins,[3,4] it makes sense to do whatever one can to bring it down. For a "stick-to-your-ribs" breakfast that may do your heart good, help yourself to a bowl of oatmeal. Other sources of fiber that are reported to be helpful include legumes such as beans, peas, lentils, and the like, barley, and pectin-rich fruits including, of all things, bananas, as well as some of the more likely high-pectin candidates.

Fighting Back with Fish

We sometimes get tired of oatmeal morning after morning. But we have a wonderful alternative. One of our favorite breakfasts is a piece of toast or half a bagel with a nice big chunk of smoked fish on it. Now, we're lucky to be able to get excellent smoked bluefish, trout, and sable from a local supplier; not everyone can, and some people don't like smoked fish. But whether it's smoked, fresh, or frozen, whatever time of day you eat it, fish is "heart food," especially the high-fat fish such as trout, salmon, whitefish, herring, mackerel, and bluefish.

The first inklings that fish might have some value in preventing heart disease came with the observation that the Greenland Eskimos, who traditionally ate diets very high in fat and low in vegetable foods, had an unexpectedly low rate of death from heart disease. Regardless of their relative freedom from heart disease, however, the Eskimos had a diet and a life-style few of us would want to adopt. But researchers began to wonder whether it was necessary to consume almost a pound of fish daily, with blubber for dessert, in order to get the cardiovascular benefits, or whether a less extreme diet might prove helpful. A 20-year study begun in the Netherlands in 1960 has come up with the answer, and the news is good. According to the scientists, who did meticulous dietary histories by interviewing each man's wife at length, fish intake averaging out to about an ounce a day—approximately one or two fish dishes each week—halved the rate of death from heart attack.[5]

This exciting finding has triggered research to uncover the biochemical and physiological reasons behind the protective action of fish. It has been suggested that fish oil lowers levels of the dangerous VLDL-type cholesterol;[6,7] studies have shown that it also keeps blood from forming clots quickly and easily.[8] Since scientists believe that some heart attacks may be triggered by a clot in a coronary artery, this anticlotting action may be part of the story.

But it appears that fish oil may also keep cholesterol from forming into atherosclerotic plaque and clogging the coronaries.[9] Researchers in Massachusetts fed two groups of young pigs a very high-fat, high-cholesterol diet. (Their standard chow was laced with lard.) On such a diet, pigs usually develop atherosclerosis, just like humans, but one group of piggies was dosed with a couple of tablespoons of cod liver oil every day. The difference in the coronary arteries, when they grew up to be big pigs, was remarkable. Those who had been given the cod liver oil had vessels that were clean and clear, while those who had none ended up looking like prime pig heart attack candidates.

Does this mean that you should start guzzling cod liver oil like a pig? Perhaps not. For one thing, pigs don't smoke, and these swine didn't have high blood pressure or diabetes or any of the other risk factors that make human heart disease so complicated. So it will take a few more studies before we'll know whether cod liver oil will work as well on human coronaries. For another thing, cod liver oil is very rich in the fat-soluble vitamins A and D. Although a bit of a bonus on these vitamins might be welcome, too much can be toxic. To avoid vitamin poisoning, you should probably keep your dose at no more than two tablespoons a day.

Both cod liver oil and the fish oil capsules rich in the omega-3 fatty acids eicosapentaenoic acid (EPA) and docosahexaenoic acid (DHA) (heavily promoted these days as **Promega**, **Proto-Chol**, **MaxEPA**, and other products) do seem to prolong bleeding time. Anyone with bleeding problems or taking an anticoagulant probably should stay away from such "dietary supplements" unless the doctor agrees to provide close supervision.

The bottom line here is that we still don't know quite enough about the appropriate dose and possible side effects of cod liver oil and fish oil capsules to recommend them for everybody. What's more, in order to really lower cholesterol and prevent blood clots, experts estimate that you might have to take dozens of capsules a day at a significant cost.[10] One aspirin daily is probably more effective at preventing clots and a whole lot less expensive. But substituting fish for a high-cholesterol serving of marbled steak, lamb chop, or macaroni and cheese at least once or twice a week is an innocuous, even tasty, way of reducing your risk of heart attack.

(Another tantalizing use for fish oil—relieving psoriasis, inflammation, and, possibly, easing arthritis—is also undergoing testing.[11,12] But there is not enough evidence yet on this potential benefit for us to be able to tell whether it really helps or not.)

The Olive Oil Option

First they told us butter was bad. They said margarine was better and millions of Americans switched, thinking they were doing something good for their hearts. If you had to cook with oil you were supposed to use polyunsaturated vegetable oil. Then they came along and said that we were still in trouble and that we had to work harder to cut more fat out of our diets.

Maybe the experts should have talked to people from Sicily, Greece, or Crete. In one large study, a group of middle-aged Cretan men was followed for 10 years—and unlike their counterparts in Finland, the United States, and several other countries, not one suffered a fatal heart attack.[13] The scientists were baffled, because they couldn't account for this phenomenal record with differences in smoking, obesity, blood pressure, or exercise. In fact, according to conventional wisdom, the Cretans should have dropped as fast as anyone, since their diets were very high in fat, in the form of olive oil.

This had some researchers scratching their heads, and Dr. Scott M. Grundy decided to check out the effects of an experimental diet simulating the olive-oil-drenched fare on Crete. In a controlled setting, he had patients subsist on three different liquid formulas for a month each—a formula high in carbohydrate and low in fat, one high in saturated fats similar to butter (actually, they used coconut oil), and one high in monounsaturated fat very much like olive oil. His results shook the nutrition establishment, for the high-fat formula resembling an olive-oil-rich diet was "at least as effective in lowering plasma cholesterol as a diet low in fat and high in carbohydrate."[14] In fact, says Dr. Grundy, "If anything, the response to monounsaturated fatty acids was somewhat greater than the response to the Low-Fat diet,"[15] because the ratio of dangerous LDL to protective HDL was more favorable while patients were getting the pseudo-olive oil formula.

Now, that is nutritional heresy, and it has made some other nutritional scientists nervous. Dr. Frank Sacks, of Harvard Medical School, thinks that testing more normal diets over a longer period of time would show that a low-fat regimen really is much better for the cholesterol profile than one that goes overboard on a fat like olive oil.[16] But researchers at Stanford studied the diets and blood pressures of middle-aged American men and found that the more monounsaturated fat these men were eating, the lower their blood pressures: "The correlations presented in this report reveal a significant, and unexplained, association between increasing levels of monounsaturated fat intake and decreasing levels of both systolic and diastolic blood pressure."[17]

We don't think anyone should try to drown his sorrows in olive oil. But if you are going to put some dressing on your green leafies, make it with olive oil. And when it comes to sauteeing onions and garlic (read on for why that's a good idea), why not use olive oil? It tastes good and it just might be good for your heart.

The Glories of Garlic and Onions

If you are an onion lover or a garlic enthusiast, you're in good luck. These pungent members of the lily family have been featured in folk medicine for millennia, at least since the time of

Tutankhamen. But medical science is finally beginning to catch up. Research worldwide shows that garlic has anticlotting activity and a positive effect on cholesterol, and onion seems to have some benefits as well.

Garlic has considerable power, not only on the breath but also on the blood. One of its effects, which occurs within an hour after eating fresh garlic, is to inhibit the ability of blood platelets to clump together.[18] The tendency these cells have to stick to each other may, researchers believe, lead to a clot and a potentially fatal heart attack. Doctors treating patients who have had heart attacks or strokes often prescribe blood thinners such as heparin or **Coumadin** (warfarin) to prevent recurrences, or they may recommend an aspirin a day to fend off a second heart attack. Scientists have found that some components of garlic also have significant anticoagulant activity. The substance called methyl allyl trisulphide, or MATS for short, keeps platelets from aggregating, but the body breaks it down rather promptly.[19] Within two and a half hours after eating garlic very little MATS remains.

One of the world's most knowledgeable experts on garlic, Dr. Eric Block, has isolated a substance from garlic called ajoene (after the Spanish word for garlic, *ajo*). He and his colleagues have found that ajoene is at least as effective at preventing blood clots as aspirin. The catch? According to Dr. Block, dehydrated garlic powder, pills, oils, and extracts that are commercially available don't have measurable levels of ajoene. He concludes, "For now the beneficial effects attributed to garlic are best obtained from fresh garlic."[20]

An apple a day may keep the doctor away, but gulping garlic for breakfast, lunch, and dinner will probably keep everyone else at arm's length as well. What about garlic breath? Well, while we have received many letters on the subject from people with a solution, the sad truth is that the garlic aroma comes not from the mouth but from the blood, by way of the lungs. A lively controversy raged in the pages of the *Journal of the American Medical Association* about 50 years ago in which this question was settled. One group of physicians claimed their experiments with a strong mouthwash suggested the odor originated in the mouth. Others disputed this with an elegant experiment. Women in labor were given garlic capsules to swallow. Within 20 minutes to an hour, they developed garlic breath. But more impressive: nearly all their infants had very noticeable garlic breath as well, as soon as they were born—strong evidence that garlic is something you have in your blood. Since none of us is about to stop breathing, it may be that the best solution to garlic breath is to time our dietary indiscretions so that we can relax and enjoy them.

Perhaps onions are more to your taste. Onions also seem to have an anticlotting effect,[21] and the indications are that even fried or boiled onions may have some impact.[22] Further research on MATS, ajoene, or the active component of onion may lead to new compounds that could lead to a new means of dealing with blood clotting. But in the interim, it makes sense for lovers of onions and garlic to indulge themselves. And if you happen to like Chinese food, help yourself to some cloud ears once in a while. This tree fungus, or *mo-er*, also seems to have anticlotting properties fairly similar to those of garlic or onions.

Preventing clots isn't the only way garlic may work against heart disease. According to several studies,[23-25] garlic has the ability to lower undesirable blood fats, including LDL-type cholesterol, and simultaneously raise the level of high-density lipoproteins. All this suggests that, in the words of one researcher, "garlic can have a role in the prevention of human thrombo-atherosclerosis."[26] That is, it may help prevent heart attacks and strokes. Don't expect your doctor to prescribe it, but if you want to tailor your diet to minimize your risk of heart problems, go for garlic, olive oil, and fish. Skip the butter and cream. And don't forget to eat your vegetables.

Wait, back up a minute. Don't, for goodness sake, get so enthusiastic about cutting back on cream that you reach for the nondairy creamer. You just might be making a big mistake while you congratulate yourself on doing your heart a favor. You see, while it's true that cream is fairly high in cholesterol (about 10 mg in that tablespoon you just poured into your coffee), we all need to worry just as much about saturated fat. Remember, the body makes its own cholesterol, using saturated fat as the raw material. So even though some foods may have no cholesterol, if they're loaded with saturated fatty acids they could be just as bad for you.

You need to read the labels on boxes and jars, and if coconut oil or palm kernel oil figure high on the list of ingredients, you might just as well enjoy the "real thing," whether it's cream or buttered popcorn. Or better yet, find your own low-fat substitute.

Dr. Gabe Mirkin, Professor of Pediatrics at Georgetown University and an expert on sports medicine, elaborates:

> **Low-cholesterol creamers are usually more atherogenic than cream. You're better off with cream in your coffee than with most substitutes because they're made with coconut oil, which is loaded with saturated fat. Frozen breaded fish is usually loaded with palm oil and coconut oil to hold the bread in place ... Most breakfast foods have zero fat, but granola cereals contain oats, which taste like cardboard unless the manufacturer adds oils to them. Confectioners and bakers use coconut and palm oils because they're so cheap.**[27]

The breakfast foods Dr. Mirkin is referring to are undoubtedly packaged cereals, not double cheese omelettes. These, along with hearty hamburgers and extra crispy deep-fried chicken, are high in both fat and cholesterol, and have their hazards for the heart. While you might not want to give up some of your favorite foods completely, you could consider a policy of moderation, especially when it comes to fats. But if you've been denying yourself shrimp, clams, and oysters for years because they were on the "high cholesterol" list, you can splurge a little. New, more accurate laboratory techniques for determining cholesterol content show that these relatively low-fat shellfish aren't frighteningly high in cholesterol either. Bon appetit!

Trace elements can have an impact on cholesterol, too. In this respect, zinc is bad, lowering HDL cholesterol significantly and lousing up the ratio of good to bad, while copper and chromium look pretty good. In one study, a chromium supplement of 200 μg (micrograms) a day for three months boosted HDL and lowered serum triglycerides (other blood fats) significantly.[28] Trouble is, most people don't get much chromium in their diets, often consuming only half the recommended amount of 50 to 200 μg.[29] Copper, too, is in short supply in most Americans' diets. Ironically, the best sources, organ meats and shellfish, are usually on the no-no list for anyone on a low-cholesterol diet. And yet, animals deprived of copper develop serious heart problems.[30] And in humans, copper deficiency seems to provoke a substantial rise in total cholesterol that can be reversed with normal copper intake, around 2 mg per day.[31]

Staving Off Strokes with
Spinach and Squash

Potassium is getting some attention from the medical community lately, but it hasn't yet become a household word. And to tell the truth, some doctors don't seem to know nearly as much as they should about dietary sources of potassium. Who cares, you want to know? Well, anyone with high blood pressure ought to be interested, for starters, because there are studies piling up suggesting that adequate levels of potassium, as well as calcium and magnesium, are important in helping to keep blood pressure normal.[32,33]

Even more exciting, there's new evidence that a diet rich in potassium may lower the risk of stroke.[34] A group of 859 people 50 to 79 years old in Rancho Bernardo, California, were examined and questioned about what they had eaten the previous day; in the next twelve years, 24 of them had suffered strokes and died. None of the 24 were among those who'd had the highest potassium intake. For women, especially, the risk of dying of stroke was more than four times higher for those who had eaten the least of this mineral. Now, what someone ate yesterday might not be a good reflection of what she usually eats, so the scientists are going to be looking at this relationship in some other studies, you can bet. The researchers aren't ready to come right out and say everybody should be going back for seconds on potassium-rich foods. But increasing the level of this mineral in your diet isn't likely to hurt you a bit, and you'll probably find some other valuable nutrients tagging along for the ride.

How do you translate that into a guide for grocery shopping? Linger longest in the produce department and at the fish counter. Potassium-rich foods aren't necessarily high in calories, and if you buy them as they come into season so you can get a wide variety, you'll likely reap some other nutritional benefits too.

Foods to look for when you want to maximize potassium (at least 2 mg of the element for each calorie) include popular veggies like **potatoes, beets, cabbage, carrots, broccoli, tomatoes, bell peppers,** and **squash,** as well as less-popular entries like **brussels sprouts, beet greens, sweet potato, spinach, cauliflower, chard, collards** and all those other great greens, **mushrooms,** and **bean sprouts**. You don't have to pay a bundle for **artichokes, asparagus,** or **avocado,** although they too are all super sources of potassium. While you're still at the greengrocer's, pick out some fruit in season. Among the best "bargains" for potassium content are **apricots,** both fresh and dried, **strawberries, blackberries,** and **raspberries, cantaloupe** and other melons, **bananas, oranges, peaches, plums, nectarines,** and some exotic stuff your market may or may not carry: **pomegranates, guavas, carambolas,** and **prickly pear**. Most any of the juices based on **oranges** or **tomatoes** will turn out to be pretty good sources of potassium, but steer clear of "juice drinks." *Tang* may have been fortified with vitamin C, but they didn't bring it up to speed in the potassium department.

Some foods that are quite rich in potassium are used mostly for flavoring. If you like **onions, parsley, raw ginger, herbs, paprika,** or **red pepper,** you might want to use them liberally. **Molasses** is another potassium source that doesn't really count as a food, but it can also enrich your diet, along with cereal-based coffee substitutes, such as **Pero** or **Postum**.

Most fish is rich in potassium: try **black bass, perch, mullet, snapper, halibut, cod,** or **catfish** when you can. **Clams, mussels,** and **oysters** are good sources, too. And **salmon**—if it's ever offered at a price you can afford. (Don't bother with the caviar, though. It may be rich, but not in potassium.)

If you prefer your protein without scales, try **veal** or **lean pork** once in a while. **Chicken** also has significant potassium, though not nearly as much, calorie for calorie, as the vegetables, fruit, and fish. When you get to the dairy case, throw some **buttermilk, skim milk,** or **low-fat yogurt** into your grocery cart. And now you're all set for a healthy high-potassium diet.

Supposing you want to boost your potassium intake just a bit more, you might want to consider one of the potassium chloride salt substitutes you will find on the grocery shelf. Don't go hog wild with the shaker, though. While you'd have a very hard time overdosing on potassium from your four daily servings of fruits and vegetables, there are reports of people getting too much potassium from a salt substitute, especially if they use it in making soup. Too much potassium can put you in the hospital with your whole system out of kilter, which is one reason potassium pills are so very tricky. That explains why a doctor who has prescribed potassium for someone on "potassium-wasting" blood pressure medicine will do regular checks of the level of potassium in the body. But as we've mentioned, even if you really ate like a rabbit, you probably couldn't get anywhere close to too much of this important nutrient from your plate or salad bowl. Besides, a lot of these wonderful foods have other benefits as well. So enjoy!

Keeping Cancer at Bay with a Carrot a Day?

Keeping your cholesterol down also looks like a good move in reducing the risk of colorectal cancer. New research is linking high levels of cholesterol in the blood to a slightly greater than average chance of coming down with this disease.[35,36] This association won't necessarily show up with any other forms of cancer, though, and that brings us to a caveat: Expect no magic. Just as there is no single nutrient that will prevent osteoporosis or heart disease, there is no one simple answer when it comes to cancer, which is actually not one disease but perhaps hundreds, which all may be a little bit different. But there is some tantalizing research suggesting that eating right might be better than eating wrong—so we'll tell you how to "eat right" according to the evidence scientists have come up with.

Most of the interest has been focused on lung cancer, partly because it is one of the most common. The evidence is piling up that Bugs Bunny and Popeye were onto a good thing. Several studies have uncovered a protective effect of those green and yellow vegetables loaded with the vitamin A building block, beta-carotene.[37,38] It makes sense that a nutrient that the body uses to manufacture its own vitamin A would have a beneficial effect on the epithelial cells lining the lung, for scientists have long recognized that vitamin A helps to control division and growth of these cells.

What we don't know, though, is whether dietary supplements of beta-carotene will have the same salutary effects as eating a variety of fruits and vegetables rich in this nutrient, such as **apricots, asparagus, avocado, broccoli, brussels sprouts, cantaloupe, carrots, chard, chili peppers, yellow corn, cress, pink grapefruit, kale, butterhead** or **romaine lettuce, mandarin oranges, mangoes, mustard** and all those other dark green leafies, **papayas, parsley, peaches, bell peppers, plums, pumpkins, tangerines, spinach, squash** (especially winter varieties), **sweet potato, tomato,** and **watermelon**. If you don't get any of these foods more often than once in a blue moon, it might be smart either to revise your eating habits or consider a supplement.

Beta-carotene vitamin pills don't come with warranties, but the nutrition scientists are interested enough in this one to have quite a few studies going on now. They are checking the effectiveness of beta-carotene against not only lung cancer but also skin and digestive tract cancers. In one study, a lot of doctors are taking a supplement to see whether it lowers their risk of cancer more than a placebo.[39] Though we don't know the results of that ongoing clinical trial yet, the fact that physicians are the guinea pigs suggests that the medical establishment feels pretty darned confident about the safety of this supplement.

Physicians appear optimistic about all of the vitamin-A-type chemicals or retinoids, in fighting off cancer. In one recent study, patients with precancerous mouth lesions were given the retinoid drug **Accutane** (isotretinoin).[40] The results were encouraging, for with nine months of treatment most of these abnormalities had regressed; but **Accutane** has a number of serious side effects, and after treatment the lesions seem to come back. One expert, Dr. Gerald Shklar of the Harvard School of Dental Medicine, suggests that chemoprevention with beta-carotene, alone or in combination with vitamin E, would avoid the side effects of **Accutane** and may someday prove useful in reversing precancerous changes in the mouth.[41]

Vitamin E is also showing up in epidemiological studies as a possible bonus against lung cancer.[42] Blood levels of this "antioxidant" nutrient (which is usually found in whole grains—get the wheat germ out and start spooning) were lower in people who later developed lung cancer than in those who escaped.[43] If you'd rather eat juicy worms than have your chicken salad on whole wheat, you might want to consider a vitamin E supplement, but of course nobody knows exactly how much is enough. The RDA is only 15 IU, but the toxic potential of this vitamin appears fairly low. It is often sold in 400-IU capsules, and one or two of these a day appear safe for most people.

Folic acid, a B vitamin essential in DNA synthesis, is also being tested for anticancer activity. Elegant test-tube studies have shown that cells deprived of adequate folic acid (or folacin, or folate) are more likely to have chromosomes break.[44] And when a chromosome snaps, it may allow an oncogene, or cancer-causing gene, to shift into action. Because folic acid is so essential in cell reproduction, there is a theoretical base for giving folic acid supplements at levels 25 times higher than the recommended dietary allowance of 400 μg (micrograms) to people at risk of cancer.

Research projects at the University of Alabama are aimed at reversing precancerous changes in the lungs of smokers and also in cervical cells of women who have had abnormal Pap smears.[45,46] The preliminary results are encouraging; it may be some time yet before we find out whether folic acid supplements can really be helpful in these cases and whether there are any dangers associated with such a high dose. In the meantime, maximizing folic acid in the diet can't possibly hurt, because it's found primarily in those very same fruits and veggies that supply the fiber, potassium, beta-carotene, and other healthful nutrients we've been talking about. The dark green leafies, like **spinach, chard,** and **kale,** are especially good sources of folate, as are **broccoli** and the **sprouts** (**bean** and **brussels**). Other folate-rich foods are hardly on the hit parade of all-time favorites: **liver, wheat bran, wheat germ,** and **brewer's yeast**. No wonder some folks would rather take supplements!

Although selenium has been suggested as an anticancer nutrient on theoretical grounds, the most recent research doesn't show that it is significant.[47] Selenium may work in concert with vitamin E, but this protective effect only shows up in populations that are quite deficient, such as those with the lowest intake in selenium-poor regions like Finland. What's more, dietary sources of selenium are kind of quirky, not altogether predictable. Some parts of the country have soil, and thus local foodstuffs, that are relatively rich in selenium, while other areas are deficient. But with food in your grocery store coming from all over the country as it does (and indeed from beyond our borders in some cases), it would be difficult to sort out anyone's diet without some very painstaking, and expensive, laboratory research. Too much of this trace mineral can definitely be poisonous, so be very careful if you decide you need a supplement, and don't go over 500 μg a day.

Although scientists are very interested in the possibility of affecting the development of lung cancer through dietary changes, some worry that certain masters of denial (also known as smokers) will think that if they eat properly they needn't worry about the negative health consequences of their nicotine addiction. No such luck. Take it from the experts: "Cigarette smoking is the major known cause of lung cancer, and smoking cessation would be of more benefit than change in any other single behavior."[48]

B₆ for Better Breathing

If someone whispered to you that a mysterious vitamin was being used in doses well above the recommended dietary allowance of around 2 mg to treat conditions as different as sickle cell anemia, asthma, and a painful inflammation of tendons in the wrist, you'd be well justified in chalking it up as hype and maintaining a skeptical stance. But that's precisely what we're going to tell you right now. What's more, the research backing up these claims has been done by scientists with excellent credentials. And what they have found establishes that this vitamin—and perhaps all vitamins— should definitely be considered a drug.

Pyridoxine, better known as vitamin B₆, is not a household name for most people. It was first identified in the late thirties. Without the vitamin, people develop very distinctive symptoms of deficiency—they may come down with sores at the corners of the mouth, and the mouth and tongue may become quite swollen and painful. Confusion, depression, and even convulsions are other possible signs of a problem. But people hardly ever develop out-and-out B₆ deficiency, even though U.S. Department of Agriculture experts estimate that half the population doesn't get even two thirds of the recommended dietary allowance (only 2 mg/ day) for this vitamin. The RDA is set up with a comfortable margin, but having so many people come up so short is pretty unusual. Nobody knows exactly what the long-term effects would be of not getting quite enough vitamin B₆.

None the less, researchers were somewhat surprised to discover, over the past several years, that pyridoxine seems helpful in treating a variety of unrelated conditions. Doctors studying sickle cell anemia, a genetic disease that affects the ability of the blood to carry oxygen, found that victims were low in vitamin B₆ and responded favorably to megadoses: 100 mg daily for a couple of months.[49] As a side effect of this research, they found that people with bronchial asthma also had low levels of vitamin B_6. Although the 100-mg supplements these asthmatics took did not raise their blood levels of the vitamin very noticeably, all 15 in the study "reported a dramatic decrease in frequency and severity of wheezing or asthmatic attacks while taking the supplements."[50]

This study is preliminary, with a handful of patients, and none of the scientific controls we expect in research. But it gave the investigators enough encouragement to launch a full-scale, properly controlled two-year study. Before 1990 we should know for sure exactly how well pyridoxine works for asthma. In the meantime, an asthmatic who wants to give B_6 a try should talk it over with his doctor, as other asthma medicines may need to be adjusted.

Doctors are also considering the benefits of B_6 for carpal tunnel syndrome. The carpal tunnel is the passage in the wrist that nerves and tendons from the hand thread through on their way to the arm. Injury to the tendons caused perhaps by a fall or by years of typing or other repetitive hand motion can make them swell and push on the nerves. Result: The fingers or hand may hurt, tingle, or feel numb. New research shows that if the hand muscles have not yet lost their strength, some patients (30 or 40 percent) get better with pyridoxine supplements.[51] The dose used by Dr. Allan Bernstein of Hayward's Kaiser Permanente in the study was 150 mg a day for four months.

But don't think that just because some is good, a lot would be better. Unh-uh! When it comes to B_6, a bunch of folks who treated themselves on that principle ended up in serious trouble. In high doses (which may be as low, actually, as 200 mg a day) vitamin B_6 can damage nerves. In 1983, a number of people who had been taking from 2 to 6 grams (that is, 2,000 to 6,000 mg) of this vitamin a day saw Dr. Herbert Shaumberg about numbness in their hands and feet, clumsiness, and difficulty walking.[52,53] Fortunately, when they stopped taking the vitamin supplements, they did recover, but that stands as a potent demonstration that this vitamin really must be considered a drug. Because of its potential for toxicity to nerves, B_6 probably should not be taken in doses of more than 100 mg.

If you're not asthmatic, don't have carpal tunnel syndrome, and don't want to run the risk of taking high-dose supplements just to make sure you're getting enough, what foods should you put on your shopping list? Foods richest in pyridoxine include **baked potato** (with its jacket), **banana, lean ground beef, broccoli, flounder, fresh ham, kidney beans, lentils, lima beans, liver, perch, prunes, raisin bran, trout, canned tuna, turkey** and **chicken meat,** and **wheat germ.** It is probably next to impossible to get dangerous amounts of vitamin B_6 in the diet, since only liver has more than half the RDA in a single serving. In fact, as we noted before, there are a lot of people who don't really get close to just 2 mg daily. If nothing on this list ever shows up on your table, you could be one of them. In that case, a modest supplement might be in order. Any dose from the RDA of 2 mg up through perhaps 25 mg should be safe. More than that, and you're taking a drug instead of a vitamin.

Watching Out for Weird Diets

Nutrition is not always an inherently exciting topic. In fact, for the past 30 years or so, the advice we've been getting from the nutrition establishment has bordered on the soporific: Eat a well-balanced diet. Get your servings from the Basic Four Food Groups daily. Don't overindulge, at least not too often. Don't worry about vitamin supplements. And, echoing all the mothers we have ever known, eat all your vegetables.

'Fess up, now. Weren't you a little disappointed a bit ago to read that your best nutritional hedge against cancer is precisely a lifetime of vegetables? What could be more boring than broccoli? The fact is, this kind of advice doesn't have any flair. So it's no wonder that books touting almost magical regimens and flouting established nutritional knowledge sell so well. Harvey and Marilyn Diamond's *Fit for Life,* for example, was the number *one* bestseller in hardcover in 1986.

Part of the appeal of diet books is the fantasy element, according to historian Hillel Schwartz—the promise that their readers will not only become slim and beautiful, but also live to a ripe old age, boost their immune systems, and stay vigorous and active right to the end. "No matter how much doctors attack the principles of a diet," he suggests, "they'll never dissuade people from it because they don't address the fantasies that the diet projects."[54]

These fantasies may involve easy or quick weight loss or marvelous health claims, and may draw upon concepts that sound familiar even though they appear in no nutrition texts, because they are derived from popular ideas of nutrition dating from a bygone era. According to Schwartz, "*Fit for Life* is based in part on ideas that were born in the health-reform movement of the 1830s." And *Dr. Berger's Immune Power Diet* has been criticized by the *Harvard Medical School Health Letter* as fiction: "What this book is selling is a collection of quack ideas about food allergies that have been around for decades."[55]

Doctors have a hard time dealing with patients who subscribe to nonstandard nutritional approaches or "food fads":

> **Most individuals who are immersed in faddism can be placed into one of two categories—the Deceived and the Deluded. The Deceived mainly need accurate information and perhaps some assistance with logical reasoning. The Deluded require much more effort and may even be beyond help.**
>
> **The Deceived and Deluded cannot be differentiated on the basis of what they believe or how strongly they *appear* to hold their convictions. The test is how they react when faced with substantive evidence that their beliefs are wrong. The Deceived will change, the Deluded will not. It may take some time to determine which type of person you are dealing with.** [56]

Doctors have two rational reasons to worry about food fads and nutty notions. First, they are afraid that some regimens may be so extreme that people will be harmed by them, as happened with the patients taking massive doses of vitamin B_6. Many other nutrients are known to be toxic in large enough quantities, so physicians shudder to think of people gulping down megadoses of selenium, copper, or vitamin D. Then, too, we do not know the effect of high doses of many other nutrients. After all, in 1980, pyridoxine was thought to be relatively harmless even in large amounts; it is a water-soluble vitamin, and few problems with water-soluble vitamins had ever been documented before.

The second problem with nonstandard nutrition arises if someone tries to "cure" potentially serious symptoms with nutritional supplements or a popular diet. Clerks in health food stores have been known to pass out advice for supplements to treat headaches, fatigue, rashes, and other sorts of complaints. Needless to say, even if your doctor doesn't know what's causing your trouble, chances are he's made some effort to rule out some of the more serious disorders that might explain it. A clerk or even a self-styled nutrition expert is usually not capable of doing that.

When should the red flag go up? Health writer Jane Brody has suggested the following sound pointers for weight-loss diets. They apply well to nearly any other kind of diet as well:

☞**Almost anyone can lose weight on almost any diet, but only a permanent change in eating and exercise habits is likely to keep the weight off. So, the first rule of dieting is: don't go on any diet that you couldn't, wouldn't and shouldn't stay on for the rest of your life.**

☞**Most diets make food and menu choices for you ... This is unlikely to teach you how to make intelligent eating decisions once you lose the desired weight.**

☞**Don't be fooled by diets that claim to use special calorie-burning devices. There is no such magic food or drug ...**

☞**Beware of all plans that eliminate or severely restrict any major food category, other than fats and sugars. These regimens seriously distort nutrient intake in ways that cannot be corrected with vitamin supplements ...**

☞**Foods rich in complex carbohydrates, such as potatoes, cereals, grains, bread, and beans, as well as fruits and vegetables, are the mainstay of any nutritious diet. They permit you to eat more food for fewer calories and provide the roughage needed to keep your digestive tract working smoothly. A healthful diet causes neither constipation nor diarrhea.**

☞**Avoid fasting as a weight-control method. Fasting is equivalent to burning your furniture, instead of wood logs, in the fireplace ...**

☞**A good diet encourages you to drink up to eight eight-ounce glasses of water a day ...**

☞**You should feel good while dieting, not weak or tired or ravenously hungry. Your hair shouldn't fall out and your nails shouldn't crack. Any untoward symptoms are warnings that your diet is unhealthful.**[57]

Some other tips: If somebody tries to tell you that you need megadoses of some nutrient, find out why. There are some diseases that require specific diets for their management, and a number of drugs that may have nutritional consequences, but get the specifics. Don't accept vague explanations like "You feel tired, don't you?" as a reason to take megadoses of anything. (Vitamins don't supply energy.)

And don't fall for hair analysis. Although it seems like a logical idea, there are too many kinks in the system to make hair analysis useful, except perhaps in some cases of lead, mercury, or other heavy metal poisoning.[58] In fact, even in this case there can be difficulties in interpreting the results. You'd hardly want to undergo treatment for the lead poisoning that showed up on hair analysis just because you forgot to mention that you had been using a lead-acetate hair coloring like **Grecian Formula**.

Another warning sign: Get suspicious if someone suggests you need to give up a lot of the foods you are used to. Cytotoxic testing is the rage in some areas, and can produce a very long list of proscribed foods, but it has a very iffy reputation in medical science. It's also very expensive. If you really suspect that some food you eat commonly gives you trouble of one sort or another and you want confirmation, why not run your own "elimination and challenge" test? Cut that one food out of your diet for two weeks or so and see if your symptoms disappear, then "challenge" your system with a serving and see if they return. This is as much information as you ought to need, and it's free. (For goodness' sake, if you know that you are allergic to something that makes you break out in a rash and start to wheeze, don't try this. You don't need the "confirmation" an anaphylactic reaction would undoubtedly bring—along with the danger of dying.)

Remember, too, the old rule of thumb: If it sounds too good to be true, be suspicious. Science has not yet discovered any particular nutrients to help you live forever, for example, or even to make you live longer. Some interesting animal research has been done on "free radical scavengers" such as vitamin E and the like,[59] but the results can not yet be extrapolated to human beings with any degree of confidence. For more on what researchers *have* turned up, and the ways in which it might possibly be stretched to apply to humans, check out Chapter 14.

So what about weight loss for seniors? First, find out if it makes sense for you. If you are well into your seventies, losing weight probably won't lower your risk of certain diseases—you're already past that stage. But perhaps it will help you control your blood pressure or put less strain on overloaded arthritic joints. Your doctor will tell you if there is a good medical reason for you to go to all that trouble. Then, *please* stay away from crash diets. They are not wise for anyone, and may be especially dangerous for older people or people taking medications. Dr. Gabe Mirkin warns:

> **The diet kings are doing Americans a terrible injustice—they're setting them up for regaining any weight they may lose. And every time they rapidly put the weight back on, they lay down arterial plaque at an accelerated rate ...[60]**

Gradual weight loss will spare your body a lot of needless wear and tear and is likely to stick with you a lot longer, too. Some kind of exercise may also be a great help. One reader wrote to tell us how his wife largely overcame intermittent claudication with blood pressure medication, a circulatory drug, **Trental** (pentoxifylline), and an exercise program:

> **In April of last year she could not walk to the end of the driveway to pick up the paper without at least once freezing in place with pain. Today she has improved so much it has changed our lives. At Old Williamsburg she can walk you (me, anyway) into the ground, all day!**
>
> **In that time she has worked up to an equivalent of 50 miles a day on the exercise bike. That's just under 3 hours while watching TV. She is also back to 120 pounds, and size 8, from a maximum 175 pounds, size 17. Interesting, since her motivation was to save her legs and her health.**

You notice he did not mention any special diet? The exercise, it seems, was largely responsible. Three hours a day of exercise may be far too much for you. And perhaps you don't like the exercise bicycle, or can't get to one. It doesn't matter much what kind of exercise you choose, as long as it is realistic for your abilities and you like it enough to do it every day or at least several times a week. (There are even exercise programs now for people in wheelchairs.) Add a reasonably prudent diet, with plenty of emphasis on the veggies we've been praising (most are quite modest when it comes to calories), and you've got a shot at some very slow but steady progress against excess pounds. It won't be easy; losing weight never is. But losing weight gradually, say no more than half a pound a week, rather than quickly, is definitely better for your health.

Another word or two about exercise for elders: Dr. William J. Evans of Tufts University believes, "Because of demonstrated beneficial effects of exercise, there is probably no segment of the population that can benefit more from increased physical activity than the elderly."[61] Exercise is not magic: it won't necessarily help you live longer[62] and it won't prevent the loss of muscle tissue that usually occurs with age.[63] But, says Dr. Evans, "We've discovered two striking things. One, sedentary older people—especially women—have remarkably low functional capacities, and two, that capacity increases substantially as a result of exercise."[64] Translation: Keep moving. You'll be stronger and feel better.

One caution, especially for those unaccustomed to working up a sweat: Make sure to drink adequate fluids, not all at once, but before, after, and possibly during an exercise session. As we get older, thirst is not sensitive enough to tell us how much to drink, so if the day is warm or you are sweating heavily, drink even though you may not feel thirsty.

Should You Take Vitamins?

It would be great if we could tell you, "Older people need more vitamin X. You should take a supplement supplying exactly 353 mg daily." But we can't, for a variety of reasons. Reason number 1: Everyone, even the teenager down the block who seems to spend all her energy and most of her allowance looking just like everyone else she hangs around with, is biochemically unique. No two people have the exact same nutritional requirements. But the older we get, the more pronounced the differences become. So, while nutritional surveys can tell us that elderly people in general seem to be getting less zinc, folic acid, vitamin B$_6$ and copper than they should,[65] that doesn't tell us anything, really, about a particular senior citizen.

The second reason is that the RDAs (recommended dietary allowances) for older people may not be very accurate. In many cases, they are "extrapolated" (read that: guessed at, by scientists) from the actual research conducted on much younger people.[66] There isn't even a set of RDAs specifically for the elderly, just one batch to cover everyone older than 51 years. The investigators in this field are becoming increasingly uncomfortable with this approach, and are even admitting openly that it's probably not the way to go. According to Dr. Walter Mertz, director of the Human Nutrition Research Center of the U. S. Department of Agriculture,

> **Most of the nutrition experiments are done in universities. They're done on college students. It's very, very questionable that we can take results from a teenager or 22-year-old who is still growing, who hasn't reached the peak of body mass yet, and translate those to an age where body mass is declining.[67]**

To make things worse, a lot of other issues get mixed up with "age" in research. As far as scientists have been able to tell, a simple accumulation of years may not have a great deal of impact on nutritional requirements. "A good diet at age 40 years is still a good diet at age 80."[68] But disease can have a significant effect on nutrient needs, and so can certain drugs. Older people often suffer from diseases, such as diabetes or hypertension, or take drugs, including blood pressure medications, that make some nutritional management necessary.

Take iron, for example. Iron deficiency anemia is fairly common among women and young children because they just don't get enough of this mineral in their diet. Iron deficiency anemia in elderly people is rarely caused by dietary inadequacy. Frequently, it may be due to gastrointestinal bleeding caused by aspirin or one of the other nonsteroidal anti-inflammatory drugs so commonly used for arthritis. If that's not applicable, anemia should be a tip-off to the doctor to look for some underlying disease. Chronic blood loss as, for example, from an ulcer or other gastrointestinal lesion, is often to blame, but the list of other possibilities is long: lead poisoning, alcoholism, liver or kidney disease, drug reactions affecting the bone marrow, chronic infections or arthritis-type conditions, and certain types of cancer can all cause anemia.[69] Clearly, treatment needs to address the underlying cause as well as the iron deficiency itself.

The other issue that can confuse research on the nutritional status of the elderly is money. One study of elderly Floridian women discovered that just 3 percent of the middle class and wealthy women had evidence of folate deficiency, while 60 percent of the poor women had low levels of folate in their blood.[70] Zinc has nutritionists worried because its main sources in the diet are milk and meats, and these are often the first to go when the tab is too high at the supermarket. Older people living on fixed incomes may be skimping on their groceries just so they can pay their bills. No wonder they may be lacking in some nutrients—most likely their diets are altogether inadequate. Less food overall often means a lower chance of hitting the bull's eye on any given element of the diet.

In fact, as we grow older, we do tend to eat less. That's partly because we usually become less active and so need fewer calories, but for some people it may also be related to dental difficulties that make it hard to chew and swallow, or to problems shopping and cooking a meal. If you or someone you know is limited to just a few foods because of problems like this, it is time to call in the troops. Many communities have a "Meals on Wheels" program delivering nutritious hot meals to senior citizens several times a week, or even daily. In other places, a senior citizens' center serves lunch. If there aren't any programs offering nutritional backup in your area, maybe you should start organizing. Your church or temple might be interested in helping to get such a project off the ground. One thing you can be sure of: If one person has problems getting out or fixing food, there are plenty of other folks in the same boat.

So, should you be taking vitamin pills? Some experts give a "knee-jerk" no. Jane Brody offers the usual stance: "... the scientific evidence supporting the benefits of supplements ranges from meager to nonexistent."[71] But she goes on to suggest that elderly people with a restricted diet (in quantity or variety) might well need a multivitamin–mineral supplement. If most of the vegetables, fruits and other nutritious foods listed earlier in the chapter are old familiar friends that show up on your dinner table often, you probably don't need supplements. But if you're not sure your regular fare qualifies as a "well-balanced diet," a multiple vitamin pill probably won't hurt and might provide some useful nutritional insurance. Don't bother with ultra-expensive super-duper formulations, though, unless you have money to spare. We haven't found any research that shows a natural or organic supplement is better utilized by the body than the cheapest drugstore kind.

All right, we can almost hear the wheels turning. "My diet's not too bad," you may be saying, "but how do I know I'm not deficient in one nutrient or another?" The answer: You don't, not unless your doctor orders a specific test to find out. And these laboratory analyses are relatively expensive. You could take a simple multivitamin supplement for a long time—several years— before it would cost as much as a single nutrient determination. Of course, if your doctor finds signs of a deficiency, he will probably check it out more closely and prescribe a supplement to treat it. (And if he diagnoses a deficiency, Medicare usually pays for the lab work.)

Older people are more likely than youngsters to have little or no acid in the stomach—or they may be taking an ulcer drug, such as **Tagamet** (cimetidine), which shuts down stomach acid production. Either way, the absorption of both vitamin B_{12} and folate may be reduced.[72] Do ask, if your doctor starts you on B_{12} shots, that she check folic acid status as well. The two often go hand-in-glove, and it is just as dangerous to supplement B_{12} without looking at folate as the other way around.[73] Folic acid deficiency, whether it results from not getting enough folate in the diet, not absorbing folate well, or taking a drug that depletes folacin in the body, is serious for older people because the symptoms—confusion and disorientation—are easily mistaken for the onset of senility.[74] And nobody needs a false diagnosis of Alzheimer's disease to mess up his life!

If you'd rather not go for a more general multiple vitamin, let's take a look at some of the B vitamins and trace minerals that are most frequently reported as low among middle-aged or older people. One study discovered that in a relatively healthy, wealthy, and wise (disease-free, well-off, and well-educated) group of Americans between 60 and 94 years old, those with the lowest levels of vitamin C and the B vitamins—folic acid, niacin, riboflavin, thiamine, pyridoxine, and vitamin B_{12}—had the poorest performance on tests of abstract reasoning and memory.[75,76] So if you're not big on **wheat germ, brewer's yeast, whole grains, liver, lean pork, peanuts,** or **collard greens,** you've got a rationale for a B-complex supplement. Stick with one that supplies between 50 and 200 percent of the RDA; there's no reason whatsoever for the popularity of a B-100 type of supplement, except that the label looks nice and tidy.

Watch out for really high doses of any single nutrient, because often they may interfere with others that can be equally important. Even RDA levels in one single pill might be a problem: 400 µg of folacin (the current RDA) can reduce the amount of zinc absorbed.[77] And zinc is a nutrient of special interest for older people. Their diets are often skimpy on zinc, but this trace element is crucial for wound healing, and for patients with bed sores, that could make a big difference.[78] Lack of zinc may also lead to a dulling of the sense of taste.[79] If you eat **oysters** or other **shellfish, meat, milk, liver, eggs,** and **whole grains,** you probably get enough zinc.[80] If most of those foods sound weird— well, look for a supplement to offer close to the 15 mg that are currently thought to be appropriate. Just to be on the safe side, though, don't take it at the same time as your B-complex pill.

Another vitamin–mineral interaction worth noting: Megadoses of vitamin C can mess up the body's use of copper,[81] another of the nutrients older people reportedly lack. The suggested intake of copper is around 2 or 3 mg per day. Look for it in **oysters, nuts, liver, whole grains, mushrooms, dried beans, peas,** and **lentils**. Zinc and copper need to work together with each other and with iron—as you notice, they're all found in many of the same food sources. Too much of one interferes with the other; what's more, they can both cause serious problems in overdose. Resist the temptation to go overboard with supplements, and here's to your health!

Drug Interactions with Vitamins and Minerals

Not only do vitamins and minerals frequently interact with each other, but many of them also interact with medications. Some drugs can really ruin a person's appetite by causing nausea or discomfort, or by wiping out the sense of taste. Anticancer drugs often cause loss of appetite; less frequently, medications such as blood pressure pills, including **Aldactone** (spironolactone), **Aldomet** (methyldopa), **Apresoline** (hydralazine), **Catapres** (clonidine), **Lasix** (furosemide), and **Wytensin** (guanabenz), may also have this effect.[82] So may digitalis-type drugs for the heart, especially when the dose is too high, and phenothiazine-type tranquilizers such as **Compazine** (prochlorperazine), **Mellaril** (thioridazine), **Permitil** and **Prolixin** (fluphenazine), **Stelazine** (trifluoperazine), and **Thorazine** (chlorpromazine) tend to decrease the appetite in older people especially. The tuberculosis drug isoniazid and the gout medicine colchicine may also make patients feel less interested in food. As a result, elderly people taking such medicines or taste-destroying drugs such as **Cuprimine** (penicillamine), **Capoten** (captopril), **Atromid-S** (clofibrate), **Fulvicin** (griseofulvin), and **Dilantin** (phenytoin) may just not eat enough food to stay well nourished, period.[83]

Some of these medications also interfere with the body's ability to absorb or use particular nutrients. **Dilantin** affects the metabolism of calcium and vitamin D quite profoundly; it also has a substantial impact on vitamin K and the B-complex vitamins, especially folic acid. But like certain other drugs, **Dilantin** does not work properly when some vitamin levels are too high. Supplements of folate and pyridoxine can decrease the anticonvulsant activity as much as 50 percent. The following table summarizes drug and nutrient interactions to watch for. Remember to check with your physician, though, before you tinker with the dose of *any* drug or prescribed supplement.

Interactions Between Medicines and Nutrients*

Drug	Nutrient	Interaction
ANTIBIOTICS		
TETRACYCLINE-TYPE **Achromycin Aureomycin Minocin Panmycin Terramycin Tetracyn** etc.	Calcium Iron Magnesium Riboflavin Vitamin C Zinc	Drug and minerals interfere with each other. Prolonged use of tetracycline may require dietary supplements, but do not take calcium or other mineral supplements within 2 hours of drug. Taken at the same time, the supplements will prevent absorption of the drug.
NEOMYCIN	Sodium Potassium Calcium Iron Vitamin D Vitamin B_{12} Folate	These nutrients are not well absorbed.
ARTHRITIS REMEDIES		
Aspirin **Anacin Ascriptin Bayer Bufferin Excedrin** etc.	Vitamin C	Less vitamin C gets into cells, and the body loses more. It is unclear whether vitamin C supplements overcome this problem.
	Folate	Folate levels are lower. Heavy aspirin users may need a supplement.
	Iron	Losing small amounts of blood from the gastrointestinal tract daily can deplete the body of iron. Iron supplements may be advisable.
Indomethacin **Indocin**	Iron	Same as aspirin. See above.
	Calcium Phosphorus	These minerals may be depleted, weakening bones.
Penicillamine **Cuprimine Depen**	Iron Magnesium	Iron supplements or iron-rich food may interfere with proper absorption of this arthritis drug. So can mineral supplements containing magnesium.
	Zinc Copper	This drug may make an insoluble complex with zinc and copper, causing deficiency. Loss of taste and slow healing are possible results.

Drug	Nutrient	Interaction
	Vitamin B_6	This drug may induce a vitamin deficiency, with symptoms of confusion or tingling or numb hands and feet. More Vitamin B_6 (pyridoxine) may be needed.
Methotrexate **Mexate**	Folate Vitamin B_{12} Carotene	The drug affects the intestinal wall and interferes with absorption of these nutrients. With methotrexate being used against psoriasis and arthritis as well as cancer, more doctors and patients need to be aware of these nutritional imbalances. Cancer patients MUST NOT take folate supplements except by prescription, for an excess of this vitamin could reduce the effectiveness of the drug.
Prednisone **Deltasone** **Meticorten**	Calcium	Long-term use of prednisone or similar corticosteroids interferes with calcium absorption and may lead to weakened bones.

BLOOD PRESSURE DRUGS

Drug	Nutrient	Interaction
THIAZIDES **Aldoril** **Diuril** **Esidrix** Hydrochlorothiazide **HydroDIURIL** **Ser-Ap-Es** etc.	Potassium Magnesium Zinc	These minerals are lost from the body. This could be a sticky problem since both potassium and magnesium appear to be helpful in keeping blood pressure normal. Periodic blood checks are a good idea.
TRIAMTERENES **Dyazide** **Dyrenium** **Maxzide**	Folate	Folic acid deficiency could become a problem unless a supplement is taken.
	Potassium	Triamterene-containing diuretics are potassium-sparing. If supplements are taken (including salt substitutes), a dangerous potassium overload (hyperkalemia) could result.
FUROSEMIDE **Lasix**	Calcium	Furosemide kicks calcium out of the body through the kidney. A deficiency is possible.

Drug	Nutrient	Interaction
HYDRALAZINES **Apresazide** **Apresoline** **Hydralazine** **Ser-Ap-Es** **Unipres**	Vitamin B_6	The body may become depleted of pyridoxine. Symptoms of a serious deficiency include numbness or tingling of hands and feet, depression, and forgetfulness. To prevent nerve damage, try to start with adequate levels of vitamin B_6 and maintain them.
METHYLDOPA **Aldomet** **Aldoril**	Folate Vitamin B_{12} Iron	These nutrients are not well absorbed.
BLOOD THINNERS **Coumadin** **Dicumarol** **Panwarfin**	Vitamin C	Large doses of vitamin C may possibly interfere with the effectiveness of the drug.
	Vitamin E	With supplements, the drug may work too well. Have your doctor check your bleeding time.
	Vitamin K	Don't binge on foods rich in this vitamin, such as beef liver, cabbage, spinach, broccoli, turnip greens, and green peas. Vitamin K can block the action of this drug.
CHOLESTEROL-LOWERING DRUGS **Colestid** **Lopid** **Questran**	Vitamin A Vitamin B_{12} Vitamin D Vitamin E Vitamin K Folate Iron	Nutrient absorption is hindered. Cholesterol-lowering medications may be risky in combination with blood thinners because of their effect on vitamin K. Frequent blood tests are advised.
EPILEPSY DRUGS Phenytoin **Dilantin**	Folate	This vitamin may become depleted. Supplementation is controversial, for too much folic acid (more than 2 mg/day) may interfere with the effectiveness of the drug. The doctor should test for folate anemia and prescribe adequate folate supplementation (0.4–1 mg) to prevent this.

Drug	Nutrient	Interaction
Phenobarbital Phenytoin **Dilantin**	Vitamin B$_6$	The drug is less effective in preventing seizures. An 80-mg supplement of B$_6$ could reduce anticonvulsant activity by half.
	Vitamin D Calcium	These anticonvulsants interfere with the action of vitamin D. Without vitamin D, calcium cannot be utilized normally. Osteomalacia (weak bones) may result unless a supplement is taken (400–800 IU). Muscle weakness, difficulty walking, and hearing problems are also possible.
Phenytoin **Dilantin** Primidone **Mysoline**	Vitamin K	The vitamin level may be lowered.

DIGESTIVE TRACT DRUGS
ALUMINUM ANTACIDS

Drug	Nutrient	Interaction
Aludrox **Delcid** **Di-Gel** **Gelusil** **Maalox** **Mylanta** **Rolaids** **WinGel** etc.	Calcium Phosphate	On a regular basis, these aluminum-based antacids could make older people more susceptible to weakened bones. Aluminum grabs on to phosphate in food and may deplete it from the body. Calcium loss may follow.
	Thiamine	These antacids inactivate thiamine. Do not take them at mealtime.
LAXATIVES Mineral Oil **Agoral** **Nujol** **Petrogalar**	Vitamin A Vitamin D Vitamin E Vitamin K	Regular use of these laxatives interferes with absorption of fat-soluble vitamins. When vitamin D is not absorbed well, calcium and phosphate are affected and bones may weaken. Depleting Vitamin K could interfere with proper blood clotting and lead to bleeding gums and more serious problems.
Phenolphthalein **Correctol** **Ex-Lax** **Feen-A-Mint** **Phenolax**	Vitamin D Calcium	Regular use of these laxatives may interfere with vitamin D and calcium, eventually causing bone weakening.
	Potassium	This nutrient may not be properly absorbed.

Drug	Nutrient	Interaction
INFLAMMATORY BOWEL DISEASE		
Sulfasalazine **Azulfidine**	Folate	Vitamin deficiency may develop. Your doctor may need to prescribe a supplement (0.4–1.0 mg).
ULCER		
Cimetidine **Tagamet**	Calcium	It is possible, but not confirmed, that long-term use of cimetidine may interfere with calcium absorption and lead to weakened bones. For maximum absorption of a supplement, take it with meals.
ESTROGENS		
Estratab **Estrocon** **Evex** **Menest** **Premarin**	Folate	Women using estrogens may be susceptible to folate deficiency. The physician may wish to check plasma folate from time to time.
GOUT MEDICINE		
Colchicine **ColBENEMID**	Vitamin D Vitamin B_{12} Sodium Potassium Carotene	Absorption of these nutrients is reduced.
HEART DRUGS		
DIGITALIS GLYCOSIDES **Crystodigin** **Digiglusin** Digitalis Digitoxin **Purodigin** Digoxin **Lanoxin**	Thiamine	Long-term use of one of these heart medicines may lead to thiamine deficiency.
	Potassium Magnesium Zinc	Body loss of magnesium and zinc is increased by these drugs. Potassium or magnesium depletion makes the body more sensitive to the toxic effects of the drugs.
	Vitamin D	Too much Vitamin D can boost the level of calcium in the blood. This may make the drug more effective—so much so that irregular heartbeats may become a danger.

Drug	Nutrient	Interaction
PSYCHIATRIC DRUGS		
LITHIUM **Cibalith** **Eskalith** **Lithobid**	Sodium	The kidney handles lithium and sodium in the same way. If there is too much sodium in the body, lithium levels will drop and the drug may become ineffective. If the body becomes depleted of sodium, lithium can build up and toxic reactions are possible.
MAJOR TRANQUILIZERS		
Chlorpromazine **Thorazine** etc.	Riboflavin Vitamin B_{12}	These vitamins are depleted. Supplementation may be necessary.
Fluphenazine **Permitil** **Prolixin** Thioridazine **Mellaril**	Vitamin C	High doses of vitamin C may reduce the effectiveness of the drug.
PARKINSON'S DISEASE DRUGS		
Levodopa **Dopar** **Larodopa** **Parda**	Vitamin B_6	Supplements of more than 5 mg of pyridoxine may interfere with the drug's effectiveness and could make symptoms worse.
POTASSIUM SUPPLEMENTS		
Potassium chloride (slow release) **Kaon-Cl** **Klotrix** **K-Tab** **Micro-K** **Slow-K**	Vitamin B_{12}	The vitamin is absorbed less efficiently. Usually a deficiency would take several years to develop, but an older person who has already begun depleting body reserves could run into trouble sooner.
SLEEPING PILLS		
Glutethimide **Doriden**	Vitamin D	Long-term use of this sleeping pill may deplete vitamin D levels, with weakened bones as a result.
TUBERCULOSIS DRUGS		
Isoniazid **INH** **Laniazid** **Nydrazid** **Rifamate**	Niacin Vitamin B_6 Folate	Deficiencies of these B vitamins are likely. Your doctor should prescribe supplements. DO NOT take them without supervision, as high doses of pyridoxine (vitamin B_6) may reduce the drug's effectiveness.

Drug	Nutrient	Interaction
P.A.S.	Vitamin B_{12} Folate	Deficiencies of these vitamins may occur.

Table Sources

Garabedian-Ruffalo, Susan M.; and Ruffalo, Richard L. "Drug and Nutrient Interactions." *Am. Fam. Physician* 33(2)165–174, 1985.

Grunfeld, Eva. "Anticonvulsant Drugs and Nutrient Interactions." *Can. Pharm. J.* 113:22–25, 1979.

Lamy, Peter P. "Effects of Diet and Nutrition on Drug Therapy." *J. Am. Geriatr. Soc.* 30(11): S99–S112, 1982.

Mangini, Richard, ed. *Drug Interaction Facts.* St. Louis: J.B. Lippincott, 1984.

Powers, Dorothy E.; and Moore, Ann O. *Food Medication Interactions.* Tucson, 1983.

Roe, Daphne A. "Interactions Between Drugs and Nutrients." *Medical Clinics of North America* 63:985–1007, 1979.

Roe, Daphne A. "Drug-Induced Malnutrition in Geriatric Patients." *Comprehensive Ther.* 38(10): 24–28, 1977.

Roe, Daphne A. "Drug-Nutrient Interactions in the Elderly." *Geriatrics* 41(3):57–74, 1986.

Smith, Christine Hamilton; and Bidlack, Wayne R. "Dietary Concerns Associated with the Use of Medications." *Am. Diet. Ass. J.* 84(8):901–914, 1984.

Vitamin Supplements. *Med. Let.* 27:66–68, 1985.

VNIS/Roche. Drug-Nutrient Interactions.

Things to Remember

1. Foods that may help minimize problems with cholesterol and the risk of heart attack include fiber from oatmeal, oat bran, legumes, barley, and high-pectin fruit; fish or fish oil; olive oil; garlic and onions; and foods or supplements providing copper and chromium in the range of safe and adequate daily intakes (2 to 3 mg for copper, 0.05 to 0.2 mg for chromium).

2. For a healthy heart, take it easy on foods high in saturated fat. Watch out for lard, butter, and cream; but also avoid "substitutes" made with coconut oil or palm kernel oil. These fats can kick your body's cholesterol-manufacturing machinery into high gear!

3. Get enough potassium if you want to keep your blood pressure and your risk of stroke as low

as possible. High-potassium foods include many vegetables: artichokes, asparagus, avocado, beets, bell peppers, broccoli, brussels sprouts, cabbage, carrots, cauliflower, chard, mushrooms, potatoes, squash, sweet potatoes, and tomatoes. Potassium-rich fruit includes apricots, bananas, blackberries, cantaloupe, nectarines, oranges, peaches, and plums. Don't forget the fish, clams, mussels, oysters, buttermilk, skim milk, and yogurt.

4. Potassium-based salt substitutes (**Adolph's Salt Substitute**, **Morton Salt Substitute**, **NoSalt**, **Nu-Salt**) are good sources of potassium, but it's not too hard to overdose. Be careful, especially with homemade soup.

5. Foods rich in carotene may be beneficial in helping to prevent cancer. Help yourself to generous portions of apricots, asparagus, avocadoes, broccoli, brussels sprouts, canteloupe, carrots, chard, chili peppers, yellow corn, cress, pink grapefruit, greens (mustard, turnip, beet, collard, etc.), kale, butterhead or Romaine lettuce, mandarin oranges, mangoes, papayas, parsley, peaches, bell peppers, plums, pumpkins, tangerines, spinach, squash, sweet potatoes, tomatoes, and watermelon.

6. Vitamin E is another nutrient that appears to be protective against lung cancer. Whole grains are the richest dietary source. Spoon on that wheat germ or take a supplement if you want extra insurance.

7. Folic acid is also promising for cancer prevention. Good foods for this vitamin include dark green leafies (spinach, chard, kale), broccoli, bean sprouts, brussels sprouts, liver, wheat bran, wheat germ, and brewer's yeast.

8. Vitamin B_6 may be useful for people with asthma and carpal tunnel syndrome. Too much of a

good thing could be toxic. Keep your intake to 100 mg or less a day.

9. Be wary of weird diets. Promises of rapid weight loss, immune boosting power, or detoxification are hard to keep.

10. Many drugs will affect your nutritional status, and some nutrients may muck up the effectiveness of your medicine. Check the table above to see whether you need extra supplements.

References

1. Kushi, Lawrence H., et al. "Diet and 20-Year Mortality from Coronary Heart Disease: The Ireland–Boston Diet–Heart Study." *N. Engl. J. Med.* 312:811–818, 1985.
2. "Reducing Your Level of Cholesterol? Try Oats." *Tufts University Diet & Nutrition Letter* 4:1–2, Nov. 1986.
3. "Cholesterol's Slippery Slope." *Science News* 128:344, 1985.
4. Kolata, Gina. "Lowered Cholesterol Decreases Heart Disease." *Science* 223:381–382, 1984.
5. Kromhout, Daan; Bosschieter, Edward B.; and Coulander, Cor de Lezenne. "The Inverse Relation between Fish Consumption and 20-Year Mortality from Coronary Heart Disease." *N. Engl. J. Med.* 312:1205–1209, 1985.
6. Wallis, Claudia. "Is Seafood Good for the Heart?" *Time*, May 20, 1985, p. 64.
7. Harris, W.S., et al. "The Comparative Reductions of the Plasma Lipids and Lipoproteins by Dietary Polyunsaturated Fats: Salmon Oil Versus Vegetable Oils. " *Metabolism* 32:179–184, 1983.
8. Knapp, Howard R., et al. "In Vivo Indexes of Platelet and Vascular Function During Fish-Oil Administration in Patients with Atherosclerosis." *N. Engl. J. Med.* 314: 937–942, 1986.
9. Weiner, Bonnie, et al. "Inhibition of Atherosclerosis by Cod-Liver Oil in a Hyperlipidemic Swine Model." *N. Engl. J. Med.* 315:814–816, 1986.
10. "Fish Oil for the Heart." *Medical Letter* 29:7–9, 1987.
11. "Fish Oil May Ease Arthritis Pain." *Med. World News* July 14, 1986, p. 9.
12. Lee, Tak H., et al. "Effect of Dietary Enrichment with Eicosapentaenoic and Docosahexaenoic Acids on In Vitro Neutrophil and Monocyte Leukotriene Generation and Neutrophil Function." *N. Engl. J. Med.* 312:1217–1234, 1985.
13. Liebman, Bonnie F. "Good Fats?" *Nutrition Action Healthletter* 13:1–6, 1986.

14. Grundy, Scott M. "Comparison of Monounsaturated Fatty Acids and Carbohydrates for Lowering Plasma Cholesterol." *N. Engl. J. Med.* 314:745–748, 1986.
15. Ibid. p. 747.
16. Liebman, op. cit., pp. 4–5.
17. Williams, Paul T., et al. "Associations of Dietary Fat, Regional Adiposity, and Blood Pressure in Men." *JAMA* 257:3251–3256, 1987.
18. Boullin, David J. "Garlic as a Platelet Inhibitor." (letter) *Lancet*, Apr. 4, 1981, pp. 776–777.
19. Ariga, Toyohiko; Oshiba, Susumu; and Tamada, Terumi. "Platelet Aggregation Inhibitor in Garlic." (letter) *Lancet*, Jan. 17, 1981, pp. 150–151.
20. Block, Eric. "The Chemistry of Garlic and Onions." *Scientific American* 252(3):114–119, 1985.
21. Makheja, Amar N.; Vanderhoek, Jack Y.; and Bailey, J. Martyn. "Effects of Onion (Allium Cepa) Extract on Platelet Aggregation and Thromboxane Synthesis." *Prostaglandins and Medicine* 2:413–424, 1979.
22. Menon, I. Sudhakaran; Kendal, R.Y.; Dewar, H.A.; and Newell, D.J. "Effect of Onions on Blood Fibrinolytic Activity." *Brit. Med. J.* 2:351–352, 10 Aug. 1968.
23. Jain, R.C. "Effect of Garlic Oil in Experimental Cholesterol Atherosclerosis." *Atherosclerosis* 29:125–129, 1978.
24. "Heavy Garlic Intake Lowers Serum Lipids." *Med. Trib.* 19(39):2, 1978.
25. Bordia, Arun. "Effect of Garlic on Blood Lipids in Patients with Coronary Heart Disease." *Am. J. Clin. Nutr.* 34:2100–2103, 1981.
26. Ibid., p. 2103.
27. Trager, James. "Saturated Fat on Menu—In Small Print." *Medical Tribune* Feb. 4, 1987, p. 6.
28. Riales, R.; and Albrink, M.J. "Effect of Chromium Chloride Supplementation on Glucose Tolerance and Serum Lipids Including High Density Lipoprotein of Adult Men." *Am. J. Clin. Nutr.* 34:2670–2678, 1981.
29. Anderson, Richard; and Kozlovsky, A.S. "Chromium Intake, Absorption and Excretion of Subjects Consuming Self-Selected Diets." *Am. J. Clin. Nutr.* 41:1177–1183, 1985.
30. Fields, M. "Newer Understanding of Copper Metabolism." *Internal Medicine* 6:91–98, 1985.
31. "Tracing the Facts About Trace Minerals." *Tufts University Diet & Nutrition Letter* 5(1):3–6, 1987.
32. Khaw, Kay-Tee; and Barrett-Connor, Elizabeth. "Dietary Potassium and Blood Pressure in a Population." *Am. J. Clin. Nutr.* 39:963–968, 1984.
33. Kromhout, D.; Bosschieter, E.B.; and Coulander, C. de L. "Potassium, Calcium, Alcohol Intake and Blood Pressure: The Zutphen Study." *Am. J. Clin. Nutr.* 41:1299–1304, 1985.
34. Khaw, Kay-Tee; and Barrett-Connor, Elizabeth. "Dietary Potassium and Stroke-Associated Mortality: A 12-Year Prospective Population Study." *N. Engl. J. Med.* 316:235–240, 1987.
35. Tornberg, Sven A.; Holm, Lars-Erik; Carstensen, John M.; and Eklund, Gunnar A. "Risks of Cancer of the Colon and Rectum in Relation to Serum Cholesterol and Beta-Lipoprotein." *N. Engl. J. Med.* 315:1629–1633, 1986.

36. Mannes, Gerd Alexander, et al. "Relation Between the Frequency of Colorectal Adenoma and the Serum Cholesterol Level." *N. Engl. J. Med.* 315:1634–1638, 1986.
37. Colditz, Graham A.; Stampfer, Meir J.; and Willett, Walter C. "Diet and Lung Cancer: A Review of the Epidemiologic Evidence in Humans." *Arch. Intern. Med.* 147:157–160, 1987.
38. Menkes, Marilyn S., et al. "Serum Beta-Carotene, Vitamins A and E, Selenium, and the Risk of Lung Cancer." *N. Engl. J. Med.* 315:1250–1254, 1986.
39. Hennekens, Charles H. "Micronutrients and Cancer Prevention." *N. Engl. J. Med.* 315:1288–1289, 1986.
40. Hong, Waun Ki, et al. "13-*cis*-Retinoic Acid in the Treatment of Oral Leukoplakia." *N. Engl. J. Med.* 315:1501–1505, 1986.
41. Shklar, Gerald. "Oral Leukoplakia." (editorial) *N. Engl. J. Med.* 315:1544–1545, 1986.
42. Colditz et al, op. cit., pp. 158–159.
43. Menkes et al, op. cit.
44. Yunis, Jorge J.; and Hoffman, William R. "Birth of an Errant Cell: A New Theory About the Cause of Cancer." *The Sciences* 25(6):28–33, 1985.
45. Johnson, Roger. "Vitamins Reverse Smokers' Lesions." *Medical Tribune,* Jan. 14, 1987, pp. 4–5.
46. "Vitamins for Cervical Cells." *Medical Tribune,* Jan. 14, 1987, p. 5.
47. Ibid.
48. Colditz et al, op. cit., p. 160.
49. Liebman, Bonnie F. "B-6: Vitamin and Drug?" *Nutrition Action Healthletter* 13(9):1–6, Oct. 1986.
50. "Can B_6 Add to Asthma Therapy?" *Medical World News* 27(15):63, 1986.
51. Liebman, "B-6: Vitamin and Drug?" op. cit., p. 5.
52. Ibid.
53. "Rx for Some Sensory Neuropathy: Discontinue Vitamin B_6 Megadoses." *Medical World News,* Oct. 10, 1983, p. 38–39.
54. Monmaney, Terence. "Diet Books with No Sugarcoating." *Newsweek* Feb. 2, 1987, p. 76–78.
55. "Power Failure for the 'Immune Power' Diet." *Consumer Reports* Feb. 1986, pp. 12, 113.
56. Jarvis, William T. "Coping with Food Faddism." *Nutrition & the M.D. Special Report: Nutrition Myths & Misinformation,* n.d. (ca. 1986).
57. Brody, Jane E. "You Do Not Have to Fall Prey to Worthless Weight-Loss Gimmicks." (NY Times News Service) *Durham Sun,* Aug. 13, 1986.
58. Ibid.
59. Blumberg, Jeffrey B. "Role of Dietary Antioxidants in Aging." Fifth Annual Bristol-Myers Symposium on Nutrition Research, Oct. 31–Nov. 1, 1985.
60. Trubo, Richard. "Fad Diets: Sorting Through the Misinformation." *Medical World News* 27(15):44–59, 1986.
61. Evans, William J. "Exercise and Muscle Metabolism in the Elderly." Fifth Annual Bristol-Myers Symposium on Nutrition Research, Oct. 31–Nov. 1, 1985.

62. Holloszy, John O. "Effect of Exercise on Longevity of Rats." Fifth Annual Bristol-Myers Symposium on Nutrition Research, Oct. 31–Nov. 1, 1985.

63. "Exercise Can't Reverse Muscle Loss Caused by Aging—But It Can Help Delay It." (press release) Fifth Annual Bristol-Myers Symposium on Nutrition Research, Oct. 31–Nov. 1, 1985.

64. Ibid.

65. Kohrs, Mary Bess. "Nutritional Benefits of Nutrition Intervention Programs for the Elderly." Fifth Annual Bristol-Myers Symposium on Nutrition Research, Oct. 31–Nov. 1, 1985.

66. Schneider, Edward L., et al. "Recommended Dietary Allowances and the Health of the Elderly." *N. Engl. J. Med.* 314:157–160, 1986.

67. Cooke, Susan. "Trace Element Needs of Elderly Not Ironed Out." *Medical Tribune* Feb. 26, 1986, p. 42.

68. Shock, Nathan W. "The Role of Nutrition in Aging." *J. Amer. College of Nutrition* 1:3–9, 1982.

69. Freedman, Michael L. "Iron Deficiency in the Elderly." *Hospital Practice* 21(3A):115–137, 1986.

70. Grinblat, Joseph. "Folate Status in the Aged." *Clinics in Geriatric Medicine* 1:711–728, 1985.

71. Brody, Jane. "Experts Question Value of Dietary Supplements." (NY Times News Service) *Durham Sun*, Feb. 5, 1987, p. 8-A.

72. Grinblat, op. cit., p. 723.

73. Ibid., p. 717–718.

74. Lamy, Peter P. "Nutrition, Drugs and the Elderly." *Currents* 1(2):21–28, 1985.

75. Goodwin, J.M.; Goodwin, J.S.; and Garry, P. "Association Between Nutritional Status and Cognitive Functioning in a Healthy Elderly Population." *JAMA* 249:2917–2921, 1983.

76. Treichel, J.A. "Food for Thought in the Elderly." *Science News* 123:358, 1983.

77. Grinblat, op. cit., 720.

78. Roe, Daphne A. "Drug-Induced Malnutrition in Geriatric Patients." *Comprehensive Ther.* 38(10)24–28, 1977.

79. Garabedian-Ruffalo, Susan M.; and Ruffalo, Richard L. "Drug and Nutrient Interactions." *Am. Fam. Physician* 33(2):165–174, 1986.

80. "Tracing the Facts About Trace Minerals." *Tufts University Diet & Nutrition Letter* 5(1):3–6, 1987.

81. Ibid.

82. Garabedian-Ruffalo, et al., op. cit., p. 170.

83. Ibid.

11

Getting the Jump
on Joint Pain

Arthritis is a gold mine for the drug companies. They may not like to admit that they are profiting from people's pain and misery, but with 40 million sufferers—one out of two people over 65—the market for medications that can offer some relief is a billion-dollar bonanza.

The trouble is, doctors don't know exactly what causes arthritis, and they don't have any cures for it. It's a total mystery why some people get so crippled up they can barely move while others are completely spared joint pain even at a ripe old age. But whether the condition creeps up slowly and insidiously or appears quite suddenly, finding a way to quell the inflammation and ease the stiffness can be a very difficult and long-term project.

There may be times when just thinking about dragging those old bones out of bed in the morning is enough to make you wish you could go back to sleep. Or perhaps getting dressed is torture because you can barely manage the buttons on your shirt. Maybe you need to go shopping but the mere prospect of walking a few blocks when every step hurts may convince you that you can live without. If you are an "old pro" with arthritis, you know that while some days are worse than others, it sometimes gets hard to find any days that are truly better.

With this kind of unrelenting pain, it's no wonder that people are ready to try just about anything that promises a little relief. **Feldene** (piroxicam), **Naprosyn** (naproxen), and **Clinoril** (sulindac) are among the most profitable medications on the doctors' top twenty hit parade. These anti-inflammatory agents bring in hundreds of millions of dollars each year.

But the big best-seller of all time is ibuprofen. Starting in 1974, it was sold only by prescription as **Motrin**. Then the drug became available under the brand name **Rufen**. Eventually the Food and Drug Administration cleared a lower dose (200-mg) ibuprofen for over-the-counter sale, and ads started appearing for **Advil, Nuprin, Medipren, Ibuprin, Haltran,** and **Trendar**. It was promoted for everything from arthritis pain and headaches to menstrual cramps and toothaches.

Americans swallowed over 3,000,000,000 (that's nine zeroes—as in *B* for billion) pills of ibuprofen last year alone, and pharmaceutical manufacturers took in more than $350 million.[1] This drug represents one of the fastest growing segments of the $1.7 billion nonprescription analgesic market.

That represents an awful lot of pain and suffering. One of the reasons such drugs are so successful is that they don't cure anything. At best they provide some temporary measure of relief. But soon the ache is back as bad as ever, and people must swallow yet another pill to make life bearable.

The Infection Connection

Perhaps if scientists better understood the nature of inflammation and the origins of the various kinds of arthritis, they would come up with more successful treatments. Ask a doctor what causes arthritis and he is likely to get a glazed look in his eyes and shrug his shoulders. Considering that this condition has been around since the cave men, it's amazing there is so little awareness about how people get arthritis. All we have are a few unproven theories and plenty of arguments about them.

Although doctors once thought that arthritis could be divided into dozens of distinct disease categories, some of the lines are becoming blurred. Osteoarthritis is usually considered to be a relatively mild condition that comes along almost inevitably with age and wear and tear on joints. No one gets surprised if Grandpa complains of his "rheumatism" when the weather changes. But now doctors are beginning to recognize that even ordinary osteo-arthritis can produce the redness, warmth, and swelling that are usually considered more typical of the inflammation associated with rheumatoid arthritis (RA), which affects up to seven million people. Other inflammatory diseases include ankylosing spondylitis, systemic lupus erythematosus, polymyalgia, rheumatica, psoriatic arthritis, and gout, to mention just a few.

Even though we don't have a clue to what causes most of the common forms of arthritis, one approach to rheumatoid arthritis that has been gaining ground lately is the infection connection. A small number of researchers speculate that microscopic beasties such as viruses and bacteria may trigger an immunological reaction that produces arthritislike symptoms in some people. One of the first clues came when several children in Old Lyme, Connecticut, developed serious arthritis in the summer of 1975. Doctors at Yale started sleuthing the cases to see if there was anything unusual going on.

They found that the children lived in the country and often played in the woods. At first they had come down with a skin rash and flu-like symptoms that lasted up to a month. Eventually arthritis developed. When one of the patients remembered being bitten by a tick, the light bulb went on.

Eventually researchers linked the joint pain to a bacterium carried by the deer tick and transmitted by a bite. They dubbed the disease Lyme arthritis and tried large doses of penicillin. For some people the results were dramatic:

> **Seven of the 20 penicillin-treated patients had complete resolution of arthritis soon after injection, whereas the 20 placebo-treated patients continued to have arthritis symptoms. In a second trial, 11 of 20 patients treated with 20 million units of IV penicillin a day for 10 days appeared to be cured of arthritis.[2]**

Now before you get your hopes up and rush off to the doctor for a shot of penicillin, you must realize that Lyme arthritis is extremely rare, with probably fewer than 2,000 cases reported each year. Researchers are excited, though, because this breakthrough is already helping them discover other infection connections. Food poisoning, for example, if caused by salmonella bacteria, occasionally provokes arthritis symptoms several weeks after the diarrhea has disappeared. FDA experts estimate that there are four million cases of salmonellosis in the United States each year, leading to chronic arthritis in 2 or 3 percent, or about 120,000 people. Apparently the bacteria trigger immune system changes in susceptible individuals. This reaction leads the immune system to attack the body's joints and tissues and is thought to be a major component in many forms of arthritis.

In 1986 Dr. Anthony Woolf reported to the American Rheumatism Association on 54 patients from Bristol, England. Forty had come down with a virus that caused a rash and flu-like symptoms. Eventually, most of these people developed pain, swelling, and morning stiffness in the joints of their hands, feet, and knees. While this arthritis went away for the majority, some of the women had repeat outbreaks as long as seven months later, causing Dr. Woolf to wonder "if—in the right people—it can go on to RA. [rheumatoid arthritis]."[3]

One doctor has believed for decades that there is a link between rheumatoid arthritis and infection. During the last 40 years Dr. Thomas McPherson Brown has used tetracycline-type antibiotics to treat over 10,000 patients. He claims that with persistence and patience (in some cases up to five years may be necessary to control the disease), the results can be impressive.

But most rheumatologists are skeptical about this octogenarian's approach, citing a lack of hard data. Nevertheless, Dr. Brown's credentials are solid. He was chairman of medicine at George Washington University and is now director of the Arthritis Institute for the National Hospital for Orthopaedics and Rehabilitation in Arlington, Virginia.

Dr. Paul Plotz, chief of connective tissue diseases at the National Institute of Arthritis, Diabetes, and Digestive and Kidney Disease, states that "though no convincing evidence, direct or indirect, implicates a particular infectious agent in RA, most of us share a conviction with Dr. Brown that RA will turn out to have a connection to infection."[4]

It may be a long time before researchers learn what really triggers arthritis and come up with a cure. Although current therapy has improved significantly in recent years, most of our drugs are still aimed at controlling symptoms. Dr. Ray Robinson, a rheumatologist from Sydney, Australia, likens the new rheumatoid arthritis research to a bomb: "We've been looking at the far-flung shrapnel of RA. Now it's time to turn back to looking at the fuse."[5] One fuse that doctors rarely consider may be medicine.

The Beta Blocker Boomerang

Is your heart medicine making your arthritis worse? It seems incredible, but it happened to Harriet. At 67 she was in pretty good health except for a few of the aches and pains that accompany garden variety arthritis (osteoarthritis). You know, some stiff fingers and a knee that sometimes acted up when the weather changed. Aspirin usually kept everything under control, or at least held the pain to a tolerable level.

Then Harriet went to the doctor for a routine physical. He had been keeping an eye on her heart for quite some time. After mild exertion she sometimes complained of some slight chest pain and he was afraid she might be developing angina. This time he decided to prescribe **Inderal** (propranolol) just to be on the safe side.

Soon after she started taking this beta blocker heart medicine, she noticed her knees started acting up. Not just her bad one—the good knee became swollen and began hurting too. And her fingers, wrists, and shoulders got quite a lot worse as well. At first she convinced herself it was the weather, but when the pain didn't go away and instead got steadily worse, she wondered what was going on.

Harriet was fortunate. Her doctor was really on the ball. When she went back to ask for something more powerful than aspirin to relieve her aching joints, he did something far better. He made the arthritis flare-up disappear simply by taking her off the **Inderal**. Within days of phasing the drug out gradually, she discovered to her delight that the swelling and joint pain were almost gone and she was back to normal.

No one knows how common drug-induced arthritis may be. Aches and pains are usually believed to be the price we pay for growing older. Most doctors would never even think to connect a patient's joint complaints with a beta blocker prescribed for high blood pressure or heart disease. However, Harriet's physician was a rare bird. He listened carefully to her story and linked her sudden deterioration to articles he had seen recently in the medical literature.

Beta blockers are among the most frequently prescribed drugs in the world today. In fact, **Inderal** has been at the top of the doctors' hit parade for years. Every day over 10 million people swallow at least one hexagonal-shaped pill with a big letter *I* stamped on it. They take it to lower their high blood pressure or ease the pain of angina, to calm irregular heart beats or reduce the risk of repeat heart attacks. Some folks use **Inderal** to prevent migraine headaches and there are even those who swallow a low dose before a speaking engagement or musical performance to ease their stage fright.

But reports in the medical literature have begun to link beta blockers like **Inderal** and **Lopressor** (metoprolol) to arthritislike symptoms in some people.[6,7] Knees and shoulders seem to be the joints most commonly affected. But wrists, feet, and fingers may also become stiff and swollen. Side effects such as dry mouth and eyes may accompany the arthritis.

Just how often does this sort of reaction crop up? That's still a mystery, but one report in the *British Medical Journal* suggests that "Joint disturbance must be considered to be a common adverse effect associated with beta blockade."[8] Other beta blockers that have been linked with arthritis include **Blocadren** (timolol), **Sectral** (acebutolol), **Tenormin** (atenolol), and **Visken** (pindolol). To be fair, we have to confide that other researchers believe this reaction is so uncommon it is almost as rare as hen's teeth.[9]

Whether it's rare or common, it still may not be easy to tell whether a beta blocker is responsible for your arthritis pain. If swelling, stiffness, and pain show up or are aggravated soon after drug therapy is started, that's a clue. But about the only way to know for sure is to ask your doctor to give you a plan for slowly tapering off the drug under medical supervision. Going off a beta blocker suddenly is a terrible idea, as it can lead to serious withdrawal symptoms including angina or even a heart attack. People with heart disease, high blood pressure, or irregular heart rhythms may need to have an alternative medication substituted as they gradually decrease the dose. There are many people who should never stop such medication.

If the beta blocker is responsible for joint pain and stiffness, these symptoms should clear up soon after stopping the drug completely. Although in one case recovery took almost a month, most people were feeling much better within two or three days. If the pain doesn't go away, it's a pretty good indication that the medicine isn't the culprit.

Beta blockers aren't the only drugs that have been associated with arthritis symptoms. Diuretics, which are often used to treat high blood pressure, can raise uric acid levels and make gout flare up. This condition results when uric acid crystals precipitate in the joints, especially the big toe. Gout affects almost two million people in this country. Ask them about the joint pain of an acute attack, and they'll tell you it can be unbearable.

Other medications that have been reported to occasionally bring on joint pain include the heart medicine quinidine (**Cardioquin, Duraquin, Quinaglute, Quinidex, Quinora**), the ulcer drug cimetidine (**Tagamet**), the antifungal agent amphotericin B (**Mysteclin-F**), and the blood pressure medication hydralazine (**Apresazide, Apresoline, Ser-Ap-Es,** and **Unipres**). Some drugs may affect muscle tissue or bone instead of joints. And certain medications can precipitate the autoimmune disease lupus (systemic lupus erythematosus), which sometimes leads to joint pain. The table below gives a more complete list of compounds that may occasionally precipitate or aggravate arthritis, muscle, or bone pain.

Drugs That May Provoke Arthritis Symptoms*

Generalized joint pain may be brought on or aggravated by:

Generic Name	Brand Name
acebutolol	**Sectral**
amphotericin B	**Fungizone, Mysteclin-F**
atenolol	**Tenormin**
barbiturates	**Alurate, Donnatal, Fiorinal, Mebaral, Nembutal,** etc.
cimetidine	**Tagamet**
isoniazid	**INH, Rifamate**

Generic Name	Brand Name
metoprolol	**Lopressor**
pindolol	**Visken**
propranolol	**Inderal**
quinidine	**Cardioquin, Duraquin, Quinaglute, Quinidex, Quinora**
timolol	**Blocadren**

Muscle pain may be brought on or aggravated by:

Generic Name	Brand Name
cimetidine	**Tagamet**
clofibrate	**Atromid-S**
diuretics	Any brand that depletes sodium or potassium
isoetharine	**Bronkosol**
labetalol	**Normodyne, Trandate**
laxatives	Excessive use of harsh laxatives may deplete magnesium, leading to muscle cramps
licorice	Overdoing could cause potassium depletion and muscle pain
lithium	**Eskalith, Lithane, Lithobid**
penicillamine	**Cuprimine, Depen**
terbutaline	**Brethaire, Brethine, Bricanyl**

Bone pain may be brought on or aggravated by:

Generic Name	Brand Name
aluminum antacids (regular, prolonged use)	**Aludrox, Alurex, A.M.T., Creamalin, Delcid, Kolantyl Gel, Maalox, Magnatril, Riopan, WinGel**, etc.
corticosteroids	Prolonged use at high doses, as after transplants, may cause pain due to osteoporosis. **Aristocort, Cortef,** Cortisone, **Cortone, Decadron, Deltasone, Hexadrol, Hydrocortone, Meticorten,** Prednisone

Generic Name	Brand Name
glutethimide	Doriden
laxatives (regular, prolonged use)	
mineral oil	Agoral, Neo-Cultol, Nujol, Petrogalar
phenophthalein	Alophen, Correctol, Ex-Lax, Phen-A-Mint, Phenolax
methotrexate	Mexate
primidone	Mysoline

Lupus (SLE) may be brought on or aggravated by:

Generic Name	Brand Name
chlorpromazine	Thorazine
hydralazine	Apresazide, Apresoline, Ser-Ap-Es, Unipres
isoniazid	INH, Rifamate
methyldopa	Aldoclor, Aldomet, Aldoril
penicillamine	Cuprimine, Depen
phenylbutazone	Butazolidin
phenytoin	Dilantin
procainamide	Procan, Pronestyl
quinidine	Cardioquin, Duraquin, Quinaglute, Quinidex, Quinora

*Some of these reactions are extremely rare, and others are have not been established beyond a shadow of a doubt. You should discuss with your physician whether one of these drugs might be contributing to pain or inflammation and whether it would be appropriate to consider an alternate medication. Remember, **NEVER** discontinue any drug without consulting your doctor!
Source: Hart, F. Dudley. "Drug-Induced Arthritis and Arthralgia." *Drugs* 28:347-354, 1984.

Arthritis Drugs: Past, Present, and Future

Assuming that any treatable causes of your arthritis have been ruled out, about the best your doctor can do is try to relieve some of the symptoms some of the time. Now this is going to blow your mind, but despite all the new-fangled arthritis medicines that have become popular in recent years, there is still nothing better than good old-fashioned, plain-Jane aspirin. You can pay three arms and a swollen knee for prescription drugs like **Anaprox, Clinoril, Dolobid, Feldene, Indocin, Meclomen, Naprosyn, Orudis,** or **Tolectin,** but you can't buy a magic wand. None of these drugs is significantly better than large doses of aspirin for relieving pain and inflammation.

Amazing Aspirin

Aspirin is a true wonder drug. Most people find that hard to believe, seeing as how they can buy a bottle of 100 tablets over the counter for less than a buck. Miracles are supposed to be more expensive. It's also pretty hard to get excited about something that has been around for so long that we take it for granted.

And that's the problem. We have been snookered into believing that it takes a prescription to get strong medicine. Anything we buy over the counter is considered by definition to be a wimp drug, sort of a weak sister. That's certainly not true for aspirin. Besides the now well-publicized benefits for heart attack and stroke prevention, there is the suggestion that aspirin may slow the progression of cataracts.

When it comes to arthritis relief, aspirin is the gold standard. But don't expect that popping down a couple of tablets is all it takes. Most experts suggest that you may need to do a fair amount of "fiddling" with the dose before you find what works best for you. Think about this dosing stuff as if you were Goldilocks visiting the bears. There's the porridge (aspirin), but you need it not too hot and not too cold. Getting it "just right" takes a lot more effort than most people realize. The confusion occurs because regular recommended doses (two tablets every four to six hours) work only for pain relief. That may be all that's necessary for mild osteoarthritis.

But many folks with severe arthritis may need as many as 14 to 20 tablets over the course of a day in order to achieve an anti-inflammatory effect. At this dose you will need a doctor's supervision. If you begin to hear ringing in your ears or get that burning pain in the pit of your stomach, by all means cut back a little. Once you start taking enough aspirin to make a real difference for your aching joints, side effects aren't rare at all. But since you live inside your body and know how it responds, you are in the best position to adjust your dose. Unless your doctor sticks a tube down your throat to see how your stomach is faring, even he can't do it much better. Remember, it may take at least two weeks at a fairly decent level before aspirin can really attack the inflammation you are suffering.

Besides its unbeatable effectiveness, aspirin's other great advantage is price. Aspirin is cheap, unless you buy a lot of fancy packaging and high-priced television advertising along with the acetylsalicylic acid. There's no reason at all why you need aspirin touted as super-duper strength especially for arthritis—it's really no different from any other aspirin except that the tablets come slightly larger so you don't have to take as many.

Don't get seduced by promises of gentle, soothing, buffered aspirin. All you'll get is a little aluminum and magnesium hydroxide—antacids that may cut down on the effectiveness of your pain relief without delivering much in the way of protection against stomach irritation.

Coated aspirin is somewhat more effective at reducing symptoms of indigestion and heartburn. There are lots of products on the market these days, including **Ecotrin, Easprin, Encaprin,** and **Cosprin**. They are designed to slide through the acid environment of the stomach untouched and dissolve in the more alkaline small intestine where theoretically they won't be as irritating. Some people do indeed seem to benefit from these "enteric" coated formulations and studies show less stomach damage from them than from regular aspirin.

But there is no guarantee you won't experience some discomfort. Older people sometimes make less stomach acid or they might be taking medications like **Zantac** (ranitidine) or **Tagamet** (cimetidine) that reduce acidity. In such a situation the coated aspirin may be fooled into dissolving in the stomach instead of the small intestine. Be alert for any symptoms of stomach pain or irritation. By the way, if some of these coated aspirin products are taken with food, their absorption may be delayed for hours and effectiveness could be reduced. There are also cases in which the tablets have ended up collecting undigested in the stomach. If you begin to develop a strange full feeling in your gut, get to a gastroenterologist pronto.

There are some other cautions for regular aspirin users. Your stomach will be bleeding on a daily basis. That's a fact of life. Now don't get all excited. We're only talking about drops, not buckets. Still, small but repeated blood loss from the intestine can deplete the body of iron, so a supplement may be necessary. Folic acid levels also become lower and a little extra of this vitamin would probably be a good idea. For reasons that aren't at all clear, vitamin C doesn't get into cells as well for people taking aspirin. Extra C makes sense to us (500 to 1,000 mg), but there is no evidence such supplementation will actually correct the imbalance.

Aspirin Alternatives

The power behind aspirin is salicylate. Though few people realize it, there are quite a few other salicylate compounds on the market and several may be a lot less irritating to the stomach than aspirin or even high-priced prescription anti-inflammatory agents. Magnesium salicylate (**Doan's Pills, Efficin, Magan,** and **Mobidin**) is one option. Choline and magnesium salicylate combined (**Trilisate**) is another.

Dr. Sanford Roth, director of the Arthritis Center in Phoenix, Arizona, is a big booster of salicylsalicylic acid (salsalate) for people who have sensitive stomachs or are allergic to aspirin. This compound is sold by prescription under the brand names **Artha-G, Disalcid,** and **Mono-Gesic**. (It is available over the counter with aspirin under the name **Persistin**). According to Dr. Roth, "Another advantage of these agents is their simple dosing format: one dose in the morning and one in the evening often achieves therapeutic salicylate levels, with a range of safety that is not surpassed by any other NSAIDs [nonsteroidal anti-inflammatory drugs like **Clinoril, Motrin, Naprosyn,** and **Feldene**]."[10]

When prescribing **Disalcid,** Dr. Roth aims for 3,000 mg a day. He usually starts his patients on two 750-mg tablets in the morning and two more in the evening. If the patient has troubles with nausea or buzzing in the ears, he cuts it back to one tablet three times a day. After a month he would probably order a blood test to see if the salicylate levels fall within the recommended therapeutic range of 10 to 30 mg per 100 ml.

Most physicians (including a fair number of rheumatologists) don't appear to be as enthusiastic as Dr. Roth about the advantages of salsalate or as concerned about the dangers of the other medications they usually prescribe. Nearly all of the usual arthritis drugs may lead to the development of ulcers, including potentially life-threatening bleeding ulcers, and the risk is especially great for older people.[11]

Not long ago, British researchers examined the hospital records of patients 60 and older. They found "the risk of admission with bleeding peptic ulcer is substantially increased in takers of NSAIDs [nonsteroidal anti-inflammatory drugs]."[12] What's so scary is that the damage is often insidious. People taking medicines like **Anaprox, Butazolidin, Clinoril, Dolobid, Feldene, Indocin, Meclomen, Motrin, Nalfon, Naprosyn, Orudis, Rufen, Suprol,** and **Tolectin** may not realize they are developing ulcer craters. According to Dr. Roth, 50 percent of the patients who are checked will have signs of redness and irritation and 20 percent will have serious erosions inside their stomachs. Half of all these patients may have few, if any, symptoms of these problems.[13] Dr. Roth thinks of these patients as time bombs, just waiting to explode.

There have been quite a few explosions in recent years. With the growing popularity of NSAIDs there has come a corresponding increase in the frequency of perforated ulcers, especially among older women.[14] When an ulcer perforates, a hole occurs in the stomach wall. This can be a life-threatening situation and indeed, deaths from this complication are increasing.

One of our newspaper column readers has had plenty of experience with the dilemma of arthritis medicine. Mrs. P writes:

> **I just got out of the hospital with a bleeding ulcer. It's the second time this year. The first time I had been taking Motrin and then Naprosyn under a doctor's supervision. After the first ulcer I took Ascriptin but it too gave me a problem. Now I can't take anything for my arthritis and just don't know what to do. Isn't it too bad us oldsters have to be guinea pigs for this medicine?**

Perhaps like Mrs. P you're feeling trapped somewhere between the proverbial rock and a hard place. Without some anti-inflammatory medicine the pain and stiffness of arthritis can make life almost unbearable. But you don't want to trade joint relief for a bleeding ulcer. So what should you do to protect yourself?

First, be vigilant! Persistent symptoms of stomach upset or indigestion should **NOT** be ignored. Dark or tarry stools are a red flag that there's bleeding going on higher up in the digestive tract. But normal bowel movements don't mean you can let down your guard. Get into the habit of doing a home stool test for blood. Several kits are now available over the counter, including **Early Detector, Fleet Detecatest,** and **Hemoccult Home Test**. If you see anything suspicious, get thee to a gastroenterologist. Even if everything appears perfectly normal, your doctor should schedule periodic evaluations including blood and kidney function tests.

If you are suffering indigestion or heartburn or your doctor finds signs of digestive tract irritation, that doesn't necessarily mean that you have to give up all arthritis medicine forever. Dr. Roth has found that the ulcer drug **Carafate** (sucralfate) can act almost like an antidote to protect the stomach lining from the irritation caused by nonsteroidal anti-inflammatory drugs. According to Dr. Roth, "If the patient takes the NSAID with the sucralfate just before the meal, both he and his stomach will be happier."[15]

Taking Care of Your Kidneys

There's something else your doctor may not have told you about your arthritis medicine. Most of the prescribed NSAIDs can affect the kidney. While a lot less common than stomach upset, kidney function problems can be very serious, especially in older people. Blood pressure medicine may interact with arthritis drugs to increase the risk. Anyone who is taking a diuretic, a beta blocker, or an ACE inhibitor (**Capoten** or **Vasotec**)[16] needs to be on the alert.

The NSAIDs are not all alike when it comes to the kidney, though. **Indocin** (indomethacin) is usually considered to be the worst culprit, while aspirin and **Clinoril** (sulindac) seem to pose the least danger.[17] If your doctor suspects that your kidneys are not quite up to snuff, he or she might want you to try one of these medications first. You should have a blood test to check kidney function before you even start taking any anti-inflammatory drug, and at regular intervals after that.

There are also a few things you, the patient, can watch out for as warnings of possible kidney problems. Invest in a quality scale and weigh yourself every day. A sudden weight gain (not the creeping kind so many of us battle over the years) often indicates that you are holding water in your system. It's a signal that you need to check in with your medic promptly.[18] Other warning signs are a change in the color of the urine and back pain you didn't have last week or last month.[19] These same cautions hold for over-the-counter ibuprofen preparations such as **Medipren, Advil, Nuprin, Ibuprin, Haltran,** and **Trendar**.

Nonsteroidal Anti-Inflammatory Drugs (NSAIDs): Not Just Super Aspirin

Feldene (piroxicam)

Feldene is one of the most successful and most controversial arthritis drugs on the market today. Within four years of its introduction in the United States, worldwide sales had rocketed to an extraordinary $500 million yearly. Convenient once-a-day dosing is responsible for both the popularity and problems of this medication. On January 8, 1986, Dr. Sidney Wolfe, Director of Nader's Health Research Group (HRG), petitioned the Food and Drug Administration to "immediately ban, as an imminent hazard to the public health, the use of Pfizer's widely sold anti-arthritis medication **Feldene** (piroxicam) in people ages 60 and older." Here are the reasons Dr. Wolfe requested the ban:

> Since Feldene was introduced in the United States in April 1982, the FDA has received a total of 2,621 nonfatal and 182 fatal adverse reaction reports associated with the drug's use. These figures include 687 nonfatal cases due to severe gastrointestinal (GI) toxicity and 99 deaths in which there was stomach and intestinal bleeding, ulcers, intestinal perforation, hematemesis (vomiting of blood), or melena (blood in the stool).

These data, taken with the results of prescription-based surveys conducted by the FDA and government drug regulatory agencies in Great Britain and Sweden, indicate that GI toxicity is more common and severe with Feldene than with similar arthritis drugs—particularly in elderly patients. This is due to the extremely long time Feldene lingers in the body and the well-documented problems that geriatric patients have with certain long-acting drugs.

Virtually all (96%) of the GI deaths and 71% of the nonfatal reactions due to GI toxicity from Feldene which have been reported in this country occurred in persons ages 60 and older. Because 55% of U.S. Feldene users are in this age group, we estimate that at least 1.75 million elderly American people now receiving this drug are at risk of developing life-threatening GI reactions.[20]

After reviewing all the data, the feds announced on July 7, 1986, that they were denying Health Research Group's request for a **Feldene** ban in older people. In his letter to HRG, Dr. Otis Bowen, Secretary of Health and Human Services, stated that the FDA "found no basis for concluding that piroxicam [**Feldene**] is more likely to cause serious gastrointestinal toxicity in the elderly than similar products."[21]

Perhaps this statement was meant to be reassuring. But it tends to obscure the fact that *all* of these arthritis drugs can sometimes cause serious GI side effects in older people. At this point we can't say whether **Feldene** is in fact more dangerous than the others or just equally hazardous. But HRG reports that both Canada and Germany have issued official warnings about **Feldene** for older people. According to HRG, the package insert for physicians in Canada now states in part that:

as elderly, frail or debilitated patients tolerate gastrointestinal side effects less well, consideration should be given to a starting dose that is lower than usual and to an increase of the dose only if symptoms remain uncontrolled. Such patients must be very carefully supervised.[22]

The **Feldene** controversy has died down, but there are still some questions. All the key players, including the FDA, Health Research Group, and Pfizer, have dug in their heels. HRG maintains that "We are sure that there will eventually be warning labels in this country on **Feldene** for older people."[23] Whether such a warning ever appears in the United States or not, it would be smart for older people on **Feldene** (and ALL other NSAIDs) to remain vigilant. Stomach pain, indigestion, nausea, diarrhea, black or tarry stools, cramps, heartburn, or any other digestive tract problem should be reported to your doctor. Periodic stool tests for blood are worthwhile.

Stomach upset and ulcers aren't the only problem with **Feldene**. Lost amidst all the confusion and brouhaha are some other serious side effects. One of our newspaper column readers reported the following reactions:

> I'm convinced the doctor I went to used me as a guinea pig, and it makes me really mad!
>
> I went to him because my knees were giving me trouble. He diagnosed my problem as tendinitis and gave me a prescription for Feldene. I took the medicine less than a week when my face turned red and swelled up. I developed hives on my neck and a painful rash all over my hands.
>
> When I called the doctor, he said it should clear up in a couple of days, but instead my eyes swelled almost shut and my rash got worse. My hands were so sore I couldn't cook or clean for myself. All the skin on my palms peeled off.
>
> I asked about side effects before I started taking Feldene, and was told not to worry. It cost me $80 to get into this mess and six weeks to recover.

Fortunately, such severe skin reactions are rare. But if you experience itching or a rash, you will probably have to stop the drug. Sunshine may bring on an uncomfortable skin reaction in some people and so it would be prudent to use a high-SPF (Sun Protection Factor) sunscreen or stay out of the sun altogether while on **Feldene**.

Other side effects to watch out for include dizziness, headache, ringing in the ears, sleepiness, and fluid retention. Sudden weight gain could be an indication that the kidneys are having trouble, and so it makes sense to weigh yourself regularly and keep a record of the normal daily fluctuation. Any changes should be reported to the doctor immediately. People with high blood pressure, heart failure, kidney, or liver disease are most vulnerable, as are those taking diuretics. Flank pain or any change in urination is also a red flag. Changes in vision, fever, fatigue, jaundice, or any other unusual symptoms require immediate medical treatment.

Given all these dangers, why have doctors prescribed **Feldene** to 12 million patients around the world? For one thing, convenience does seem to matter. Once-a-day dosing makes **Feldene** a lot easier to deal with than four **Motrins** or 20 aspirin. Also, the longer action of **Feldene** keeps the anti-inflammatory effect going all night for most patients, to make morning stiffness a lot more bearable. Only you and your doctor can decide whether these benefits are worth the risk.

Motrin, Rufen, Advil, Nuprin, Haltran, Trendar, Medipren, Ibuprin (ibuprofen)

The history of ibuprofen sounds like one of the greatest shell games ever played. First, there was Boots. No, we're not talking about rubbers, but rather a big British pharmaceutical manufacturer with a very low profile in the United States. The company had a hot arthritis drug on its hands and no sales force in America. In order to cash in on the lucrative U.S. market, the drug was licensed to Upjohn, which ushered ibuprofen through the FDA and started selling it under the name **Motrin** in 1974.

It wasn't long before Boots realized that its foreign-born baby was growing up fast. The drug was going bonkers and becoming incredibly successful. In 1977 Boots decided to move into the United States itself and bought a small drug company in Louisiana. By 1981 Boots was ready to go into competition with Upjohn and entered the market with its own brand of ibuprofen, **Rufen**.

To make matters even more confusing, ibuprofen was approved for over-the-counter sale in 1984 in a 200-mg dose. Upjohn wasn't positioned for a strong OTC marketing program, and so it in turn licensed ibuprofen to Bristol-Myers, which sold it under the name **Nuprin**. Meanwhile, Boots sold a license to Whitehall (maker of **Anacin**), which put its "new" nonprescription drug out as **Advil**. McNeil, maker of **Tylenol** (acetaminophen), saw a challenge to its position in the lucrative pain reliever market. The company sued the FDA and suggested that many doctors were strongly opposed to the OTC switch.

Confused? Wait, it gets worse. Just before ibuprofen went off patent, Upjohn, realizing what a gold mine this drug had become, (and what it had given up when it licensed **Nuprin** to Bristol-Myers) started marketing its own over-the-counter version, called **Haltran**, for menstrual cramps. Whitehall was ready with its "new formula" **Trendar** for "menstrual pain and cramps, headaches, backaches, and muscular aches and pains associated with Premenstrual Syndrome." Obviously, this multipurpose pain reliever had become a hot item.

Now remember, it's all the same ibuprofen started by Boots back in Britain. To add complexity to chaos, when the drug came off patent in September 1986, other players entered the market. McNeil, the **Tylenol** tycoon, decided that if you can't lick 'em, join 'em, and launched **Medipren** with a heavy-duty marketing blitz ("You haven't got time for the pain"), designed to make its ibuprofen a market leader. Thompson, manufactuer of **Dexatrim** diet pills and **Aspercreme** arthritis rub, promoted **Ibuprin**. And of course there were all sorts of house brand generic ibuprofens, not to mention the prescription products available in stronger doses. In just over a decade more than 130 million prescriptions were filled for this nonsteroidal anti-inflammatory drug and countless millions of bottles were sold over the counter. Worldwide, over 25 billion tablets have been swallowed.[24]

Does ibuprofen deserve its exalted position? Is it more effective than other NSAIDs? No way. Is it significantly safer? Read the physicians' package insert and judge for yourself:

> **Peptic ulceration and gastrointestinal bleeding, sometimes severe, have been reported in patients receiving MOTRIN Tablets (ibuprofen). Peptic ulceration, perforation, or severe gastrointestinal bleeding can have a fatal outcome . . .**
>
> **Blurred and/or diminished vision, scotomata [an area of no vision], and/or changes in color vision have been reported. . . .**
>
> **Severe hepatic reactions, including jaundice and cases of fatal hepatitis, have been reported with ibuprofen as with other nonsteroidal anti-inflammatory drugs.[25]**

Clearly, ibuprofen is not perfectly safe. And just because the FDA gave it a "Seal of Approval" for over-the-counter use, the leopard hasn't lost its spots. Even though the nonprescription dose is low, that doesn't mean people can't get into trouble. Three Veterans Administration doctors worried that "the present product labeling, as approved by the Food and Drug Administration, is grossly inadequate." They pointed out that even moderate doses of ibuprofen can trigger kidney failure in some patients.[26] Older people, those on diuretics, and anyone with heart, liver, or kidney problems are especially vulnerable.

Symptoms to be alert for include puffiness, sudden weight gain, skin rash, any change in vision, dizziness, ringing in the ears, stomach pain, nausea, heartburn, and elevated blood pressure. Even with all these possible side effects, ibuprofen appears to be one of the safer NSAIDs. Whether this should entitle it to be the only one of them available without a prescription, only time and the FDA will tell—and the FDA may not be talking.

One advantage of ibuprofen is its age. Because its patent protection period has expired, you should be able to shop around for an inexpensive generic form, either as a prescription drug or over the counter. This could save you plenty if you have to take this kind of medication regularly. Next to aspirin, ibuprofen is probably the cheapest anti-inflammatory agent on the market. But remember, even though you may not see all the side effects listed on the nonprescription packaging, nobody has waved a magic wand to make them go away. It's more important than ever to stay in touch with your doctor.

Clinoril (sulindac)

We suppose if you pushed us into a corner and forced us to choose one NSAID over all the others, our first pick would be **Clinoril**. There are several reasons why we favor this arthritis drug. First, it's relatively convenient. Twice-daily dosing makes it almost as easy to take as **Feldene**. More important, it appears to be easier on the kidneys than most of its cousins.

An extra bonus is that **Clinoril** seems far less likely to interact with blood-pressure-lowering drugs than other NSAIDs.[27] Many doctors are unaware that arthritis medications like **Feldene, Indocin** (indomethacin), **Naprosyn,** and **Anaprox** (naproxen) may reduce the effectiveness of beta blockers. So if a patient is taking **Tenormin** or **Tenoretic** (atenolol), **Inderal** or **Inderide** (propranolol), **Blocadren** or **Timolide** (timolol) for hypertension and is unfortunate enough to need an NSAID for arthritis pain, there is a possibility his blood pressure won't respond as expected. For such a person, **Clinoril** would probably be the best arthritis medication.

Like all NSAIDs, however, **Clinoril** does have side effects. Stomach pain (10 percent), indigestion, nausea, vomiting, diarrhea, constipation, gas, skin rash, wheezing, itching, dizziness, headache, fluid retention, and ringing in the ears should be reported to a doctor without delay. Unexplained fever, jaundice, or any strange skin reaction will require a liver function test. If there is a sudden weight gain or change in urination, the kidneys could be in trouble.

Although **Clinoril** is less likely to interfere with beta blockers than other arthritis medicines, it can interact with some drugs. Anyone taking aspirin and **Clinoril** simultaneously will get less anti-inflammatory relief. That's because aspirin prevents the active form of the drug from reaching adequate levels in the bloodstream. The same thing occurs if you use DMSO (dimethyl sulfoxide). But all things considered, **Clinoril** is a reasonable choice for relieving arthritis pain, especially for people with high blood pressure who are being treated with beta blockers.

> **Dolobid** (diflunisal)
> **Meclomen** (meclofenamate)
> **Nalfon** (fenoprofen)
> **Naprosyn, Anaprox** (naproxen)
> **Orudis** (ketoprofen)
> **Ponstel** (mefenamic acid)
> **Tolectin** (tolmetin)

Over the years NSAIDs have multiplied a lot like rabbits. There are subtle variations between them but few major differences. **Anaprox, Dolobid,** and **Naprosyn** are swallowed twice a day, whereas **Nalfon, Orudis, Meclomen,** and **Tolectin** are usually taken three or four times daily. That's hardly a big deal. The price of a prescription may be one of the biggest disparities. At the time of this writing our local pharmacy is charging about $30 for a month's supply of **Tolectin,** whereas **Meclomen** would run almost $50 for the same amount of time.

Side effects are remarkably similar for most of these medications. As expected, stomach pain, heartburn, nausea, indigestion, gas, diarrhea, and constipation are not uncommon. **Ponstel** should always be taken at meal time to reduce stomach irritation. If diarrhea occurs, the drug should be stopped immediately and the doctor notified. In fact, the doctor should always be told if symptoms develop while you're taking any of these compounds.

Other adverse reactions to watch out for include visual changes, ringing in the ears, headache, depression, fluid retention, sudden weight gain, swollen ankles or feet, frequent urination, bloody or cloudy urine, black or tarry stools, unusual bruising, mouth sores, unusual thirst, jaundice, chills, and fever.

People who are allergic to one of these drugs (or to aspirin) are often allergic to all. If you develop a skin rash, itching, hives, or difficulty breathing while on any NSAID, you are pretty much out of luck for the rest. **Tolectin** has been reported to produce severe allergic reactions for some people, especially if they phase on and off the drug periodically. This may mean that continuous use is safer for most folks than stop-and-go therapy. Finally, it is crucial to realize that many arthritis medicines may make you pretty spacey. If you feel drowsy, dizzy, or fuzzy-headed, DO NOT drive or try to do anything that requires coordination or concentration.

Butazolidin, Azolid (phenylbutazone)
Indocin (indomethacin)

These two drugs are the granddaddies of modern-day NSAIDs. **Butazolidin** became available in 1952 and was the first nonsteroidal anti-inflammatory agent to come along after aspirin. **Indocin** showed up in 1965. Because they've been around so long, both are available in generic form at considerable savings. But these drugs should not be thought of as just another couple of arthritis meds. They are potent and pose significant risks, especially for older people.

Many people on these drugs experience nasty stomachaches or other signs that the GI tract is under attack. The last thing you want to do is give one of these pills a chance to linger on the way down, or it could begin to wear a hole in the lining of the gullet. So *always* swallow these drugs with a full 8-ounce glass of liquid (water, juice, milk, iced tea, or whatever you like except anything with even a hint of alcohol) at meal time. Never, ever take this sort of medicine lying down. That could be an open invitation to trouble. Stomach pain, indigestion, nausea, vomiting, and diarrhea can be severe. Don't try to ignore them (as if you could!). All of these symptoms may serve as an early warning system that an ulcer is on the way.

Stay away from all other anti-inflammatory agents (including aspirin) while on these medicines. Instead of getting extra relief, you'll probably only double up on the risk of stomach upset. Be prepared for dizziness and drowsiness. If you feel light-headed, DO NOT drive, fly a plane, run a lawnmower, use a sewing machine, or attempt anything else that requires coordination or concentration. Headaches are awfully common—and pretty awful—with **Indocin**. Though they may fade away after two or three weeks, plenty of people stop taking this medicine because they can't handle the headache.

There are quite a few other side effects you need to be on the lookout for: fever, chills, aches and pains, fatigue, skin rash, sore throat, difficulty breathing, mouth sores, bruising, sudden weight gain or fluid retention, swollen legs or feet, trouble urinating, black or tarry stools, blood in the urine, psychological depression, forgetfulness, confusion, visual changes, ringing in the ears, and jaundice. If you notice such reactions or anything else out of the ordinary, contact your doctor immediately! Even though you might think you are just feeling a little under the weather, your body could be trying to tell you there's a serious drug reaction going on.

Indocin and **Butazolidin** can interact with a number of other medications. For example, **Capoten** or beta blockers like **Tenormin, Inderal, Corgard, Visken, Sectral,** and **Blocadren** may not lower blood pressure as well as they should if a person is also taking **Indocin**. Blood thinners, digitalis heart medicine, diuretics, and many other commonly prescribed drugs can also be affected by these NSAIDs. If you are taking ANY other medicines at the same time you are prescribed either **Indocin** or **Butazolidin,** have your physician and pharmacist check to make sure that they aren't incompatible.

Arthritis Artillery:
Bringing Out the Heavy Guns

Until now we've been discussing mostly garden variety arthritis (osteoarthritis) treatment. Sure, these drugs can be used for bursitis, tendinitis, ankylosing spondylitis, and a host of other joint conditions, but they're at best a holding action. When it comes to the severe, debilitating joint inflammation that's associated with rheumatoid arthritis (RA), such medicines serve more as a finger in the dike than a way to push back the tides. On occasion it may be necessary to break out the reserve ammunition.

Methotrexate

In the last several years physicians have started experimenting aggressively with a whole host of new and more powerful medications. Many don't like to admit it in public yet, but they have begun prescribing methotrexate in low "pulsed" doses—three 2.5-mg tablets once a week at meal time (total dose = 7.5 mg/wk). The results can be startling in as little as six or eight weeks.

But methotrexate is definitely NOT just another arthritis drug. It's a potent and extremely toxic anticancer medicine that can have life-threatening consequences if not used with great caution. No one knows exactly why it can be so effective for rheumatoid arthritis (and also psoriasis). It has been suggested that methotrexate may modulate the immune system. Remember, severe arthritis is thought to be in large part an autoimmune disease. Responding to a trigger that is as yet unidentified, the immune system, which normally protects your body against outside invaders—bacteria, viruses, etc.—starts to run amok and attacks your own joints and tissue. Medications like methotrexate and **Imuran** (azathioprine), a drug used to prevent organ transplant rejection, may somehow cool things down.

For someone who is faced with constant pain the promise of relief can be very tempting. Methotrexate relieves swelling and stiffness for many and often takes away pain. But the drug is no cure. Once methotrexate is discontinued, there is a strong likelihood that the disease will return. There is also fear that even at low doses side effects could be a serious problem, especially if taken for long periods of time.

Before anyone starts down the methotrexate road, he must have a long heart-to-heart talk with a doctor. The package insert offers the following:

> WARNING: METHOTREXATE MUST BE USED ONLY BY PHYSICIANS EXPERIENCED IN ANTIMETABOLITE CHEMOTHERAPY. BECAUSE OF THE POSSIBILITY OF FATAL OR SEVERE TOXIC REACTIONS, THE PATIENT SHOULD BE FULLY INFORMED BY THE PHYSICIAN OF THE RISKS INVOLVED AND SHOULD BE UNDER HIS CONSTANT SUPERVISION.[28]

It is absolutely crucial that liver and kidney function tests be run before a patient can be considered for methotrexate therapy. Unless they are perfectly normal, this drug is out. Even if everything is fine, it will be necessary to have monthly lab checks to make sure the body stays that way. Common side effects include mouth sores, itching, and skin rash. The doctor should be notified if they occur or if you experience fever and chills, fatigue, sore throat, yellow skin or eyes, dark or bloody urine, nausea, stomach pain, diarrhea, black or tarry stools, difficulty breathing, headache, dizziness, blurred vision, or swelling of the legs or feet. Anything out of the ordinary also merits an immediate call to the doctor.

Anyone taking methotrexate must ABSOLUTELY AVOID ASPIRIN! That means in any form including salicylates. No **Alka-Seltzer, Anacin, Artha-G, Arthritis Pain Formula, Ascriptin, Aspergum, BC Powder, Bufferin, Cosprin, Darvon Compound, Disalcid, Doan's Pills, Easprin, Ecotrin, Empirin, Encaprin, Fiorinal, 4-Way Cold Tablets, Magan, Midol, Mono-Gesic, Pepto-Bismol, Percodan, Persistin, Sine-Off, Trilisate, Vanquish,** or **Zorprin**. These drugs can all make methotrexate more toxic by increasing its concentration in the blood stream. Alcohol is also out as it may raise the risk of liver damage. Other drug interactions to look out for include sulfa and tetracycline antibiotics, seizure medicine (**Dilantin**) and the arthritis drug **Butazolidin**.

With such warnings it's easy to understand why people might doubt the wisdom of even considering a drug like methotrexate. Yet when used cautiously, with constant medical supervision, such a drug can produce dramatic improvement for severe rheumatoid arthritis. The balance between risks and benefits is one that will have to be weighed carefully between family and physicians.

Imuran (azathioprine)

Like methotrexate, **Imuran** is a very big gun. It's an immune system modulator and should be considered only for severe rheumatoid arthritis that hasn't responded to more traditional therapies. This drug was originally used only to help prevent organ transplant rejection by suppressing the immune system. More recently it has been found to reduce the swelling and inflammation of RA. Increased susceptibility to infections is one serious side effect of this medicine; it makes medical vigilance essential. Other possible adverse reactions include nausea and vomiting, diarrhea, skin rash, sore throat, mouth sores, unusual bruising, dark urine, stomach pain, and fever. If any such side effects occur, the doctor should be informed. The greatest drawback to the widespread use of **Imuran** is its carcinogenic potential. Long-term reliance on this drug could increase the risk of cancer.

Ridaura (auranofin)

It's easy to understand why some doctors might well keep methotrexate and **Imuran** in reserve for times when all else has failed. Although they do produce impressive relief for many patients, the dangers are not to be taken lightly. That's why traditional treatments are usually tried first. Gold shots date back over 50 years. For reasons that are still unclear, gold also seems to modulate the immune system and reverse some of the devastating effects of rheumatoid arthritis. But the expense and inconvenience of injections has made this kind of therapy barely tolerable. People often complain about a terrible itchy skin rash and mouth ulcers. Regular blood and urine tests are necessary to monitor liver and kidney function as well as bone marrow status. All that can be expensive. But for about 30 percent of the people who go for the gold, the benefit can be worth the cost. After five or six months pain and inflammation may all but disappear.

A new and far more convenient form of gold therapy involves an oral pill called **Ridaura**. Like gold shots, this drug can ease morning stiffness, take away pain, improve grip strength, and reduce fatigue and weakness. Because this drug eliminates the cost and trouble of weekly injections, a lot more people are willing to give gold a try these days. Since it appears safer than "old gold," doctors are often willing to start therapy earlier in the disease, when this kind of medicine can do the most good. But diarrhea is a fact of life for as many as 40 percent of those on **Ridaura**. A skin rash can also be a problem. Clearly, gold is not good for everyone, though it is an important advance in our drug armamentarium.

Cuprimine, Depen (penicillamine)

Penicillamine may sound like it's an antibiotic, but believe me, this drug won't kill germs. When gold is too toxic or just doesn't produce much improvement, rheumatologists may turn to this powerhouse. In the old days it was usually considered a very hard medication to handle. But in recent years doctors have adopted the "go slow—go low" approach. This means that they start with the smallest possible dose, usually 125 mg a day. If the patient manages well at that level, the dose is raised after two to four weeks by another 125 mg. Gradually the dose can be raised in this manner with the goal to keep the total amount of medication as low as possible (definitely below 750 mg a day). It usually takes three to six months before any benefit can be detected.

As with all the arthritis drugs we have discussed, the dropout rate is very high with **Cuprimine**. Anywhere from 30 to 50 percent will give it up as either too toxic or just not worth the discomfort. Some people complain of loss of taste, appetite, and smell. Nausea, vomiting, mouth sores, and diarrhea are not uncommon side effects. Skin rashes and itching can also become unbearable. A major concern is kidney damage or severe blood disorders. If you experience fever, chills, wheezing, sore throat, unusual bruising, or any other strange symptom, contact your doctor immediately. Frequent lab tests during the first few months of treatment may provide an early warning of danger. Your doctor will probably encourage you to drink lots of water to maximize the drug's effectiveness. The more water you drink, the lower the dose and the smaller the risk of side effects. When they tell you to drink a pint of water at bedtime and another pint when you have to get up in the middle of the night, they aren't kidding. Now you know why **Cuprimine** isn't one of the most popular of arthritis drugs.

Steroids: cortisone, prednisone, prednisolone, etc.

Here we are at the court(isone) of last resort. No doubt about it, steroids work like gangbusters to relieve the swelling, redness, heat, and pain associated with all sorts of inflammatory conditions. Arthritis, bursitis, tendinitis, ankylosing spondylitis, lupus, asthma, allergies, poison ivy, psoriasis, polymyalgia rheumatica, sunburn, seborrheic dermatitis, and hives all respond amazingly well to treatment with one of the corticosteroids. In fact, back when these drugs were first introduced in the fifties, patients and doctors both were completely dazzled by the marvelous relief these drugs provided. It almost seemed too good to be true, and of course it was.

Before long, the very serious side effects cortisone and its cousins provoke began to crop up. Some physicians began to wonder whether easing inflammation was worth the risk of cataracts, glaucoma, greater susceptibility to infection, ulcers, high blood pressure, fluid retention, potassium and calcium depletion, osteoporosis, psychological reactions, muscle weakness, and weight gain. Not surprisingly, corticosteroids began to fall out of favor, especially when the nonsteroidal alternatives began proliferating.

Does this mean you should run the other way if your doctor suggests prednisone? Absolutely not. Steroid phobia can be taken too far. When used for short periods of time or in low doses, these drugs can be extraordinarily useful. Polymyalgia rheumatica responds to cortisone-type medications like magic. What's more, in low doses (7.5 mg of prednisone or less per day) steroids can be gentle to the GI tract and may be helpful for patients who are caught in an NSAID nightmare. If your doctor thinks it's appropriate, take your medicine every other day. This may reduce the risks of many common steroid side effects. Used cautiously, cortisone can play an important role in the relief of arthritis symptoms, but it's not the sort of drug your doctor should stick you on and walk away.

Helping Yourself with Home Remedies

By now you've probably gotten the picture that there are no perfect arthritis medicines. If the truth be known, there aren't even any good, friendly ones. At best this whole business is a careful balancing act, like walking a high wire between pain relief on one side and stomach ulcers, kidney problems, and other unpleasant consequences on the other. We can send men to the moon, create powerful computers that fit in a briefcase, and devise space-based weapons that will take warfare to a new dimension. But we still can't seem to do a heck of a lot to cure the aches and pains of arthritis. It's hardly any wonder that so many people try all sorts of home remedies and old-fashioned treatments.

Curious to learn what patients actually do to cope with their rheumatism, three British researchers asked a lot of people what alternative therapies they used. Actually, they had a pharmacist administer the questionnaire and promise anonymity so that people would not worry that their answers would get back to their doctors. Of 158 patients, only one relied exclusively on the medicine his doctor had prescribed. Everyone else had experimented with a range of remedies including herbs, diet, liniments, heat treatments, olive oil massage, cod liver oil, copper bracelets, acupuncture, and faith healing.[29]

Physicians often react with outrage to the idea that patients would take their treatment into their own hands. Certainly, home remedies are no substitute for medical care, but how can you knock something that helps people feel better? Many arthritis patients swear that a hot bath goes a lot further to ease morning stiffness than four aspirin before breakfast. In the British study a lot of patients found that their maverick treatments were about as good as their prescription drugs. Hot water bottles got a vote of confidence from 85 percent of the people who had tried them. About 60 percent of those who had taken **Indocin** found it helpful, whereas almost 70 percent were helped by a liniment.[30] Nearly half of the people with RA who tried special diets reported benefit.

Now, we'd never suggest that anyone down gallons of comfrey tea, gulp Chinese herbal medications, sit in an abandoned uranium mine, or bury himself in horse manure. All of these approaches have been tried at one time or another and some (like the herbal remedies) could be dangerous. Speaking of unapproved treatments, whatever happened to DMSO (dimethyl sulfoxide)? Over the years enthusiasts have proclaimed this industrial solvent to be a wonder drug that prevents cancer, replaces insulin, relieves arthritis, and soothes sprains and strains.

But DMSO is still in FDA limbo land. It is sold legally as a chemical solvent, and many people are buying it up and using it as a drug without medical supervision. Some claim it really helps, while others feel they wasted their money.

After 20 years there are still more questions than answers about the safety and effectiveness of DMSO. Reports that this drug may cause cataracts, blurred vision, and night blindness make us nervous. The scandal that surrounded its FDA approval for a rare bladder ailment (interstitial cystitis) is still hanging over the drug like a cloud. The *Mayo Clinic Health Letter* offers the following recommendation:

> **Don't use DMSO. The substance is available "underground," through certain athletic publications and at unregulated "pain clinics" in foreign countries. It is also available as a chemical solvent in America. Our Food and Drug Administration has not approved DMSO for general human use as a drug. If you get it through unauthorized channels, you risk price gouging and a product of uncertain purity.**
>
> **Based upon current evidence, we must say that DMSO—despite the claims—is not worth your while. Don't use it as a medication.**[31]

We're not quite as negative as the folks at the Mayo Clinic, but until there is solid scientific evidence proving the drug's safety and effectiveness, we're erring on the side of caution. We wouldn't suggest it to any arthritis sufferers, but if someone was already using it and finding it helpful, we might not scream and jump up and down either. The bottom line on all of these therapies, including prescription medicines, is that different things work for different people. Arthritis treatment requires a lot of tinkering.

Diet does seem to help some people. A well-controlled scientific study of rheumatoid arthritis patients found that "there was significant objective improvement during periods of dietary therapy."[32] It is still unclear which foods are the most common culprits. Milk, grains, chocolate, nitrates (found in spinach and preserved foods), shrimp, and red meat have all been implicated for some people. A low-fat diet has also been recommended. Fish oils, especially those high in omega-3 fatty acids such as EPA (eicosapentaenoic acid), may also provide noticeable relief. Cod liver oil, which is high in omega-3s, has long been touted as beneficial for arthritis. Now it looks as if today's high-tech researchers are finally beginning to catch up with their grandmothers' home remedies.

If you can't stand the smell of cod liver oil, you might want to look around for EPA fish oil capsules. There are now lots of products available and some of the major drug companies and vitamin suppliers are hopping on the bandwagon with brands like **MaxEPA, Promega, Proto-Chol,** and **SuperEPA**. Other do-it-yourself approaches include moist heat or warm paraffin. If your local hospital has a walk-in clinic for arthritis, they'll probably have the paraffin bath available. If you would like one of your own, it can be ordered through the *Medical Self-Care Catalog*. For a free copy of this magnificent self-help ordering service, write to Medical Self-Care; 11 Chapel Street; P.O. Box 1099; Augusta, Maine 04330. Another catalog which carries aids to make daily life easier for arthritis victims is *Comfortably Yours* (52 West Hunter Ave; Maywood, N.J. 07607).

There are lots of things arthritis patients can do that may help. A physical therapist can supervise an appropriate exercise program to strengthen muscles without risking damage to joints. Swimming or water exercise is often at the top of the list for arthritis benefit, because it takes most of the stress of gravity off the joints. Whatever combination of "tricks" and treatment you settle on, P & P—Persistence and Patience—are the key to success.

Hope for the Future

It hasn't escaped the drug companies' eagle eyes that the market for arthritis drugs is big and getting bigger. As a result, there are dozens of new medications in various stages of development. Most of them are NSAIDs and will probably turn out to be pretty similar, overall, to the ones we've already got. Their makers will be looking for advantages, of course, and trumpeting them to the world. One anti-inflammatory, **Rimadyl** (carprofen), is supposed to be easier on the tum, but company officials will be watching for other potential problems, especially skin rash.

Voltaren (diclofenac sodium) is another new NSAID. The manufacturer, Ciba-Geigy, claims that their experience with **Voltaren** in 90 other countries shows that it may be somewhat better than competitors because it doesn't accumulate in the body and put a strain on the kidneys. According to Dr. Joanne Burcher, "That's especially important in the elderly or other patients with renal [kidney] problems."[33] **Maxicam** (isoxicam) is also being ballyhooed as safe for older people. The manufacturer would like us to believe that it's more effective than aspirin, but they will have to produce some powerful data to convince the FDA.

Ultradol (etodolac) may offer some slight benefit over traditional NSAIDs. Stomach upset is purported to be less common and it doesn't look as though it poses any particular hazard to the kidneys. Another company that's hoping to cash in on the NSAID market actually named their drug **Ansaid** (flurbiprofen). We've been told that stands for "Another NSAID," but it looks as though this drug may be prescribed as often by dentists as by doctors. The grapevine has it that **Ansaid** may be useful in slowing gum disease.

With so many new arthritis medications coming on line, it's entirely possible that your doctor may become overwhelmed. Other products that will be showing up on drugstore shelves include **Benoral** (benorylate), **Cinopal** (fenbufen), **Flenac** (fenclofenac), **Froben** (flurbiprofen), **Oxapro** (oxaprozin), **Rengasil** (pirprofen), and **Surgam** (tiaprofenic acid). Sorting out all of the claims and counterclaims for these drugs that sound like they come from outer space will be a messy and monumental task, so be patient. Don't beg to be the first on your block to try out one of these newer NSAIDs unless you like being a guinea pig. We've had too many scandals and disasters with this type of medication over the past several years, and we'd hate to have you become a statistic.

Perhaps one of the most exciting new developments in the treatment of rheumatoid arthritis involves an experimental cancer treatment. Gamma interferon, a product of the biotechnology revolution, was being tested in cancer patients when some of them noticed that the pain and swelling they usually suffered from their RA was mysteriously disappearing. This drug, which may work its magic by modulating the immune system, is now in clinical trials for rheumatoid arthritis. Another fascinating new anticancer agent, interleukin-2, will also be undergoing tests. Specially tailored monoclonal antibodies may offer yet another high-tech approach to getting the immune system back under control.

Even more promising may be TIMP (tissue inhibitor of metalloproteinase). This substance, which occurs in the body naturally, has recently been created in the laboratory by biotechnology wizards at Celltech in England. TIMP appears to have an important role in preventing the breakdown of connective tissues, and the company believes it will "have potential in controlling the advance of rheumatoid arthritis and possibly arresting the disease completely."[34]

It may take several years before any of these bioengineering projects produce drugs that people can really use, but we're delighted to see research rolling along in this direction. Learning more about the immune system and how to make it behave offers the best chance so far of someday finding a compound that acts like a cure. Maybe we'll even discover what causes arthritis in the first place. Until then P&P (Patience and Persistence) are where it's at.

Things to Remember

1. Doctors still don't know much about arthritis: you should be wary of any remedy that purports to be a cure. If it were easy, no one would still be suffering.

2. Some drugs may bring on symptoms of arthritis or make them worse. If you have a sudden flare-up after starting a new drug regimen or if you suspect one of your medicines is making you worse, talk it over with your physician.

3. Aspirin is still the gold standard for arthritis treatment, both for pain relief (which you can get at low doses) and inflammation (which comes only at significantly higher doses, often up to 14 to 20 tablets a day under a doctor's supervision). Coated aspirin (**Ecotrin, Easprin, Encaprin, Cosprin,** etc.) may be gentler on the stomach. Don't take them with food.

4. Other salicylates can relieve inflammation without as much stomach upset. **Disalcid, Artha-G,** and **Mono-Gesic** (salsalate) are available by prescription with convenient twice-a-day dosing. Nonprescription **Persistin** contains aspirin and salsalate, a combination that may be beneficial in that it provides both pain relief and anti-inflammatory action.

5. NSAIDs (nonsteroidal anti-inflammatory drugs) commonly used for arthritis include **Anaprox, Butazolidin, Clinoril, Dolobid, Feldene, Indocin, Meclomen, Motrin, Nalfon, Naprosyn, Orudis, Rufen,** and **Tolectin.** All can be irritating to the digestive tract. Bleeding and perforated ulcers are potential hazards of these drugs, especially for older people. Watch out for dark or tarry stools, abdominal pain, and persistent heartburn.

6. An antidote to the stomach problems caused by these drugs could be **Carafate.** This prescription ulcer medicine may help protect the stomach lining when taken with the NSAID before meals.

7. NSAIDs may also affect kidney function in some people. Symptoms to watch out for include sudden weight gain, puffiness, swollen feet and ankles, change in the color of urine, and sudden back pain. Periodic kidney function tests are recommended.

8. Over-the-counter ibuprofen products (**Advil, Haltran, Ibuprin, Medipren, Nuprin, Trendar,** etc.) have the same side effects as their prescription counterparts **Motrin** and **Rufen.** If you are going to play doctor with these nonprescription drugs, make sure you know what you are doing. No matter what NSAID you are taking, watch out for skin rash, changes in vision, headache, depression, fluid retention, stomach pain, nausea, heartburn, diarrhea, constipation,

sudden weight gain, puffiness, ringing in the ears, difficulty in breathing, mouth sores, jaundice, and elevated blood pressure.

9. **Clinoril** may be somewhat safer for the kidneys than other NSAIDs and appears to be less likely to reduce the effectiveness of beta blocker blood pressure drugs such as **Inderal, Tenormin,** and **Blocadren**.

10. Many NSAIDs may affect concentration. Do not drive or try anything else that requires attention or coordination if your drug makes you feel sleepy, dizzy, or fuzzy-headed.

11. If your doctor prescribes such heavy duty medicines for rheumatoid arthritis as methotrexate or **Imuran,** regular blood tests are important. Be vigilant for symptoms of complications such as mouth sores, skin rash, sore throat, dark or bloody urine, fever and chills, diarrhea, stomach pain, unusual bruising, and jaundice.

12. Drugs aren't the only answer to arthritis. Carefully designed exercise programs, home remedies such as hot water bottles or paraffin baths, and liniments can all be helpful. If you suspect that something you're eating is making your arthritis worse, why not check with a dietician to design a nutritionally balanced meal plan that eliminates the offending foods.

13. There are lots of new arthritis drugs on the way. Most are similar to NSAIDs like **Clinoril, Motrin,** and **Naprosyn,** but people respond differently to these various compounds and so you may benefit from one or another of the new ones. Just don't be the "first on your block" to be a guinea pig. Sometimes it takes a year or more to find out if there are any rare but serious side effects.

14. No matter what medicines you take for arthritis, remember that YOU'RE IN CHARGE! Listen to your body and if you notice anything out of the ordinary, speak up.

References

1. Owen, Vicki, Boots Pharmaceuticals. Personal communication, Sept. 9, 1986.
2. Fuerst, Mark L. "Arthritis." *Medical World News* 26(17):74–96, 1985.
3. "Arthritis-Parvovirus Link Shown." *Medical World News* 27(15):16, 1986.
4. Fuerst, *op. cit.*
5. Ibid.
6. Sills, Judith M.; and Bosco, Lynn. "Arthralgia Associated with b-Adrenergic Blockage." *JAMA* 255:198–199, 1986.
7. "More Beta-Blocker Joint Problems." *Physicians' Drug Alert* 7(2):9, 1986.
8. Savola, Jaakko. "Arthropathy Induced by Beta Blockade." *British Medical Journal* 287:1256–1257, 1983.
9. Waller, Patrick C.; and Ramsay, Lawrence E. "Do β Blockers Cause Arthropathy? A Case Control Study." *British Medical Journal* 291:1684, 1985.
10. Roth, Sanford H. "Arthritis Update: A Guide to Therapeutic Options." *Modern Medicine* 54(10):46–55, 1986.
11. Caradoc-Davies, T. "Nonsteroidal Anti-inflammatory Drugs, Arthritis, and Gastro-intestinal Bleeding in Elderly In-patients." *Age and Ageing* 13:295–298, 1984.
12. Somerville, Kevin; Faulkner, Gail; and Langman, Michael. "Non-Steroidal Anti-inflammatory Drugs and Bleeding Peptic Ulcer." *Lancet* 1 (8479):462–464, 1986.
13. Roth, Sanford H., Personal communication, Aug. 20, 1986.
14. Walt, Robert, et al. "Rising Frequency of Ulcer Perforation in Elderly People in the United Kingdom." *Lancet* 1(8479): 489–492, 1986.
15. Roth, "Arthritis Update." *op. cit.*, p. 55.
16. Zipser, R.; and Henrich, W. "Implications of Nonsteroidal Anti-inflammatory Drug Therapy." *American J. of Medicine* 80(suppl 1A):78–84, 1986.
17. "Minimizing NSAID Effects on the Kidneys." *Physicians' Drug Alert* 7(5):40, 1986.
18. Ibid.
19. Porter, G.; and Bennet, W. "The Effects of Drugs on the Kidney." *Harrison's Principles of Internal Medicine, Update VI*, 1985, pp. 68–69.
20. Wolfe, Sidney M.; and Sobel, Pauline. Petition to the Department of Health and Human Services (HHS) and the FDA on behalf of Public Citizen and Health Research Group to ban Feldene as an imminent hazard in people ages 60 and older. Jan. 8, 1986, pp. 1–2.
21. Bowen, Otis R. Letter to Sidney Wolfe from The Secretary of Health and Human Services, July 7, 1986.
22. "Feldene: Canada and Germany Protect Older People Better." *Public Citizen Health Research Group Health Letter* 2(4):14, 1986.
23. Ibid.
24. Busson, M. "Over-The-Counter Status for Ibuprofen." *S. Afr. Med. J.* 70(3):178, 1986.

25. Huff, Barbara B., ed. "Motrin Product Information." *Physicians' Desk Reference*, 40th ed. Oradell, N.J.: Medical Economics Co., 1986. pp. 1854–1855.
26. Nashel, D.J.; Shalhoub, R.J.; and O'Connell, J.M. "Labeling of Ibuprofen for Over-the-Counter Use." *N. Engl. J. Med.* 312:377, 1985.
27. "Nonsteroidal Anti-Inflammatory Drugs: Effects on Antihypertensive Activity of Beta Blockers." *Drug Interactions Newsletter* 6(1):1–2, 1986.
28. Huff, Barbara B., ed. *Physicians' Desk Reference*, 40th ed. Oradell, N.J.: Medical Economics Co., 1986, p. 1016.
29. Higham, Carol, et al. "Non-prescribed Treatments in Rheumatic Diseases." *The Practitioner* 227:1201–1205, 1983.
30. Ibid.
31. "DMSO Promises Much, but Delivers Little." *May Clinic Health Letter* 4(10):3–4, 1986.
32. Darlington, L.G., et al. "Placebo-Controlled, Blind Study of Dietary Manipulation Therapy in Rheumatoid Arthritis." *Lancet* 1:236–238, 1986.
33. White, John P. "New Nonsteroidals Coming to the Rescue." *Drug Topics* 130(14):38–42, 1986.
34. "Celltech Plans to License TIMP, Rheumatoid Arthritis Inhibitor, to Marketer in U.S.: Firm Says TIMP Has Also Shown Efficacy in Cancer and Periodontal Disease." *F-D-C Reports* 48(45):12, 1986.

12

Staying Sexy After Sixty

Too many people, including a surprising number of doctors, believe that libido and sexual ability should dry up once you become a senior citizen. There's a kind of Norman Rockwell perspective that says grandparents should restrict their passion to a peck on the cheek and holding hands. If by some mysterious process you still show a spark of interest in sex, you are labeled a "dirty old man" or a "sex-starved little old lady." That's just plain, unadulterated balderdash!

Many older people have a very satisfying love life. Sex can be even more enjoyable than when they were younger because there is less pressure to perform. With age comes a degree of patience and perspective. Affection, closeness, and romanticism all take on greater significance. There is tremendous satisfaction in being held closely, snuggled, and treated tenderly.

A survey of 800 people between the ages of 60 and 91 carried out by Dr. Bernard Starr from the Center for Gerontological Studies at the University of New York and Marcella Baker Weiner from Brooklyn College uncovered some fascinating statistics:

- **In the 60–79 age category, 97 percent of the respondents said sex was a crucial part of their lives, "providing a general sense of well-being and**

good feeling about themselves." For the older age
group, that response dropped only slightly, to 93
percent.

- When asked about their frequency of orgasm, 68
percent of the seniors said it was the same as
when they were young and 20 percent said it was
higher. Only 14 percent reported their frequency
of orgasm had decreased.[1]

One of the nice things that comes with age and wisdom is a
recognition that there's no need to rush lovemaking. People can
take time to relax and really enjoy themselves. In fact, as people
get older, they may tend to reverse roles, with men becoming
more sensitive, giving, and vulnerable and women becoming more
assertive.

Over the years we have received many frank letters from
women who have become concerned about their husband's ability
to participate sexually. Here is one just one example:

> I am 67 and my husband is 71. We have had a very
> happy sex life for over forty years. But about two
> years ago my husband was put on a beta blocker for
> high blood pressure. There were little problems at
> first, but recently he has had a complete lack of libido
> and he says that he is impotent. His doctor will barely
> even talk about this subject and then only lightly
> after we prod him. I needn't tell you what this is
> doing to what once was a beautiful relationship.

What a tragedy! Doctors have a responsibility to discuss *all*
drug side effects—including sexual ones—with their patients. When
it comes to issues of human sexuality, the medical profession
hasn't evolved much further than the Spanish Inquisition. That's
not just our opinion, that is the conclusion of Dr. John Morley,
Professor of Medicine at the University of California, Los Angeles:

> *When the member is no way stirred and can never*
> *perform the action of coition, this is a sign of*
> *frigidity of nature, but when it is stirred and yet*
> *cannot become erect, it is a sign of witchcraft.*
> *Malleus Maleficarum, 1487*

In essence, general medical beliefs concerning impotence have not advanced much over the last 500 years since this edict was issued by the Spanish Inquisition. Most practitioners still believe that in the majority of patients, impotence is psychologic, with fears, phobias and feelings of guilt associated with the sexual act being responsible for the impotence. In addition, the ability to have nocturnal [nighttime] or early morning erections is considered to be pathognomonic [particular to] psychologic ("witchcraft") impotence. The one major change has been in the treatment of psychogenic [psychologic in origin] impotence—in 1487, the "witch" was burned at the stake, leading to the cure of the male, whereas in the 1980s, the male is often psychologically "burned at the stake" with inappropriate psychotherapy when the cause of his disease is organic ("frigidity of nature").[2]

Right on, Dr. Morley! What he's saying is that doctors have a tendency to blame the victim when it comes to sexual problems. If a man is "impotent," it must be because of some deep-seated psychological fears or phobias. If a woman isn't interested in sex or can't experience orgasm, she is labelled "frigid." What horrible words. It is time for doctors to emerge from the Middle Ages.

We now know that most sexual difficulties are biological, not psychological. They can be traced to some underlying physiological problem that may be correctable. How can we contradict conventional medical wisdom with such authority? Research carried out by doctors at the Minneapolis Veterans Administration Medical Center has turned up some fascinating statistics. They studied 1,180 men who visited an outpatient clinic for routine medical problems. The physicians found that 401 men (a whopping 34 percent) suffered from impotence. But the real story was that the overwhelming majority (80 percent) of those cases of erection difficulties were caused by drugs or some physical ailment such as hormonal imbalance, thyroid disease, or diabetes. The Minneapolis investigators concluded that communication between physicians and patients is pretty dismal when it comes to sex:

The patients with impotence secondary to medications used a variety of medications. However, the medications most often implicated were diuretics, antihypertensives, and vasodilators. These patients usually gave a history of normal sexual function before the use of the inciting medication and rapid decrease after the onset of use. In many instances the patients stopped taking the medication but were hesitant to tell their physican why. It was not uncommon for these patients to be considered noncompliant in regard to their medical therapy. The reason for their noncompliance was erectile dysfunction, a complication they were uncomfortable in discussing with their primary physician. In our study, where administration of medications could be stopped, many of the patients improved . . .

By virtue of our experience with this group of patients, it is clear that sexual impotence is a common problem in middle-aged and elderly men with associated medical problems. It also became obvious early in the study that when physicians broached the topic of impotence, patients were eager to discuss and seek evaluation for the problem and yet had been reluctant to call attention to the problem to their primary physician. Before our inquiries regarding sexual function, only six of the 401 men with impotence had been identified as having this problem.[3]

Sure we have trouble talking about intimate issues. Impotence, ejaculatory difficulties, and lost libido are not conversations for "polite" company. But physicians *must* encourage candor. They have a responsibility to discuss sexual side effects and offer alternate remedies when drugs cause problems. The following table lists medications that have been purported to produce sexual dysfunction. Side effects may range from loss of libido and impotence to inability to ejaculate or achieve orgasm. Some of these drugs may be more likely to cause problems than others. Keep in mind that most studies on this subject leave a lot to be desired and that many of the following drugs are included on the basis of anecdotal reports in the medical literature, not well-planned research.

Drugs That May Adversely Affect Sexuality

Brand Name	Generic Name
Adapin	doxepin
Aldoclor	methyldopa, chlorothiazide
alcohol	
Aldactazide	spironolactone, hydrochlorothiazide
Aldactone	spironolactone
Aldomet	methyldopa
Aldoril	methyldopa, hydrochlorothiazide
Amen	medroxyprogesterone
Amicar	aminocaproic acid
Amitril	amitriptyline
Anaprox	naproxen
Anhydron	cyclothiazide
Antabuse	disulfurem
Apresoline	hydralazine (uncommon)
Aquastat	benzthiazide
Aquatag	benzthiazide
Artane	trihexyphenidyl
Asendin	amoxapine
Atromid-S	clofibrate
Aventyl	nortriptyline
Banthine	methantheline
barbiturates	
Bentyl	dicyclomine
Blocadren	timolol
Brevicon	norethindrone, ethinyl estradiol
Calan	verapamil
Catapres	clonidine
Cogentin	benztropine
Combipres	chlorthalidone, clonidine
Cordarone	amiodarone
Delalutin	hydroxyprogesterone
Depo-Provera	medroxyprogesterone
DES	diethylstilbestrol
Diamox	acetazolamide

Brand Name	Generic Name
Dianabol	methandrostenolone
Dibenzyline	phenoxybenzamine
Dilantin	phenytoin
Diupres	chlorothiazide, reserpine
Diuril	chlorothiazide
Dolophine	methadone
Dopar	levodopa
Dyazide	hydrochlorothiazide, triamterene
Elavil	amitriptyline
Endep	amitriptyline
Enduron	methyclothiazide
Esidrix	hydrochlorothiazide
Eskalith	lithium
Ethamide	ethoxzolamide
Eutonyl	pargyline
Exna	benzthiazide
Flagyl	metronidazole
Flexeril	cyclobenzaprine
Fluidil	cyclothiazide
Haldol	haloperidol
Homapin	homatropine
HydroDIURIL	hydrochlorothiazide
Hydropres	reserpine, hydrochlorothiazide
Hygroton	chlorthalidone
Hylorel	guanadrel
Inderal	propranolol
Inderide	propranolol, hydrochlorothiazide
Inversine	mecamylamine
Ismelin	guanethidine
Isoptin	verapamil
Janimine	imipramine
Lanoxin	digoxin
Larodopa	levodopa
Librax	chlordiazepoxide, clidinium
Librium	chlordiazepoxide
Limbitrol	chlordiazepoxide, amitriptyline
Lioresal	baclofen

Brand Name	Generic Name
Lithane	lithium
Lithobid	lithium
Lopressor	metoprolol
Lozol	indapamide
Ludiomil	maprotiline
Marplan	isocarboxazid
Maxzide	triamterene, hydrochlorothiazide
Megace	megestrol
Mellaril	thioridazine
Mesopin	homatropine
Metahydrin	trichlormethiazide
Metatensin	trichlormethiazide, reserpine
Mexitil	mexiletine
Micronor	norethindrone
Midamor	amiloride
Minipress	prazosin (uncommon)
Moban	molindone
Modicon	norethindrone, ethinyl estradiol
Mysoline	primidone
Naprosyn	naproxen (uncommon)
Naqua	trichlormethiazide
Nardil	phenelzine
Naturetin	bendroflumethiazide
Navane	thiothixene
Neptazane	methazolamide
Nizoral	ketoconazole
Norlutate	norethindrone
Norlutin	norethindrone
Normodyne	labetalol
Norpace	disopyramide
Norpramin	desipramine
Nor-Q.D.	norethindrone
Oretic	hydrochlorothiazide
Ortho-Novum	norethindrone, ethinyl estradiol
Ovcon	ethinyl estradiol, norethindrone
Ovrette	norgestrel
Pamelor	nortriptyline

Brand Name	Generic Name
Parnate	tranylcypromine
Pathilon	tridihexethyl
Permitil	fluphenazine
Pertofrane	desipramine
Pondimin	fenfluramine
Presamine	imipramine
Pro-Banthine	propantheline
progesterone	
Prolixin	fluphenazine
Provera	medroxyprogesterone
Quarzan	clidinium
Reglan	metoclopramide
Renese	polythiazide
reserpine	
Robinul	glycopyrrolate
Salutensin	hydroflumethiazide, reserpine
Sandril	reserpine
Ser-Ap-Es	reserpine, hydralazine
Serpasil	reserpine
Serax	oxazepam
Serentil	mesoridazine
Sinequan	doxepin
Stelazine	trifluoperazine
Tagamet	cimetidine
Taractan	chlorprothixene
Tegretol	carbamazepine
Tenormin	atenolol (less common)
Thorazine	chlorpromazine
Timolide	timolol, hydrochlorothiazide
Timoptic	timolol
Tofranil	imipramine
Trandate	labetalol
Trecator	ethionamide
Triavil	perphenazine, amitriptyline
Trilafon	perphenazine
Valium	diazepam
Valpin	anisotropine

Brand Name	Generic Name
Visken	pindolol
Vivactil	protriptyline
Wytensin	guanabenz
Xanax	alprazolam
Zantac	ranitidine (uncommon)

Sources:

"Drugs That Cause Sexual Dysfunction. *Medical Letter* 25(641):73–76, 1983.

Soyka, Lester F.; and Mattison, Donald R. "Prescription Drugs That Affect Male Sexual Function." *Drug Therapy*, Aug. 1981, pp. 46–58.

Smith, P.J.; and Talbert, R.L. "Sexual Dysfunction with Antihypertensive and Antipsychotic Agents." *Clin. Pharm.* 5:373–384, 1986.

Aldridge, S.A. "Drug-induced Sexual Dysfunction." *Clin. Pharm.* 1(2):141–147, 1982.

Morley, John E. "Impotence," *Am. J. Med.* 80:897–905, 1986.

Now don't panic just because a medication you are taking is included on this list. If you haven't experienced any problems, don't start looking for trouble. In some cases sexual side effects are quite uncommon. The ulcer drug **Tagamet**, for example, rarely causes impotence unless it is taken in high doses for something unusual called Zollinger-Ellison syndrome.

Even if a particular drug is associated with lowered libido or erection problems, that doesn't mean that all users will suffer from it. Some people are more sensitive, or resistant, than others. And just because your medicine is not mentioned doesn't mean it's not the cause of sexual difficulties. Most drugs have not been tested for their effects on sexuality, and physicians rarely ask their patients about this situation or report such side effects in the medical literature.

One of the real dilemmas in detecting drug-induced sexual dysfunction is that the onset can be slow, subtle, and insidious. Most people don't keep careful records of how many times they have relations. And so a gradual loss of libido or interest in sex may not even be noticed for months or years. Or it might be chalked up to that old bugaboo, "aging." That's why it is important to pay attention to your body and think back to when sexual vitality began to wane. Could it have been associated with a new prescription?

So what should you do if your medication *is* on the list and you are having trouble? Do NOT stop taking your drug!!! First and foremost, talk it over with your doctor. She should know about all important side effects, and sexual difficulties *are* important! Ask if an alternate medicine is available. Sometimes just switching from one beta blocker to another will work wonders. For example, someone may develop impotence with **Inderal** but not with **Tenormin** or **Visken**. Or the calcium channel blocker **Calan** might cause erection problems whereas **Procardia** might actually be helpful against impotence.[4]

Going for the Gold

If you have heard one message repeated throughout this book, it is that "quality of life" is not a trivial issue. And there are choices that can be made to enhance that quality. We can't think of a better motivation to lose weight, give up smoking, and control blood pressure through nondrug alternatives than to maintain a healthy and vigorous sexual appetite and ability into one's sixties and beyond. And if medicine is necessary to prevent a stroke or heart attack, then drugs that are less likely to muck up the machinery may be worth trying.

Antihypertensives have a horrible reputation for causing all manner of sexual side effects, but these drugs are not created equal in this regard.[5-7] **Minipress** (prazosin) and **Apresoline** (hydralazine), for example, may be less likely to cause impotence than diuretics like **HydroDIURIL** (hydrochlorothiazide).[8] **Capoten** (captopril) has been shown to produce less sexual dysfunction than **Inderal** (propranolol) or **Aldomet** (methyldopa).[9] **Vasotec** (enalapril), which is similar in action to **Capoten**, would presumably also have this benefit. Of course, both of these "ACE inhibitor" drugs must be approached with caution in older people. Kidney function tests are crucial. For more information about side effects and other precautions see page 228. The calcium channel blockers **Adalat** and **Procardia** (nifedipine), and **Cardizem** (diltiazem) may also turn out to be surprisingly helpful alternate medicine for hypertension.[10] No matter which drug is ultimately selected, it will continue to be important to maintain good communication with your physician so progress can be constantly monitored.

Blood pressure treatment isn't the only place where sexual problems crop up. Even something as seemingly benign as **Timoptic** (timolol) eye drops for glaucoma have been reported to cause sexual dysfunctions.[11] Changing glaucoma medicine could make a difference for some people. And let's not forget anti-anxiety agents and sleeping pills. They may create a subtle lowering of libido. Here is an interesting case reported in the medical literature:

> **A 42-year-old woman who had been taking diaze-pam [Valium] 5 mg three times daily and flurazepam [Dalmane] 30 mg at night for more than 5 years had these drugs abruptly stopped by her general practitioner. Before this she had had regular sexual intercourse, about weekly, generally without orgasm. During the months after the benzodiazepines were stopped she had severe withdrawal symptoms—notably, insomnia, nightmares, muscle cramps, stomach pains, anxiety, and a disabling sense of the ground slowly swaying. However, her libido increased and she became regularly orgasmic. This improved sexual function diminished when she was restarted on diazepam [Valium] (10 mg daily) to deal with the other withdrawal symptoms.[12]**

Valium shouldn't take all the flack. Most anti-anxiety agents that belong to the benzodiazepine class might have a similar effect. Other such drugs include **Ativan** (lorazepam), **Centrax** (prazepam), **Halcion** (triazolam), **Librium** (chlordiazepoxide), **Paxipam** (halazepam), **Restoril** (temazepam), **Serax** (oxazepam), **Tranxene** (clorazepate), and **Xanax** (alprazolam).

Maybe an Aphrodisiac?

Antidepressants are also notorious for messing up one's love life. MAO inhibitors like **Nardil** (phenelzine), **Marplan** (isocarboxazid), and **Parnate** (tranylcypromine) can produce erection and ejaculation difficulties in men and an inability to achieve orgasm in women. More commonly prescribed antidepressants such as **Adapin** (doxepin), **Asendin** (amoxapine), **Elavil** (amitriptyline), **Sinequan** (doxepin), **Tofranil** (imipramine), and **Vivactil** (protriptyline) may also cause sexual problems. There are two possible exceptions—**Wellbutrin** (bupropion) and **Desyrel** (trazodone). Preliminary reports indicate that **Wellbutrin** can restore sexual function for patients who have suffered problems while taking other antidepressants. There have even been suggestions that **Wellbutrin** may improve libido for many people whose sexual difficulties are not caused by depression. At this writing, however, **Wellbutrin** is still not available. For more on this interesting drug, turn to page 197.

Desyrel is another relatively new antidepressant. Dr. Nanette Gartrell, a psychiatrist at Harvard Medical School, offered the following experience:

> Although clinicians have been alerted to the possible association between trazodone and priapism [prolonged male erection], a review of the literature failed to reveal any information about trazodone's effects on female sexual functioning. I have used trazodone to treat major depression . . . in a variety of female patients in the past 3 years. In this report I describe three cases of depressed women who experienced an increase in libido to above premorbid levels with therapeutic doses of trazodone . . .
>
> *Case 2.* Ms. B, a 44-year-old psychologist with good premorbid functioning, had a 2 1/2-year history of dysthymic disorder that had begun after a mastectomy and relationship loss. She suffered from chronic fatigue, social isolation, and poor self-esteem. Whereas she had previously had positive and satisfying sexual relationships, her sex drive had diminished to the point that she had given up masturbating.
>
> After a year of psychotherapy and no remission of symptoms, Ms. B agreed to a trial of trazodone in gradually increasing doses up to 150 mg/day. The week after she had begun taking 150 mg/day, she reported that she thought trazodone might be an aphrodisiac. Although she was orgasmic, as she had

been before the onset of her dysthymic disorder, she began to feel as though she was constantly sexually driven. She began masturbating again, and she also reestablished sexual relationships with three former sexual partners (she had previously been sexually monogamous). Concurrently, her level of energy improved and she regained her self-confidence.

Ms. B's trazodone was tapered off 6 months later. Although she did not experience any recurrent symptoms of depression, she did lament the diminution of her sex drive to its premastectomy levels within 2 weeks after discontinuing the trazodone.[13]

Now before anyone rushes out to beg some **Desyrel**, it is important to recognize that Dr. Gartrell's report is preliminary at best. And not everyone responded so favorably. She reported that

Of the 13 women I have treated with trazodone, six ... experienced a substantial increase in libido ... It is important to point out that the increased libido experienced by these patients was described as highly pleasurable ... In fact, when these patients realized that the increased sex drive might be associated with trazodone, they were reluctant to discontinue the medication.[14]

Desyrel is not without unpleasant side effects, however. It can make people drowsy, disoriented, dizzy, light-headed, fatigued, or incoordinated (all very dangerous for older people). Patients have also complained of dry mouth, nausea, and constipation. Nevertheless, if depression is a problem and other antidepressants have inhibited libido, it might be worth discussing **Desyrel** with a doctor to see if this drug is appropriate. Oh yes, there is one additional potentially serious side effect with this drug. In men it has been occasionally reported to produce a prolonged and painful erection (priapism) that in some cases required emergency surgery.

Speaking of erections, are you ready for something wild and wacky? *Science News* reported the following case from the *Annals of Internal Medicine*:

Not tonight, dear, I'll have a headache

Sometimes scientific discoveries are made not by
white-coated scientists but by backyard tinkerers.
Such was the case of a Georgia man with heart
disease.

According to Emory University researchers, the
man had noticed that the nitrate skin patches he
was wearing on his chest to control heart pain gave
him a headache, a known side effect of the drug: the
headache didn't occur if he wore the patch on his
leg. His curiosity aroused, the man rubbed a used
patch on his penis. Within five minutes he became
sexually aroused, and had sexual intercourse with
his wife. "Several minutes later ... she wondered
why she had the worst headache she ever had in her
life."

The case, the researchers say, "illustrates two previously undescribed points concerning topical nitrates
[nitroglycerin]: their ability to induce vasodilation
and resulting erection, and their absorption through
the mucosal membranes of the vaginal walls." The
authors expressed doubt that further research in
this area will be done.[15]

Okay, enough of such silliness. This is a serious matter. But
then again, a little comic relief doesn't hurt once in a while. The
real issue, though, is what to do if erection problems can't be
improved by changing medications or if drugs are not the culprits. You would be surprised at how much can be done. In
recent years there have been some revolutionary changes in our
understanding and treatment of this common condition. Dr. John
Morley encourages his colleagues to "ask all male patients if they
are impotent. If they reply in the affirmative, they should be
asked whether they want the condition corrected; if so, they
should be fully evaluated."[16]

Now, the kind of evaluation Dr. Morley is suggesting probably
can't be done by a family physician. Here's a case where proper
diagnosis and treatment requires a specialist, usually a urologist.
First off, an expert will want to check for hormonal imbalances,
diabetes, thyroid disease, nutritional deficiencies, epilepsy, mini-

strokes, multiple sclerosis, or vascular disease in the penis (arteriosclerosis).

The doctor will also want to rule out psychologic factors. One of the quickest, easiest, and cheapest tricks we've heard of is the stamp test. You see, it is normal for men to get erections while they are sleeping (or more likely, dreaming), and those who do probably do not suffer from "organic" impotence. That is, there may not be anything wrong physically. There are all kinds of sophisticated testing equipment to measure nighttime erections, but the stamp test is, according to Dr. Morley, "disarmingly simple."

> **In this technique, four Christmas seals are wrapped snugly around the penis with the overlapping stamp being wet to seal the stamp ring. A positive test result represents the stamp being broken along the perforations when the patient awakens in the morning. The developers of this test calculated a cost of 30 cents for three nights' outpatient testing (nothing if the Christmas seals that come in the mail are just taken without an appropriate donation being made) compared with approximately $500 for three nights of in-hospital nocturnal penile tumescence testing![17]**

If the stamps are not broken, it is a preliminary indication that no erection occurred and that the patient is suffering organic impotence. Now what? Well, there's a lot that can be done. First, if there is a clearly diagnosed cause such as thyroid disease or a zinc deficiency, thyroid replacement or zinc supplements may work wonders.[18,19]

If the problem is not associated with hormonal or nutritional deficiencies, perhaps it's worth considering yohimbine. Canadian scientists recently proved what West African witch doctors have known for centuries. Yohimbine, a drug made from the bark of the yohimb tree, overcame erection problems in nearly half of the men tested (*Lancet,* vol 2, 1987, pages 421–423). Surprisingly, yohimbine seemed to work equally well whether the source of the difficulty was physical or psychological.

Now, this drug is not innocuous. Although the Canadian researchers concluded that yohimbine "is a safe treatment for psychogenic impotence that seems to be as effective as sex and marital therapy for restoring satisfactory sexual functioning," there are potential risks. Yohimbine can cause heart palpitations, increased pulse, high blood pressure, headache, nausea, attacks of anxiety, sweating, and tremors. While some unscrupulous mail order houses have promoted the medication as an "aphrodisiac," it should be taken only under a doctor's supervision.

If all else fails, some patients may benefit from one of the hottest new therapies in urology—papaverine injections. Papaverine is a drug that is often used by surgeons to dilate blood vessels. It is also occasionally injected during heart or anginal attacks in an attempt to improve blood flow. In 1982 a French researcher, Dr. R. Virag, reported that if papaverine was injected directly into the penis, it produced an almost instant erection.[20]

Since that initial preliminary report there have been many more studies that seem to confirm these amazing results.[21-25] In most cases papaverine is combined with another drug called **Regitine** (phentolamine) and injected directly into the penis. Sounds gruesome, right? Not to worry. Urologists tell us that it is virtually painless because an extremely small needle is used. With proper instruction, men can be easily taught how to self-inject the medication, or their partners can learn. Within seconds there is a noticeable effect and usually within four to ten minutes full erection is apparent. An erection is usually maintained up to two hours, although much longer erections have been reported. That may sound exciting, but we assure you prolonged erection can become painful and very dangerous. Allowed to last too long, this condition (priapism) can cause permanent damage to delicate penile tissues. That is why a specialist must carefully determine the appropriate dose for each patient and provide instructions about what to do in the event an erection lasts longer than two or three hours. Dr. Virag cautions that a drug-induced erection should never exceed four hours.[26]

Not everyone will benefit from papaverine, but the initial results are certainly encouraging. Even patients with spinal cord damage have had an excellent response. Researchers at the University of Minnesota Health Sciences Center and Minneapolis VA published the following observations:

> **In our hands this method has proved to be effective**
> **for the treatment of erectile dysfunction in a se-**

lected population with neurogenic impotence, and virtually 100 percent of the patients responded. In fact, most of these patients described the quality of erections as close to perfect. In a selected group of men suffering from vascular impotence the response rate also was surprisingly high (65.7 percent). However, these men described the drug-induced erections in less enthusiastic terms than men in the neurogenic impotence group, with most rating the quality of response as about 70 to 80 percent of normal . . .

However, it should be emphasized strongly that the long-term effects of intracavernous drug-induced erection are yet to be determined. Consequently, all patients practicing the method as therapy should be followed closely by physicians experienced in the evaluation and treatment of penile abnormalities.[27]

Dr. Floyd Fried is chief of the urology division of the University of North Carolina School of Medicine. In his clinic 30 out of 40 men have had favorable results. He sums up his work:

Impotence means that for some reason, the spongy tissue within the penis is not filling with blood, allowing it to become erect and capable of sexual intercourse.

By injecting a drug that helps increase the blood supply directly into the base of the penis, we can help some men achieve an erection that lasts from one to three hours.[28]

A nurse in the urology clinic described patients' acceptance this way: "Some are a little embarrassed at first, but most would rather be embarrassed than impotent, so they are willing to spend the time learning how to do the injection."[29]

Urologists are cautiously optimistic that these results will continue to be duplicated. As yet, the papaverine/phentolamine injections must still be considered experimental. Neither drug has been approved by the FDA for this purpose though both drugs are available and doctors can legally prescribe them for any purpose they believe is appropriate.

In addition, alprostadil (prostaglandin E_1) has shown some promise for this application. Dr. Arnold Melman, a consultant for the *Journal of the American Medical Association*, believes that "Men with diabetes, hypertension, and atherosclerosis are good candidates for this method of treating impotence."[30]

There are concerns that long-term side effects may yet show up. Some reports of fibrosis (toughened tissues) have begun to circulate, so there may be serious risks down the road. Doctors also worry that infection is possible if patients do not observe sterile techniques for their injections.

People with sickle cell anemia or liver disease or those taking major tranquilizers (phenothiazines) should not be allowed to try papaverine. For the moment patients should only consult skilled specialists who are familiar with the proper workup, testing, and treatment with this exciting new approach to erection difficulties. And even if injection therapy proves unsuccessful or inappropriate, penile implants offer another alternative. The urologist doing the workup will explain the advantages and disadvantages of each style. The bottom line is that with a caring, sensitive, knowledgeable physician, there is hope for many couples who have suffered with erection problems.

Oh, That Pesky Prostate

One cause of erection problems is prostate surgery. That's why a lot of men fear to go under the knife and instead prefer to suffer with what doctors refer to as urinary hesitancy and we call problem peeing. Let's clear up some myths right away. Prostate surgery does *not* inevitably lead to impotence. A lot depends on the kind of surgery that is being done and who's doing the cutting.

Before we get into the details and differences between TURP (transurethral resection of the prostate) and the far more drastic radical prostatectomy, let's have a quick anatomy lesson. Think of the prostate gland as a small donut. It is located under the bladder with the urethra running through the hole in the donut.

When we are young, the gland is about the size of an almond. When we become teenagers, the gland has begun to respond to male hormones and enlarges to the size of a walnut. At 50, there is already significant enlargement for some men, leading to benign prostatic hypertrophy (BPH). And by age 70, more than half of the male population will have an overgrown gland, reaching the size of a grapefruit in some cases. When your prostate gets that big you can bet it will be pretty hard to pee. The gland squeezes the urethra and in so doing blocks the flow of urine.

Please understand that an enlarged prostate gland does *not* mean you have cancer. Although prostate cancer is extremely common, we don't honestly understand much about this disease. Doctors have done autopsies on men who died between the ages of 40 and 50 from other causes and found that up to 20 percent had microscopic signs of prostate cancer. When they did autopsies on men who lived to their seventies and eighties, they found that up to 60 percent had signs of cancer. But the vast majority of men with cancer cells (five out of six) never show signs of disease, and the cancer never spreads to other parts of the body. Dr. Ira Sharlip, a urologist at the University of California, San Francisco, Medical Center, puts it this way: "Most men die *with* prostate cancer, not *from* it."[31] In other words, the cancer cells may be there, but for most men they never seem to cause any problems. Mysterious.

Assuming an enlarged prostate is not cancerous, what can be done to help eliminate the discomfort of urinary hesitancy? Here is where TURP comes in. This is the surgical equivalent of the Roto-Rooter man. The urologist inserts a small tube into the penis and up into the urethra. Yes, I know you just said ouch, but this is done under spinal or general anesthesia. An electrical wire loop is then turned on and it burns and/or chisels away all that excess prostate tissue. Urologists consider such a procedure routine, but believe us when we say it is major surgery with a lot of blood and some inflammation. Infection is rare (occurring in about 1 percent of cases). Incontinence is also unlikely (again about 1 percent). And lost erections, while a concern, are not common (ranging from 1 to 5 percent).

By the way, if prostate cancer is a problem and a radical prostatectomy (prostate removal) is called for, you might want to contact Dr. Patrick Walsh, head of the Brady Urological Institute at Johns Hopkins University in Baltimore, Maryland. Before Dr. Walsh refined his surgical procedure, impotence was almost guaranteed (90 percent or more). Dr. Walsh has developed a careful technique that has preserved erection potential in up to 80 percent of patients.

In the case of the far more common TURP, Michael Castleman, writing in the magazine *Medical Self-Care*, describes a more likely side effect:

> **In most cases TURPs result in "dry orgasm." Scarring from the electrocautery usually closes the ejaculatory ducts, thus blocking the flow of seminal fluid. After a TURP, orgasm feels as pleasurable as ever, but the man does not ejaculate. If seminal fluid still flows at all, it is released backward into the bladder. Backward ejaculation, called retro-ejaculation, may sound strange, but it's of no medical concern. Any semen mixes with the urine and passes out during urination.[32]**

Is there any alternative to surgery? Maybe, just maybe, there will be a drug for prostate enlargement in the not too distant future. Israeli researchers have been experimenting with a drug called **Dibenzyline** (phenoxybenzamine). Dr. Marco Caine of Hadassah Medical Center in Jerusalem has reported that "the last word has not yet come, but until we find another drug to shrink the size of the prostate and cure the condition, **Dibenzyline** is by far the most effective orally administered preparation."[33]

> **In a subjective study cited by Dr. Caine, Dibenzyline brought relief to 137 of 171 patients with benign prostatic hypertrophy, or 80 percent of the participants. The drug also improved urinary flow in 133, according to patient reports.**
>
> **About one-third of men over age 60 can expect to have prostate trouble, Dr. Caine said, and "most men will experience BPH if they live long enough.[34]**

Dibenzyline is sold in this country for special cases of hypertension. But it's not without risks. It can cause weakness, dizziness, stuffy nose, and palpitations and can inhibit ejaculation. There is also worry that it causes cellular mutations and has promoted tumor formation in animals. No one knows if **Dibenzyline** is carcinogenic in humans. Although any risk of cancer is probably small, we caution against treating benign prostatic hypertrophy with the drug at this time. But Dr. Caine's preliminary success is spurring U.S. drug companies to come up with newer, safer and more effective treatments.

The most exciting experimental compound comes from Merck Sharpe & Dohme, and is currently called MK-906. It blocks an enzyme that is responsible for converting the male hormone testosterone to a more potent hormone thought responsible for contributing to acne, male pattern baldness, excess hair growth in women (hirsutism), prostate enlargement, and prostate cancer.[35-37] In a 1987 report to stockholders, the company offered the following optimistic assessment:

> **MK-906 is a drug that is the subject of unusual scientific and medical interest in our laboratories. It is a Merck discovery designed to relieve prostatic hypertrophy—that is, to reduce the size of an enlarged prostate gland. This condition, which affects the vast majority of men over fifty, can result in symptoms that cause a great deal of suffering and which often require surgery with its attendant risks.**
>
> **There is now strong evidence that a hormone called dihydrotestosterone causes overgrowth of the prostate gland. Dihydrotestosterone is formed in the body by a specific enzyme which converts testosterone, the essential male hormone, to dihydrotestosterone. Merck scientists designed MK-906 to inhibit that enzyme and thus block the formation of dihydrotestosterone.**
>
> **MK-906 has been tested in three species of animals and has proved successful in reducing the size of enlarged prostates. . . . We are moving ahead with tests in patients with enlarged prostates to determine whether this compound does in fact reduce the size of the affected gland.[38]**

For the millions of men who suffer with enlarged prostate glands, that most common and vexing fixture of male aging, the future looks extremely bright. If these drugs turn out to be half as good as the researchers expect, prostate surgery may become a thing of the past.

Women Have Problems Too

After menopause, most women experience a decrease in the natural lubrication produced in the vagina during sexual arousal. This can often lead to painful intercourse, but the problem is easily remedied with any of several lubricating substances. The use of lubricants is quite common in sex, and many couples use them even if the woman's natural lubrication is normal. In some cases, they find that lubricants can heighten their sexual experience.[39]

Perhaps one of the safest and more effective lubricants is the one used by doctors when doing rectal or gynecological exams: **K-Y Jelly**. It has the advantage of being water soluble, which means it doesn't feel greasy and is easily washed off. During lovemaking it may dry out though, so you may have to keep reapplying it. Oil is also an acceptable alternative. There are a number of romantic-sounding massage oils on the market that you may find appealing. Or you might want to use prelubricated condoms. Petroleum jelly (**Vaseline**) is not high on our list of recommended lubricants because it is just too greasy and doesn't wash off.

Sometimes the vaginal walls become thin and so dry that even a lubricant may not protect them adequately. That's when estrogen, either taken orally or applied as a cream, may well be justified. There are risks (see pages 250–251) but for many women the benefits of osteoporosis prevention and improved intercourse are worth the risks.

Sex is an important part of many people's lives, and there's no reason why they should have to give it up just because they reach some arbitrary age. We hope that with some of the clues you have found in this chapter and a supportive physician you will be able to overcome any sexual difficulties that interfere with your enjoyment of life.

Things to Remember

1. Sex can be even more enjoyable as we get older. Patience and affection are great assets in a romantic relationship. (It may take a little longer

to get there, but who cares, if you enjoy the
trip?)

2. Some sexual difficulties may be side effects of
one or more medications. As the problem may
have a gradual onset, it is not always easy to
identify the culprit. But if you suspect that a
drug you are taking is having an adverse effect
on your love life, talk it over with your doctor.
There may be alternative treatments available
that are less likely to cause trouble. Blood pressure medications such as **Adalat, Apresoline,
Capoten, Cardizem, Minipress, Procardia,** and
Vasotec have reasonably good track records.
Antidepressants like **Desyrel**, **Prozac**, and **Wellbutrin** (when it becomes available) also may be
better tolerated than older drugs.

3. Some of the medicines that may lead to impotence or loss of libido in men can also interfere
with women's sexuality. Sexual side effects in
women are not reported in the medical literature
as often, but that does not mean they do not
occur. Clear communication with a sensitive physician is important for people of both sexes.

4. When erection difficulties interfere with sexual
relations, a complete workup by a qualified urologist is called for. Hormone imbalances, nutritional deficiencies, diabetes, and vascular disease
must be carefully treated, if responsible.

5. Be suspicious of over-the-counter aphrodisiacs
or erection aids. Ground up rhinoceros tusk, gin-
seng, Spanish fly, or special vitamins are unlikely to produce the desired results.

6. Organic impotence may respond to injection therapy with a combination of either papaverine or
alprostadil and phentolamine. Careful adjustment
of dose is critical to prevent prolonged and painful erection. This treatment is still highly experimental, however, and long-term risks have not
yet been established.

7. Prostate enlargement may not be an inevitable result of aging. Exciting drug advances could soon make it possible to reverse this common ailment without surgery.

8. After menopause, low estrogen levels may affect vaginal tissue. If intercourse becomes painful, lubrication is important. Estrogen therapy is appropriate for some people.

References

1. "Sex for Senior Citizens Is No Longer Shrouded in Shame, Secrecy." Reprinted from the *Fort Lauderdale News and Sun-Sentinel* in *The News and Observer,* Sept. 7, 1986, pp. C1.
2. Morley, John E. "Impotence." *Am. J. Med.* 80:897–905, 1986.
3. Slag, Michael, et al. "Impotence in Medical Clinic Outpatients." *JAMA* 249:1736–1740, 1983.
4. Morley, op. cit.
5. Williams, Gordon H. "Quality of Life and Its Impact on Hypertensive Patients." *Am. J. Med.* 82:98–104, 1987.
6. Kaplan, Norman M. "Antihypertensive Drugs: How Different Classes Can Impact Patients' Coronary Heart Disease Risk Profile and Quality of Life." *Am. J. Med.* 82(suppl 1A):9–14, 1987.
7. Virag, R., et al. "Is Impotence an Arterial Disorder? A Study of Arterial Risk Factors in 440 Impotent Men." *Lancet* 1:181–184, 1985.
8. Grimm, Richard H., Jr. "Thiazide Diuretics and Selective Alpha Blockers: Comparison of Use in Antihypertensive Therapy, Including Possible Differences in Coronary Heart Disease Risk Reduction." *Am. J. Med.* 82(suppl 1A) 26–35, 1987.
9. Croog, Sydney H., et al. "The Effects of Antihypertensive Therapy on the Quality of Life." *N. Engl. J. Med.* 314:1657–1664, 1986.
10. Morley, op. cit.
11. Katz, Irving M. "Sexual Dysfunction and Ocular Timolol." *JAMA* 255:37–38, 1986.
12. Nutt, David, et al. "Increased Sexual Function in Benzodiazepine Withdrawal." *Lancet* 2:1101–1102, 1986.
13. Gartrell, Nanette. "Increased Libido in Women Receiving Trazodone." *Am. J. Psychiatry* 143:781–782, 1986.
14. Ibid.
15. "Not Tonight, Dear, I'll Have a Headache." *Science News,* Dec. 14, 1985, pp. 377.
16. Morley, op cit.
17. Ibid.
18. Ibid.

19. Billington, C.J., et al. "Zinc Status in Impotent Patients." *Clin. Res.* 31:714A, 1983.

20. Virag, R. "Intracavernous Injection of Papaverine for Erectile Failure." *Lancet* 2:938, 1982.

21. Zorgniotti, Adrian W.; and Lefleur, Richard S. "Auto-Injection of the Corpus Cavernosum with a Vasoactive Drug Combination for Vasculogenic Impotence." *J. Urol.* 133:39–41, 1985.

22. Virag, R., et al. "Intracavernous Injection of Papaverine as a Diagnostic and Therapeutic Method in Erectile Failure." *Angiology J. of Vascular Diseases* 35(2):79–87, 1984.

23. Brindley, G.S. "Maintenance Treatment of Erectile Impotence by Cavernosal Unstriated Muscle Relaxant Injection." *Br. J. Psychiatry* 149:210–215, 1986.

24. Wyndaele, J.J., et al. "Intracavernous Injection of Vasoactive Drugs, an Alternative for Treating Impotence in Spinal Injury Patients." *Paraplegia* 24:271–275, 1986.

25. Kiely, E.A., et al. "Impotence: Science and Sciencibility." *Br. Med. J.* 292:1137–1138, 1986.

26. Virag, R. "About Pharmacologically Induced Prolonged Erection." *Lancet* 1:519–520, 1985.

27. Sidi, Abraham Ami, et al. "Intracavernous Drug-Induced Erections in the Management of Male Erectile Dysfunction: Experience with 100 Patients." *J. Urol.* 135:704–706, 1986.

28. *News*, The University of North Carolina at Chapel Hill. "UNC Study Shows Injections Can Help Impotent Men." July 28, 1986.

29. Ibid.

30. "Impotence Cure by Injection," Questions and Answers. *JAMA* 258:700, 1987.

31. Castleman, Michael. "The Puzzling Prostate." *Medical Self-Care.* July-August, 1986, pp. 26–31.

32. Ibid.

33. "Oral Therapy Cuts Prostate Surgery." *Medical World News*, Sept. 23, 1985, pp. 43.

34. Ibid.

35. Tehming, Liang, et al. "Species Differences in Prostatic Steroid 5α-Reductases of Rat, Dog, and Human." *Endocrinol.* 117:571–579, 1985.

36. Rasmusson, Gary H., et al. "Azasteroids: Structure-Activity Relationships for Inhibition of 5α-Reductase and of Androgen Receptor Binding." *J. Med. Chem.* 29:2298–2315, 1986.

37. Stoner, Elizabeth, et al. "Administration of MK-906, A 4-Azasteroid Compound, Results in Marked Suppression of Serum Dihydrotestosterone in Healthy Men." *Clin. Res.* 35(3):4–2A, 1987.

38. Merck & Co., Inc. *First Quarter Report*, 1987, pp. 11–12.

39. "Using Lubricants to Enhance Sexual Sensations." *Sex Over Forty* 4(11):6–7, 1986.

13

Developing Your Rubber Ducky Detector (Quack, Quack)

Now we're going to tell you perhaps the most important information of all. This chapter is your key to the biggest savings on medications. It will absolutely save you money. It will also save you pain and suffering, both physical and mental. And it just might save your life.

You see, this chapter is about things that don't really work. It's about cures that don't cure, about remedies that remedy nothing, about unproven, untested, unapproved, and untried medications and devices that are sold to the American public to the tune of more than 10 BILLION dollars every year.[1]

It's a very sad story, because it's about callous, knowing, deliberate attempts to take advantage of those whose illnesses don't readily yield to treatment or cure. It's the story of those who would trade on people's fears, lack of knowledge, and hopes just to make a few bucks for themselves.

And the saddest part of all is that those bucks are most often

extracted from older people, whose bodies and budgets are both
at their most vulnerable. Almost half of those over 65 years of
age have at least one chronic (long-term) condition, which is the
most fertile hunting ground of the medical fraudster. The beguil-
ing ad promises to do what no doctor has done—cure your
arthritis, make your hearing perfect, improve your vision, rid you
of those aches and pains. Make no mistake: as an older American,
YOU are the prime target of the rip-off merchants.

We're going to look at some of the reasons these phony-baloney,
hyped-up "cures" exist, and show you some surefire ways to spot a
scam coming a mile away. In the end we hope that you'll join us
in promising yourself not to be tempted and taken in by those
who would use and abuse your aches and pains, your fears and
hopes, and your very understandable desire to feel as well and
look as good as possible.

We're also going to ask something even more difficult. We're
going to ask that, in order to protect yourself, you understand
and accept that medicine has some very real limits. When those
are reached, there really is nothing more that can be usefully
done. We're going to try and puncture the overinflated balloon
that has carried aloft the message saying everything can be
perfectly treated, that doctors always work miracles, or that
there are magic cures that a conspiracy of evil physicians has
prevented from coming to market just so they can profit from
your continued illness.

Who's Watching Whom?

You are more vulnerable today than ever before to shady health
scams, and it's going to have to be *YOU* who looks out for you.
No, the FDA (Food and Drug Administration) won't do it. The
FTC (Federal Trade Commission) won't do it. The Postal Service
is trying valiantly, but it's fighting a losing battle. As you read
about some of the outrageous attempts to separate people from
their money, you'll find yourself saying, as we often do, "There
ought to be a law." And in fact, there usually is a law. The problem
has to do with enforcement.

The 1980s have brought unprecedented changes to the health
field. Lots of them have definitely not been to your benefit. In its

zeal to promote deregulation, the administration told the regulatory agencies to "lay off." Stop hampering those poor, innocent companies that are just out there plowing the fields of entrepreneurship in the best American tradition. Don't hassle them. Don't write lots of rules. Don't work too hard at enforcing the ones that exist. Government and paperwork and rules are what's wrong with this country. Let business be, and let there be business, so everyone can prosper.

Sounds like a great idea. Unfortunately, the scam merchants of medicine also prospered. Freed of the few restraints they'd previously had, these fringe elements have come forth in unprecedented numbers to perpetrate unbelievable frauds on very believing people, while the FDA and other agencies largely stood by and watched.

Which is not to say that medical quackery is anything new, far from it. The tradition of the snake oil salesman goes way, way back. What has changed are the methods. What was once peddled from the back of a wagon is today sold through sophisticated advertising, either mail order or on television, or sometimes by high-pressure person-to-person techniques applied by salespeople involved in a pyramid marketing scheme. But until several years ago the government gave off the illusion, at least, that it was intervening to protect consumers from the very worst of these scams. The original Food, Drug and Cosmetic Act gave the FDA broad powers and removed the need even to prove fraud. All the agency had to do to convict was establish that a company had made false therapeutic claims.

Now, understand, dear reader, that the Food and Drug Administration and the Federal Trade Commission (which between them share the responsibility for overseeing the advertising and promotion of most over-the-counter and prescription medications, food supplements, and medical devices) were, even at their best, never particularly aggressive in tracking down and prosecuting the purveyors of worthless cures. But at least once upon a time the regulatory watchdog had some teeth and would occasionally bite.

Not in the Era of Deregulation. In the early 1980s, the FDA's head said in a speech, "We are ... simply overmatched." Perhaps that's largely because the agency spends only 0.5 percent of its budget on quackery enforcement and prevention, with virtually every cent of that going for consumer pamphlets.[2]

There are many reasons why enforcement has traditionally been so lax. Part of the problem is that jurisdictions overlap, which means no agency sees itself in charge. The FDA, for example, is supposed to approve and regulate drugs, but the Postal Service is involved if someone's peddling phony pills that look like drugs (but aren't) through the mail.

In fact, the Postal Service has been successful in zapping mail order quackery a number of times. The Postal Service has the authority, in the case of mail fraud, to seize the company's incoming mail. This may put a temporary crimp in the shysters' style, especially if the undelivered mail is full of orders and payments. Unfortunately, a big outfit may just take out another box in a different post office, sometimes even a different state, running an elaborate shell game in which it stays a half step ahead. Some of the companies pushing ridiculous remedies have made an end run around the Postal Service by advertising on TV and having orders placed only by toll-free numbers, using credit card payments over the phone. If false claims are made on television, the Federal Trade Commission is supposed to spring into action and protect the public exposed to the airwaves. However, actually sinking its teeth into a case is time-consuming and, as a result, expensive for the FTC, and what's more, it doesn't fit the current federal philosophy. The agency has almost dropped that act from its repertoire.

This lack of will has been exacerbated by the utter failure of Congress to update the laws and provide the necessary legal tools for dealing promptly and effectively with these promoters. Laws for combating quackery are horse-and-buggy-era relics, leftovers from the days of the traveling medicine show, that simply won't and don't work in the current environment. The legal gymnastics required to stop a company from selling nothing for something are so complex that many offenders manage to profit for months, or even years, while cases work their way through the courts. The outcome, even when adverse to the companies, often involves a fine that's a minuscule portion of their ill-gotten gains.

In one case, a company purveying a worthless and dangerous "natural fiber" product that was claimed to cause amazing weight loss was prosecuted by the local authorities in Los Angeles. The company readily agreed to a $500,000 fine, which investigators found was a mere 15 percent of the profits from the prior eight months. The "fine" was actually more like a tax, and the company went right on doing business, though forced to modify some of its more outrageous claims for instant weight loss.[3]

So where's the FDA, protector of the people? One official (since banished) confided to us the agency's quack attack efforts were mostly "smoke and mirrors." Oh, they still chase down an occasional miscreant, mostly to keep Congress happy. Why, in 1985, they seized ten phony products! Pretty aggressive, huh? (If you think there were only ten health scams tried in this country that year, we have a bridge in Brooklyn you'd be very interested in bidding on.)

"It's like holding back the tide," pleads FDA Deputy Commissioner John Norris.[4] "It costs the agency $200,000 to $300,000 for each criminal prosecution. We get much more bang for our buck attacking the demand side." Translation: The FDA is going to concentrate on the consumer, to whom it can send leaflets, rather than the perpetrator, whom it would have to take to court.

To give you some idea of just how unprotective the agency is, you need only know that they have pursued exactly *one* criminal prosecution of health fraud in the last dozen years. That case was brought against the huge national chain of General Nutrition Center stores for claiming that a substance called evening primrose oil could cure high blood pressure. The case is an interesting illustration of how the game is played. Follow along.

When Is a Claim Not a Claim?

The Food and Drug Administration has responsibility for ruling on the safety and effectiveness of anything that claims to be a medicine or cure. The term "drug," according to the law, includes "articles intended for use in the diagnosis, cure, mitigation, treatment, or prevention of disease in man or other animals, and articles (*other than food*) intended to affect the structure or any function of the body of man or other articles."[5]

The emphasis on the words "other than food" is ours, because that's the loophole an awful lot of shysters try to slip through. A drug, you see, is supposed to have some therapeutic benefit. As a result, it becomes part of the FDA drug approval process. *That* means years of scientific studies and testing in order to meet the law's requirement for establishing that a drug is both safe and effective and will in fact do what it says it does.

If something is a food, however, the FDA has no power to insist on proof of safety and effectiveness. The only requirement for a food is that it be clean. Being no dummies, the scamsters quickly leaped on (and through) the loophole and have marketed one worthless thing after another as a "food supplement." Of course, if you ask at the counter, or look around the store (maybe even right next to the product, surprise, surprise), you just might find information about what evening primrose oil, or glucomannan or guarana, will do to cure almost everything under the sun. The *label* says, gosh, gee, this is just a plain ol' food supplement. You can take it if you want, in any old dosage, and, my goodness, we can't imagine what medical purpose that would have. One bottle was so bold as to recommend a dose of several capsules daily— under the heading "Suggested Serving." Nobody would dream of taking a serving of drug, right? So, *voilà*, clearly whatever is in those capsules must be a plain old food.

Look at the books or pamphlets nearby. Or ask the friendly clerk (perhaps called a "nutritional counselor"). He or she will be more than happy to fill in what isn't on the bottle. It won't take you long to find out about the claims that this wondrous food supplement will cure arthritis, or allergies, or warts, or cancer. And maybe all of them at once.

That's the way General Nutrition was playing the game. Its attitude seemed to be *Us, selling drugs? Dont be silly. Why, we're just offering the public these fine food supplements, which you know you can't regulate.* The catch was that FDA investigators found that the company was also sending more than a thousand stores in its nationwide chain literature for distribution claiming that evening primrose oil cured hypertension ... oh yes, also arthritis and multiple sclerosis. Isn't Nature great? In the annals of medicine, no drug has ever been found that cures any of those three diseases, yet along comes this mysterious evening primrose oil to deliver a knockout blow to all these scourges of mankind. And only the health food stores know about it.

Needless to say, this delivered more money for the pockets of the promoters than health benefits for their customers. When the evening primrose oil case finally got to court, General Nutrition, its former president and a vice president pleaded guilty to selling a misbranded drug. The company's fine was $10,000 (about what it might spend on one ad in a major newspaper).

So that's the enforcement story. Basically, there isn't much. As long as it adds up to a profit, you can expect people to keep mispromoting things, and for the foreseeable future you can *not* expect the FDA or anybody else to be watching out for you. Just because a product is being marketed does not mean it has been approved, or even that it's legal. It may mean nothing more than that the FDA and other agencies have failed to do their job, again. The trick is not to let their failure literally be at your expense.

The Fantasia Pharmacopoeia

If it looks like a duck, walks like a duck, and goes "quack," what kind of quackery is it? Well, for your edification, education, and amusement, let's take a look into what we call the Graedons' People's Pharmacy Fantasia Pharmacopoeia. It's a list of some of the most amazing, fantastic, unbelievable, remarkable . . . well, that's the way the peddlers want you to see their wares. What we see is a calculated attempt to separate you from your money with some of the most imaginative concoctions ever dreamed of.

These items would all be quite funny if we didn't know they were part of a multibillion-dollar industry that's draining vitally needed money from folks just like you every day . . . money that could be used to pay rent, buy food, and put a little pleasure into the lives of those who've worked all their days in the hopes of enjoying their retirement. It's that thought, more than anything, which makes us angry. We're hoping it will have the same effect on you, and keep you from even thinking of filling out the coupon in the Sunday supplement for the amazing, wonderful, stupendous Superbalm that will cure everything at once.

Just take a look at some of these creations. There is, for instance, biotin. Biotin is actually a vitamin in the B-complex family that is needed in the diet in very minute amounts for normal metabolism. It is very hard to induce a biotin deficiency (you have to eat gobs of raw egg whites for months), and there is no reason whatever that biotin would have much effect, if any, when smeared on the skin. But that doesn't keep the hucksters from claiming that biotin restores hair growth by combating "the buildup of testosterone." These folks want you to believe that built-up testosterone is the reason Yul Brynner didn't look like Gorgeous George. According to the ads, all you have to do is just rub in some biotin solution (available by mail, of course) morning and evening, and your sleeping hair will wake up. It's sort of a hirsute version of sleeping beauty. One kiss from their cream and you're on your way to the barber. Stand back, Mabel, my hair is gonna grow!

Will biotin grow hair on your head? Nope. Will it eliminate evil testosterone buildup? Nope. Will it make bald people hairy? Nope. How do we know it won't? Well, let's turn the question around. If there were indeed such a substance, wouldn't every medical journal in the world have published an article about it? Wouldn't every physician with male patients past the age of puberty be using it? How is it that only the "research laboratory" cranking out the ads has heard the news?

We could go on for pages about baldness remedies, but onward, explorers, for there's much ground to cover here in medical Fantasyland. Let's take a look in this corner, where we find—ah, yes, one of our favorites, **Gerovital**. This amazing substance is (and we quote from the accompanying material) "for preventive and curative treatment of specific phenomena and physical and mental asthenia in elderly persons." Sounds serious. Hope nobody we know ever gets any of those specific phenomena. And you'd certainly want to avoid "mental asthenia," whatever it is.

Oh, in case you don't have any of those things, the drug is also good for "degenerative rheumatism, dystrophia of the skin, nails and hair, neurodermatitis, eczema, alopecia [baldness], psoriasis, scleroderma, vitiligo." But wait—there's more. This wonder substance cures all that PLUS "preventing vasospasm in angina pectoris, sequelae of myocardial infarction [heart attack], Raynaud's disease, arteritis, hemiplagia [sic: stroke] sequelae. GH_3 can give good results in bronchial asthma and peptic ulcer." Gee, does it do windows, too?

It's hard to understand why thousands of people every year spend oodles of money on this cure-all. Some go halfway around the world to Dr. Ana Aslan's clinic in Rumania, where it was developed. Perhaps part of the appeal has been the widespread notion that **Gerovital** has special powers against aging. But according to Dr. Roy Walford, an expert on the scientific study of longevity, the initial research on **Gerovital** was flawed because it was not done on the most appropriate strain of rat:

Although trumpeting the alleged age-retarding po-
tency of Gerovital for almost thirty years, Aslan
has not repeated (or at least not published) her
work with any other rat strains, nor with any other
genetically inbred long-lived mouse strains (which
are readily available), nor with hamsters or other
animals whose life spans are substantially shorter
than man's, so that effects on maximum life span
could be evaluated without having to wait for years
and years. Why haven't other gerontologists run
survival tests? It's because the supporting evidence
for something that has been around now for thirty
years and been so highly touted is so marginal that
good scientists won't invest their time in a doubtful
experiment requiring three years of work. They have
better options ... Gerovital has never been adequately tested for life-span extension in animals.[6]

How about **Blue-Green Manna**? That was hot for awhile. It's
algae, folks, sort of like the green scum you wouldn't go near
when you see it floating on quiet ponds. Some folks decided that
they could harvest a special variety, *Aphanae klamathomenon
flos-aquae*. If your Latin is up to speed, you'll recognize this as
algae that floats on the water in Upper Klamath Lake. They
figured that if it were properly packaged, you could be persuaded
not only to get near it, but to eat it to provide "food for the
brain" and to "detoxify" the system. The promoters also claim
to have looked in some depth at the use of this algae for
"allergies, herpes virus, arthritis, leprosy, Mediterranean fever,
Alzheimer's disease, the general aging process, narcolepsy, sickle
cell anemia and anorexia nervosa." They were right about one
thing: People snapped it up, unaware that flies, ants, cicadas,
water fleas and parts of other insects were found contaminating
one sample.[7]

These and dozens of other items have been around for years.
They're the mainstays of the business. But what makes this game
hard to keep up with is the ever-changing nature of the items
being peddled. Certain things get hot, run their course, and then
are replaced by others as either the public's enthusiasm or its
willingness to be duped wanes. Fashions come and fashions go,
both in legitimate medicine and in quackery. And when it comes

to making a fast buck, it's especially useful to have a brand new product that sounds impressive and hasn't yet been debunked.

If you don't think that explanations wax and wane, with another picking up in popularity just as the first fades away, think about the yeast phenomenon. Several years ago, these lowly single-celled entities were suddenly blamed for a myriad of human ills. Tired? Anxious? Depressed? Irritable? Sex drive low? It must be because of those pesky yeast, which run wild because we eat too much bread and sugar and take too many antibiotics. People followed a special diet and took antifungal drugs when they could get their doctors to prescribe them. A lot of doctors, though, hadn't been able to find any organic reason for their patients' problems earlier and decided the root of the trouble was in the head. When people said they had yeast throughout their body, the doctors became sure of it.

Almost overnight virtually an entire industry grew up to cater to people with *Candida albicans*. There were yeast labs, and yeast tests, and yeast diets, and of course lots of pills you could take. Still the medical profession is skeptical that there even is a Candida epidemic. Vaginal infections *are* common, especially after broad-spectrum antibiotic therapy. But most doctors insist that fungal infections that spread throughout the body are rare. People who succumb to such infections usually have compromised immune systems and are in serious shape.

Now, we have to admit that we have run into people who absolutely insist that both diet and drugs have changed their lives for the better. We can't say they're wrong. There may well be something to this approach, but until there is well-controlled scientific research published in reputable medical journals, we urge caution. Some antifungal drugs are quite toxic.

The Magic Potion Effect

Whenever people are suffering from vague symptoms like fatigue, lethargy, depression, irritability, anxiety, and so on, they may be vulnerable to unproven therapies. These problems are general, common, and difficult to diagnose. And while lasting relief is hard to come by for such difficulties, short-term treatment is often quite successful: Take 100 people who are generally not feeling well, though suffering from nothing specific, do something to them, and many will report feeling better.

The amazing thing is, it doesn't matter what you do. Give them a pill, or take one away. Talk to them. Wave a magic wand over their heads. Give them lotions, or potions. Just tell them you know what the problem is, do something, and watch the miracle cures come rolling in. These people will swear that they were sick, and now they're well. And they'll be very sincere and convincing.

It's this Magic Potion Effect, as we call it, that is the real driving force behind unproven remedies. People who don't feel well want to feel better. Nothing wrong with that. Then they get charged a significant sum of money by someone who claims to know what's wrong and how to make it better. Are you surprised that a lot of these people, having invested both their money and their faith, are cured of vague complaints, at least for a time?

In fact, we're willing to make a bet that you have yourself effected this kind of cure. What? You haven't? Think carefully, now. Did a child ever come running to you, crying, with a cut or a sliver or a bee sting? Did you ever tell her you could make it stop hurting by kissing it, or by counting to 10, or by some other magic means that parents and grandparents seem to know? And it worked—at least some of the time—didn't it? It's the Magic Potion Effect in action.

The only difference between that and the "cures" of the scam merchants is that they charge a lot, offer less, and there's no love lost in the bargain. On the assumption you would prefer not to get caught up in such things, we're going to give you some surefire ways to spot medical rip-offs.

Ten Claims That Are Hardly Ever True

After reading a few dozen (or a few hundred) of these huckster pitches, certain things begin to stand out. Almost like beacons, these advertising claims announce that what's being sold is 100 percent unadulterated BS, unfit for consumption by anyone who doesn't want to sacrifice their money, their dignity and their health all at once. Here are the words you want to run from:

1. **"BREAKTHROUGH"**—This generally means an idea the promoters haven't thought of before. Medicine, alas, usually works its way forward by inches, not by breakthroughs. Frustrating, we know, but that's really the way it is. Ads with this word will go on to claim that there's been some amazing new discovery that will save your X, make your Y bigger, shrink your Z, or perhaps restore your ABC. Just send $24.95 and you can be among the first on this continent to get Royal Goo.

To combat this nonsense, it's important that you understand how medicine and science work. No, you don't need an advanced degree. All you really need to know is that medical science finds things out by carefully testing new ideas. When someone thinks he's on to something, the results are published in a scientific journal after careful review by several other scientists. This is called peer review, and it serves as a screening device to weed out experiments that have been carelessly conceived, performed, or analyzed.

After the results are published, other scientists may say, "Hmm, sounds interesting." They then try to duplicate the experiments, and their results will be published. So it goes, until the weight of evidence either confirms or denies the truth of the claim. It's slow, tedious, difficult going, but the end result is very likely to be true. And because the process works the way it does, there are rarely any great leaps forward that might be called breakthroughs. If there are, they too get duly exposed in journals for comment and criticism by others who are competent to judge the scientific validity of what has been found.

Believe us, this kind of "breakthrough" is *not* what the ad in the Sunday paper is screaming about.

For the same reasons, beware the word **"SECRET."** This is another favorite of the schlockmeisters. Their super good glop contains a secret ingredient. Sorry, ma'm, can't tell you what it is, but it sure will be good for what ails you. In real medicine, active ingredients are never secrets.

2. **"MIRACLE"**—These are mighty scarce in the realm of science and medicine. There are unexpected recoveries or remissions that are difficult to explain. But these are also almost impossible to predict. Miracles *don't* come in bottles, so don't let anyone try to sell you one. If a product is advertised as a "miraculous" discovery, or a "miracle" substance, turn the page.

3. "A DOCTOR'S FORMULA"—Or "A doctor's discovery" or a doctor's anything. This is one of the great come-ons. It adds a bit of credibility to the schlock. After all, if a doctor is associated with it, the stuff must be real, right?

Wrong. On several counts. First, it is remarkably easy to get a doctor (remember, it only takes one) to endorse almost anything. Have you seen your favorite star hawking beer or pantyhose? You know they're paid for that endorsement, and that for a bit more money they'd just as soon squeal the virtues of another brand's beer or pantyhose. Do you think that doctors are different?

Second, keep in mind that there are many kinds of "doctors." Besides MD doctors, which is what they want you to assume the person endorsing their stuff is, there are also PhD doctors, and Doctors of Education, and Doctors of Chiropractic. And there are doctorates granted by Harvard and then there are those from some mail-order school where the only graduation requirement is money. Some of the doctors are as phony as the stuff being peddled.

Even when it's a real doctor we're talking about, keep in mind that there are lots of them, just like there are lots of plumbers and insurance salespeople. Doctors, too, are a diverse lot. Most are incredibly honest, hardworking, and committed to their patients' welfare. Others are not. Some can be bought (sometimes surprisingly cheaply) to endorse things that any high school science student knows can't, don't, and won't work. There may be doctors who are greedy, incompetent, or otherwise not the ideal model of what a professional should be, but do not dignify these doctor testimonials with the same credibility you give your family physician.

4. "IT WORKED FOR ME!"—Or "It saved my life," or "I lost 900 pounds in 15 minutes," or any other kind of testimonial.

The testimonial is one of the most obvious clues to a scam that you can find. First of all, testimonials are often entirely fiction. When they do come from real people, they're often paid endorsements like any other kind of advertisement. And even when they're unsolicited testimonials, they fall far short of credible scientific evidence.

Remember our discussion a while ago of the Magic Potion Effect, whereby you can cure a kid of a hurt finger by kissing it? Same effect, but a slightly different technique. Let's say a magic grapefruit–avocado weight loss pill is sold to 1,000 people. Ten of those people will lose weight, and will be willing to write any kind of letter the promoters want saying they lost weight because they took the grapefruit–avocado pill. Of course, the other 990 will lose nothing except their money.

In a scientific study of anything, the people would be divided into two groups. Half would get the real thing, half would get an identical-looking pill that contained no effective ingredients. If there were no significant differences in the number of people who lost weight (or were cured of some disease, or whatever), then we would know that the "active" ingredient hadn't really done a thing. Sure, 10 of those taking it got better. But so did 12 of the people taking the sham pill.

It is *always* possible to get a testimonial-type endorsement about anything. Its value is exactly nothing, except as a red flag that should tell you to STAY AWAY.

5. "NEW FROM EUROPE"—or Outer Winnebago, or the Orient, or someplace other than nearby. This is the mystique factor. They're trying to sell you the notion that somehow this mysterious essence, wrought from the rare tutsitutsi flower found only in the Netherlands, is the cure for X, Y, or Z.

This plays, to some extent, on a sort of reverse cultural chauvinism. Many of us seem to think that things from Europe, particularly those having to do with health and beauty, are inherently good. It also plays on a tendency of people to be lulled into the notion that this incredible item is even now, as we speak, "sweeping Europe." You should sweep these kinds of claims from your sight immediately, or you're going to find yourself plucked of your money.

6. "CONTAINS OOGOO"—Or walrus nasal hairs, or royal bee dandruff, or some other strange, weird, and vaguely nauseating ingredient. Sometimes it will have a neat name of its own, unknown to anyone but the perpetrator of this week's scam. It will be "Zevulex-23" or "Amino Nitroimulon" or some other name made up to sound somewhat scientific, just a bit long and complex, and definitely important.

Come on, customers, let's get smart, OK? Tens of thousands of scientists look ceaselessly for the drugs to mitigate or eliminate all manner of human ills. When they find it, the word is announced to every medical person in the world. So here's this unheard of "laboratory" (a lab in name only), which has found this magic substance that nobody ever had any knowledge of before, about which they've written nothing anywhere, which has been tested on nobody, and they want you to send your $10.95 (plus shipping). Please don't be suckered in.

7. "THE DOCTORS DON'T WANT YOU TO KNOW THIS"— One of our favorites, this ruse has many forms, all of which might be lumped under the heading of "Conspiracy Theories." The copy generally runs along the lines of "We've found this amazing stuff. It can cure (fill in the name of some dread, usually fatal disease), but all the doctors have gotten together to keep knowledge of it from the public because if you ever got hold of it you'd all be cured and they wouldn't make as much money. But we alone have been able to learn the secret, and are now making it available, etc., etc., yak, yak, yak."

If we didn't see people responding, we'd assume this is so ridiculous as to need no rebuttal. But just think about this. If some marvelous cure for a deadly disease were discovered, and all the doctors in the country knew about it, what are the odds on keeping it a secret? Ask anyone who has ever tried to organize a group of doctors to do anything and see what they think the chances are of getting a bunch of physicians to agree on whether it's day or night, let alone agree on keeping a deep dark secret like not releasing the cure for cancer.

Doctors are only human, but they're not deliberately blocking anything. Nontraditional approaches may be "frozen out," so to speak, but only because many docs don't believe anything credible could come from anywhere but within the halls of the establishment. So a maverick physician with a different idea may have a hard time getting funding for research. And until the research is done, the data collected and analyzed, the study written up and accepted and published by a major medical journal, few clinicians will give it any credence.

If that's a conspiracy, it's a conspiracy of conservatism. It is regrettable that it sometimes slows down some promising research, but it is, by and large, to the doctors' credit and to the patient's advantage. It's truly unethical for a doctor to prescribe a regimen he knows won't help the patient; and it's only slightly less ethical to experiment with an unproven therapy unless the patient has no other hope and agrees, with full knowledge of the potential risks, to be part of a study. But you're not likely to find an "informed consent" form in the newspaper ad. If there's a true conspiracy out there, it's more likely to be among a bunch of shady characters plotting how to trick the gullible into paying dearly for a worthless preparation.

8. "FDA APPROVED"—Hogwash. The FDA regulates drugs. Advertisements for real drugs don't have to convince anyone that they're legitimate. So if you see "FDA approved" in the Sunday supplement, you can almost assuredly assume that the FDA has *not* approved whatever it is the ad is trying to peddle. In fact, if its enforcement people had any staff, money, and guts, they'd probably put the peddlers in the slammer.

As we noted earlier, most of the quack stuff sold skirts the law by being (or trying to be) a food, while getting as close as possible to making the claims that are the province of drugs. The Food, Drug and Cosmetic Act requires that foodstuffs not include rat droppings and pieces of metal, but even if a batch of sugar pills passes inspection for that kind of filth, it still isn't "approved." It just wasn't seized as contaminated or adulterated. But if you believe that there has been any testing for the safety and efficacy of the stuff, forget it.

Real drugs that have been proven to work don't have to claim to be "FDA Approved," because everyone should *know* that. There's no need to shout it from the rooftops. If something is flashing the FDA at you as an implied endorsement, ignore it, and ignore what's being sold.

9. "CURES EVERYTHING"—Or at least lots of things. Of all the legitimate drugs available these days, fewer than a handful work against more than a limited number of things (either a limited number of diseases, or a limited number of bacteria). How could **Magic Goo 80 Super Formula** cure (*cure*, not just help) everything from lumbago to cancer? The reason, dear friends, is that it's a scam. The heftier the claims, the larger your suspicions should be that this stuff and the people selling it are up to no good.

There's one very easy test to be applied: If it sounds too good to be true, most likely it is. Somewhere, deep down in the hearts of almost all the people being duped, there lies the knowledge that what they're buying probably really can't cure baldness, arthritis, hemorrhoids, hoof-and-mouth disease, and prostate trouble all at once. But this good and reasonable common sense is somehow overwhelmed by wishful thinking, a combination of a desire for relief from a very real ailment and a tendency to want to believe, to want the claims to be true.

We sympathize with you, but not with those who would steal from you. Beware, we say, the potion that does too much.

10. "CURES AN INCURABLE DISEASE"—If you would promise yourself never, ever to go for a "remedy" for any of seven conditions, you could avoid about 90 percent of the fraud come-ons. If you hear, read, divine, or otherwise start to be fed information about someone claiming they have something that will magically cure any of the following, but which isn't available from a doctor, run. The Big Seven are WEIGHT LOSS, ARTHRITIS, CANCER, IMPOTENCE, BALDNESS, WRINKLES, and AGING.

We hate to be glum, but nothing has been found to cure aging except death, which halts it completely. If you need to refresh your memory on wrinkle removers, flip back to Chapter 5 right now. Other than creams that temporarily puff up the skin for a few hours and make wrinkles appear momentarily less visible, anything else that might reverse wrinkles is strictly prescription only. The same goes for male pattern baldness, which will not yield to any nonprescription gunk rubbed into the scalp, or vitamin pills. Impotence is quite treatable, but not by anything you will buy from an ad.

Legitimate cancer treatments are dispensed only under strict medical supervision in a hospital or medical center, or through one of their outpatient clinics. No one needs to double his trouble by becoming a victim of a charlatan as well as of cancer. You will find solid information on a range of cancer therapies, both accepted and experimental, in an excellent book, *Understanding Cancer*, by John Laszlo, M.D. (1987, Harper & Row).

Arthritis is a cruel and difficult disease whose progress can be slowed and whose pain can be dampened, but nothing yet developed will make it go away completely. And as for weight loss, there has never been a pill that gobbles fat or melts it away. If you want to lose weight, you must expend more calories than you take in. Period. Some weight loss pills "work" for the first few days because they are really diuretics—pills that make you pass water. This will indeed cause some weight loss, but it can't go on more than a few days, and it's hardly permanent. There are appetite suppressants, but most people should know by now that a weight problem is rarely a result of hunger. We snack because we're anxious, bored, lonely, or have developed poor eating habits. For the time being, weight loss means eat less, exercise more. Besides that temporary deception, no mail order pill will do the trick.

We know this is hardly as upbeat and enthusiastic as those ads, but then again, we aren't trying to take your money away and give you hot air in return.

Actually, the best guard against quackery is simply to use your head. Start to see it as a battle, with your pocketbook as the potential victim. This is nothing less than an all-out assault and battery, and only the use of common sense will enable you to prevent it. We can help by posting a warning of some of the common ways these things are marketed, but in the end, you'll have to use your noodle, your experience, and the wisdom of your years to avoid being sucked in by these scam merchants.

Things to Remember

1. Older people with chronic health problems need to be especially cautious to avoid becoming the victims of health fraud.

2. If the warning is too late and you feel you've already been cheated, yell like hell. Report it to the local Consumer Protection Agency. Local and state officials are often more vigorous in pursuing charlatans than the feds, so cooperate as fully as you can. If more victims complained, the hucksters would have a harder time of it.

3. Be wary of extravagant medical claims for vitamins and food supplements.

4. The following words and phrases are scam tip-offs. Don't send your hard-earned bucks to any company that claims to have a corner on a non-prescription "breakthrough," a "secret," a "miracle," or a "doctor's discovery" that's "new from

Europe" or anywhere else far away. If instead of a secret ingredient, the active component of the remedy is an Amazonian plant, a Malaysian root, or the tonsils of a deep-sea fish, get suspicious.

5. Be leery of testimonials, whether they're from pleased-sounding patients or a doctor who's made a discovery. Run the other way if you hear that "your doctor doesn't want you to know about this."

6. Do not believe claims for any over-the-counter products claiming a "cure" for obesity, arthritis, cancer, impotence, baldness, wrinkles, or aging. There are no surefire remedies for any of these, although with the proper medical treatment arthritis can sometimes be controlled, some cancers can be cured (especially if they are discovered early enough), impotence can often be relieved, and perhaps as many as 30 percent of bald heads can grow hair again under minoxidil (see page 151).

7. Don't trust any claims for a nostrum that works for everything.

References

1. "Foods, Drugs, or Frauds?" *Consumer Reports* 50(5): 275–283, 1985.
2. Ibid.
3. "New Snake Oil, Old Pitch." *U.S. News and World Report* 101(23):68–70, 1986.
4. Ibid.
5. Federal Food, Drug and Cosmetic Act, as amended. U. S. Government Printing Office, 1981.
6. Walford, Roy L. *Maximum Life Span.* New York: Avon Books, 1984.
7. "Foods, Drugs, or Frauds?" op. cit., p. 280.

14

Finding the Fountain of Youth

Searching for the Fountain of Youth can be a hazardous under-
taking. Ponce de Léon, sloshing through the swamps of southern
Florida, would undoubtedly have lived longer had he stayed at
home, for at the age of only 61 he was mortally wounded by a
hostile Indian's arrow. (It must be admitted, the Indian may have
been somewhat justified: as governor of Puerto Rico, Ponce de
Léon had crushed political resistance by killing off most of the
native Carib Indian population.)

In any event, he evidently never found any magical elixir. But a
few scientists believe that one or more breakthroughs allowing
physicians to retard the human aging process are due within the
next decade. These latter-day fountains of youth will not make
people live forever, but drugs that affect enzymes, "free radicals,"
"cross-linked" molecules, or the activity of the immune system
may make for a healthier, and longer old age.

Despite the optimism in scientific circles, there are as yet no
drugs known to slow down human aging, let alone stop it. There
are a few compounds being tested for specific purposes, but
most are still in the preliminary phase of study. The fact is, even
the experts do not know precisely what causes the physical
changes we see with aging. We will take a look at some of the
many theories researchers have proposed to account for the

deterioration, and at a few ideas clinicians and investigators are entertaining about why some individuals seem to stay healthy and vigorous so much longer than others.

But let's not forget the lesson of Ponce de Léon in our quest to live longer and better. Do-it-yourself dosing with various vitamins, minerals, and other nutritional supplements that have been recommended may be as risky as a hike through the Everglades. We simply have no idea of the short-term and long-term effects of many of these chemicals. So before we dive in, let's scout the territory.

The Fascination with Extending Life

For this expedition, you may need a compass and a map. There is a veritable forest of information out there in books, newspapers, magazines, fliers, and, last but by no means least, advertisements. While none of the books are actually saying "You can live forever," the titles are enticing. *Life Extension* and *Fit for Life* have been big best-sellers. Others, written by people with impressive academic credentials, sound just as promising: *How to Live Longer and Feel Better,* by Nobel Laureate Linus Pauling; *Longevity: Fulfilling Our Biological Potential,* by psychologist and noted author Kenneth R. Pelletier; and *Maximum Life Span,* by Roy L. Walford, a pathologist and leading gerontological researcher. And then, of course, there are diets: *The 120 Year Diet, The 21st Century Diet,* and a whole host of others. If they all agreed, the choice would be easy. But there are serious discrepancies among them, and even sometimes within the same work. In one chapter of *Life Extension,* Durk Pearson and Sandy Shaw advise:

> **1. Don't eat too much. Obesity is associated with a markedly shortened life span.**
> **2. Eat the types of foods you like, including some proteins, carbohydrates, fats, and fiber.**
> **... 6. A diet high in fiber and fresh fruits and vegetables (which contain natural antioxidants), relatively low in total fat, and very low in polyunsaturated fat appears to be the safest.**[1]

Then they seem to thumb their noses at this with the example they are setting:

> **The two of us together in a week consume: 1 to 2 dozen eggs; about a pound or two of butter; several pounds of beef, poultry, and pork; and 4 to 5 gallons of whole (not low-fat) milk.**

To be fair, they point out in the same paragraph, in italics:

> *Remember that this approach must still be considered a personal experiment. It cannot be assumed that other people will respond well to a high fat diet as we seem to have so far.*[2]

How can anyone hope to figure out how to live longer without knowing whom—and what—to believe?

It may help to step back from the trees just a few steps to get some perspective on this forest. At the time Pearson and Shaw wrote those words, they were not yet 40. As one observer notes, "Over the past few years it dawned upon me that most of the best-selling books on fitness, health, and longevity were written either by people who did not live much past 70 (if they even made it at all), or are now not even 40 or 50."[3] Before you bet *your* chances of a long, healthy old age on somebody else's "personal experiment," you might want to watch and see that they get to be at least as old on their regimen as you are now.

In fact, personal experiments don't necessarily lead to the kind of knowledge we'd need to make "life-extending" recommendations for anyone. If you polled a sample of the oldest people you could find and asked them what accounts for their longevity, one might attribute it to a shot of whiskey every day, another to complete abstention from alcohol, some to lifelong sexual moderation, others to vigorous sexual activity, a few to a diet of raw vegetables and fruits, and more to a variety of other regimens, including such practices as not worrying about things too much. This is not the best way to collect scientific data for study, because we can't know whether Aunt Bella is right in crediting her daily consumption of yogurt for her good health at 79, or whether she was lucky to get good genes from her grandmother, who died in her nineties.

Fortunately, there are a number of other ways for scientists to find out how to improve our chances of becoming nimble nonagenarians. (That's in relative terms, of course. Reflexes, reaction times, and the strength to follow through are reduced in a 90-year-old below what they were at younger ages.) One source of clues is to look at the life-styles of populations with high proportions of elderly persons. Although researchers dispute the actual ages attained by oldsters among the Vilcabambans of Ecuador, the Hunzas of the Himalayas, and the Abkhazians of the Caucasian Mountains in the Soviet Union, a greater number of people in these societies and some others around the globe do seem to stay active and healthy into old age, regardless of whether that's really only 95 instead of over 100.

Another source of data is laboratory experimentation on animals, especially small mammals whose basic biochemistry is probably pretty similar to ours but who have short life spans (a mouse lives two or three years, a guinea pig about eight). It takes only years instead of centuries to try out a diet or a drug on a cageful of such critters and see if they live any longer than the ones in the next cage who didn't get the special treatment.

Laboratory rodents have other advantages, too, for they can be selectively bred, and genetically long-lived and short-lived strains are available. But when we start to apply rat research, we should be as cautious as investigators developing new drugs. Nobody assumes that just because a drug is good for mice, it will work well in humans. Animal research is just the first step in drug development. Any new agent that looks promising in the lab then undergoes extensive clinical testing in humans—and not all drugs pass! Remember to check out the potential dangers as well as the purported benefits before you start treating yourself like a guinea pig got treated.

Still other data on the nature of aging is coming out of laboratories working on cells in tissue culture or on one-celled animals. Many gerontologists (scientists who study aging) are excited about the research Dr. Joan Smith-Sonneborn is doing on DNA (genetic material) repair mechanisms in the microscopic beasties called paramecia, for example. This is "basic research," which is aimed at helping scientists understand the biology and chemistry of aging. Once the underlying causes are understood, it may be possible for physicians to intervene in the process. But for now, researchers have not yet determined the root causes of aging, and there are at least half a dozen theories that have enough evidence behind them to spur further research.

Why Do We Age? A Survey of Theories

There is no dearth of hypotheses that may someday give us the "bottom line" on why the kidney works more slowly as we age, or the immune system becomes less efficient, or everyday short-term memory fails to serve as well, or the bone-building cells fall behind those that break bone down.

One line of approach puts the emphasis on the inherent genetic "program." Normal human cells seem to have a preset number of times they can divide before, for still mysterious reasons, they stop dividing and die. This "Hayflick limit" (named after the scientist who discovered two decades ago that a certain type of cell could not be made to divide more than 50 times) is apparently coded by the genes within the cell's nucleus, a sort of "genetic clock ticking away within each cell [that] determines when old age sets in."[4] If scientists could find a way of changing this genetic material or slowing the clock down, they might be able to delay the onset of physiological aging.

Dr. Hayflick now suggests that perhaps as the body and the cells in it age, little glitches begin to accumulate: "enzymes that don't do their job, DNA that malfunctions."[5] Dr. Smith-Sonneborn's work on how one-celled organisms repair their damaged DNA has shown that when DNA repair is activated, paramecia live half again as long as they normally would. "One thing's for sure," she says. "When we tap into the mechanism of DNA repair, we're tapping into a great many of the things that make us age." She dreams of a time when "we'll be able to identify and clone the genes that make the different repair enzymes and transfer them into our cells."[6]

Many researchers now believe that much of the damage in the cells is done by "free radicals," molecules that have become chemically unhooked and will react wildly with almost any other molecule in the vicinity. While oxygen itself is essential to life, oxygen free radicals are thought to be especially nasty, raising the specter that every time we take a breath we are hastening our own demise. In fact, clinical applications are already being found for antioxidants, agents that protect cells from these oxygen free radicals. One place these may become important is in protecting heart tissue from oxygen damage after a heart attack.[7] Animal models look promising for strokes as well as heart attacks, and clinical trials in human heart attack patients are beginning at the University of Michigan and Johns Hopkins Medical Centers. One researcher, Dr. Richard G. Cutler, has recently implanted a gene controlling antioxidant enzymes into mice hoping to increase their life span with its protective effect.[8]

Some current theories blame free radicals for a number of the crippling diseases that become more common as people grow older, including coronary artery disease, diabetes, cancer, and rheumatoid arthritis. In study animals with arthritis, the free radicals doing the damage are produced by the white blood cells of the immune system, which rush to the inflamed joint by the billion.[9]

It's probably not just a coincidence that the immune system itself is the focus of an aging theory. Scientists have known for a long time that the thymus gland begins to shrink and founder long before the rest of the body, practically disappearing by the time most people get past 50.[10] This gland is now known to be important in the development of the T-cells, which are a critical component of the immune system.

Researchers who favor an immune system theory of aging point out that the immune system becomes far less reliable in the elderly. It may fail to attack invading microorganisms as it should, and so older people may succumb to pneumonia or other infections. On the other hand, it may not recognize the body's own tissues, and start to attack them as if they were "invaders." It is believed that a number of diseases that become more common as we grow older may be due to such autoimmune processes, including certain forms of diabetes and arthritis. Dr. Roy Walford suggests that the immune system, together with the brain and the many potent hormones and other neurochemicals it puts out, may act as a sort of "pacemaker" for aging.[11]

If medical science can find some way to strengthen the immune system and maintain its function, some of the diseases that kill people off before they reach a ripe old age may become less threatening. The immune system is thought to be important in patrolling for cancer cells and squelching them as they arise, for example, but as immune function diminishes, the risks of cancer getting a foothold go up. Needless to say, there is plenty of research being done on drugs to stimulate the immune system to more vigorous function. It's possible that some of the research on that new "Black Death," AIDS (acquired immune deficiency syndrome), will have unexpected benefits in showing how to boost immune function in healthy aging people. Researchers are looking into the immune-stimulating activity of a natural substance called coenzyme Q_{10} (a ubiquinone). The jury is out as to whether it will prolong life in humans, but if you want to know more, we suggest you read *The Miracle Nutrient: Coenzyme Q_{10}* by Emile G. Bliznakov, M.D. and Gerald L. Hunt (Bantam Books).

Some investigators believe that a simple, nondrug means of retarding the age-related decline of the immune system is already available. Ever since the 1930s laboratory animals of almost every species you can imagine have shown that they live longer— sometimes much longer—if they eat less than usual but their diets are well balanced. Not only that: the older rats are in better shape, too. Their blood cholesterol is lower. Their kidneys don't deteriorate. Their bones and muscles are stronger. And their immune systems are more active. According to Edward J. Masoro, who has done some of the important research in this field, "It would be very remarkable if an animal as complicated as a rat does not age pretty much for the same reason and by the same mechanisms as humans."[12] If you want to know more about the potential of diet for prolonging life, keep reading.

Taking Steps to Stay Young

Investigators may get excited about extending the average age of mice or guinea pigs. Some gerontologists get even more worked up over the idea of pushing maximum life spans beyond their current limits (for humans, around 115 years). But most of us have a particular and personal interest, not in average life spans, nor in maximum life spans, but in our very own life span and whether it is likely to be much longer, and whether it can be healthy. Some folks are grateful for whatever time they spend on this earth; others want to seize their time and stretch it as far as possible. They want Ponce de León's magic elixir.

What can you do about living longer? There are any number of outfits that will be happy to sell you "anti-aging and rejuvenation therapies," including vitamin and mineral preparations, skin creams, amino acid cocktails, and even prescription drugs such as **Hydergine** (ergoloid mesylates), **Parlodel** (bromocriptine), **Inderal** (propranolol), or **Dilantin** (phenytoin) through the mail.

There is an underground movement for individuals to sidestep the FDA's safeguards and import prescription and unapproved medications from overseas without a doctor's supervision. The advertising claims are certainly tempting. One product, centrophenoxine, theoretically "improves memory and intelligence, rejuvenates brain cells, and removes age pigment from the skin." Vasopressin is advertised to "imprint new information within the memory centers of the brain" and "improve learning and intelligence" as well as "reverse memory loss in the elderly." Other products are purported to revitalize and rejuvenate, and to be good for arthritis, cancer, heart disease, and diabetes. Don't believe everything you read!

Some of the drugs or nutritional supplements have been featured in popular books. In others, the mail order offer evidently stands on its own. **Dilantin**, for example, is listed in *Life Extension* as a drug that "improves animal and/or human intelligence,"[13] but it is not discussed in depth. A flier for a mail order company operating from out of the country proclaims that **Dilantin**: "stabilizes bioelectrical activity throughout the body. It is effective as a treatment for depression, high blood pressure, heart disease, hypoglycemia, epilepsy, drug and alcohol withdrawal, and compulsive eating." Now, if that doesn't sound great! A separate insert on dosages recommends: "Take three tablets a day for continuous use in alleviating depression, elevating your mood, and extending lifespan." Not a word about side effects, either long or short term. Why ruin a good sales prospect with a discouraging word?

Now read along with us as we check **Dilantin** in the *PDR* (*Physicians' Desk Reference*). We're only going to point out a few little things here and there, because the entire entry on **Dilantin**, as required by the FDA, takes up considerably more than a large page of small print. After the clinical pharmacology and indications (epilepsy is all the FDA has approved it for) come the "Warnings": don't let a patient stop taking it suddenly, do check out any changes a patient reports in lymph nodes because of reports "suggesting a relationship" between this drug and the development of lymph gland problems, possibly even cancer, do tell your patient not to drink alcohol while taking **Dilantin**.

How about "Precautions"? "The liver is the chief site of bio-transformation of phenytoin; patients with impaired liver function, *elderly patients*, or those who are gravely ill may show early signs of toxicity [emphasis added]." Other precautions cover the possibility of skin rash, including a very rare but potentially lethal variety, osteomalacia, or weakened bones, and, in the case of sustained high blood levels of the drug, "confusional states referred to as 'delirium,' 'psychosis,' or 'encephalopathy' ..."[14]

There's more; that doesn't include the information on "Drug Interactions," "Adverse Reactions" (a very common one is gum overgrowth), or "Overdosage," but the point is clear. **Dilantin**, like other prescription drugs, can only be administered safely under the supervision of a health care professional who can monitor blood levels, watch for signs of toxicity, and protect the patient from harm. And there is no scientific evidence that proves it prolongs human life. Knowing this, how would you weigh your possible benefits of elevating your mood or extending your life (by how much?) or "stabilizing bioelectrical activity" against the potential risks of side effects or interactions with other drugs you might be taking?

All right, we can hear you saying, *so maybe messing around with prescription drugs by mail order isn't such a good idea. I wasn't all that interested in taking **Dilantin** anyway. But what about something like SOD? I hear that's a free radical scavenger, and from what I've just read, I'd sure like to have all my free radicals mopped up as quick as can be.*

Well, superoxide dismutase (SOD) is in fact a free radical scavenger, one the body makes itself. It looks as though it may have several important medical applications, and in fact is being injected into heart attack patients in several clinical trials now, as we mentioned earlier. But evidence that taking SOD in pill form would do anything whatsoever to make a person live longer is lacking.

SOD is marketed in "health food" circles as a miraculous youth pill. Like most proteins, which it is, SOD is broken down into its amino acids in the digestive tract. And if it is enteric-coated to protect it from digestion, it passes through the small intestine unabsorbed. Biochemists Irwin Fridovich and Joe McCord, who discovered SOD in 1967, have not been enthusiastic about the commercial claims made for the pills. Dr. McCord, at the University of South Alabama, worries that the longevity claims being made for oral SOD "may destroy the credible aspects of its use." And Dr. Fridovich has opined, "I would say that the only people getting any benefit from SOD [pills] are the people manufacturing and selling it."

Probably SOD and perhaps other free-radical-scavenging enzymes, such as the xanthine dehydrogenase Dr. McCord is currently studying, may well turn out to have significant medical uses.[15] But adding antioxidants to the diet of lab animals doesn't always make them live longer,[16] perhaps because the system tends to be self-adjusting. In a creature that has an optimum amount of antioxidants already, feeding more of one simply tends to lower the levels of the others.[17] Gerontological researcher Richard G. Cutler of the National Institute of Aging (NIA) is currently devising a test to determine the levels of antioxidant an individual has available, so that persons with low levels *could* be given supplements. But Cutler, who has successfully extended the life spans of mice by injecting various chemicals that "trick" mouse cells into producing greater than usual amounts of free radical scavengers, is not about to experiment on himself. Asked if he has considered applying his developing technology to himself, the 50-year-old Cutler admits:

> Not yet; I'm afraid of it. These substances could turn out to be dangerous. My father will be eighty this December and is concerned about his aging, but I can't help him. I myself simply take vitamin D and beta-carotene capsules after every meal, hoping to reduce the possible mutagenic effects of food.[18]

So that's the word from one researcher. What do others think? Cancer specialist Bill Regelson at the Medical College of Virginia is enthusiastic about aging research but dubious about supplements:

> "Right now everyone's caught up with this overblown vitamin-supplementation faddism believing that taking this pill or that pill will make a difference—but there's simply no data to support that,"

he says. (Regelson does, however, take vitamin E, selenium, magnesium, pyridoxine, and Q-10.) "Then you've got ... Pearson and Shaw," he continues, "who are pushing things like arginine and BHT, which might be harmful."[19]

If there's no magical pill to help us live longer, what about some simple things, like exercise or diet? Laboratory animals live longer when their intake of food is quite restricted. In fact, exciting work has been done on a strain of mice that are genetically prone to immune system diseases that lead them to develop kidney problems, high blood pressure, and coronary artery disease and to die at a relatively early age (for mice, who don't live all that long anyway). When they are fed limited rations of a low-fat, high-carbohydrate diet with vitamin and mineral supplements, they live four times longer than usual—just as long as mice with genetic longevity.[20]

So far, however, there is just one scientist out there suggesting that people ought to be systematically underfed (although a low-fat diet has a lot of support). Even Dr. Roy Walford, though, doesn't know exactly how much, or even whether, going hungry for five years might increase a person's life span. And we'd hate to have to say if it would be worth the deprivation!

Walford is experimenting upon himself, and has written two popular books, *Maximum Life Span* (Avon) and *The 120 Year Diet* (Simon & Schuster) to get his ideas out to the public. He's not suggesting that people should starve themselves willy-nilly; he recommends "undernutrition without malnutrition." The potential risks of a meager but carefully balanced diet may not be great, to judge from Dr. Walford's long-lived mice, but we don't yet have much data on how this can affect human beings. If you want to be a guinea pig, why not check out what Walford has to say? Be prepared, though: the diet is rigorous. He writes, "You may have to give up angel food cake, but to those for whom sight, sense, and sexuality are less important than cake, I have nothing to offer. Let them eat cake."[21]

For now, the Fountain of Youth is still nearly as elusive as when Ponce de León met his untimely end. But these visionary gerontologists—biochemists, geneticists, endocrinologists, immunologists, and other scientists—are working hard on unlocking the secret of aging. The future may yield a real bonus in years. According to Dr. Edward Schneider, the deputy director of NIA:

> I don't foresee a magic bullet, an antiaging pill that you could take to restore youth. But I do predict that our increased knowledge about the aging of different organs will enable us to prevent various body functions from deteriorating. We might be able to restore immune function, for instance, and even prevent short-term memory loss. In the next decade or so, we might see average life span increase from seventy-five to about eighty-five years for men and ninety years for women. Perhaps in the next few years someone will eventually live to be as old as one hundred and thirty. Barring some unforeseen breakthrough, though, I don't think we'll see people living to one hundred fifty in the near future.[22]

Even the prospect of a relatively healthy old age is enough to keep most of us from quibbling about the 15 years between 115 and 130. After all, who would want to live until 150 if he were plagued with arthritis, forgetfulness, impotence, and all sorts of other problems? Seems like the quality of life is every bit as important as the quantity, and *that* can be affected right here and now. It may not even take a lot of high technology.

For starters, we want you to stay as healthy as you can, and we hope that this book has been of some help in that regard. We don't have to tell you that people age more successfully when they stay as independent as they can manage; you probably know it intuitively. But in case anyone starts giving you a hard time about it, you can let them know there's a tall pile of scientific studies proving that the more control older people have over their lives, the better they do on all kinds of health measures.[23]

Gerontologists are beginning to discover that loneliness may be as deadly as hardening of the arteries.[24] Stay active; keep up with your old friends, and keep making new ones. In at least three epidemiological studies focusing on older Americans, scientists found that folks with more contacts with friends and family were more likely to live longer.[25] A good social support system may have practical advantages as well as psychological benefits for all of us. Stay involved with the things that matter to you. Making a valuable contribution, even if it's a relatively small one, is important for self-esteem at any time of life. Keep moving and thinking; whether or not it'll rejuvenate you, you'll feel better than if you let body and mind rust in a rocking chair. Our parting advice is really a wish for all of us: May we savor the rest of our lives!

References

1. Pearson, Durk; and Shaw, Sandy. *Life Extension.* New York: Warner Books, 1982, p. 370–371.
2. Ibid., p. 367–368.
3. Inlander, Charles B. "From the Horse's Mouth. Living Long By People Who Have." *People's Medical Society Health Bulletin.* Emmaus, PA: Rodale Press, n.d.
4. Walford, Roy L. *Maximum Life Span.* New York: Avon Books, 1983, p. 75.
5. Bagley, Sharon. "Why Do We Grow Old?" *Newsweek,* June 16, 1986, p. 61.
6. Fettner, Ann Giudici; and Weintraub, Pamela. "Elixirs of Youth." *Omni* 9(1):60–128, 1986.
7. Marx, Jean L. "Oxygen Free Radicals Linked to Many Diseases." *Science* 235:529–531, 1987.
8. "Enzymes May Extend Life Spans." *Durham Sun,* Jan. 17, 1987, p. B1.
9. "New Therapies Target Free Radicals." *Medical World News,* Dec. 8, 1986, pp. 56–57.
10. Schmeck, Harold M., Jr. "Mysterious Thymus Gland May Hold the Key to Aging." *New York Times,* Jan. 26, 1982, pp. C1–C2.
11. Walford, op. cit., p. 92.
12. Hallowell, Christopher. "New Focus on the Old." *New York Times Magazine,* Dec. 15, 1985, p. 42.
13. Pearson and Shaw, op. cit., p. 168.
14. Huff, Barbara B., ed. *Physicians' Desk Reference,* 41st ed. Oradell, N.J.: Medical Economics Co., 1987, p. 1478.
15. Marx, op. cit., p. 530.
16. Bagley, op. cit.
17. "Interview: Richard Cutler." *Omni* 9(1):109–181, 1986.
18. Ibid.
19. Lowry, Katharine. "Death Avengers." *Omni* 9(1):85–157, 1986.
20. Good, Robert A. "Aging, Nutrition and Immunity: Animal Models." Fifth Annual Bristol-Myers Symposium on Nutrition Research, Oct. 31–Nov. 1, 1985.
21. "Lean-Lived. Eating for Life." *Longevity* 1(2):9, 11, 1986.

22. Fettner and Weintraub, op. cit., p. 128.
23. Rowe, John W., and Kahn, Robert L. "Human Aging: Usual and Success-ful." *Science* 237:143–149, 1987.
24. Gelman, David. "Why We Age Differently." *Newsweek*, Oct. 20, 1986, pp. 60–61.

Afterword

At the very beginning of this book we explained why we felt we had to write it. We have seen the trouble our older relatives, friends, and neighbors have trying to find information about their health problems and the medications they take. We wote this book for them and for you, and we hope you have found it helpful.

If you have a suggestion, question, or comment, please drop us a line. Many of the issues in this book were brought to our attention by our faithful readers. We can't promise to answer each letter personally, but we value your ideas.

All correspondence will be forwarded to the Graedons if you address it:

Joe and Terry Graedon

50+

Bantam Books

666 Fifth Avenue

New York, NY 10103

For information about the authors, see page 460.

Appendix:
Drugs That Require Special Attention
for Older People

No matter what medicine you take, it makes sense to be careful. A little extra vigilance is in order for the following drugs. Some have a greater potential to interact dangerously with other commonly prescribed medications. Others may be somewhat more likely to cause trouble for older people. But even drugs that are not mentioned below may give an older person some difficulty and should be treated with caution.

Just because a drug is on this list does not mean it will produce problems. But if you are on one of them, you and your doctor should both be alert for signs of toxicity. Some possible side effects are summarized, but this list is by no means comprehensive. Your pharmacist and physician should be consulted if you suspect you are having an adverse reaction to any medicine you are taking.

Medicine—Possible Problems

Achromycin (tetracycline)—Nausea, diarrhea, kidney trouble, altered vitamin K levels

Acylanid (digitalis)—Confusion, depression, visual changes, nausea, vomiting, loss of appetite; potential drug interactions

Adapin (doxepin)—Dry mouth, constipation, urinary problems, glaucoma, blurred vision, drowsiness, confusion, memory impairment, dizziness; potential drug interactions

Alcohol (**Nyquil, Geritol, Geritonic,** etc)—Sedation; potential drug interactions

Aldactazide (spironolactone, HCTZ*)—Frequent urination, dry mouth, dizziness, increased blood sugar, muscle weakness or cramps, gout, elevated cholesterol

Aldoclor (methyldopa, chlorothiazide)—Dry mouth, sedation, forgetfulness, dizziness, liver disorders, nightmares, hallucinations, headache, depression; potential drug interactions

Medicine—Possible Problems

Aldomet (methyldopa)—Dry mouth, sedation, forgetfulness, dizziness, liver disorders, nightmares, hallucinations, headache, depression; potential drug interactions

Aldoril (methyldopa, HCTZ*)—Dry mouth, sedation, forgetfulness, dizziness, liver disorders, nightmares, hallucinations, headache, depression; potential drug interactions

Alurate (aprobarbital)—Drowsiness, dizziness, may be addicting, sometimes can cause agitation instead of the usual sedation; withdrawal can cause insomnia, confusion, anxiety; potential drug interactions

Amcill (ampicillin)—Skin rash, itching, digestive tract upset, altered vitamin K levels

Amitril (amitriptyline)—Dry mouth, constipation, urinary problems, glaucoma, blurred vision, drowsiness, confusion, memory impairment, dizziness; potential drug interactions

amitriptyline—Dry mouth, constipation, urinary problems, glaucoma, blurred vision, drowsiness, confusion, memory impairment, dizziness; potential drug interactions

amoxicillin—Skin rash, itching, digestive tract upset

Amoxil (amoxicillin)—Skin rash, itching, digestive tract upset

ampicillin—Skin rash, itching, digestive tract upset, altered vitamin K levels

Amytal (amobarbital)—Drowsiness, dizziness, may be addicting, sometimes can cause agitation instead of the usual sedation; withdrawal can cause insomnia, confusion, anxiety; potential drug interactions

Anaprox (naproxen)—Stomach upset, nausea, indigestion, vomiting, reduced appetite, diarrhea, constipation, stomach ulcer, dizziness, drowsiness, lightheadedness, headache, high blood pressure, kidney damage, anemias, visual disturbances, skin rash, asthma; potential drug interactions

Anhydron (cyclothiazide)—Frequent urination, dry mouth, dizziness, increased blood sugar, muscle weakness or

Medicine—Possible Problems

cramps, gout, elevated cholesterol, increased calcium, lowered potassium, rash; potential drug interactions

Aquatag (benzthiazide)—Frequent urination, dry mouth, dizziness, increased blood sugar, muscle weakness or cramps, gout, elevated cholesterol, increased calcium, lowered potassium, rash; potential drug interactions

Aquatensen (methyclothiazide)—Frequent urination, dry mouth, dizziness, increased blood sugar, muscle weakness or cramps, gout, elevated cholesterol, increased calcium, lowered potassium, rash; potential drug interactions

Aquazide (trichlormethiazide)—Frequent urination, dry mouth, dizziness, increased blood sugar, muscle weakness or cramps, gout, elevated cholesterol, increased calcium, lowered potassium, rash; potential drug interactions

Aristocort (triamcinolone)—Bone weakening, psychological instability, insomnia, stomach ulcer, fluid retention, high blood pressure, diabetes, potassium loss; potential drug interactions

Artane (trihexyphenidyl)—Confusion, drowsiness, disorientation, hallucinations, nervousness, dry mouth, constipation, urinary difficulties, blurred vision, glaucoma

Asendin (amoxapine)—Dry mouth, constipation, urinary problems, glaucoma , blurred vision, drowsiness, confusion, memory impairment, dizziness, tardive dyskinesia (involuntary muscle spasms and movements); potential drug interactions

Ativan (lorazepam)—Drowsiness, incoordination, difficulty walking, falls, difficulty driving, confusion; prolonged use (more than 8 months) may lead to habituation—sudden discontinuation of drug may cause symptoms such as insomnia, irritablity, depersonalization, nerves jerking, headache

Augmentin (amoxicillin, clavulanate)—Skin rash, itching, digestive tract upset

Aventyl (nortriptyline)—Dry mouth, constipation, urinary

Medicine—Possible Problems

problems, glaucoma, blurred vision, drowsiness, confusion, memory impairment, dizziness; potential drug interactions

Benadryl (diphenhydramine)—Drowsiness, fatigue, unsteadiness, confusion, blurred vision, dry mouth, stomach upset, urinary problems; sometimes excitation instead of sedation is a paradoxical side effect in older people

Blocadren (timolol)—Fatigue, depression, lethargy, drowsiness, insomnia, strange nightmares, cold hands and feet, asthma, slower pulse, hallucinations, forgetfulness, joint pain, impotence; sudden discontinuation of drug may lead to angina or heart attack; potential drug interactions

Bristacycline (tetracycline)—Nausea, diarrhea, kidney trouble, altered vitamin K levels

Bronkodyl (theophylline)—Nausea, vomiting, stomach pain, loss of appetite, diarrhea, jitteriness, anxiety, insomnia, headache, dizziness, muscle twitching, depression, palpitations; many potential drug interactions; monitor blood levels

Butalan (butabarbital)—Drowsiness, dizziness, may be addicting, sometimes can cause agitation instead of the usual sedation; withdrawal can cause insomnia, confusion, anxiety; potential drug interactions

Butazolidin (phenylbutazone)—Severe stomach upset, ulceration, serious anemias and other blood disorders, fluid retention, asthma, blurred vision, drowsiness; potential drug interactions

Butisol (butabarbital)—Drowsiness, dizziness, may be addicting, sometimes can cause agitation instead of the usual sedation; withdrawal can cause insomnia, confusion, anxiety; potential drug interactions

Calan (verapamil)—Constipation, nausea, headache, dizziness, depression, fluid retention, impotence; potential drug interactions

Capoten (captopril)—Rash and itching, loss of taste (usually disappears after several weeks), kidney problems (requires periodic testing), fluid retention

Medicine—Possible Problems

Catapres (clonidine)—Dry mouth, drowsiness and sedation, dizziness, constipation, nausea; sudden discontinuation of this drug could lead to a rapid and severe elevation in blood pressure

Centrax (prazepam)—Drowsiness, incoordination, difficulty walking, falls, difficulty driving, confusion; prolonged use (more than 8 months) may lead to habituation; sudden discontinuation of this drug may cause symptoms such as insomnia, irritability, depersonalization, nerves jerking, headache

chlordiazepoxide—Drowsiness, incoordination, difficulty walking, falls, difficulty driving, confusion; prolonged use (more than 8 months) may lead to habituation; sudden discontinuation of drug may cause symptoms such as insomnia, irritability, depersonalization, nerves jerking, headache

chlorothiazide—Frequent urination, dry mouth, dizziness, increased blood sugar, muscle weakness or cramps, gout, elevated cholesterol, increased calcium, lowered potassium, rash; potential drug interactions

chlorpromazine—Drowsiness, dizziness, fainting, dry mouth, skin rash, nasal congestion, blurred vision, parkinsonism, tardive dyskinesia (uncontrollable muscle twitching and spasms—possibly irreversible); potential drug interactions

Cleocin (clindamycin)—Nausea, abdominal cramps, loss of appetite, diarrhea (possibly severe), dehydration, electrolyte imbalance, skin rash, itching

Clinoril (sulindac)—Stomach upset, nausea, indigestion, vomiting, reduced appetite, diarrhea, constipation, stomach ulcer, dizziness, drowsiness, lightheadedness, headache, high blood pressure, kidney damage, anemias, visual disturbances, skin rash, asthma; potential drug interactions

codeine—Drowsiness, dizziness, nausea, constipation; potential drug interactions

Cogentin (benztropine)—Confusion, drowsiness, disori-

Medicine—Possible Problems

entation, hallucinations, nervousness, dry mouth, constipation, urinary difficulties, blurred vision, glaucoma

Compazine (prochlorperazine)—Drowsiness, dizziness, fainting, dry mouth, skin rash, nasal congestion, blurred vision, parkinsonism, tardive dyskinesia (uncontrollable muscle twitching and spasms—possibly irreversible); potential drug interactions

Cordarone (amiodarone)—Fatigue, unsteadiness, incoordination, nausea, vomiting, constipation, loss of appetite, headache, insomnia, nightmares, visual problems, sun sensitivity leading to rash, liver disorders; potential drug interactions

Corgard (nadolol)—Fatigue, depression, lethargy, drowsiness, insomnia, strange nightmares, cold hands and feet, asthma, slower pulse, hallucinations, forgetfulness, joint pain, impotence; sudden discontinuation of drug may lead to angina or heart attack; potential drug interactions

Cortef (hydrocortisone)—Bone weakening, psychological instability, insomnia, stomach ulcer, fluid retention, high blood pressure, diabetes, potassium loss; potential drug interactions

Coumadin (warfarin)—Hemorrhage (bleeding from gums or other mucous membranes, black tarry stools), diarrhea, blood disorders; avoid aspirin and large amounts of green leafy vegetables; potential drug interactions

Crystodigin (digitoxin)—Confusion, depression, visual changes, nausea, vomiting, loss of appetite; potential drug interactions

Cuprimine (penicillamine)—Skin rash, stomach pain, nausea, vomiting, ulceration, diarrhea, blood disorders, mouth ulcers, fever, kidney problems, ringing in ears

Dalmane (flurazepam)—Drowsiness, incoordination, difficulty walking, falls, difficulty driving, confusion; prolonged use (more than 8 months) may lead to habituation; sudden discontinuation of drug may cause symptoms such as insomnia, irritability, depersonalization, nerves

Medicine—Possible Problems

jerking, headache; drug accumulates in the body—do not drink alcohol; potential drug interactions

Darvocet-N (propoxyphene, acetaminophen)—Sedation, drowsiness, dizziness, slower breathing, nausea, constipation, skin rash; possible drug interactions

Darvon (propoxyphene)—Sedation, drowsiness, dizziness, slower breathing, nausea, constipation, skin rash; possible drug interactions

Decadron (dexamethasone)—Bone weakening, psychological instability, insomnia, stomach ulcer, fluid retention, high blood pressure, diabetes, potassium loss; potential drug interactions

Delta-Cortef (prednisolone)—Bone weakening, psychological instability, insomnia, stomach ulcer, fluid retention, high blood pressure, diabetes, potassium loss; potential drug interactions

Deltasone (prednisone)—Bone weakening, psychological instability, insomnia, stomach ulcer, fluid retention, high blood pressure, diabetes, potassium loss; potential drug interactions

Demerol (meperidine)—Slowed breathing, dizziness, drowsiness, confusion, disorientation, nausea, vomiting, constipation, dry mouth, blurred vision, impotence, urinary difficulties; regular reliance on this drug may lead to habituation; potential drug interactions

Depakene (valproic acid)—Nausea, vomiting, stomach upset, diarrhea, loss of appetite, drowsiness, skin rash, hair loss; potential drug interactions

Depen (penicillamine)—Skin rash, stomach pain, nausea, vomiting, ulceration, diarrhea, blood disorders, mouth ulcers, fever, kidney problems, ringing in ears

Desyrel (trazodone)—Drowsiness, constipation, urinary problems, glaucoma, blurred vision, dry mouth, confusion, memory impairment, dizziness; potential drug interactions

DiaBeta (glyburide)—Low blood sugar (hypoglycemia manifested as fatigue, sweating, hunger, and numbness in hands and feet), nausea, vomiting, stomach pain, loss of

Medicine—Possible Problems

appetite, skin rash, blood disorders; potential drug interactions

Diabinese (chlorpropamide)—Low blood sugar (hypoglycemia manifested as fatigue, sweating, hunger, and numbness in hands and feet), nausea, vomiting, stomach pain, loss of appetite, skin rash, blood disorders; potential drug interactions

digoxin—Nausea, vomiting, loss of appetite, stomach upset, diarrhea, confusion, disorientation, weakness, visual disturbances (green/yellow effect, halos, or blurring), depression, nightmares, hallucinations, skin rash, headache; very serious potential for drug interactions; monitor blood levels

Dilantin (phenytoin)—Confusion, dizziness, unsteadiness, slurred speech, insomnia, hallucinations, headache, nausea, vomiting, stomach pain, bone weakening, gum overgrowth, skin rash, liver problems; potential drug interactions; monitor blood levels

Dimetane (brompheniramine)—Drowsiness, fatigue, unsteadiness, confusion, blurred vision, dry mouth, stomach upset, urinary problems; sometimes excitation instead of sedation is a paradoxical side effect in older people

Disipal (orphenadrine)—Confusion, drowsiness, disorientation, hallucinations, nervousness, dry mouth, constipation, urinary difficulties, blurred vision, glaucoma

Diucardin (hydroflumethiazide)—Frequent urination, dry mouth, dizziness, increased blood sugar, muscle weakness or cramps, gout, elevated cholesterol, increased calcium, lowered potassium, rash; potential drug interactions

Diuril (chlorothiazide)—Frequent urination, dry mouth, dizziness, increased blood sugar, muscle weakness or cramps, gout, elevated cholesterol, increased calcium, lowered potassium, rash; potential drug interactions

Dolene (propoxyphene)—Sedation, drowsiness, dizziness, slower breathing, nausea, constipation, skin rash; possible drug interactions

Medicine—Possible Problems

Dolophine (methadone)—Slowed breathing, dizziness, drowsiness, confusion, disorientation, nausea, vomiting, constipation, dry mouth, blurred vision, impotence, urinary difficulties; regular reliance on this drug may lead to habituation; potential drug interactions

Dopar (levodopa)—Involuntary movements, nausea, vomiting, stomach upset, loss of appetite, dry mouth, tremor, headache, hallucinations, insomnia, nightmares, dizziness, anxiety; potential drug interactions

Duraquin (quinidine)—Stomach upset, nausea, vomiting, dizziness, headache, ringing in the ears, visual disturbances, confusion, skin rash, blood disorders; potential drug interactions

Dyazide (HCTZ,* triamterene)—Stomach upset, nausea, diarrhea, skin rash, weakness, frequent urination, dry mouth, dizziness, increased blood sugar, gout, elevated cholesterol, increased calcium; potential drug interactions

Dymelor (acetohexamide)—Low blood sugar (hypoglycemia manifested as fatigue, sweating, hunger, and numbness in hands and feet), nausea, vomiting, stomach pain, loss of appetite, skin rash, blood disorders; potential drug interactions

Elavil (amitriptyline)—Dry mouth, constipation, urinary problems, glaucoma, blurred vision, drowsiness, confusion, memory impairment, dizziness; potential drug interactions

Empirin w/codeine (aspirin, codeine)—Drowsiness, dizziness, nausea, constipation; potential drug interactions

Endep (amitriptyline)—Dry mouth, constipation, urinary problems, glaucoma, blurred vision, drowsiness, confusion, memory impairment, dizziness; potential drug interactions

Enduron (methyclothiazide)—Frequent urination, dry mouth, dizziness, increased blood sugar, muscle weakness or cramps, gout, elevated cholesterol, increased calcium, lowered potassium, rash; potential drug interactions

Medicine—Possible Problems

Esidrix (HCTZ*)—Frequent urination, dry mouth, dizziness, increased blood sugar, muscle weakness or cramps, gout, elevated cholesterol, increased calcium, lowered potassium, rash; potential drug interactions

Eskalith (lithium)—Nausea, vomiting, diarrhea, tremor, confusion, speaking difficulty, muscle weakness, drowsiness, incoordination, thirst; potential drug interactions

Exna (benzthiazide)—Frequent urination, dry mouth, dizziness, increased blood sugar, muscle weakness or cramps, gout, elevated cholesterol, increased calcium, lowered potassium, rash; potential drug interactions

Feldene (piroxicam)—Stomach upset, nausea, indigestion, vomiting, reduced appetite, diarrhea, constipation, stomach ulcer, dizziness, drowsiness, lightheadedness, headache, high blood pressure, kidney damage, anemias, visual disturbances, skin rash, asthma; potential drug interactions.

Fioricet (acetaminophen, butalbital, caffeine)—Drowsiness, dizziness, may be addicting, sometimes can cause agitation instead of the usual sedation; withdrawal can cause insomnia, confusion, anxiety; potential drug interactions

Fiorinal (butalbital, aspirin, caffeine)—Drowsiness, dizziness, may be addicting, sometimes can cause agitation instead of the usual sedation; withdrawal can cause insomnia, confusion, anxiety; potential drug interactions

Fluidil (cyclothiazide)—Frequent urination, dry mouth, dizziness, increased blood sugar, muscle weakness or cramps, gout, elevated cholesterol, increased calcium, lowered potassium, rash; potential drug interactions

Furadantin (nitrofurantoin)—Nausea, loss of appetite, vomiting; nerve damage can become severe if vitamin B deficiency occurs

Gemonil (metharbital)—Drowsiness, dizziness, may be addicting, sometimes can cause agitation instead of the usual sedation; withdrawal can cause insomnia, confusion, anxiety; potential drug interactions

Medicine—Possible Problems

Glucotrol (glipizide)—Diarrhea, stomach upset, nausea, vomiting, loss of appetite, weakness, skin rash, headache, low blood sugar (hypoglycemia manifested as fatigue, sweating, hunger, and numbness in hands and feet), blood disorders; potential drug interactions

Halcion (triazolam)—Drowsiness, incoordination, difficulty walking, falls, difficulty driving, confusion; prolonged use (more than 8 months) may lead to habituation; sudden discontinuation of drug may cause symptoms such as insomnia, irritability, depersonalization, nerves jerking, headache

Haldol (haloperidol)—Drowsiness, dizziness, fainting, dry mouth, skin rash, nasal congestion, blurred vision, parkinsonism, tardive dyskinesia (uncontrollable muscle twitching and spasms—possibly irreversible); potential drug interactions

hydrochlorothiazide (HCTZ)—Frequent urination, dry mouth, dizziness, increased blood sugar, muscle weakness or cramps, gout, elevated cholesterol, increased calcium, lowered potassium, rash; potential drug interactions

hydrocortisone—Bone weakening, psychological instability, insomnia, stomach ulcer, fluid retention, high blood pressure, diabetes, potassium loss; potential drug interactions

Hydrocortone (hydrocortisone)—Bone weakening, psychological instability, insomnia, stomach ulcer, fluid retention, high blood pressure, diabetes, potassium loss; potential drug interactions

HydroDIURIL (HCTZ*)—Frequent urination, dry mouth, dizziness, increased blood sugar, muscle weakness or cramps, gout, elevated cholesterol, increased calcium, lowered potassium, rash; potential drug interactions

Hygroton (chlorthalidone)—Frequent urination, dry mouth, dizziness, increased blood sugar, muscle weakness or cramps, gout, elevated cholesterol, increased calcium, lowered potassium, rash; potential drug interactions

Medicine—Possible Problems

Imodium (loperamide)—Constipation, nausea, drowsiness, dizziness, dry mouth, intestinal obstruction

Inderal (propranolol)—Fatigue, depression, lethargy, drowsiness, insomnia, strange nightmares, cold hands and feet, asthma, slower pulse, hallucinations, forgetfulness, joint pain, impotence; sudden discontinuation of drug may lead to angina or heart attack; potential drug interactions

Indocin (indomethacin)—Stomach upset, nausea, indigestion, vomiting, reduced appetite, diarrhea, constipation, stomach ulcer, dizziness, drowsiness, lightheadedness, headache, high blood pressure, kidney damage, anemias, visual disturbances, skin rash, asthma; potential drug interactions

Ismelin (guanethidine)—Dizziness, fainting, diarrhea, weakness, fluid buildup, stuffy nose, sweating, sexual problems, urinary difficulties, depression, asthma, muscle fatigue

Isoptin (verapamil)—Constipation, nausea, headache, dizziness, depression, fluid retention, impotence; potential drug interactions

Janimine (imipramine)—Dry mouth, constipation, urinary problems, glaucoma, blurred vision, drowsiness, confusion, memory impairment, dizziness; potential drug interactions

Kenacort (triamcinolone)—Bone weakening, psychological instability, insomnia, stomach ulcer, fluid retention, high blood pressure, diabetes, potassium loss; potential drug interactions

Lanoxin (digoxin)—Nausea, vomiting, loss of appetite, stomach upset, diarrhea, confusion, disorientation, weakness, visual disturbances (green/yellow effect, halos or blurring), depression, nightmares, hallucinations, skin rash, headache; very serious potential for drug interactions; monitor blood levels

Larodopa (levodopa)—Involuntary movements, nausea, vomiting, stomach upset, loss of appetite, dry mouth,

Medicine—Possible Problems

tremor, headache, hallucinations, insomnia, nightmares, dizziness, anxiety; potential drug interactions

Larotid (amoxicillin)—Skin rash, itching, digestive tract upset

levodopa—Involuntary movements, nausea, vomiting, stomach upset, loss of appetite, dry mouth, tremor, headache, hallucinations, insomnia, nightmares, dizziness, anxiety; potential drug interactions

Librax (chlordiazepoxide, clidinium)—Drowsiness, incoordination, difficulty walking, falls, difficulty driving, confusion; prolonged use (more than 8 months) may lead to habituation; sudden discontinuation of drug may cause symptoms such as insomnia, irritability, depersonalization, nerves jerking, headache

Libritabs (chlordiazepoxide)—Drowsiness, incoordination, difficulty walking, falls, difficulty driving, confusion; prolonged use (more than 8 months) may lead to habituation; sudden discontinuation of drug may cause symptoms such as insomnia, irritability, depersonalization, nerves jerking, headache

Librium (chlordiazepoxide)—Drowsiness, incoordination, difficulty walking, falls, difficulty driving, confusion; prolonged use (more than 8 months) may lead to habituation; sudden discontinuation of drug may cause symptoms such as insomnia, irritability, depersonalization, nerves jerking, headache

Lithane (lithium)—Nausea, vomiting, diarrhea, tremor, confusion, speaking difficulty, muscle weakness, drowsiness, incoordination, thirst; potential drug interactions

Lithobid (lithium)—Nausea, vomiting, diarrhea, tremor, confusion, speaking difficulty, muscle weakness, drowsiness, incoordination, thirst; potential drug interactions

Lithonate (lithium)—Nausea, vomiting, diarrhea, tremor, confusion, speaking difficulty, muscle weakness, drowsiness, incoordination, thirst; potential drug interactions

Lithotabs (lithium)—Nausea, vomiting, diarrhea, tremor, confusion, speaking difficulty, muscle weakness, drowsiness, incoordination, thirst; potential drug interactions

Medicine—Possible Problems

Lomotil (diphenoxylate, atropine)—Drowsiness, dizziness, headache, dry skin, urinary problems, nausea, itching, depression; potential drug interactions

Lopressor (metoprolol)—Fatigue, depression, lethargy, drowsiness, insomnia, strange nightmares, cold hands and feet, asthma, slower pulse, hallucinations, forgetfulness, joint pain, impotence; sudden discontinuation of drug may lead to angina or heart attack; potential drug interactions

Lopurin (allopurinol)—Skin rash, itching, drowsiness, confusion, dizziness, nausea, stomach pain, vomiting, diarrhea, headache; potential drug interactions

lorazepam—Drowsiness, incoordination, difficulty walking, falls, difficulty driving, confusion; prolonged use (more than 8 months) may lead to habituation; sudden discontinuation of drug may cause symptoms such as insomnia, irritability, depersonalization, nerves jerking, headache

Lotusate (talbutal)—May be addicting, sometimes can cause agitation instead of the usual sedation; withdrawal can cause insomnia, confusion, anxiety; potential drug interactions

Ludiomil (maprotiline)—Dry mouth, constipation, urinary problems, glaucoma, blurred vision, drowsiness, confusion, memory impairment, dizziness; potential drug interactions

Macrodantin (nitrofurantoin)—Nausea, loss of appetite, vomiting; nerve damage can become severe if vitamin B deficiency occurs

Marplan (isocarboxazid)—Dizziness, unsteadiness, weakness headache, jitteriness, forgetfulness, muscle twitching, urinary problems; very serious drug and food interactions

Maxzide (triamterene, HCTZ*)—Stomach upset, nausea, diarrhea, skin rash, weakness, frequent urination, dry mouth, dizziness, increased blood sugar, gout, elevated cholesterol, increased calcium; potential drug interactions

Medicine—Possible Problems

Mebaral (mephobarbital)—Drowsiness, dizziness, may be addicting, sometimes can cause agitation instead of the usual sedation; withdrawal can cause insomnia, confusion, anxiety; potential drug interactions

Meclomen (meclofenamate)—Stomach upset, nausea, indigestion, vomiting, reduced appetite, diarrhea, constipation, stomach ulcer, dizziness, drowsiness, lightheadedness, headache, high blood pressure, kidney damage, anemias, visual disturbances, skin rash, asthma; potential drug interactions

Medrol (methylprednisolone)—Bone weakening, psychological instability, insomnia, stomach ulcer, fluid retention, high blood pressure, diabetes, potassium loss; potential drug interactions

Mellaril (thioridazine)—Drowsiness, dizziness, fainting, dry mouth, skin rash, nasal congestion, blurred vision, parkinsonism, tardive dyskinesia (uncontrollable muscle twitching and spasms—possibly irreversible); potential drug interactions

Metahydrin (trichlormethiazide)—Frequent urination, dry mouth, dizziness, increased blood sugar, muscle weakness or cramps, gout, elevated cholesterol, increased calcium, lowered potassium, rash; potential drug interactions

Meticorten (prednisone)—Bone weakening, psychological instability, insomnia, stomach ulcer, fluid retention, high blood pressure, diabetes, potassium loss; potential drug interactions

Micronase (glyburide)—Diarrhea, stomach upset, nausea, vomiting, loss of appetite, weakness, skin rash, headache, low blood sugar (hypoglycemia manifested as fatigue, sweating, hunger, and numbness in hands and feet), blood disorders; potential drug interactions

Minipress (prazosin)—The first dose can produce severe dizziness and fainting during the first two hours (extreme caution is required initially); angina, fluid retention, headache, drowsiness, nausea, dry mouth

Medicine—Possible Problems

Minocin (minocycline)—Nausea, vomiting, diarrhea, dizziness, unsteadiness

Moban (molindone)—Drowsiness, dizziness, fainting, dry mouth, skin rash, nasal congestion, blurred vision, parkinsonism, tardive dyskinesia (uncontrollable muscle twitching and spasms—possibly irreversible); potential drug interactions

Mogadon (nitrazepam)—Drowsiness, incoordination, difficulty walking, falls, difficulty driving, confusion; prolonged use (more than 8 months) may lead to habituation; sudden discontinuation of drug may cause symptoms such as insomnia, irritability, depersonalization, nerves jerking, headache

Motrin (ibuprofen)—Stomach upset, nausea, indigestion, vomiting, reduced appetite, diarrhea, constipation, stomach ulcer, dizziness, drowsiness, lightheadedness, headache, high blood pressure, kidney damage, anemias, visual disturbances, skin rash, asthma; potential drug interactions

Nalfon (fenoprofen)—Stomach upset, nausea, indigestion, vomiting, reduced appetite, diarrhea, constipation, stomach ulcer, dizziness, drowsiness, lightheadedness, headache, high blood pressure, kidney damage, anemias, visual disturbances, skin rash, asthma; potential drug interactions

Naprosyn (naproxen)—Stomach upset, nausea, indigestion, vomiting, reduced appetite, diarrhea, constipation, stomach ulcer, dizziness, drowsiness, lightheadedness, headache, high blood pressure, kidney damage, anemias, visual disturbances, skin rash, asthma; potential drug interactions

Naqua (trichlormethiazide)—Frequent urination, dry mouth, dizziness, increased blood sugar, muscle weakness or cramps, gout, elevated cholesterol, increased calcium, lowered potassium, rash; potential drug interactions

Nardil (phenelzine)—Dizziness, unsteadiness, weakness, headache, jitteriness, forgetfulness, muscle twitching,

Medicine—Possible Problems

urinary problems; very serious drug and food interactions

Naturetin (bendroflumethiazide)—Frequent urination, dry
mouth, dizziness, increased blood sugar, muscle weakness or cramps, gout, elevated cholesterol, increased
calcium, lowered potassium, rash; potential drug interactions

Navane (thiothixene)—Drowsiness, dizziness, fainting, dry
mouth, skin rash, nasal congestion, blurred vision, parkinsonism, tardive dyskinesia (uncontrollable muscle
twitching and spasms—possibly irreversible); potential
drug interactions

Nembutal (pentobarbital)—Drowsiness, dizziness, may be
addicting, sometimes can cause agitation instead of the
usual sedation; withdrawal can cause insomnia, confusion, anxiety; potential drug interactions

Nitro-Bid (nitroglycerin)—Headache, dizziness, unsteadiness, faintness, weakness, nausea, vomiting, palpitations,
rash, blurred vision, dry mouth; potential drug interactions

Nitrodisc (nitroglycerin, transdermal)—Headache, dizziness, unsteadiness, faintness, weakness, nausea, vomiting, palpitations, rash, blurred vision, dry mouth; potential
drug interactions

Nitro-Dur (nitroglycerin, transdermal)—Headache, dizziness, unsteadiness, faintness, weakness, nausea, vomiting, palpitations, rash, blurred vision, dry mouth; potential
drug interactions

nitrofurantoin—Nausea, loss of appetite, vomiting; nerve
damage can become severe if vitamin B deficiency occurs

Nitroglyn (nitroglycerin)—Headache, dizziness, unsteadiness, faintness, weakness, nausea, vomiting, palpitations,
rash, blurred vision, dry mouth; potential drug interactions

nitroglycerin—Headache, dizziness, unsteadiness, faintness,
weakness, nausea, vomiting, palpitations, rash, blurred
vision, dry mouth; potential drug interactions

Medicine—Possible Problems

Nitrostat (nitroglycerin)—Headache, dizziness, unsteadiness, faintness, weakness, nausea, vomiting, palpitations, rash, blurred vision, dry mouth; potential drug interactions

Normodyne (labetalol)—Fatigue, dizziness, lethargy, drowsiness, insomnia, strange nightmares, cold hands and feet, asthma, slower pulse, hallucinations, forgetfulness, tingling of scalp, nausea, joint pain, impotence; sudden discontinuation of drug may lead to angina or heart attack; potential drug interactions

Norpace (disopyramide)—Dry mouth, urinary problems, dizziness, headache, blurred vision, dry nose, constipation, muscle weakness, skin rash, heart failure, low blood pressure

Norpramin (desipramine)—Dry mouth, constipation, urinary problems, glaucoma, blurred vision, drowsiness, confusion, memory impairment, dizziness; potential drug interactions

Omnipen (ampicillin)—Skin rash, itching, digestive tract upset, altered vitamin K levels

Oretic (HCTZ*)—Frequent urination, dry mouth, dizziness, increased blood sugar, muscle weakness or cramps, gout, elevated cholesterol, increased calcium, lowered potassium, rash; potential drug interactions

Orinase (tolbutamide)—Low blood sugar (hypoglycemia manifested as fatigue, sweating, hunger, and numbness in hands and feet), nausea, vomiting, stomach pain, loss of appetite, skin rash, blood disorders; potential drug interactions

Orudis (ketoprofen)—Stomach upset, nausea, indigestion, vomiting, reduced appetite, diarrhea, constipation, stomach ulcer, dizziness, drowsiness, lightheadedness, headache, high blood pressure, kidney damage, anemias, visual disturbances, skin rash, asthma; potential drug interactions

Panwarfin (warfarin)—Hemorrhage (bleeding from gums or other mucous membranes), black tarry stools, diar-

Medicine—Possible Problems

rhea, blood disorders; avoid aspirin and large amounts of green leafy vegetables; potential drug interactions

Parlodel (bromocriptine)—Nausea, vomiting, dizziness, confusion, headache, fatigue, stomach pain, constipation, involuntary movements, agitation, hallucinations, urinary problems, insomnia, constipation, depression, unsteadiness

Parnate (tranylcypromine)—Dizziness, unsteadiness, weakness, headache, jitteriness, forgetfulness, muscle twitching, urinary problems; very serious drug and food interactions

Paxipam (halazepam)—Drowsiness, incoordination, difficulty walking, falls, difficulty driving, confusion; prolonged use (more than 8 months) may lead to habituation; sudden discontinuation of drug may cause symptoms such as insomnia, irritability, depersonalization, nerves jerking, headache

penicillin—Skin rash, itching, digestive tract upset

Pentids (penicillin G)—Skin rash, itching, digestive tract upset

Permitil (fluphenazine)—Drowsiness, dizziness, fainting, dry mouth, skin rash, nasal congestion, blurred vision, parkinsonism, tardive dyskinesia (uncontrollable muscle twitching and spasms—possibly irreversible); potential drug interactions

Pertofrane (desipramine)—Dry mouth, constipation, urinary problems, glaucoma, blurred vision, drowsiness, confusion, memory impairment, dizziness; potential drug interactions

Phenergan (promethazine)—Drowsiness, dizziness, fatigue, unsteadiness, confusion, blurred vision, dry mouth, stomach upset, urinary problems; sometimes excitation instead of sedation is a paradoxical side effect in older people

phenobarbital—Drowsiness, dizziness, may be addicting, sometimes can cause agitation instead of the usual sedation; withdrawal can cause insomnia, confusion, anxiety; potential drug interactions

Medicine—Possible Problems

Polycillin (ampicillin)—Skin rash, itching, digestive tract upset, altered vitamin K levels

Polymox (amoxicillin)—Skin rash, itching, digestive tract upset

Ponstel (mefenamic acid)—Nausea, diarrhea, stomach pain, ulceration, headache, kidney problems, skin rash, reduced appetite, constipation, headache, lightheadedness, visual disturbances, drowsiness, dizziness, asthma; potential drug interactions

prednisolone—Bone weakening, psychological instability, insomnia, stomach ulcer, fluid retention, high blood pressure, diabetes, potassium loss; potential drug interactions

prednisone—Bone weakening, psychological instability, insomnia, stomach ulcer, fluid retention, high blood pressure, diabetes, potassium loss; potential drug interactions

Principen (ampicillin)—Skin rash, itching, digestive tract upset, altered vitamin K levels

Procan (procainamide)—Nausea, vomiting, loss of appetite, skin rash, itching, confusion, light-headedness, blood disorders, fever, chills; potential drug interactions

Prolixin (fluphenazine)—Drowsiness, dizziness, fainting, dry mouth, skin rash, nasal congestion, blurred vision, parkinsonism, tardive dyskinesia (uncontrollable muscle twitching and spasms—possibly irreversible); potential drug interactions

Pronestyl (procainamide)—Nausea, vomiting, loss of appetite, skin rash, itching, confusion, light-headedness, blood disorders, fever, chills; potential drug interactions

propranolol—Fatigue, depression, lethargy, drowsiness, insomnia, strange nightmares, cold hands and feet, asthma, slower pulse, hallucinations, forgetfulness, joint pain, impotence; sudden discontinuation of drug may lead to angina or heart attack; potential drug interactions

Quinaglute (quinidine)—Stomach upset, nausea, vomiting, dizziness, headache, ringing in the ears, visual disturbances, confusion, skin rash, blood disorders; potential drug interactions

Medicine—Possible Problems

Quinidex Exentabs (quinidine)—Stomach upset, nausea, vomiting, dizziness, headache, ringing in the ears, visual disturbances, confusion, skin rash, blood disorders; potential drug interactions

quinidine—Stomach upset, nausea, vomiting, dizziness, headache, ringing in the ears, visual disturbances, confusion, skin rash, blood disorders; potential drug interactions

Quinora (quinidine)—Stomach upset, nausea, vomiting, dizziness, headache, ringing in the ears, visual disturbances, confusion, skin rash, blood disorders; potential drug interactions

Reglan (metoclopramide)—Drowsiness, dizziness, jitteriness, fatigue, uncontrollable muscular movements, insomnia, depression, nausea; potential drug interactions

Renese (polythiazide)—Frequent urination, dry mouth, dizziness, increased blood sugar, muscle weakness or cramps, gout, elevated cholesterol, increased calcium, lowered potassium, rash; potential drug interactions

reserpine—Nausea, vomiting, diarrhea, stomach pain, loss of appetite, drowsiness, dizziness, depression, headache, anxiety, nightmares, rash, asthma, stuffy nose, breast enlargement, weight gain, sexual difficulties; potential drug interactions

Restoril (temazepam)—Drowsiness, incoordination, difficulty walking, falls, difficulty driving, confusion; prolonged use (more than 8 months) may lead to habituation; sudden discontinuation of drug may cause symptoms such as insomnia, irritability, depersonalization, nerves jerking, headache

Rufen (ibuprofen)—Stomach upset, nausea, indigestion, vomiting, reduced appetite, diarrhea, constipation, stomach ulcer, dizziness, drowsiness, lightheadedness, headache, high blood pressure, kidney damage, anemias, visual disturbances, skin rash, asthma; potential drug interactions

Saluron (hydroflumethiazide)—Frequent urination, dry mouth, dizziness, increased blood sugar, muscle weak-

Medicine—Possible Problems

ness or cramps, gout, elevated cholesterol, increased calcium, lowered potassium, rash; potential drug interactions

Sandoptal (butalbital)—Drowsiness, dizziness, may be addicting, sometimes can cause agitation instead of the usual sedation; withdrawal can cause insomnia, confusion, anxiety; potential drug interactions

Seconal (secobarbital)—Drowsiness, dizziness, may be addicting, sometimes can cause agitation instead of the usual sedation; withdrawal can cause insomnia, confusion, anxiety; potential drug interactions

Sectral (acebutolol)—Fatigue, depression, lethargy, drowsiness, insomnia, strange nightmares, cold hands and feet, asthma, slower pulse, hallucinations, forgetfulness, joint pain, impotence; sudden discontinuation of drug may lead to angina or heart attack; potential drug interactions

Serax (oxazepam)—Drowsiness, incoordination, difficulty walking, falls, difficulty driving, confusion; prolonged use (more than 8 months) may lead to habituation; sudden discontinuation of drug may cause symptoms such as insomnia, irritability, depersonalization, nerves jerking, headache

Serentil (mesoridazine)—Drowsiness, dizziness, fainting, dry mouth, skin rash, nasal congestion, blurred vision, parkinsonism, tardive dyskinesia (uncontrollable muscle twitching and spasms—possibly irreversible); potential drug interactions

Serpasil (reserpine)—Stomach upset, nausea, vomiting, dizziness, headache, depression, anxiety, nightmares, asthma, stuffy nose, skin rash, diarrhea, loss of appetite, drowsiness, breast enlargement, weight gain, sexual difficulties; potential drug interactions

Sinequan (doxepin)—Dry mouth, constipation, urinary problems, glaucoma, blurred vision, drowsiness, confusion, memory impairment, dizziness; potential drug interactions

Medicine—Possible Problems

Sparine (promazine)—Drowsiness, dizziness, fainting, dry mouth, skin rash, nasal congestion, blurred vision, parkinsonism, tardive dyskinesia (uncontrollable muscle twitching and spasms—possibly irreversible); potential drug interactions

Slo-Phyllin (theophylline)—Nausea, vomiting, stomach pain, loss of appetite, diarrhea, jitteriness, anxiety, insomnia, headache, dizziness, muscle twitching, depression, palpitations; many potential drug interactions; monitor blood levels

Stelazine (trifluoperazine)—Drowsiness, dizziness, fainting, dry mouth, skin rash, nasal congestion, blurred vision, parkinsonism, tardive dyskinesia (uncontrollable muscle twitching and spasms—possibly irreversible); potential for drug interactions

Symmetrel (amantadine)—Dizziness, confusion, difficulty in concentrating, hallucinations, nausea, loss of appetite, depression, urinary problems, constipation, unsteadiness, insomnia, strange dreams

Tagamet (cimetidine)—Mental confusion, dizziness, restlessness, drowsiness, nausea, vomiting, slurred speech, hallucinations, breast enlargement, headache; serious potential for drug interactions

Talwin (pentazocine)—Slowed breathing, dizziness, drowsiness, confusion, disorientation, nausea, vomiting, constipation, dry mouth, blurred vision, impotence, urinary difficulties; regular reliance on this drug may lead to habituation; potential drug interactions

Tenormin (atenolol)—Fatigue, lethargy, drowsiness, nausea, diarrhea, dizziness, dry skin, insomnia, strange nightmares, cold hands and feet, asthma, slower pulse, hallucinations, forgetfulness, depression, joint pain, impotence; sudden discontinuation of drug may lead to angina or heart attack; potential drug interactions

Terramycin (oxytetracycline)—Nausea, diarrhea, kidney trouble, altered vitamin K levels

Medicine—Possible Problems

tetracycline—Nausea, diarrhea, kidney trouble, altered vitamin K levels

theophylline—Nausea, vomiting, stomach pain, loss of appetite, diarrhea, jitteriness, anxiety, insomnia, headache, dizziness, muscle twitching, depression, palpitations; many potential drug interactions; monitor blood levels

Theo-Dur (theophylline)—Nausea, vomiting, stomach pain, loss of appetite, diarrhea, jitteriness, anxiety, insomnia, headache, dizziness, muscle twitching, depression, palpitations; many potential drug interactions; monitor blood levels

Thorazine (chlorpromazine)—Drowsiness, dizziness, fainting, dry mouth, skin rash, nasal congestion, blurred vision, parkinsonism, tardive dyskinesia (uncontrollable muscle twitching and spasms—possibly irreversible); potential drug interactions

Tofranil (imipramine)—Dry mouth, constipation, urinary problems, glaucoma, blurred vision, drowsiness, confusion, memory impairment, dizziness; potential drug interactions

Tolectin (tolmetin)—Stomach upset, nausea, indigestion, vomiting, reduced appetite, diarrhea, constipation, stomach ulcer, dizziness, drowsiness, lightheadedness, headache, high blood pressure, kidney damage, anemias, visual disturbances, skin rash, asthma; potential drug interactions

Tolinase (tolazamide)—Low blood sugar (hypoglycemia manifested as fatigue, sweating, hunger, and numbness in hands and feet), nausea, vomiting, stomach pain, loss of appetite, skin rash, blood disorders; potential drug interactions

Tonocard (tocainide)—Nausea, vomiting, dizziness, lightheadedness, unsteadiness, forgetfulness, confusion, palpitations, tingling sensation, anxiety, constipation, rash

Totacillin (ampicillin)—Skin rash, itching, digestive tract upset, altered vitamin K levels

Trandate (labetalol)—Fatigue, depression, lethargy, drowsiness, insomnia, strange nightmares, cold hands and feet,

Medicine—Possible Problems

asthma, slower pulse, hallucinations, forgetfulness, joint pain, impotence; sudden discontinuation of drug may lead to angina or heart attack; potential drug interactions

Transderm-Nitro (nitroglycerin, transdermal)—Headache, dizziness, unsteadiness, faintness, weakness, nausea, vomiting, palpitations, rash, blurred vision, dry mouth; potential drug interactions

Tranxene (clorazepate)—Drowsiness, incoordination, difficulty walking, falls, difficulty driving, confusion; prolonged use (more than 8 months) may lead to habituation; sudden discontinuation of drug may cause symptoms such as insomnia, irritability, depersonalization, nerves jerking, headache

Triavil (perphenazine, amitriptyline)—Dry mouth, constipation, urinary problems, drowsiness, blurred vision, glaucoma, skin rash, nasal congestion, fainting, confusion, memory impairment, parkinsonism; tardive dyskinesia (uncontrolled muscle twitching and spasms—possibly irreversible); potential drug interactions

Trilafon (perphenazine)—Drowsiness, dizziness, fainting, dry mouth, skin rash, nasal congestion, blurred vision, parkinsonism, tardive dyskinesia (uncontrollable muscle twitching and spasms—possibly irreversible); potential drug interactions

Trimox (amoxicillin)—Skin rash, itching, digestive tract upset

Tuinal (amobarbital, secobarbital)—Drowsiness, dizziness, may be addicting, sometimes can cause agitation instead of the usual sedation; withdrawal can cause insomnia, confusion, anxiety; potential drug interactions

Tylenol w/codeine (acetaminophen)—Drowsiness, dizziness, nausea, constipation; potential drug interactions

Utimox (amoxicillin)—Skin rash, itching, digestive tract upset

Valium (diazepam)—Drowsiness, incoordination, difficulty walking, falls, difficulty driving, confusion; prolonged

Medicine—Possible Problems

use (more than 8 months) may lead to habituation; sudden discontinuation of drug may cause symptoms such as insomnia, irritability, depersonalization, nerves jerking, headache

Vasotec (enalapril)—Kidney problems (requires periodic testing), rash, itching, fluid retention, dizziness early in treatment, blood disorders, headache, rapid pulse

Visken (pindolol)—Depression, drowsiness, fatigue, dry skin, nausea, diarrhea, tingling in hands and feet, dizziness, insomnia, impotence, strange nightmares, breathing problems; sudden discontinuation of drug could lead to angina or heart problems; potential drug interactions

Vivactil (protriptyline)—Dry mouth, constipation, urinary problems, glaucoma, blurred vision, drowsiness, confusion, memory impairment, dizziness; potential drug interactions

Wymox (amoxicillin)—Skin rash, itching, digestive tract upset

Xanax (alprazolam)—Drowsiness, incoordination, difficulty walking, falls, difficulty driving, confusion; prolonged use (more than 8 months) may lead to habituation; sudden discontinuation of drug may cause symptoms such as insomnia, irritability, depersonalization, nerves jerking, headache

Zantac (ranitidine)—Confusion, headache, dizziness, diarrhea, nausea, constipation

Zyloprim (allopurinol)—Skin rash, itching, drowsiness, confusion, dizziness, nausea, stomach pain, vomiting, diarrhea, headache; potential drug interactions

*HCTZ = hydrochlorothiazide

Table Sources

Caird, F.I. and Scott, P.J.W. *Drug-Induced Diseases in the Elderly: A Critical Survey of the Literature in Drug-Induced Disorders*, vol.2. New York: Elsevier, 1986.

Olin, Bernie R., ed. founding ed. Erwin K. Kastrup. *Facts and Comparisons*. St. Louis: Lippincott, 1987

Rocci, Mario L., et al. "Geriatric Clinical Pharmacology." *Cardiology Clinics* 4:213–225, 1986.

German, Pearl S., and Klein, Lawrence E. "Side Effects of Drugs in the Elderly." *Comp. Ther.* 12(4):3–6, 1986.

Schmucker, Douglas L. "Drug Disposition in the Elderly." *J. Amer. Geriat. Soc.* 32:144-149, 1984.

Zarlengo, David G., and Uhl, Henry S.M. "Drug Therapy: The Geriatric Patient." *Hospital Formulary* 18:196–202, 1983.

Bressler, Rubin. "Geriatric Prescribing: Hazards of Common Drugs." *Drug Therapy*, March, 1981, pp. 135–139.

Ensom, Robin J., and Nakagawa, Robert S. "Phenytoin Absorption in Adults: Effect of Aging." *N. Engl. J. Med.* 313:697, 1985.

Kiechel, J.R. "Biotransformation of Drugs During Aging." *Gerontol.* 28(Suppl.1): 101–112, 1982.

Gleckman, Richard A., and Esposito, Anthony L. "Antibiotics in the Elderly: Skating on Therapeutic Thin Ice." *Geriatrics*, Jan., 1980, pp. 26–37.

Ouslander, Joseph G. "Drug Therapy in the Elderly." *Ann. Int. Med.* 95:711–722, 1981.

Index

About the Authors

Joe and Teresa Graedon and *The People's Pharmacy*

Joe and Terry Graedon are quite a team. They've been working together for almost ten years, collaborating on books, syndicated newspaper columns, and radio shows. Watching them work is a little like listening to Stiller and Meara. They bat ideas back and forth like a shuttle cock in a fast-paced game of badminton. They complete each other's sentences—almost as if each knows what the other is thinking.

But they couldn't be any more different. Joe is a high-energy, Type-A pharmacologist, while Terry exudes Type-B calm amidst the chaos Joe seems to create wherever he goes. Joe and Terry met in Ann Arbor in 1969 when they were both graduate students at the University of Michigan. Joe was getting a master's degree in pharmacology while Terry was laying a foundation in medical anthropology.

Prior to graduate school, Joe did research on mental illness, sleep, and basic brain physiology at the New Jersey Neuropsychiatric Institute in Princeton. He had graduated from Pennsylvania State University in 1967. Terry graduated magna cum laude from Bryn Mawr College in 1969.

From Ann Arbor, Joe and Terry went to Oaxaca, Mexico from 1972 to 1974, where Terry did field work for her dissertation, studying nutrition, growth, and community health in an urban squatter settlement. Joe taught pharmacology to second-year medical students in the local university, a job which left his afternoons free. Life in Oaxaca was idyllic. The weather was beautiful, the life-style was relaxed, and from the hammock on their second-floor balcony they could look down on bougainvilleas blooming below.

Terry measured children, collected blood and stool samples, and filled in hundreds of questionnaires about food intake and health status while she trudged up and down the hills of the settlement. Joe found that after teaching all morning he still had too much energy to lie in the hammock all afternoon. He figured he'd give writing a whirl. He had become aware that there was a real need for information about drugs. Neighbors, friends, relatives, and a lot of other people too, were asking about their medicine. It was obvious they didn't know beans about what they were taking, didn't know its name or possible side effects, and they sure didn't know anything about drug interactions. Joe looked around and saw there was nothing much available for people to turn to except the *Physicians' Desk Reference*. Besides being hard to obtain (at that time it was not sold in bookstores), the book was written in "doctor-speak."

Joe started work on *The People's Pharmacy* in Oaxaca, and when he and Terry returned to the States he finished it off while Terry wrote her dissertation. In August of 1975 they moved to Durham, NC where Terry had a joint appointment at Duke University's School of Nursing and Department of Anthropology. The unexpected success of Joe's book led to a newspaper column, "The People's Pharmacy," syndicated by King Features to over 100 papers around the country. And a 1977 interview with National Public Radio in Washington, DC led to an offer to be a regular contributor to NPR information programming through WUNC radio in Chapel Hill. Besides regular weekly commentaries on WUNC-FM, Joe now hosts a call-in show where Terry often joins him as a co-host.

Over the intervening years, Joe and Terry have written a number of other books, including *The People's Pharmacy-2*, *The New People's Pharmacy-3: Drug Breakthroughs of the '80s*, and *Totally New and Revised The People's Pharmacy*. During 1982 and 1983 Terry was a postdoctoral fellow in the Medical Anthropology Program at the University of California, San Francisco (UCSF), and Joe spent that time as assistant clinical professor at the University's School of Pharmacy.

These days Terry is still teaching medical anthropology part-time at Duke while she shares equally in their writing ventures. Joe appears weekly on the noon news for WTVD-TV (channel 11 in Durham) and guest lectures frequently to civic organizations and health career students at Duke University and the University of North Carolina at Chapel Hill. He was a consultant to the Federal Trade Commission from 1978 to 1983, and is on the Advisory Board for the Drug Studies Unit at UCSF. He and Terry contribute a regular column on self-medication for the journal *Medical Self-Care*.

Joe belongs to the American Association for the Advancement

of Science, the Society for Neuroscience, the Sleep Research Society, the New York Academy of Science and the American Medical Writers Association. Terry is a member of the American Public Health Association, the American Association for the Advancement of Science, the American Anthropological Association, the Society for Applied Anthropology, and the Society of Medical Anthropology.

All correspondence will be forwarded to the Graedons if you address it:

Joe and Terry Graedon
50+
Bantam Books
666 Fifth Avenue
New York, NY 10103